The New Wor...

by Charles Giuliani

Introduction

Stop a few average people on the street today, and ask them if they are happy with the way that the government is being run; ask them if they are satisfied with the economy; ask them if they feel hopeful about where society is heading; ask them if they believe and trust their political and religious leaders; ask them if they approve of the moral standards, or lack thereof, that are being imposed upon the young, impressionable minds of our youth through the media, educational institutions, and the entertainment industry--ask these questions and see how many (how VERY many) people will respond in the negative, and understandably so. For as we look out at our world today, it is obvious that things just aren't right. Most people who are even mildly acquainted with current events can easily discern that something is going on, but a good many of them can't quite put their finger on it.

Is all the chaos and confusion that we see in society today an accident? Are we to believe that the turmoil in our modern world is due to a series of random, haphazard events that have no connection with each other? Or is it possible that the troubles we see around us are somehow related? Can it be that there is a hidden force at work that is responsible for it all (or most of it), and thus these problems are merely symptoms of a much bigger problem which has escaped detection by the general public?

For most people, making sense of the workings of society today is like trying to assemble an extremely complex jigsaw puzzle without the convenience of having the cover of the box in front of them, to serve as a guide. Not knowing the nature of the finished product, the puzzle pieces look to them like a jumble of hopeless chaos. Thus most people today don't even bother trying to assemble this puzzle because it seems to them to be in the realm of impossibility. But is this puzzle really impossible to put together?

Our modern society does indeed, at first glance, appear to be a jumbled, chaotic mass of disassociated puzzle pieces. However, it IS possible to assemble this puzzle, once we have taken a glance at the picture on the cover of the box. But there are many today who, occupying high positions of power, do not want us to see this picture on the box. They want us, instead, to be in the dark as to how each individual piece fits together as an operative part of the whole. In fact, they present to us an entirely different picture, from the cover of another box, with the hope that we will never be able to properly assemble the pieces. Therefore, before we begin to sort out and group together these pieces, let us start by glancing at the right box cover.

But before we even do this, it is important to be aware of the fact that the picture of our modern world that is about to be presented will, without a doubt, be shocking and, at least at first, very difficult to believe. But as we proceed to examine, sort, and assemble each individual puzzle piece, it will be clearly seen that the reason for our past failure to have successfully assembled this puzzle is because we have indeed been looking at the cover of the wrong box.

During Hitler's Germany, the Nazi-controlled media were employed as powerful propaganda tools to portray a box-cover puzzle picture that was much prettier than the one that matched the actual Nazi puzzle. Those who knew what the real puzzle picture looked like, and tried to display it to the public, were quickly silenced. Either their names were dragged in the dust by the media, or, worse yet, they were killed. The name of this Nazi puzzle was *conspiracy*. And it is the position of this present author that *conspiracy* is also the name of the puzzle of our modern society--a conspiracy to form a world government (the "New World Order")[Endnote 1], where the ultra-rich have total domination over the ultra-poor, and the middle class becomes extinct. In this conspiracy, dominating the masses involves far more than mere economic control and exploitation, however. It extends into every aspect of societal life, in order that the control exerted by the conspirators may be complete and all-pervasive.

There are many today who simply do not want to believe that such a thing could be happening. These folk want to live in a cozy, comfy world where they can continue to pretend that all is well, and that all will continue to be well. But the simple fact is that all is NOT well. And as we look toward the future, it's quite obvious that things are not going to get better, should present trends continue.

Every page of man's history is tainted by accounts of greedy, tyrannical power-mongers who sought to conquer the world. Why should our present age be any different? The reality is that it is NOT different. The only change is that today's world-control tyrants are working together, exercising power from behind the curtain, away from public scrutiny; and their weapons of warfare are far more subtle, and thus far more effective, than those of their predecessors, as we shall soon see.

* * * * * * *

"[The U.S.] cannot escape, and indeed should welcome...the task which history has imposed on us. This is the task of helping to shape a <u>new world order</u> in all its dimensions--...economic, political, social." - "The Mid-Century Challenge to U.S. Foreign Policy,"a study sponsored by the Rockefeller Brothers' Fund, 1959.

"[There is] a new...order struggling to be born...[and] the nation-state is becoming less and less competent to perform its international political

tasks....pressing us to lead vigorously toward the true building of a new world order..." - Nelson Rockefeller, *The Future of Federalism.* Cambridge, MA: Harvard University Press, 1962.

"Two centuries ago our forefathers brought forth a new nation; now we must join with others to bring forth a new world order. Narrow notions of national sovereignty must not be permitted to curtail that obligation." - "The Declaration of Interdependence," written by historian Henry Steele Commager and signed by 32 Senators and 92 Representatives at the nation's Capitol on January 30, 1976(319, p. xiii).

"Out of these troubled times [referring to the 1990-91 Persian Gulf crisis] *our...objective--a New World Order--can emerge. A new era....A hundred generations have searched for this...while a thousand wars raged across the span of human endeavor. And today that new world is struggling to be born. A world quite different from the one we've known."* - President George Bush Sr., *U.S. News and World Report*, December 31, 1990, p. 24 (this speech was actually delivered to Congress on September 11, 1990).

"Further global progress is now possible only through a quest for universal consensus in the movement towards a new world order." - Mikhail Gorbachev, speaking before the U.N. on December 7, 1988(18, p. 165).

"A new world order is taking shape so fast that governments as well as private citizens find it difficult to absorb 'the gallop of events'..." - Don Oberdorfer, "New World Order Galloping into Position," *Washington Post*, February 25, 1990.

"When Franklin Roosevelt died during the closing days of World War II, it fell to Truman to end the war and formulate policies for a new world order." - Frederick S. Voss, *The Smithsonian Treasury: The Presidents*, 1991.

"We are not going to achieve a new world order without paying for it in blood as well as in...money." - Arthur Schlesinger Jr., *Foreign Affairs*, July/August 1995.

"Loyalty to the New World Order is disloyalty to the Republic [of the U.S.]. *In nation after nation, the struggle between patriotism and globalism is underway....We don't want to be citizens of the world, because we have been granted a higher honor--we are citizens of the United States."* - Pat Buchanan, during a speech he gave at the Boston World Affairs Council, titled "The

Millennium Conflict: America First or World Government," January 6, 2000(18, pp. 262, 263).

The plan

The modern effort to form a New World Order first began in the late 1700s by a man named Adam (Spartacus) Weishaupt. Weishaupt was a master, Jesuit-trained anarchist with a diabolical lust for power. In 1776 he formed an occultic secret society called the Bavarian Illuminati, whose purpose it was to infiltrate governments in order to control them, and ultimately to control the whole world. How did he attempt to pull this off? Simply by befriending enormously rich international bankers (particularly Baron Nathan Meyer de Rothschild) and convincing them that, through their immense wealth and his crafty, Jesuit-learned tactics of infiltration, they could become the uncontested masters of the world.

In 1785 the Bavarian government caught wind of Weishaupt's twisted plans to take over Bavaria. They immediately set out to arrest Weishaupt, who, having heard of their plans to arrest him, fled Bavaria and went even deeper into the underground. The Bavarian government decided to send out warnings to all other European states/countries, to alert them to Weishaupt's far-reaching plans to topple other governments. But, unfortunately, nobody took Bavaria's warning seriously. Thus Weishaupt's plan was able to march on, although this time he changed his approach--he formed many small splinter groups, all with different names and seemingly different goals [Endnote 2]. This approach proved to be far more effective, as it became impossible (for most people, anyway) to make any connection between these various conspiring groups. Weishaupt also secured assistance, earlier on, from several already-existing secret societies, such as the Masons, which found his ambitions most appealing.

It was at the Masonic Conference in Wilhelmsbad, on July 16, 1782, that the Bavarian Illuminati first recruited Masonry to work as its partner in covertly creating a world government, over which they would have total control. Speaking of this secret meeting, historian Nesta H. Webster wrote: "What passed at this terrible Congress will never be known to the outside world, for even those men who had been drawn unwittingly into the movement, and now heard for the first time the real designs of the leaders, were under oath to reveal nothing. One such honest Freemason, the Conte de Virieu, a member of a Martiniste lodge at Lyons, returning from the Congres de Wilhelmsbad, could not conceal his alarm, and when questioned on the 'tragic secrets' he had brought back with him, replied: 'I will not confide them to you. I can only tell you that all this is very much more serious than you think. The conspiracy which is being woven is so well thought out that it will be, so to speak, impossible for the Monarchy and the Church to escape from it.' 'From this time onwards,' says his biographer, M. Costa de Beauregard, 'the Conte de Virieu could only speak of Freemasonry with horror'"(2, p. 18)[Endnote 3].

Weishaupt was well aware that his dream of world government would not be realized within his lifetime, but this didn't seem to matter much. For him it was enough to see the first steps taken toward the fulfillment of his dream, to reap the financial and political rewards that these early steps had brought, and to know that his dream's ultimate fulfillment would be accomplished by his descendants, along with the descendants of his co-conspirators, to whom they would pass on the torch.

And pass on the torch they did! As time progressed, Weishaupt's twisted plan, operating through various secret societies, has continued to grow larger and stronger. All the while there have been, on occasion, prominent, scrupled government officials (along with certain media personnel) who have recognized and exposed this secret plot. George Washington was one such individual. He was very much aware of the existence and influence of the Illuminati in his day, and, regarding it, once wrote: "I have heard much of the nefarious and dangerous plan and doctrines of the Illuminati. It was not my intention to doubt that the doctrine of the Illuminati...had...spread to the United States. On the contrary, no one is more satisfied of this fact than I am"(6, p. 518).

As the years marched on, several other notable officials began to speak out about what was going on behind the political curtain. In the year 1800, Alexander Addison, President of the County Courts of the Fifth Circuit of the State of Pennsylvania, observed that "an absolute and despotic tyranny...by the sect of the Illuminati directed by Weishaupt...[has] the daring ambition of ruling the whole world....That there are secret societies, in regular subordination, which direct the movement of vast bodies of people, no man, who looks at the results of elections, will doubt....That the Press is used, to promote the views of such societies, will not be doubted by any who see the unprincipled similarity of publications....It is evident that every exertion is made to fill public stations and places of instruction with men who will promote this spirit, and bring it into action"(7).

This hidden plot for global domination was further exposed years later by Benjamin Disraeli, an English statesman who became prime minister in 1868. Speaking in the House of Commons on July 14, 1856, he said: "There is...a power which we seldom mention in this House....I mean the secret societies....It is useless to deny, because it is impossible to conceal, that a great part of Europe-- the whole of Italy and France and a great portion of Germany, to say nothing of other countries--is covered with a network of those secret societies....And what are their objects?...They do not want constitutional government...they want to change the tenure of land, to drive out the present owners of the soil....Some of them may go further"(9).

Winston Churchill was also well aware of the ugly, power-hungry political machine that Weishaupt had set into motion, and was keenly acquainted with its workings in his day. In the *London Sunday Illustrated Herald*, February 8, 1920, he was quoted as saying: "From the days of Spartacus [Weishaupt], to those of Karl Marx [more will be said on Marx shortly]...this world-wide conspiracy for the overthrow of civilization and reconstruction of society...has been steadily growing. It has been the main spring of every subversive movement during the 19th century, and now, at last, this band of extraordinary personalities from the underworld of the great cities of Europe and America have gripped the Russian people by the hair of their heads and have become the undisputed masters of that enormous empire [speaking of the Bolshevik Revolution and the years of chaos that followed]."

In the June 19, 1920 issue of the *Christian Science Monitor*, the following similar observation was made: "What is important is to dwell upon the increasing evidence of the existence of a secret conspiracy, throughout the world, for the destruction of organized government and the letting loose of evil." In further regards to this "secret conspiracy" involving the "letting loose of evil," note the following relevant statement made by 33rd-degree Mason J. Edgar Hoover, back in 1956: "[T]he individual is handicapped by coming face to face with a conspiracy so monstrous he cannot believe it exists. The American mind simply has not come to a realization of the evil which has been introduced into our midst. It rejects even the assumption that human creatures could espouse a philosophy that must ultimately destroy all that is good and decent"(309).

Today Weishaupt's dream is alive and well. It continues to operate, in full swing, under a variety of different names and in cooperation with a number of different secretly-affiliated organizations, such as the Bilderbergers, the Club of Rome, the Order of Skull and Bones, the Rosicrucians, the Trilateral Commission (TC), the Council on Foreign Relations (CFR)[Endnote 4], the United Nations, etc. Though some of these groups may seem, at first glance, to have no connection, there is one thing that they ALL have in common: the advancement of Weishaupt's monstrous dream of a dictatorial, totalitarian world government (which, by the way, they have made their greatest forward strides, in pursuit of this goal, through their most willing servant--the U.S. government).

Yes, the U.S. government is, and has been for a long time, under the control of a very powerful crime syndicate that has been using the political, economic, and military power of this government to bring about its plan of global domination. As we progress through this study, this point will be thoroughly demonstrated and documented in detail, showing exactly what these criminals have done and how they have done it. But for now, let us take a look at some very interesting and authoritative quotes that reveal this "hidden force" lurking in the shadows, secretly controlling the power structure in Washington.

Back in 1987, Senator Jesse Helms stated before Congress: "[The] campaign against the American people...is orchestrated by a vast array of interests....[A] careful examination of what is happening behind the scenes reveals that all of these interests are working in concert...to create...a new world order. Private organizations such as the Council on Foreign Relations, the Royal Institute of International Affairs, the Trilateral Commission, the Dartmouth Conference, the Aspen Institute for Humanistic Studies, the Atlantic Institute, and the Bilderberg Group serve to disseminate and to coordinate the plans for this so-called new world order in powerful business, financial, academic, and official circles....The viewpoint of the Establishment [Endnote 5] today is called globalism....[T]he phrase 'one-world' is still apt because nothing has changed in the minds and actions of those promoting policies consistent with its fundamental tenets....[I]n the globalist point of view, nation-states and national boundaries do not count for anything....Indeed, even constitutions are irrelevant to the exercise of power [Endnote 6]....In this point of view, the activities of international financial and industrial forces should be oriented to bringing [about] this One-World design"(12).

Going back a few decades, to February 23, 1954, we find that Senator William Jenner had warned Americans about what was (and still is) REALLY going on in our government, when he said: "Outwardly we have a constitutional government. [However], [w]e have operating within our government and political system another body representing another form of government, a bureaucratic elite which believes our Constitution is outmoded....All the strange developments in foreign policy agreements may be traced to this group who are going to make us over to suit their pleasure....

"We have a well-organized political-action group in this country, determined to destroy our Constitution and establish a one-party state....The important point to remember about this group is not its ideology but its organization. It is a dynamic, aggressive, elite corps, forcing its way through every opening, to make a breach for a collectivist one-party state. It operates secretly, silently, continuously to transform our Government without [the people] suspecting that change is under way....If I seem to be extremist, the reason is that this revolutionary clique cannot be understood unless we accept the fact that they are extremist. It is difficult for people governed by reasonableness and morality to imagine the existence of a movement which ignores reasonableness and boasts of its determination to destroy, which ignores morality, and boasts of its cleverness in outwitting its opponents by abandoning all scruples. This ruthless power-seeking elite is a disease of our century....This group...is answerable neither to the President, the Congress, nor the courts. It is practically irremovable"(13).

In the light of such quotes as these, the following words of Weishaupt seem so profoundly prophetic: "We must do our utmost to procure the advancement of Illuminati into all important civil offices....By this plan we shall direct all mankind. In this manner, and by the simplest means, we shall set all in motion and in flames. The occupations must be so allotted and contrived, that we may, in secret, influence all political transactions"(1, pp. 74, 84).

If Weishaupt was alive today, he would surely be proud to see that all is going according to plan. Notice what former Justice of the U.S. Supreme Court, Felix Frankfurter (1882-1965), once said: "The real rulers in Washington are invisible, and exercise power from behind the scenes"(14, p. 3).

John F. Hylan, a former mayor of New York City, made the proceeding similar statement back on March 26, 1922: "The real menace of our republic is the invisible government which, like a giant octopus, sprawls its slimy length over our city, state and nation. At the head is a small group of banking houses generally referred to as 'international bankers.' This little coterie of powerful international bankers virtually run our government for their own selfish purposes"(15).

President Woodrow Wilson was also aware of this problem. He once wrote: "Since I entered politics, I have chiefly had men's views confided to me privately. Some of the biggest men in the United States, in the field of commerce and manufacturing, are afraid of somebody, are afraid of something. They know there is a power somewhere so organized, so subtle, so watchful, so interlocked, so complete, so persuasive, that they had better not speak of them above their breath when they speak in condemnation of it"(16).

In 1973, Colonel L. Fletcher Prouty, who worked at the Pentagon from 1955 to 1964 and had later served as chief of special operations with the U.S. Joint Chiefs of Staff, published his book called *The Secret Team: The CIA and its Allies in Control of the United States and the World.* In this revealing book, the "Secret Team" is a title used to refer to the network of globalist conspirators which, as Prouty states, "consists of security-cleared individuals in and out of government who receive secret intelligence data gathered by the CIA [Endnote 7] and the National Security Agency....The power of the Team derives from its vast intragovernmental undercover infrastructure and its direct relationship with great private industries, mutual funds and investment houses, universities, and the news media, including foreign and domestic publishing houses. The Secret Team has very close affiliations with elements of power in more than threescore foreign countries and is able when it chooses to topple governments, to create governments, and to influence governments almost anywhere..."(403).

Philip Agee, who worked as an agent for the CIA for 12 years, explained that the CIA, FBI, and a whole host of other government security and intelligence agencies can only be "understood as logical, necessary manifestations of a ruling class's determination to retain power and privilege"(19, p. 597).

In 1970, Thomas R. Dye and L. Harmon Zeigler co-authored a book called *The Irony of Democracy: An Uncommon Introduction to American Politics*, in which we find these revealing words: "Elites, not masses, govern America. In an industrial, scientific, and nuclear age, life in a democracy, just as in a totalitarian society, is shaped by a handful of men. In spite of differences in their approach to the study of power in America, scholars--political scientists and sociologists alike--agree that the key political, economic, and social decisions are made by tiny minorities"(417).

Suzanne Keller, sociology professor at Princeton University, wrote: "The notion of a stratum elevated above the mass of men may prompt approval, indifference, or despair, but regardless of how men feel about it, the fact remains that their lives, fortunes, and fate are and have long been dependent on what a small number of men in high places think and do"(20, p. 3).

In *Issues 2002*, a special edition of *Newsweek* that was published in January 2002, Michael Hirsh made the following astonishing remarks: "While the isolationists [those wanting to keep the U.S. free from foreign entanglements]...tempted millions with their siren's appeal to nativism [nationalism]--the internationalists [globalist conspirators] were always hard at work in quiet places making plans for a more perfect global community. In the end the internationalists have always dominated national policy [Endnote 8]. Even so, they haven't bragged about their globe-building for fear of reawakening the other half of the American psyche...and so they have always done it in the most out-of-the-way places and with little ado. In December of 1917 the Inquiry, a group of eager reformers who included a young Walter Lippmann [columnist for the *New York Times*], secretly met in New York to draw up Wilson's Fourteen Points. In 1941, FDR concocted the Atlantic Charter in the mists off Newfoundland. The dense woods of New Hampshire gave birth to the Bretton Woods institutions--the IMF [International Monetary Fund] and World Bank--in 1944. And a year later the United Nations came to life [Endnote 9]....We had built a global order...bit by bit, era by era....Like it or not--and clearly large numbers of Americans still don't--we Americans are now part of an organic whole with the world that George Washington wanted to keep distant."

Notice also the next similar quotation, from *New York* magazine, regarding "the Inquiry": "The [Council on Foreign Relations] grew out of the Inquiry, a secretive group of well-educated bankers and lawyers who accompanied Woodrow Wilson to the Paris Peace Conference of 1919. The Council saw [as] its mandate the calling of signals from the sidelines....[T]he [elites] govern, while the lowly men of elective office...dirty their hands with politics....[I]nternational institutions [such as] the UN, the World Bank, and the International Monetary Fund were anticipated in studies done at the Council"(23).

Can you not see that there is indeed a "hidden force" working behind the scenes, leading us toward a world dictatorship? And can you not also see that it is primarily the CFR, working mostly through the U.S. government, that has led out in this conspiracy?

* * * * * * *

"A nation can survive its fools, and even the ambitious. But it cannot survive treason from within. An enemy at the gates is less formidable, for he is known and carries his banner openly. But the traitor moves amongst those within the gate freely, his sly whispers rustling through all the alleys, heard in the very halls of government itself. For the traitor appears not a traitor; he speaks in accents familiar to his victims, and he wears their face and their arguments, he appeals to the baseness that lies deep in the hearts of all men. He rots the soul of a nation, he works secretly and unknown in the night to undermine the pillars of the city, he infects the body politic so that it can no longer resist. A murder is less to fear."
-Marcus Tullius Cicero.

"At what point shall we expect the approach of danger? By what means shall we fortify against it? Shall we expect some transatlantic military giant, to step the Ocean, and crush us at a blow? Never! All the armies of Europe, Asia and Africa combined, with all the treasure of the earth (our own excepted) in their military chest; with a Buonaparte for a commander, could not by force, take a drink from the Ohio, or make a track on the Blue Ridge, in a trial of a thousand years. At what point, then, is the approach of danger to be expected? I answer, if it ever reach us it must spring up amongst us. It cannot come from abroad. If destruction be our lot, we must ourselves be its author and finisher. As a nation of freemen, we must live through all time, or die by suicide." - Abraham Lincoln, address before the Young Men's Lyceum of Springfield, Illinois, January 27, 1838(449).

"The world is governed by very different personages from what is imagined by those who are not behind the scenes." - Benjamin Disraeli, *Coningsby, the New Generation,* 1844.

"The history of the last century shows that...the advice given to governments by bankers...was consistently good for the bankers, but often disastrous for governments...and the people generally. Such advice could be enforced if

necessary by manipulation of exchanges, gold flows, discount rates, and even levels of business activity. " - Carroll Quigley(28, p. 62).

Implementing the plan

Not many years after Weishaupt formed the Illuminati, Karl Marx arrived on the scene. Marx was an obvious disciple of Weishaupt. His famous *Communist Manifesto* was basically a plagiarized piece of work based almost entirely on Weishaupt's writings [Endnote 10]. In Marx's *Manifesto*, he laid out a plan containing a list of criteria that must be met in order to transform a government into a socialistic/communistic system. Though Marx intended for these criteria to be implemented in a short time, during an explosive period of political revolution, it has been found that the same results can be achieved, and even far more effectively so, when these criteria are carried out at a much slower pace, without the public perceiving what is happening [Endnote 11]. Marx's dream was to see his plan followed around the world, one country at a time, until all of civilization was enslaved under this system (a system which he deceptively claimed would "liberate" the masses of the laboring class). This plan has been followed to the letter in this country, as well as abroad, primarily through the gradual, well-calculated planning of international bankers, in cooperation with major multinational corporations and various organizations like the ones mentioned above. Sound crazy? Read on...

One of the first things that Marx said must be accomplished was to establish a centralized banking system, in order to gain control of a nation's economy (for it is money that lies behind the power of any nation). This happened, in this country, back in 1913, with the establishment of the Federal Reserve Act [Endnote 12].

Few are aware that the Federal Reserve is NOT run by the government, but is instead a privately-owned and privately-run banking system. This fact was confirmed by the Circuit Court when it ruled on June 24, 1982, in the case of Lewis vs. United States: "We conclude that the [Federal] Reserve Banks are not federal...but are independent, privately owned...corporations...without day to day direction from the federal government." Note also what Congressman Charles Lindbergh had to say on this matter: "It is a common practice of congressmen to make the title of acts promise aright, but in the body or text of the acts to rob the people of what is promised in the title....[T]he government does not own one dollar of stock in the Federal Reserve Banks....The first words of the [Federal Reserve] act are definite promises which the people assumed Congress made, that the banks established were Federal Reserve--that is, *government* banks. That promise was a deliberate lie!"(25, pp. 70, 71). Here's another related quote, from Representative John R. Rarick: "The Federal Reserve is not an agency of government. It is a private banking monopoly"(26). Finally, Congressman Louis T. McFadden, who had served as the Chairman of the House Banking and

Currency Committee, made these remarks before Congress on May 23, 1933: "Some people think the Federal Reserve Banks are United States Government institutions. They are not government institutions. They are private credit monopolies which prey upon the people of the United States for the benefit of themselves and their foreign customers; foreign and domestic speculators and swindlers; and rich and predatory money lenders"(41).

You won't find any Federal Reserve bank listed in the phone book under government agencies. Instead, you'll find them all in the white pages, along with other private businesses. Yes, the Federal Reserve is no more a federal institution than Federal Express.

Interestingly, the Federal Reserve, a private, big profit organization, pays no federal or state tax. The only taxes that it pays are the minuscule property taxes on its buildings.

This banking system has total control over the printing of our money (via the Treasury) and the setting of our interest rates, and it operates totally outside of the voting power of the American people. Ever since its inception it has been wreaking incredible havoc on the U.S. economy, thus bringing this nation down without ever having to fire a single bullet or launch a single missile. In fact, this non-militaristic conquest is a favorite method of the globalists. For instance, in the April 1974 issue of *Foreign Affairs*, the official journal of the Council on Foreign Relations, Richard Gardner, himself a CFR member and an affiliate of the Aspen Institute for Humanistic Studies in Aspen, Colorado, was quoted as saying: "The House of the World Order will have to be built from the bottom up rather than from the top down....[A]n end run around national sovereignty, eroding it piece by piece, will accomplish much more than an old fashioned frontal assault."

Commenting further on this silent take-over, particularly through central banks like the Federal Reserve, a former Georgetown professor, Dr. Carroll Quigley, wrote in his book *Tragedy and Hope*: "The powers of financial capitalism had...[a] far-reaching aim, nothing less than to create a world system of financial control in private hands able to dominate the political system of each country and the economy of the world as a whole. This system was to be controlled in a feudalist fashion [a return to serfdom!] by the central banks of the world [such as the Federal Reserve] acting in concert [Endnote 13], by secret agreements arrived at in frequent private meetings and conferences [such as the annual CFR and Bilderberger meetings--more on these later]"(28, p. 324). (More will also be said on the Federal Reserve later, along with the sinister role it has been playing in the establishment of world government.)

In this same book, Quigley, an "insider" of the global government conspiracy, stated: "I know of the operations of this network because I have studied it for twenty years and was permitted for two years, in the early 1960s, to examine its papers and secret records. I have,...for much of my life, been close to it and to many of its instruments....[I]t wishes to remain unknown, [but] I believe its role in history is significant enough to be known." Please understand that these are not the words of a "paranoid conspiracy theorist." Instead, they are the words of one who was an eyewitness to the inward workings of this monstrous system.

Sadly, Quigley, not exactly what you would call a champion of civil liberties, raised no objection to the aims of the globalists to enslave the world. His only complaint was that their operations were being conducted covertly.

Another item on Marx's list called for the enactment of a graduating income tax. This happened, in this country, just prior to the establishment of the Federal Reserve Act, through the addition of the 16th Amendment to the Constitution. And how this all came about is a most interesting story.

In 1912, Colonel Edward Mandell House (President Woodrow Wilson's globalist-appointed chief advisor) published a book titled *Philip Dru: Administrator*. In this book he described, in novel form, three main characters that, as it turned out, were actually representations of real-life figures, as was later revealed in *The Intimate Papers of Colonel House*, published in 1926. In *Philip Dru*, House was actually writing history a year in advance, relating events that he knew would soon be played out in the real world. His novel portrayed "Senator Selwyn" (representing himself) who acted as a middle man between Wall Street and the White House. Selwyn manipulated "James R. Rockland" (representing Wilson), who he guided along the road to the presidency on behalf of a powerful financier, "John Thor" (representing Jacob Schiff)[Endnote 14]. House relates in this book how Rockland, once elected as president, was manipulated to bring about "socialism as dreamed of by Karl Marx," and that this involved the creation of a central bank and a graduating income tax(418). Perhaps not so surprisingly, Wilson once said of House: "Mr. House is my second personality. He is my independent self. His thoughts and mine are one"(69).

For the globalists, creating a graduating income tax is just as important as creating a central bank. In fact, they can't have one without the other, since central banks are used (amongst other things) to create debt, while income taxes are utilized to pay off this debt. And what convenient timing for the creation of the Federal Reserve and the income tax in this country--just before the outbreak of WW I. For, just a few short years later, once the U.S. entered this war, the Federal Reserve reaped handsome profits from interest on loans for U.S. military build-up, while the income tax was used to pay off these loans and their interest [Endnote 15]. At the same time, the very industries that supplied the U.S. war machine were owned by the globalists as well--the Rockefellers, the Morgans, the Schiffs, the Carnegies, the Kuhns, the Loebs, the Warburgs, the Sachs, the

Goldmans, etc. And, believe it or not, these same families profiteered from selling supplies and lending money to Germany and other enemy nations.

Perhaps you're thinking that this couldn't have been possible (U.S. corporations and banks profiting from doing business with nations that the U.S. was at war with), since the Trading With the Enemy Act, passed on October 6, 1917, forbids such treasonous acts. Well, guess again. Who do you think created this legislation in the first place? It actually allows for "certain" U.S. companies-- those that have approval from the president--to trade with belligerent nations. In other words, this law was designed simply as a measure to protect the monopolies of the globalist-owned banks and industries [Endnote 16]. Just look at Section 5 of this farce piece of legislation, which states that the president has the right to "...suspend the provisions of this Act so far as they apply to an ally of [an] enemy,...and the President may grant licenses, special or general, temporary or otherwise, and for such period of time and containing such provisions and conditions as he shall prescribe, to any person or class of persons to do business...and to perform any act made unlawful without such license..." Can you see what a fraud this is?

Yes, WW I made the world-government conspirators very rich (as if they weren't already rich enough!)[Endnote 17]. But there was another, higher "benefit" behind WW I, aside from its money-making potential. It was hoped that this war would bring the nations of the world to desperation, to the point where they would be willing to submit to an international system of government (or to an early precursor thereof), under the pretext that such a system would be the only hope of preventing another world war from happening again. Thus, just after this war, the League of Nations was established by the international bankers (through their duped puppet, President Woodrow Wilson)[Endnote 18], as their next major step toward world domination.

In the June 1923 edition of *Foreign Affairs*, Colonel Edward Mandell House wrote that "if war had not come in 1914 in fierce and exaggerated form, the idea of an association of nations [the League of Nations] would probably have remained dormant, for great reforms seldom materialize except during great upheavals."

The January 1919 edition of *International Conciliation* (connected with the Carnegies) focused upon "A League of Nations." A cover letter sent out with this edition, drafted up by the American Association for International Conciliation, headed up by people like J.P. Morgan, began with these words: "The peace conference [at Versailles, where the League of Nations was established] has assembled. It will make the most momentous decisions in history, and upon these decisions will rest the stability of the new world order and the future peace of the world"(18).

Of course, the League of Nations failed. The people of the United States, smelling a rat, refused to join [Endnote 19]. But the globalists were relentless. When this one tactic had failed, they simply regrouped and planned their next move [Endnote 20].

And what was their next move?--The 1929 stock market crash, of course, which was orchestrated to teach the United States a lesson for rejecting the League of Nations. But even more importantly, this crash was intended to help tighten the power grip that the conspirators had on this "rebellious" nation, and to create the need for an economic revival in the U.S., which would later be conveniently provided by WW II.

Little did the American people realize that the 1929 crash, along with the ensuing Great Depression, were both planned. Speaking of this period of economic crisis, Congressman Louis T. McFadden, who, as stated earlier, had served as the Chairman of the House Banking and Currency Committee, stated before Congress in 1933 that "It was not accidental. It was a carefully contrived occurrence....The international bankers sought to bring about a condition of despair here so that they might emerge as rulers of us all"(14, p. 56).

How exactly was the 1929 crash brought about? This next quote from author William Bryan provides us the answer: "When everything was ready, the New York financiers started calling 24 hour broker call loans. This meant that the stock brokers and the customers had to dump their stock on the market in order to pay the loans. This naturally collapsed the stock market and brought a banking collapse all over the country because the banks not owned by the oligarchy were heavily involved in broker call claims at this time, and bank runs soon exhausted their coin and currency and they had to close. The Federal Reserve System would not come to their aid, although they were instructed under the law to maintain an elastic currency"(32).

Far from the Federal Reserve doing anything to prevent this crisis, it raised the minimum reserve requirement, which ensured the collapse of many rival banks.

Economist Milton Friedman (along with his wife, Rose) had this to say about the Great Depression: "The Great Depression in the United States...is a testament to how much damage can be done by missteps on the part of a few men [meaning the administrators of the Federal Reserve] when they wield vast power over the monetary system of a country"(34).

It was the next step, WW II (and the events that followed as a result thereof), which finally brought the results that the world-government conspirators sought. Where the League of Nations had failed, the United Nations, founded just after this war, and built right on America's front doorstep, was finally embraced by the American people, who, by that time, had become willing to submit to such a system, thinking that it would prevent another world war [Endnote 21]. But ever since joining the United Nations, the U.S. has been soft putty in the sinister hands of the globalists. (More will be said about the United Nations later. But for now, take note of the following revealing quotes about this globalist institution.)

* * * * * * *

"I challenge the illusion that the U.N. is an instrument of peace. It could not be less of a cruel hoax if it had been organized in Hell for the sole purpose of aiding and abetting the destruction of the United States." - J. B. Matthews, former chief investigator for the House Committee on Un-American Activities(140, p. 288).

"The UN is the biggest fraud in all history. Its purpose is to destroy the United States." - John Rankin, U.S. Congressman(17, p. 33).

"It is the sacred principles, enshrined in the UN Charter, to which we will henceforth pledge our allegiance [treason!].*"* - President George Bush Sr., U.N. Building, February 1, 1992(17, p. 33).

"It's long past time to make good on our debt to the United Nations....In this new era, our freedom and independence are actually enriched, not impoverished, by our increasing interdependence with other nations....As we move into...a global economy, a truly new world...America must...stand against the poisoned appeals of extreme nationalism." - President Bill Clinton, State of the Union address, January 27, 1998.

"The UN is but a long-range, international-banking apparatus neatly set up...by a small group of powerful One-World Revolutionaries, hungry for profit and power." - Curtis B. Dall, *FDR: My Exploited Father-in-Law.* Washington, D.C.: Action Associates, 1970.

"There can be no doubt that there now exists a widespread understanding and agreement made between the agents of this [U.S.] *Government and the United Nations and North Atlantic Treaty Organization* [NATO] *to build a world government, and to make the United States a part of it, regardless of our Constitution, laws, and traditions. This is to be done in the name of peace, but will result in the total destruction of our liberty."* - Congressman Usher Burdick, in a speech he titled "The Great Conspiracy to Destroy the United States." *Congressional Record*, April 28, 1954.

"The time has come to recognize the United Nations for the anti-American, anti-freedom organization that it has become [or always was!]. *The time has come for us to cut off all financial help, withdraw as a member, and ask the United Nations to find a headquarters location outside the United States that is more in keeping with the philosophy of the majority of voting members, someplace like Moscow or Peking."* - U.S. Senator Barry Goldwater, *Congressional Record*, October 26, 1971.

"[Members of the CFR want] a One World Socialist State governed by 'experts' like themselves....[They seek] policies which favor...gradual surrender of United States sovereignty to the United Nations." - Edith Kermit Roosevelt (granddaughter of President Theodore Roosevelt), *Indianapolis News*, December 23, 1961.

"The United Nations...deserves the support of all who are concerned with the building of a New World Order." - Dr. Ewen Cameron (Canadian psychiatrist who would later earn fame for his psychotic mind control experiments, conducted under the CIA's MK Ultra program in the 1950s and 1960s), from a speech he gave, entitled "The Building of the Coming World Order," aired live by the Canadian Broadcasting Corporation on May 5, 1946.

"The American people see the United Nations aspiring to establish itself the central authority of a new international order of global laws and global governance....Americans look with alarm at UN claims to a monopoly on international moral legitimacy. They see this as a threat to the...freedoms of the American people, a claim of political authority over America and its elected leaders without their consent....As the UN seeks to impose its Utopian vision of international law on Americans, we can add this question: Where do we go when we don't like the laws of the world?...[A] United Nations that seeks to impose its presumed authority on the American people without their consent begs for confrontation..." - Senator Jesse Helms, addressing the U.N. Security Council on January 20, 2000(18, p. 264).

A rigged game

It is no secret that money is a very powerful force, either for good or for evil--either to make the world go around or to turn it upside down. The globalist conspirators realized this very early on, and have used money as a tool to control governments, and thereby to enslave the masses.

Back at the turn of the 19th century, a famous international banker, Baron Nathan Meyer de Rothschild, who, as mentioned earlier, was a personal friend of Weishaupt, had thusly bragged: "Let me issue and control a nation's money and I care not who makes the laws"(35, p. 9). Another revealing statement about money being used as a tool for political power was made by John Maynard Keynes, a famous English economist and a member of the Fabian (socialist) Society of England (another globalist front group): "There is no subtler, no surer means of overturning the existing basis of society than to debauch the currency. The process engages all the hidden forces of economic law on the side of destruction, and does it in a manner which not one man in a million is able to diagnose"(36).

Yes, Karl Marx was right--gaining control of a nation's wealth is a must if the conquest of that nation's political system is to be achieved. And this is exactly what has been done in the United States, through the Federal Reserve System (as well as in many other countries, through their respective central banking systems).

Just how did the Federal Reserve Act actually come about? In a nutshell, a secret meeting was held in 1910 at an elite "clubhouse," known today as the Jekyll Island Club Hotel, at Jekyll Island, Georgia, between some of the biggest names in international banking at that time. Among those in attendance at this private meeting were:

- Banker/Senator Nelson Aldrich
- Paul Warburg
- Henry P. Davison (representing J.P. Morgan & Company)
- Frank A. Vanderlip (President of the Rockefeller-owned National City Bank)
- Benjamin Strong (of Morgan's Bankers Trust Company)
- A. Piatt Andrew (the bought-off Assistant Secretary of the Treasury)

Speaking of this secret gathering, Frank Vanderlip later wrote: "There was an occasion near the close of 1910 when I was as secretive, indeed as furtive, as any conspirator. I do not feel it is any exaggeration to speak of our secret expedition to Jekyll Island as the occasion of the actual conception of what eventually became the Federal Reserve System....We were told to leave our last names behind us. We were told further that we should avoid dining together on the night of our departure. We were instructed to come one at a time...where Senator Aldrich's private car would be in readiness, attached to the rear end of the train for the South....Once aboard the private car we began to observe the taboo that had been fixed on last names. Discovery, we knew, simply must not happen, or else all our time and effort would be wasted....If it was publicly exposed that our group had gotten together and had written a banking bill, that bill would have no chance whatsoever of passage by Congress"(37).

In order to prep the American people for, and coerce them into, acceptance of the soon-coming Federal Reserve central banking system, J.P. Morgan precipitated the panic of 1907 by spreading false rumors about the insolvency (or insufficient reserves) of rival banking institutions. Note the following *Life* magazine quote, which confirms this: "Oakleigh Thorne, the president of that particular trust company [the Trust Company of America], testified...before a congressional committee that his bank had been subjected to only moderate withdrawals,...that he had not applied for help, and that it was...[Morgan's] 'sore point' statement alone that had caused the run on his bank. From this testimony, plus the disciplinary measure taken by the Clearing House against the Heinze, Morse and Thomas banks,...certain chroniclers have arrived at the ingenious conclusion that the Morgan interests took advantage of the unsettled conditions during the autumn of 1907 to precipitate the panic, guiding it shrewdly as it progressed so that it would kill off rival banks and consolidate the preeminence of the banks within the Morgan orbit....The lesson of the panic of 1907 was clear, though not for some six years was it destined to be embodied in legislation: the United States gravely needed a central banking system"(38).

Before the panic of 1907 (which occurred in October of that year), the globalist banker clansmen initially tried to verbally frighten the United States into accepting a central bank, hoping to avoid the more troublesome route of staging a full-blown panic. Thus, in early 1907, Jacob Schiff, a German-born Rothschild agent, in a speech to the New York Chamber of Commerce, warned that "unless we have a Central Bank with adequate control of credit resources, this country is going to undergo the most severe and far reaching money panic in its history"(486, p. 37).

Obviously this warning didn't have enough of a chill effect to con Americans into accepting a central bank, necessitating the staged panic later that year.

Just prior to the establishment of the Federal Reserve Act, Congressman Charles Lindbergh warned: "This act establishes the most gigantic trust on earth....When the President signs this act the invisible government by the money power, proven to exist by the Money Trust investigation, will be legalized....They control the banking interests....The money power overawes the legislative and executive forces of the Nation and of the States. I have seen these forces exerted during the different stages of this bill....Wall Street will control the money....The new law will create inflation whenever the trust wants inflation....From now on, depression will be scientifically created"(39). Too bad that nobody listened to Congressman Lindbergh!

It is precisely because nobody listened to Lindbergh's warning that Senator Nelson Aldrich, back in July of 1914, just seven months after the passage of the Federal Reserve Act, was able to boast: "Before the passage of this Act, the New York bankers could only dominate the reserves of New York. Now we are able to dominate the bank reserves of the entire country"(40).

Less than eighteen years later, Congressman Louis T. McFadden, speaking before Congress on May 23, 1933, made the following scathing remarks about the Federal Reserve System: "We have in this country one of the most corrupt institutions the world has ever known. I refer to the Federal Reserve Board and the Federal Reserve Banks...

"In that dark crew of financial pirates there are those who would cut a man's throat to get a dollar out of his pocket; there are those who send money into the states to buy votes to control our legislation; and there are those who maintain an international propaganda for the purpose of deceiving us and wheedling us into the granting of new concessions which will permit them to cover up their past misdeeds and set again in motion their gigantic train of crime....

"When the Federal Reserve Act was passed, the people of these United States did not perceive that a world banking system was being set up here....

"[It amounts to a] super-state controlled by international bankers and international industrialists acting together to enslave the world for their own pleasure.

"Every effort has been made by the Fed to conceal its powers but the truth is--the Fed has usurped the government....It controls everything here [in Congress] and it controls all our foreign relations. It makes and breaks governments at will"(41).

How the international bankers are pulling off their sinister secret takeover of this country (and indeed, the whole world) was perhaps best summed up by author Sheldon Emry: "It is easy to see that no matter how skillfully they [the common people] play, eventually the 'banker' will end up with all of his original chips back, and except for the very best players, the rest, if they stay in long enough, will lose to the 'banker' their homes, their farms, their businesses, perhaps even their cars, watches, rings, and the shirts off their backs (whatever they have mortgaged). Our real life situation is MUCH WORSE than any poker game. In a poker game, none [are] forced to go into debt, and anyone can quit at any time and keep whatever he still has. But in real life, even if we borrow little ourselves from the bankers, the local, provincial, and federal governments borrow billions in our name, squander it, then confiscate our earnings from us and pay it back to the bankers with interest. We are forced to play the game and none can leave except by death. We pay as long as we live, and our children pay after we die. If we cannot pay, the same government sends the police to take our property and give it to the bankers. The bankers risk nothing in the game; they just collect their percentage and 'win it all'"(42, p. 21).

One of the most profitable games that the international bankers like to play is the stock market--a game that they simply cannot lose. Here's roughly how it works: First they raise interest rates, creating a panic, and causing many to sell out their stocks cheap. Their next step is to buy up these stocks in great hoards. After this, they wait for a while, so as not to arouse suspicions, and then lower the interest rates. This, of course, soon results in an upsurge in the economy. Next they begin selling their cheaply-purchased stocks at a tremendous profit.

Another foolproof, profit-making venture for these bankers is the bond market. This is one of their favorite games to play, as it is most successful, not just for making a financial killing, but for putting a strangle hold on the nation which they target through this game. The rules of this game are quite simple. All that needs to be done is for the "big boys" to send out their agents to buy up thousands, even millions, of government bonds. Soon an artificial, temporary condition of prosperity will ensue in that nation, as this action will quickly raise the value of its bonds, fooling the masses into taking out large loans and making huge credit purchases, thinking that the booming economy is there to stay. After waiting a while, so as to not arouse suspicions and to allow time for the people to go into debt, our banker friends then suddenly dump all of these bonds on the market, plummeting their value. Soon the economy of the target nation takes a huge plunge, and nearly all of its citizens are left wondering what in the world happened. The bankers then walk away, exulting in the high-interest debts that the people now owe them, both collectively and individually, which are impossible, or nearly impossible, to pay because the economy now lies in ruins (in which case the bankers offer enormously profitable loans to the government for "economic revival," which drive up banker profits even more). Once again the bankers win and the people lose. Quite a deal, wouldn't you say?

The globalists have an unending list of tricks up their sleeves through which they work to amass tremendous wealth while driving millions into desperate poverty. But perhaps their most favorite game of all, and one that is easiest to play, is to simply spread false, panic-inducing rumors in financial publications, gloomily speculating about a particular targeted nation's economy, which results in a massive withdrawal of foreign investments. This, in turn, brings the nation to its knees, on the verge of a total economic collapse, and thus unable to resist the temptation to take enormously oppressive, high-interest loans from the international monetary scavengers.

Understand that the real objective for these unscrupulous thieves is not so much to make more money, but to take more of ours--to drive us ever further into poverty and to make us helpless dependents.

Coming back to our discussion of the Federal Reserve, Representative Ron Paul (R-Texas), one of the few people in Congress who has fought valiantly against this fraudulent banking system over the years, wrote the following remarks back in 1983, in one of his newsletters: "As a member of the House Banking Committee, I have long believed that present economic difficulties are caused principally by our centralized banking system headed by the Federal Reserve, and by the use of irredeemable paper money.

"Article 1, Section 8 of the Constitution grants Congress the exclusive power of coining money, not printing it [Endnote 22]. But 70 years ago, in 1913, Congress enacted the Federal Reserve Act establishing our present banking system. At the time we were still on a gold standard, and the harmful effects of the Federal Reserve System were meliorated by the continued use of gold and silver as coins and as backing for paper currency. Still, the Federal Reserve has succeeded in causing the worst depressions, inflations, recessions, unemployment, and interest rates in our history [Endnote 23]...

"I am convinced that there is no permanent solution to our severe economic problems that does not involve thorough monetary reform. This is why I have introduced [several] ...major pieces of legislation. The first bill, H.R. 875, would repeal the Federal Reserve Act of 1913, thus ending our 70-year experiment with paper money, an experiment that has obviously failed. To achieve that end, I have also introduced a bill requiring, for the first time in history, a complete audit of the Federal Reserve, H.R. 877. I believe that a thorough audit and investigation of the Federal Reserve would reveal enough damning information about the Fed that virtually all members of Congress would support its abolition..."(43, pp. 135, 136)[Endnote 24].

It is frightening enough to realize that the Federal Reserve, which exercises total control over our economy, is privately owned and operated. But it is even more frightening when one realizes that a large percentage of this private ownership and directorship is foreign. In this regard, Congressman Henry B. Gonzalez made these revealing statements back in 1993: "There is no question that the Fed runs our nation's monetary policy because it has complete and final governmental authority to manage the United States money supply....The American public should know that of the Federal Reserve System member banks that vote for...Reserve Bank directors, approximately 60 banks, with 130 billion dollars in assets, are foreign owned....In the New York Federal Reserve District, 33% of the medium-sized member banks and 25% of the large member banks are foreign owned"(44).

The Rockefellers are some of the most powerful international bankers in the world. Through John D. Rockefeller Sr., this family played a major role in the development of the Federal Reserve. And, not so surprisingly, this same family has also been pushing quite forcefully, from behind the scenes, for the establishment of global government. It was John D. Rockefeller Jr., for example, who donated the plot of land upon which the U.N. building was constructed in New York.

Regarding the Rockefellers, Congressman Larry P. McDonald wrote the proceeding remarks in the introduction to Gary Allen's book, *The Rockefeller File*: "The Rockefeller File is not fiction. It is a compact, powerful and frightening presentation of what may be the most important story of our lifetime-- the drive of the Rockefellers and their allies to create a one-world government combining super-capitalism and communism under the same tent, all under their control.

"For more than one hundred years, since the days when John D. Rockefeller Sr. used every devious strategy he could devise to create a gigantic oil monopoly [Endnote 25], enough books have been written about the Rockefellers to fill a library. I have read many of them. And to my knowledge, not one has dared to reveal the most vital part of the Rockefeller story: that the Rockefellers and their allies have, for at least fifty years, been carefully following a plan to use their economic power to gain political control of first America, and then the rest of the world.

"Do I mean conspiracy? Yes I do. I am convinced there is such a plot, international in scope, generations old in planning, and incredibly evil in intent"(50).

To illustrate just how evil the intent of the Rockefellers is, notice what former Arizona Senator Barry Goldwater, commenting on the Trilateral Commission (founded by David Rockefeller), once wrote: "David Rockefeller's newest international cabal...is intended to be the vehicle for multi-national consolidation of the commercial and banking interests, by seizing control of the political government of the United States"(46, p. 203).

Bill Moyers, who had served as J.F.K.'s press secretary, once had this to say about David Rockefeller: "David Rockefeller is the most conspicuous representative today of the ruling class, a multinational fraternity of men who shape the global economy and manage the flow of capital. Rockefeller was born to it, and he has made the most of it....Rockefeller sits at the hub of a vast network of financiers, industrialists, and politicians whose reach encircles the globe....But what some critics see as a vast international conspiracy, he considers a circumstance of life and just another day's work"(321).

During the same PBS show on which Moyers made the above statement about Rockefeller, he interviewed Ridgeway Knight, a retired American ambassador and a former assistant secretary of state, who made this remark about the tycoon: "I represent David personally....What impresses me most is that I represented a number of presidents, and I've spoken for a number of secretaries of state, but I've never seen doors open more easily than when I say I'm coming from David Rockefeller--it's fantastic!"

The comment that follows, made by David Rockefeller himself, lucidly illustrates the total indifference that the Rockefellers and their fellow globalists have toward the millions (or billions) around the world who suffer from the corrupt policies that they advance: "The social experiment in China under Chairman Mao's leadership is one of the most important and successful in human history"(47).

You might be interested to know that over 60 million people were murdered under Mao's tyrannical reign. This "successful" social "experiment" was but one of many such "practice runs" conducted by the Rockefellers and their cohorts, in preparation for the totalitarian world government that they long for.

Not so surprisingly, a good friend of David Rockefeller, Zbigniew Brzezinski, who helped Rockefeller create the Trilateral Commission, on various occasions, just like Rockefeller cited above, has praised Marxist leaders. Here's one such example: "Marxism represents a further vital and creative stage in the maturing of man's universal vision....Though Stalinism may have been a...tragedy..., there is the intellectually tantalizing possibility that for the world at large it was...a blessing in disguise"(48, pp. 72, 134).

Stalinism MAY HAVE been a tragedy? It was a blessing in disguise? Just how are we to interpret the reign of a man who was responsible for the death of over 100 million of his own people as a "blessing in disguise"?

The Rockefellers and their comrades at the Federal Reserve have totally rigged our economy, turning us into their serfs. Just consider the national debt, for example. Do you suppose that this unfathomably-high obligation is an accident? Through Fractional Reserve Banking, a system whereby money is created out of nothing by the Federal Reserve, thus saturating our country with worthless, interest-accruing pieces of paper, the globalists are destroying our economy and condemning us to an oppressive perpetual debt.

Fractional Reserve Banking is literally the creation of money out of thin air. The Boston Federal Reserve Bank admitted this in its publication "Putting It Simply": "When you or I write a check there must be sufficient funds in our account to cover that check, but when the Federal Reserve writes a check, it is creating money." Instead of "Fractional Reserve Banking," perhaps it should be called "legalized counterfeiting"!

Once this counterfeit money is printed, it is then put into circulation (in the form of loans to the government, at our expense) at full face value plus interest. Since future loans must be issued to create the money to pay these loans and their interest, the federal debt can never mathematically be repaid, in spite of all the political rhetoric. (But the amazing truth is that this debt is not a real debt, because the money borrowed is not real money!) Congressman Wright Patman summed it all up this way: "The dollar represents a one dollar debt to the Federal Reserve System. The Federal Reserve Banks create money out of thin air...lending money into circulation at interest...which the American people are obligated to pay..."(51).

Perhaps some elaboration is in order, to better explain how the Fractional Reserve Banking fraud actually works: The government only requires the Federal Reserve to have 10% in "reserve" of what it actually prints into circulation (or loans out). In other words, it only needs to have $10 (of worthless paper money) in its vault to loan out $100. And where does the $100 come from?--It is created out of nothing but paper and ink! And then they take this magically-created $100 and loan it out to the government, at our expense, at high interest. This means that our paper "dollars" not only have no value of themselves, but they are, in reality, debt receipts (or "promissory notes"). As you can see, the Federal Reserve boys come up with a winning hand in this game every time. The only ones who lose are the millions of duped Americans who allow this fraud to perpetuate.

Yes, the title "Federal Reserve" is an absolute joke. Not only is this institution not run by the federal government, but there are no authentic reserves. The government and the bankers have a good thing going, and they intend to keep it that way. Just think about it: The bankers get filthy rich as the government borrows unlimited amounts of high-interest-bearing funny money from them, which we then pick up the tab for, through extortion. Notice what Walter Wriston had to say on this matter, while chairman of Citicorp Bank back in 1982: "If we had a truth-in-Government act comparable to the truth-in-advertising law, every note issued by the Treasury would be obliged to include a sentence stating: 'This note will be redeemed with the proceeds from an identical note which will be sold to the public when this one comes due'"(52, p. 28). Josiah Stamp, former director of the Bank of England, put it so well back in 1937: "The modern banking system manufactures money out of nothing. The process is perhaps the most astounding piece of sleight of hand that was ever invented....If you want to be slaves of the bankers, and pay the costs of your own slavery, then let the banks create money"(53, p. 177). Daniel Webster further said: "Of all the contrivances for cheating the laboring class of mankind, none has been more effectual than that which deludes them with paper money"(54). So much for slavery being abolished!

"But wait," someone interjects. "Doesn't our government have a lot of gold reserves locked away at Fort Knox?" The reality is that, all the while that the Federal Reserve has been pumping the U.S. economy with worthless paper money, it has been slowly raping our country of its gold reserves (remember that gold has _real_ value; paper does not). As author Christopher Weber pointed out, a lot of very strange things have been going on in this country, regarding its gold reserves: "Fact 1: From 1958 to 1968, 52 percent of the nation's gold reserves left this country. Fact 2: These shipments were made with the knowledge and acquiescence of government officials. Fact 3: For 35 years [as of 1988], the government had failed to conduct a physical inventory of its gold. Fact 4: Inquiries into the history of America's gold reserves and the policies behind that history have been consistently stonewalled"(55, p. 3).

In further regards to our gold reserves leaving this country, on September 30, 1963, President John F. Kennedy, addressing a meeting of the International Monetary Fund, stated: "Twenty years ago...[s]ixty percent of the gold reserves of the world were here in the United States. [But]...[t]here was a need for redistribution of the financial resources of the world....It did not come about by chance but by conscious and deliberate...planning [as if the IMF didn't already know this!]....We are now entering upon a new era of economic and financial interdependence....Our gold reserves are...[now] forty percent of the world's holdings"(57)[Endnote 26].

Although F.D.R. had already taken the U.S. off the gold standard in 1933, the globalist bankers have been progressively removing the gold reserves of this country, in order to ensure that it will have nothing to fall back on in an emergency.

But it's not just the gold reserves of the government that the globalist bankers have seized. In 1933, F.D.R. conducted, on behalf of his Federal Reserve buddies, the greatest gold heist in world history. Through the passage of the scandalous Emergency Banking Relief Act of March 9, 1933 (along with a subsequent Executive Order passed on April 5), Roosevelt mandated that all U.S. citizens turn over their privately-owned gold to the Federal Reserve, in exchange for worthless paper funny money (only to devaluate this same paper currency by 59%, less than a year later!). The consequence of not complying with this legalized grand theft fiasco was either a maximum 10-year prison sentence or a maximum fine of $10,000 [Endnote 27]. The bankers, needless to say, made billions, while an already-suffering working class was sunk further into the hole

[Endnote 28].

As you might guess, this Emergency Banking Relief Act, like so many other pieces of globalist-created legislation passed over the years, came about in a most dubious manner. Regarding this bill, Congressman McFadden stated: "Mr. Speaker [Henry T. Rainey], I regret that the membership of the House has had no opportunity to consider or even read this bill. The first opportunity I had to know what this legislation is was when it was read from the Clerk's desk"(56). Representative Ernest Lundeen said of this bill: "Today the Chief Executive sent...a banking bill for immediate enactment. The author of this bill seems to be unknown. No one has told us who has drafted the bill. There appears to be a printed copy at the Speaker's desk, but no printed copies are available for House members. The bill has been driven through the House with cyclonic speed after 40 minutes debate--twenty minutes for the minority and twenty minutes for the majority!...We...have the spectacle of the great House of Representatives of the United States of America passing, after a 40-minute debate, a bill its members never read and never saw; a bill whose author is unknown!...I want to put myself on record against a procedure of this kind and against the use of such methods in passing legislation affecting millions of lives and billions of dollars. It seems to me that under this bill...money and credit control will be still further concentrated in the hands of those who now hold the power....I am suspicious of this railroading of bills through our House of Representatives, and I refuse to vote for a measure unseen and unknown!"(56).

By the way, Roosevelt didn't stop there. The final straw came on June 10, 1933, with the passage of the Banking Act of 1933. This bill allowed the Federal Reserve, from that time forward, to retain 100% of its profits, without any going to the government. It is indeed a strong testament to the power of propaganda that Roosevelt, to this day, is considered one of the greatest presidents in American history, when in reality he was a monstrous traitor.

When confronted with such facts as what we have been discussing, many have argued the point, "If you don't like the way that the government or the economy is being run, then vote to change things!" But the reality is that it matters not how one votes anymore, since candidates don't even make it on the ballot in the first place today unless they belong to "the club"--unless they hold membership in one or more of the globalist organizations that we have been discussing. For example, every president from Eisenhower to Clinton, with the single exception of Ronald Reagan, was a member of either the CFR or the TC [Endnote 29] (and the same holds true for a large percentage of the members of Congress). So, no matter who gets into office, "the plan" will always march forward.

Yes, the election process is yet another rigged game of the globalists, as the next several insightful quotes point out:

- In the book *Billions for the Bankers, Debts for the People*, Sheldon Emry wrote: "An economic conquest takes place when nations are placed under 'tribute' without the use of visual force, so the victims don't realize they've been conquered. The conquest begins when the conquerors gain control of the monetary system of the nation. The conquerors do not want to arouse suspicion, so they make gradual changes to their benefit. They slowly usurp the financial assets of a nation. Tribute is collected from them in the form of 'legal' debts and taxes, which the people are led to believe is for their own good....[A]lthough this method is much slower than a military conquest, it is longer lasting because the captives do not see any military force used against them. <u>The people are free to participate in the election for their rulers although the outcome is manipulated by those in control</u>. Without realizing it, a nation is conquered. Their wealth is transferred to their captors and the conquest is complete"(42).

- In *Tragedy and Hope*, Quigley wrote: "[T]he business interests...intended to contribute to both [the republican and democratic parties] and allow an alternation of the two parties in public office in order to conceal their own influence...and allow the electorate to believe that they were exercising their own free choice"(p. 73).

- A famous and well-respected defense attorney, Gerry Spence, penned these words: "[T]he modern election has degenerated into choosing between whomever the power structure has put up for the job....Shall we vote for the Republican supported by the big money, or the Democrat supported by the big money? In short, our candidates are pre-bought by money interests. What we are provided is the illusion of representation"(58, p. 211).

- MIT professor Noam Chomsky had this to say: "Modern 'democratic theory' takes the view that the role of the public...is to be spectators, not participants. They're supposed to show up every couple of years to ratify decisions made elsewhere, or to select among representatives of the dominant sectors in what's called an 'election.' That's helpful, because it has a legitimizing effect"(59, p. 12).

- Back in 1996, Senator Bill Bradley stated: "Money not only determines who is elected, it determines who runs for office. Ultimately, it determines what government accomplishes--or fails to accomplish"(60, p. 405).

- Finally, let's take a look at what Curtis B. Dall had to say on this matter, in his book *FDR: My Exploited Father-in-Law*: "It appears to me that politics is the gentle art of having to pretend to be something that you know you are not, for vote-catching purposes, while being aided by our press....Usually, carefully screened leading 'actors' are picked well in advance of election day by a small group, picked for both major parties....It is desirable for [candidates] to have great personal ambition and, perchance, to be vulnerable to blackmail...for some past occurrences; hence, someone not apt to become too independent in time"(82).

And let's not forget how the Supreme Court illegally overrode the voting power of the American people by self-appointing George W. Bush as president in the 2000 "election" [Endnote 30]. Not that Al Gore would have been any better, of course. But it's quite obvious that Bush Jr. was the man that the globalists really wanted in office. So much for the "right to vote."

Have you noticed how election campaigns hardly ever focus on real issues anymore, but focus instead on the opposing candidates taking turns cutting each other down? You would think that this alone would open people's eyes to the fraudulent nature of the whole election campaign process. It's actually much like "professional" wrestling, where the opponents put on a public show of mock fighting, including insults, but then later laugh it all off over a few beers at the local pub.

In a political campaign, any differences over issues, programs, or policies that do pop up between opposing political candidates are simply part of the public show of mock fighting. Understand that neither "competing" candidate has any authentic intention of carrying out any type of program or policy that would actually benefit the general public in any significant fashion. As with "professional" wrestlers, the political actors must simply follow the pre-written script and deliver what the masses want to hear.

If our "elected officials" were truly interested in the general public, then why would they pass, or allow to be passed, programs, policies, and legislation that are entirely antagonistic to the public's interests? Just think of NAFTA (North American Free Trade Agreement), for example, which has been stealing jobs away from us as companies move to Mexico, where workers are paid much lower wages, and where the general costs of running a business are much lower. These same companies then turn around and sell their products back here, at a very high price, which we can barely afford because these very companies have put us out of work [Endnote 31].

What better way to bring down a nation than to destroy its economy? The U.S. is under siege and is sinking fast, right before our eyes, and our "elected officials" are rolling out the red carpet for our aspiring conquerors. Welcome to the New World Order. Yes, our "elected officials" care more about pleasing their "pocket feeders" (campaign contributors and lobbyists) than they care about blue-collar, hard-working Americans. No wonder politicians have such a hard time remembering their campaign "promises" once the elections are over.

Perhaps no one summarized this whole mess better than CNN's Lou Dobbs, who stated on his October 11, 2006 show: "I don't know about you, but I can't take seriously anyone who takes either the Republican Party or Democratic Party seriously--in part because neither party takes you and me seriously; in part because both are bought and paid for by corporate America and special interests. And neither party gives a damn about the middle class.

"Our country's middle class is not just collateral damage in what has become all-out class warfare. Political, business and academic elites are waging an outright war on working men and women and their families, and there is no chance the American middle class will survive this assault if the dominant forces unleashed over the past five years continue unchecked.

"They've accomplished this through large campaign contributions, armies of lobbyists that have swamped Washington, and control of political and economic think tanks and media. Lobbyists, in fact, are the arms dealers in the war on the middle class, brokering money, influence and information between their clients [and] our elected officials.

"Yet in my entire career, I've literally never heard anyone in Congress argue that lobbyists are bad for America. In 1968 there were only 63 lobbyists in Washington. Today, there are more than 34,000, and lobbyists now outnumber our elected representatives and their staffs by a 2-to-1 margin.

"According to the nonpartisan Center for Public Integrity, from 1998 through 2004, lobbyists spent nearly $12 billion to not only influence legislation, but in many cases to write the language of the laws and regulations.

"Individual firms, corporations and national organizations spent a record $2.14 billion on lobbying members of Congress and 220 other federal agencies in 2004, according to PoliticalMoneyLine. That's nearly $6 million a day spent to influence our leaders. We really do have the best government money can buy"(552).

Coming back to our discussion of central banking and the Federal Reserve, it is important to point out that every U.S. president that has been assassinated, and almost every one that has had an attempt made on his life, has been "guilty" of the "crime" of standing up to the international bankers who have pushed for and supported central banking in this country.

As a case in point, consider J.F. Kennedy's assassination. There have been many proposals over the years as to the real reason for this crime, but most of them have knowingly or unknowingly overlooked the real issue: Kennedy was opposed to the Federal Reserve System, and sought to relieve the American people of the death grip that it held them in. To counteract the Federal Reserve, Kennedy, through Executive Order 11110, began printing non-interest-bearing United States Bank Notes (greenbacks)--an unspeakable act of "treason" against the money masters.

This is not to imply that there weren't other reasons for Kennedy's assassination. He did do other things that aroused the wrath of the globalists, such as changing the power structure of the out-of-control CIA. One thing he did was to take from it the management of covert operations, transferring this function over to the Joint Chiefs of Staff. He had also fired the agency's director, Allen Dulles, as well as two other key CIA officials, primarily because of the Bay of Pigs fiasco, which he took the blame for. He had even threatened, according to the April 25, 1966 *New York Times*, to "splinter the CIA in a thousand pieces and scatter it to the wind."

Another "mistake" Kennedy made was announcing his plans to call off U.S. involvement in Vietnam, which he did through National Security Action Memorandum #263, in October 1963. But, of course, he was murdered before being able to carry out this directive. As former Speaker of the House, Tip O'Neill, in a nationally-broadcast television documentary produced in 1992, in the wake the Oliver Stone film *JFK*, stated: "My last conversation with him [Kennedy], I'll always remember it. He said: 'As soon as the election is over, I'm going to get the boys out of Vietnam.' To myself I've always said there never would have been that great disaster we had--the loss of lives that we had-- had he lived"(64).

As further proof that Kennedy wanted to prevent full-scale armed conflict with Vietnam, the *Boston Globe* reported on June 6, 2005: "Newly uncovered documents from both American and Polish archives show that President John F. Kennedy and the Soviet Union secretly sought ways to find a diplomatic settlement to the war in Vietnam, starting three years before the United States sent combat troops"(474).

Although many reasons could be cited for Kennedy's assassination, all of them legitimate, it was surely his threat to the Federal Reserve System, more than anything else, that sealed his fate, since control of the U.S. economy has played a key role in the accomplishment of globalist goals. (For more information on Kennedy's assassination, see Appendix 4.)

It is most enlightening to take note of the fact that Mr. "Loyal to the System," Lyndon B. Johnson, was quick to rectify J.F.K.'s "crime" against the Federal Reserve. Once in office, he saw to it that the issuance of non-interest-bearing United States Notes (greenbacks) was banned (through an executive order that he passed the day after Kennedy's funeral). Later, with the passage of the

Coinage Act of 1965, Johnson discontinued the use of silver in the minting of all dimes and quarters, and had reduced the silver content of the half dollar to 40%. Finally, in 1968, Johnson had all silver removed from all U.S. coins, completing what the Federal Reserve Act had begun in 1913--the degradation of the U.S. monetary system to a valueless currency. Johnson also made sure that Vietnam War plans were whipped into high gear, just four days after Kennedy's death, through National Security Action Memorandum #273. In addition, he restored covert operations management to the CIA, so that they could continue with "business as usual."

Presidents Abraham Lincoln and James Garfield, who were also assassinated, were both opposed to a centralized banking system in this country as well. After the National Banking Act of 1863 was passed by Congress, which was one of many attempts by the bankers to gain control of our monetary system, Lincoln stated: "The money power preys upon the nation in times of peace and conspires against it in times of adversity. It is more despotic than monarchy, more insolent than autocracy, more selfish than bureaucracy. I see in the near future a crisis approaching that unnerves me and causes me to tremble for the safety of my country. Corporations have been enthroned, an era of corruption in high places will follow, and the money power of the country will endeavor to prolong its reign by working upon the prejudices of the people until the wealth is aggregated in a few hands and the republic is destroyed"(65). In 1880, President Garfield declared: "Whoever controls the volume of money in any country is master of all its legislation and commerce"(36).

Regarding the Lincoln assassination, in his 1970 book *Bitter Harvest*, author John Steinbacher wrote: "Seeking in a time of great crisis to develop their money power over the United States, the big international financiers tried to ambush President Lincoln during the dark days of the civil war, a war which some astute historians claim to have been brought on by the international money powers in order to divide and conquer this nation in the resulting chaos....Federal reserves and expenses then were small, and...Lincoln was desperate for money to finance and equip his Union armies in the field....Although hard pressed by the European money masters,...the President would have no part in their scheme to provide the funds in return for interest bearing U.S. obligations....Rather than cave in to the bankers offers to lend the government money at usurious rates of interest, in 1863 President Lincoln caused to be issued $430 million in non-interest bearing currency....With the credit of the nation behind it, the new money in the form of United States Notes was readily accepted by military suppliers....Abraham Lincoln was killed over his insistence that the United States should coin its own money rather than turn that right over to the international money changers"(318). Further along this same line, the German Chancellor, Otto von Bismarck, made this remark in 1876 about Lincoln's assassination: "They [the bankers] understood at once [because Lincoln wouldn't play their game], that the United States would escape their grip. The death of Lincoln was resolved upon. Nothing is easier than to find a fanatic to strike"(532).

President Andrew Jackson was also opposed to having a central bank in this country. In 1836 he finally succeeded in shutting down the so-called "Second Bank of the United States" (1816-1836). Speaking of this bank, Jackson once said: "The bold effort the present bank has made to control the government, the distress it had wantonly produced...are but premonitions of the fate that awaits the American people should they be deluded into a perpetuation of this institution or the establishment of another like it"(66).

In the early stages of his efforts to shut down this bank, Jackson directed the following statement at the bankers who ran it, which was surely what prompted a failed attempt on his life in 1835: "You are a den of vipers. I intend to rout you out, and by the Eternal God I will rout you out. If the people only understood the rank injustice of our banking system, there would be a revolution before morning!"(36)[Endnote 32].

President William McKinley was also assassinated. His presidency was at a time when the international bankers were again pushing heavily for a central bank in this country, not too long before the passage of the Federal Reserve Act. Also, McKinley was a strong proponent of tariffs, which are not, and never have been, popular with the globalists (tariff removals have been, and continue to be, a major part of the NAFTA and WTO agenda, except on the few occasions where tariffs can be used to hinder any competition to globalist corporations). Do you suppose that there was a connection between McKinley's assassination and his resistance to the globalist money power?

Another U.S. president who was staunchly supportive of tariffs was Warren G. Harding. Although not considered a victim of assassination, Harding, nevertheless, died under rather mysterious circumstances. On August 2, 1923, he collapsed and remained unconscious until he died the next day. White House physician General Charles E. Sawyer later declared, without ever performing an autopsy, that the cause of death was an "embolism," case closed. Did the globalist money masters have Harding murdered as well? He certainly had aroused their anger. For not only was he a strong proponent of tariffs, but he was doggedly opposed to world government. Notice what he said during his inaugural address on March 4, 1921: "We recognize the new order in the world....But America, our America, the America builded on the foundation laid by the inspired fathers, can be a party to no permanent military alliance....Every commitment must be made in the exercise of our national sovereignty....[A] world supergovernment is contrary to everything we cherish and can have no sanction by our Republic. This is not selfishness, it is sanctity. It is not aloofness, it is security. It is not suspicion of others, it is patriotic adherence to the things which made us what we are....It has been proved again and again that we cannot, while throwing our markets open to the world, maintain American standards of living and opportunity, and hold our industrial eminence in such unequal competition. There is a luring fallacy in the theory of banished barriers of trade, but preserved American standards require our higher production costs to be reflected in our tariffs on imports"(18, pp. 42, 43). (Would you be surprised to discover that Marx was a major advocate of tariff removals?) [Endnote 33]

Harding was also opposed to the Federal Reserve. In 1921, he said of it: "The Federal Reserve Bank is an institution owned by the stockholding member banks. The government has not a dollar's worth of stock in it"(532).

The push for a central bank in this country goes way back to the earliest days of U.S. history. The first attempt at such a bank was the First Bank of the United States (1791-1811). One of its most eager antagonists, Thomas Jefferson, was well-aware of the corrupt, far-reaching plans of its creators. Here is one particularly intriguing warning he gave about their enslaving intentions: "If the American people ever allow private banks to control the issue of their currency [which is just what the Federal Reserve System does], first by inflation, and then by deflation, the banks and the corporations that will grow up around them will deprive the people of all property until their children wake up homeless on the continent their fathers occupied. The issuing power of money should be taken from the banks and restored to Congress and the people to whom it belongs"(70, p. 84). Jefferson also stated back in 1791: "I place economy among the first and foremost of virtues, and public debt as the greatest of dangers to be feared. To preserve our independence, we must not let our rulers load us with perpetual debt.

"If we run into such debts, we must be taxed in our meat and our drink, in our necessities and in our comforts, in our labor and in our amusements. If we can prevent the government from wasting the labor of the people under the pretense of caring for them, they will be happy"(36)[Endnote 34].

Jefferson was never shot at or killed for his resistance to centralized banking in the United States. The reason for this was probably the fact that his brazen outspokenness against central banking would certainly have drawn unwanted attention to the international banking crowd as the culprits behind this scheme--attention that they clearly couldn't afford at this early stage in their game.

As an interesting side note, I want to point out that the timing of the War of 1812 was impeccable. It came at a time when the European bankers (particularly the House of Rothschild which ran, and still runs, England) were furious with Congress for not rechartering the First Bank of the United States.

But Congress soon had a change of heart, creating the Second Bank of the United States just four years after this war had started, solely because of the enormous debt created by it. In 1812, the national debt of the United States was $45 million. But by 1816, it rose to a staggering $127 million. In other words, the War of 1812 conveniently created the need for another central bank (or what was hoped would become a fully-functioning central bank).

Almost immediately after its creation in 1816, the Second Bank of the United States began pressuring President James Monroe to take high interest loans to help pay off the 1812 war debt. When he refused to do so, the bank simply flooded the economy with exorbitant amounts of worthless paper currency which created massive inflation, culminating in the 1819 depression. Are you seeing how this game works? Is history starting to make a little more sense now?

This method of bringing a nation to its knees through the economic sorcery of centralized banking, which began with the Bank of England in the seventeenth century, had proved so successful, and required so little effort, that, as the decades of the nineteenth century rolled on and it became clear that such economic witchcraft truly was the best and fastest way to attain control of the entire planet, central banks began popping up all over Europe. Here are a few glaring examples:

1800 - France
1813 - Denmark
1814 - Netherlands
1816 - Austria
1840 - Finland
1841 - Greece
1846 - Portugal
1850 - Belgium
1856 - Spain
1870 - Germany
1893 - Armenia
1893 - Italy
1907 - Switzerland

As you can see, our globalist banker friends were quite busy during this period, setting the stage for global conquest [Endnote 35]. But the grand prize didn't come for them until 1913, with the establishment of what they had lusted after for over 100 years--total control over the U.S. economy through the establishment here of a permanent, full-fledged central bank--the Federal Reserve.

* * * * * * *

The information we have been looking at is, no doubt, shocking and hard to believe. This is because we have been lied to through both the media and our educational system. As you may have guessed by now, the conspirators have full control over these avenues as well. In fact, they haven't left ANY stone unturned. We will be looking at their takeover of our media and educational system shortly. But for now, let us first closely examine some of the false beliefs that these avenues of public information and learning have been propagating regarding our government and economy.

False beliefs [Endnote 36]

<u>False Belief #1: We live in a democracy.</u>

The government that our Constitution is based upon is NOT a democracy, but a republic--a constitutional republic. "But wait," one might object, "Doesn't our own president keep referring to America as a 'democracy,' whose job it is to make the whole world 'safe for democracy'?" Well, the sad fact is that our president, better yet, ALL of our presidents for a good many years now, have been telling us a LOT of things that just aren't true. But what IS true is that America was never a democracy--it has always been a republic, and will continue to be such for as long as the Constitution stands.

Article 4, Section 4 of the U.S. Constitution states: "the United States shall guarantee to every State in this Union a Republican form of Government." Think about it: When we pledge allegiance to the flag, do we not say "to the *Republic*, for which it stands"? The word "democracy" does not appear anywhere in the Constitution, the constitutions of any of the 50 states, or the Declaration of Independence. Our Founding Fathers never intended for this country to be a democracy. Why? Well, for one thing, all democracies throughout history have failed. John Adams stated in a letter to John Taylor on April 14, 1814: "Democracy never lasts long. It soon wastes itself, exhausts and murders itself. There never was a democracy yet that did not commit suicide." Back in 1928, the U.S. Army defined democracy as follows: "Democracy: A government of the masses....Results in mobocracy [total chaos]. Attitude toward property is communistic--negating property rights....Result is demagogism [the act of politicians appealing to the emotions and prejudices of the people], license, agitation, discontent, anarchy"(316).

As for the claim that it is America's job to make the whole world "safe for democracy," this isn't true either. For one thing, democracy isn't safe! For another thing, it's not America's job to stick its nose in the affairs of other nations. It IS America's job, however, to defend, protect, and uphold our constitutional republic--something that is no longer being done in this country.

"So what's the difference," you may be asking, "between a democracy and a republic?" Well, in a republic, the law (in conformance with the Constitution, in the case of the U.S.) is the supreme rule of the land (which for U.S. citizens means that each one of us has certain natural, inalienable rights that the government has no authority to tamper with). In a democracy, however, the supreme rule of the land is determined by the current opinion of the masses. Thus the rights of the individual are subject to majoritarian leanings (which can easily be manipulated through propaganda)[Endnote 37]. This is totally contrary to the system of government that this country was constitutionally designed to uphold and enforce.

<u>False Belief #2: The government grants us our rights, and it is the job of the courts to defend our rights for us.</u>

The fact is, your rights come from God (or, for you atheists, they are your natural entitlement from birth)--not from any creation of man. And it is not the job of the courts to assert and defend your God-given rights [Endnote 38]; it's YOUR job, and MY job ("we the people"). It's the job of the courts to merely see to it that justice is equally served. The problem is that nearly everyone has forgotten this, and has thus sat back and let despots take control of how the government and the courts are run. And now we are seeing the consequences of our apathy.

<u>False Belief #3: The Federal Reserve System is owned and run by the government.</u>

Though this issue has already been dealt with in considerable detail, and will yet be elaborated on even more in the coming pages, it seems fitting at this time to cite a few excerpts from perhaps the most powerful speech ever delivered before Congress on the Federal Reserve, which brilliantly summarizes the enslaving nature of this system. The speaker was Representative James Traficant [Endnote 39]; the date was March 17, 1993: "Members of Congress are official trustees presiding over the greatest reorganization of any Bankrupt entity in world history, the US Government. We are setting forth hopefully, a blueprint for our future. There are some who say it is a coroner's report that will lead to our demise.

"It is an established fact that the United States Federal Government has been dissolved by the Emergency Banking Act, March 9, 1933, 48 Stat. 1, Public Law 89-719; declared by President Roosevelt, being bankrupt and insolvent. H.J.R. 192, 73rd Congress m session June 5, 1933--Joint Resolution To Suspend The Gold Standard and Abrogate The Gold Clause dissolved the Sovereign Authority of the United States and the official capacities of all United States Government offices, Officers, and Departments and is further evidence that the United States Federal Government exists today in name only.

"The receivers of the United States Bankruptcy are the International Bankers, via the United Nations, the World Bank and the International Monetary Fund. All United States Offices, Officials, and Departments are now operating within a de facto status in name only under Emergency War Powers.

"With the Constitutional Republican form of Government now dissolved, the receivers of the Bankruptcy have adopted a new form of government for the United States. This new form of government is known as a Democracy, being an established Socialist/Communist order...

"It is essential that we comprehend the distinction between real money and paper money substitute. One cannot get rich by accumulating money substitutes, one can only get deeper into debt. We the People no longer have any 'money.' Most Americans have not been paid any 'money' for a very long time, perhaps not in their entire life. Now do you comprehend why you feel broke? Now do you understand why you are 'bankrupt,' along with the rest of the country?

"Federal Reserve Notes (FRNs) are unsigned checks written on a closed account. FRNs are an inflatable paper system designed to create debt through inflation (devaluation of currency). Whenever there is an increase of the supply of a money substitute in the economy without a corresponding increase in the gold and silver backing, inflation occurs....

"[T]he Federal Reserve System agreed to extend the federal United States corporation all the credit 'money substitute' it needed. Like any other debtor, the federal United States government had to assign collateral and security to their creditors as a condition of the loan. Since the federal United States didn't have any assets, they assigned the private property of their 'economic slaves,' the U.S. citizens, as collateral against the un-payable federal debt. They also pledged the unincorporated federal territories, national park forests, birth certificates, and nonprofit organizations, as collateral against the federal debt. All has already been transferred as payment to the international bankers.

"...Why are 90% of Americans mortgaged to the hilt and have little or no assets after all debts and liabilities have been paid? Why does it feel like you are working harder and harder and getting less and less?

"We are reaping what has been sown, and the results of our harvest is a painful bankruptcy, and a foreclosure on American property, precious liberties, and a way of life. Few of our elected representatives in Washington DC have dared to tell the truth. The federal United States is bankrupt. Our children will inherit this unpayable debt, and the tyranny to enforce paying it"(443).

False Belief #4: Inflation is a natural and unavoidable phenomenon.

The truth is that inflation is engineered as each new paper dollar that is printed into circulation reduces the value of all dollars already in existence. To help hide this ugly deed, experience has taught the Federal Reserve that a 5% annual devaluation of the money supply can be consistently maintained without alarming the public [Endnote 40]. To date, this insidious practice has gradually robbed Americans of over 90% of their purchasing power. It has also generated trillions of dollars in profits for the private banking monopoly that rents us our money supply.

False Belief #5: Our government owes the national debt to itself.

If this were true, the government could simply forgive itself its own debt and start over. The fact is that the government owes most of this debt, as was already mentioned, to the Federal Reserve System (some is owed to foreign countries). Or, more accurately, most of it is owed to the elite foreign and domestic families who lobbied certain Congressmen to ramrod through the Federal Reserve Act back in 1913, who to this day comprise the "Class A" voting stockholders of the Federal Reserve System.

False Belief #6: The 16th Amendment to the U.S. Constitution, the so-called "income tax amendment," authorized the income tax.

Not so! The Supreme Court ruled in 1916, in Stanton vs. Baltic Mining (a case that has never been overturned), that the 16th Amendment conferred "no new power of taxation" [Endnote 41]. Imagine that! The highest court in the land ruled that the 16th Amendment changed absolutely nothing! Why? Because it couldn't, since Article 1, Section 2, Clause 3 and Article 1, Section 9, Clause 4 of the Constitution entirely forbid Congress from directly taxing U.S. citizens [Endnote 42]. Therefore, the 16th Amendment does not give the IRS any legally-binding authority to seize one-third of each U.S. citizen's paycheck from week to week. So why, you may ask, was the 16th Amendment even written in the first place? Simply to create the illusion of a new authority to directly tax the wages of U.S. citizens--an illusion upon which the IRS still relies.

The IRS loves illusion games. Just look at the IRS Code, for example. Its mere size alone has served to discourage most people from attempting to make any sense of it. Often it happens that different sections of the Code contradict each other, while other sections are very obscure and difficult to follow, even for many IRS agents themselves. The Code was specifically designed this way, to overwhelm and confuse citizens into thinking that they are liable for something that the IRS, at the highest levels, knows they are not.

Yet, all the while that the IRS plays such manipulative word games, many of its own publications ironically state that it operates under a system of "voluntary compliance." For example, former IRS Commissioner Mortimer Chaplin stated in the 1975 Internal Revenue Audit Manual: "Our tax system is based on individual self-assessment and voluntary compliance." Though this is indeed an ironic admission, the IRS, in fact, has to say this because it knows that there is no law that gives it taxation authority over U.S. citizens' paychecks. But it sure rigged things up nicely with every employer across the country, to see to it that we practice such "voluntary compliance" if we desire a job. This is nothing but extortion. Notice what the Supreme Court declared in 1875 (back in the good old days, before we had a fraudulent income tax), in the case of Savings and Loan Association vs. Topeka: "To lay with one hand the power of the government on the property of the citizen and with the other to bestow it upon favored individuals to aid private enterprises and build up private fortunes [such as what the IRS does today for the Federal Reserve!] is none the less a robbery because it is done under the forms of law and is called taxation"(313, p. 292).

It is truly because of our ignorance and apathy, to a large extent, that the government is able to perpetuate this tax fraud against us (and so many other frauds, for that matter). With this thought in mind, notice what the U.S. Supreme Court stated in the case of United States vs. Minker: "Because of what appears to be a lawful command on the surface, many citizens, because of their respect for what appears to be law, are cunningly coerced into waiving their rights due to ignorance." In 1969, former Senator Henry Bellmon made this astonishing statement: "In a recent conversation with an official at the Internal Revenue Service, I was amazed when he told me: 'If the taxpayers of this country ever discover that the IRS operates on 90% bluff, the entire system will collapse.'"

But perhaps an even bigger factor that has enabled the government to pull off the income tax hoax has been our fear, as the next two quotes will confirm: "Fear is the key element for the IRS in achieving its mission. Without fear, the IRS would have a difficult time maintaining our so-called system of voluntary compliance." -Santo Presti, former Treasury agent(317). "More tax is collected by fear and intimidation than by the law. People are afraid of the IRS." - Former IRS District Chief David Patnoe(72)[Endnote 43].

But the IRS is also afraid of us--afraid of us finding out the truth about the income tax. As a case in point, in section 5221 of the Internal Revenue Manual, titled "Returns Compliance Programs," we find this warning for IRS agents: "[S]ome techniques [of tax collecting] can be used only in connection with a full-scale program due to the nature of the tax situation and the need to avoid unnecessary taxpayer reaction."

Could this "nature of the tax situation" be the fact that the income tax is something other than what we've always assumed it to be? Could this "unnecessary taxpayer reaction," which the IRS seeks to "avoid," be the American public finally waking up to the truth?

Foreseeing the dangers of the passage of the 16th Amendment, roughly three years before it was passed, Richard E. Byrd, Speaker of the Virginia House of Delegates, voiced the following prophetic words of warning and opposition: "This Amendment...will extend the Federal power so as to reach the citizen in the ordinary business of life. A hand from Washington will be stretched out and placed upon every man's business; the eye of a Federal inspector will be in every man's counting house. The law will of necessity have inquisitorial features, it will provide penalties. It will create a complicated machinery. Under it businessmen will be hauled into courts distant from their homes. Heavy fines imposed by distant and unfamiliar tribunals will constantly menace the taxpayer. An army of Federal inspectors, spies and detectives will descend....They will compel men of business to show their books and disclose secrets of their affairs. They will dictate forms of bookkeeping. They will require statements and affidavits....When the Federal government gets a strangle hold on the individual businessmen, state lines will exist nowhere but on the maps. Its agents will everywhere supervise the commercial life of the states"(73). Sound familiar?

There have actually been many IRS employees over the years who have woken up to the fact that the income tax is illegal, and consequently left their job with the agency. One such person was Joseph Banister. On March 26, 1999, WorldNetDaily reported on his awakening experience in an article called "IRS Special Agent Challenges System," which stated: "'The Internal Revenue Service is everything the so-called tax protesters said it was; non-responsive, unable to withstand scrutiny, tyrannical, and oblivious to the rule of law and the U.S. Constitution.'

"That's how Joseph Banister--a certified public accountant who, until last month, was an investigator and gunslinger for the Criminal Investigation Division of the IRS--now regards his former employer. His conclusion is based in part on a personal two-year investigation into the agency's history and purpose--an investigation he began somewhat reluctantly, never expecting he'd reach the conclusion he did.

"His research led him to question its very legality and constitutionality. Deeply disturbed by his discoveries, he summarized these in a report which, in February, he sent to his supervisors, and asked them to respond to three allegations:

1. That the filing of federal income tax returns is voluntary and the filing of federal income tax returns is not required

2. That the 16th Amendment to the U.S. Constitution was never ratified [Note: This is true--the 16 Amendment was never properly ratified. You can read about this in a fascinating 2-part book called *The Law That Never Was: The Fraud of the 16th Amendment and Personal Income Tax* by Bill Benson (ISBN:

B0006ELT78). I generally don't use this argument, however, since, as the Supreme Court itself admits, this amendment doesn't grant Congress new powers of taxation, which we saw above.]

3. That income taxes are not used to pay for daily government operations, but to pay the interest on the national debt [we will cover this in the next False Belief]."

And what kind of response do you think Banister got from the IRS? WorldNetDaily quoted these opening words of the response letter: "'The Internal Revenue Service will not be responding to your request and will provide you with the necessary paperwork to tender your resignation,' his supervisor wrote....

"Banister says he was 'astonished' and 'confused,' at the response--or rather 'the lack of it.' After all, he had worked for the agency five years. He believed his allegations were serious enough to warrant a response. Even a personal plea to Commissioner Charles Rossotti himself, wasn't enough. His career as a special agent was so much dust"(476).

What do you suppose became of Mr. Banister? On November 18, 2004, he was arrested for--you guessed it--"tax crimes." He was later released, after paying out a handsome $25,000 bond. They couldn't answer his questions about what makes a person liable for paying the fraudulent income tax, but they arrested him anyway. This is nothing but pure harassment and intimidation. Actually, he is one of the lucky ones. Usually they send in a SWAT team that results in the death of the "tax protester." It's all part of living in a "free" country [Endnote 44].

False Belief #7: The purpose of the income tax is to raise revenue to pay for the day-to-day operations of the federal government.

Not so! In the January 1946 issue of *American Affairs*, Beardsley Ruml, at that time the Chairman of the powerful New York branch of the Federal Reserve System, wrote an article titled "Taxes For Revenue Are Obsolete." In the introduction to this article, the editor of the magazine summarized Ruml's views by saying: "His thesis is that, given...a central banking system and an inconvertible currency [money not backed by gold], a sovereign national government is finally free of money worries and needs no longer levy taxes for the purpose of providing itself with revenue"(52, p. 204).

Ruml, incidentally, was the one who devised the system of automatic withholding during WW II. Thus he is an obvious reliable authority on the purpose and nature of the federal income tax.

So if our federal income tax is not needed to fund the federal government, then what, exactly, is this tax money used for? On January 15, 1984, the Grace Commission, a private-sector, blue ribbon committee impaneled by President Ronald Reagan to find ways to cut government spending, stated in its final report to the president: "...100% of what is collected is absorbed solely by interest on the Federal Debt....[A]ll individual income tax revenues are gone before one nickel is spent on the service taxpayers expect from government"(67).

Yes, you have read correctly--not one nickel (or even one penny!) of personal income tax collected by the IRS goes to pay for government services/programs. Instead, this money is used to pay the interest on our "debt" to the Federal Reserve.

But there is another, even more sinister reason for imposing this unconstitutional tax on American citizens. In the same *American Affairs* article mentioned a moment ago, Beardsley Ruml wrote: "[T]he most important single purpose to be served by the imposition of federal taxes is the maintenance of a dollar which has stable purchasing power over the years. Without the use of federal taxation, all other means of stabilization...are unavailing." In other words, the true purpose of the income tax is to maintain relative economic stability. The siphoning off of excess dollars from circulation provided by the income tax helps to hide the inflation--perhaps even the hyperinflation--that would result from issuing too much paper money. But what Ruml failed to mention above is the fact that the income tax was never intended to PREVENT dollar devaluation, but to help to CONTROL this process so that it would happen more subtly, without alerting the public. This is the only "stabilization" that the income tax provides.

The income tax, of course, has still another purpose, perhaps no less important than that of disguising inflation. The globalists know all-too-well that money equals power. By robbing significant amounts of our income each week, they have made "we the people" much less of a threat to their plans. This situation becomes all the more pathetic, and seems most ironic, when one considers the fact that the American Revolution started over protests against unjust taxes. Yet those taxes were indirect taxes and only amounted to between one and three percent of a person's wages. By contrast, the bulk of the taxes we pay today are direct taxes, and, looking at our modern tax burden collectively (local, state, and federal combined), it amounts to well over fifty percent of our wages!

So now you know the truth behind the income tax.

But a question still remains: If the taxes on our wages are not what funds government services/programs, then what does the government subsist on? Today the government subsists primarily on loans that it takes from the Federal Reserve--loans that "we the people" get stuck paying for (although, remember, as we saw earlier, that these loans mathematically can never actually get paid off--all that gets paid is the interest, or a portion thereof; but, as we also saw earlier, when we pay this portion of the interest, the national debt actually increases, since this money paid out was itself initially borrowed from the Federal Reserve, as this is how money is now put into circulation).

It would be bad enough if the government just illegally taxed our wages each week to directly fund itself. But when we realize that it works through the Federal Reserve "middle man," which serves no practical (or legal) function whatsoever, except to drown us in a bottomless pit of debt, our dilemma becomes all the more alarming.

What a contrast this is from how the government originally funded itself. Prior to the establishment of the Federal Reserve and the "income tax," the government subsisted solely on indirect taxes (such as purchase taxes) and tariffs. All during that time, the national budget was balanced every year, except during the Civil War period.

While some might argue that today's government couldn't function on tariffs and indirect taxes alone, this is only partially true. The only reason it couldn't thusly function today is because of its presently over-extended size and unrestrained spending habits. But if it were forced to "downsize" and cut out so very many unnecessary (and often undesirable, if not downright despicable) programs and bureaucracies, and cease from sending billions overseas in the name of so-called "foreign aid" [Endnote 45], and learn to function on a limited budget like the rest of us, then it most certainly could function adequately on tariffs and indirect taxes alone, as it once did (of course, this all presupposes a return to a legal, constitutional money system backed by precious metals, and an abolition of the Federal Reserve System). Understand that, when still on the gold standard, the U.S. government was restrained from over-spending, by the amount of gold that it had--it couldn't spend more than it had in reserve. But under the current system, this barrier is removed so that the government spends without restraint, and all at our expense. Thus it is open season on our wallets and pocketbooks.

False Belief #8: All American citizens are required to file and pay income tax.

Though this issue, too, was already dealt with earlier, it requires a little further elaboration here.

Repeated warnings from the government and the media have probably led you to believe that all citizens have an obligation to file income tax returns, and that they owe their "fair share" of this tax burden, whether they like paying it or not. But is this really true? Are all U.S. citizens liable to pay tax on their "income" (wages)? To see where Congress made the U.S. citizen, working within the fifty states, liable for this tax on his/her own "income," simply read chapters one through six of the IRS Code, which cover the tax on "income," and locate the corresponding liability statute. Well, good luck, because it doesn't exist! That's right--you can scan the entire Code by computer on a CD-ROM, or on the Internet, and you can rest assured that you won't find it. Tens of thousands have looked with a fine tooth comb and have discovered that it's just not there. If you doubt this, try it yourself. Yes, the IRS can't even rely on its own Code to compel us to comply with its fraudulent "income" tax.

The only ones liable for this tax are foreigners, or U.S. citizens working overseas in a foreign country that is under a current tax treaty with the U.S. Although your tax professional may point to Code section 1 which imposes the income tax on "individuals," researching the underlying Treasury regulations for code section 1 will reveal that the "individual" referred to is one with foreign-source income only. Which is why, as outrageous as it may sound, it is absolutely correct to state that, unless in receipt of foreign-source income, you are not now paying the income tax, nor have you ever paid one dime in income tax your entire life. So what tax HAVE you been paying? We will deal with that question in a moment. But first we must deal with another question you may be asking yourself: How could it possibly be true that I have never paid a single dime in income tax when I, as a taxpayer, have always been required to file Form 1040 to report my income? This question brings us to our next false belief...

False Belief #9: Form 1040 is required to be used by all working Americans to report their income.

Not so! The Department of the Treasury, which supervises the IRS, made the following declaration back in 1916: "The responsible heads, agents, or representatives of nonresident aliens...shall make a full and complete return of the income there-from on...Form 1040..."(81).

So Form 1040, just like the income tax, is for foreigners (or U.S. citizens with foreign-source income). As further proof of this fact, under the 1980 Paperwork Reduction Act, Congress made the Office of Management and Budget (OMB) the watchdog required to approve any government agency form that asks for information from a U.S. citizen. According to the OMB and the National Office of the IRS, the required form for a U.S. citizen to use to report income is not Form 1040--it's Form 2555, titled "Foreign Earned Income." The top of Form 2555 says, "attach to front of Form 1040." Form 1040, "U.S. Individual Income Tax Return," is merely a supplemental worksheet to the required Form 2555, which states, "for use by U.S. citizens" (with foreign-source income, of course). Apparently the IRS does know the difference between an "individual" and a "citizen."

Now back to our other question: If you haven't been paying the income tax, then what have you been paying? You've been paying the employment tax, otherwise known as the wage, or Social Security (socialism) tax. The employment tax is found in chapters twenty-one through twenty-five of the IRS Code, and has nothing whatsoever to do with the income tax under the law [Endnote 46]. And who is liable for the employment tax? The "employee." But not just any employee--only one who volunteers to apply for a Social Security number; one who volunteers to use that number to build up credits toward retirement and other federal benefits; one who volunteers to sign a Form W-4, "Employee's Withholding Allowance Certificate," and allows taxes to be withheld from his/her paychecks. This leads us to our next false belief...

False Belief #10: Submitting the W-4 is required by law.

Wrong again! The fact is that there is no law requiring any worker to execute a Form W-4. It's strictly elective. Of course, it appears mandatory, since most employers won't hire you without one. Why not? Because they've never read the actual law, and thus they believe, like everyone else believes, that it is required. But the truth is that the W-4 is simply a permission slip that allows an "employer" to withhold taxes from an "employee."

"So," the question is asked, "is everyone who hires others automatically an 'employer'?" No--only those who have signed Form SS-4, "Application for Employer Identification Number." And, as you may have guessed by now, this form is not required either. After all, an application is always voluntary, isn't it? Otherwise there would be no reason to apply. The proper paperwork to stop tax withholding in the workplace is explained in 26 Code of Federal Regulations, section 1.1441-5 and in IRS Publication 515, which, in speaking to the withholding agent, states: "If an individual gives you a written statement stating that he or she is a citizen or resident of the United States, and you do not know otherwise, you do not have to withhold tax" [Endnote 47]. Imagine that! One who hires others does not need to be an unpaid bookkeeper for the federal government, or an accomplice in the government's theft of the wages of its workers!

False Belief #11: All U.S. citizens are required to obtain a Social Security number.

Not true, and never has been! The fact is, as the Social Security Administration readily admits in its standard form letter to anyone who asks: "The Social Security Act does not require a person to have a Social Security number in order to live and work in the United States, nor does it require a [number] simply for the sake of having one." Title 42 of the United States Code, Section 405(B), states under Subsection II that Social Security numbers are assigned "to an individual who is an applicant for, or recipient of, benefits."

So, once again, there simply is no law that requires a U.S. citizen to obtain or use a number, or to get one for his or her child. Shocked? It gets worse: The IRS can't even establish a record in its computer systems (by law) for any entity that does not volunteer to number itself, whether a corporation, a partnership, or an individual person. This is why those who choose not to apply for a Social Security number are non-taxpayers (or non-income-taxpayers), and are never contacted by the IRS their entire lives.

Social Security numbers are the primary means through which the banker boys have been able to efficiently track, exploit, and control us from the cradle to the grave. Notice what Carroll Quigley had to say on this matter, in *Tragedy and Hope*: "[H]is [the individual's] freedom and choice will be controlled within very narrow alternatives by the fact that he will be numbered from birth and followed, as a number, through his educational training, his required military or other public service, his tax contributions, his health and medical requirements, and his final retirement and death benefits." In this quote, Quigley was, of course, talking about more than just Social Security numbers--he was talking about an as-yet-future global numbering system. However, we can see that the Social Security numbering system has been serving as a good prep for what is to come.

Incidentally, not only have the globalists been using the Social Security system to their advantage, but they were the ones who created it in the first place. Though we have been told that F.D.R. masterminded this government program, he was merely the puppet who presented it to the American people on behalf of his string pullers (the same is true, of course, for Welfare and other socialist "New Deal" programs that were introduced during F.D.R.'s administration). Notice what F.D.R.'s son-in-law had to say about this: "For a long time I felt that F.D.R. had developed many thoughts and ideas that were his own to benefit this country, the U.S.A. But, he didn't. Most of his thoughts, his political 'ammunition' as it were, were carefully manufactured for him in advance by the CFR-One World Money Group. Brilliantly with great gusto, like a fine piece of artillery, he exploded [this] prepared 'ammunition' in the middle of an unsuspecting target, the American people--and thus paid off and retained his internationalist political support"(82, p. 185). Lyndon Johnson, of course, later carried the socialist torch to new heights in the U.S., with his so-called "Great Society."

The push for socialism has been, and continues to be, an important piece of the twisted globalist puzzle. H.G. Wells, who wrote extensively about the coming world government, made this point very clear in his 1939 book that he fittingly titled *The New World Order*: "This new and complete [global] Revolution we contemplate can be defined in a very few words. It is a) outright world-socialism, scientifically planned and directed, plus b) a sustained insistence upon law, law based on a fuller, more jealously conceived restatement of the personal Rights of Man [such as the 'right' to follow whatever the globalist masters dictate], plus c) ...a sedulous expansion of the educational organization to the ever growing demands of the new order [more on this shortly]....Putting it at its compactest, it is the triangle of Socialism, Law, and Knowledge which frames the Revolution that may yet save the world"(148). The former Soviet president, Mikhail Gorbachev, himself a dedicated globalist, echoed these same sentiments of pushing for socialism around the world, in his book *Perestroika*: "We will proceed toward better socialism rather than away from it....Any hopes that we will begin to build a different, non-socialist society and go over to the other camp are unrealistic and futile. Those in the West who expect us to give up socialism will be disappointed"(83).

And why is socialism so important to the globalist cause? Well, for one thing, it increases government power over people by intruding more and more into every aspect of their private lives, and it makes them dependent upon their government for its "favors," to say nothing of the financial rewards that it brings to the globalists, as social programs tend to be very costly, resulting in huge borrowings from the Federal Reserve. (Note: While it can be rightly argued that some of these social programs are needed today, it can also be rightly argued that such needs have been manufactured.) Marx, of course, was a major advocate of socialism, recognizing it as the best way to subtly achieve dictatorial control en route toward a communistic government.

One globalist organization that has helped tremendously to advance socialism is the Fabian Society of England (of which, incidentally, H.G. Wells was a pioneering member). The methodology that the Fabians have faithfully followed has been to slowly introduce socialism in countries around the world, never labeling it outright as socialism (at least not in the U.S.) so that public awareness and suspicion would not be aroused. This deceptive Fabian tactic was clearly revealed by Roger Baldwin, an American Fabian and former Executive Director of the ACLU (American Civil Liberties Union--itself a globalist/socialist institution), when he gave the following caution to other ACLU leaders: "Do steer away from making it [the ACLU] look like a Socialist Enterprise. We want also to look like patriots in everything we do. We want to get a good lot of flags, talk a good deal about the Constitution and what our forefathers wanted to make of the country, and to show that we are really the folks that really stand for the spirit of our institutions"(84, p. 222).

To help illustrate just how twisted the Fabian mind-set really is, take note of the following: The headquarters of the Fabian Society of England are located at the Beatrice Webb House in Surrey, England. This building originally contained a stained glass window upon which was found the proceeding verse from a poem written by Omar Khayyam, himself a dedicated Fabian Socialist, which served as a summation of Fabian philosophy and purpose: "Dear love, couldst thou and I with fate conspire, to grasp this sorry scheme of this entire, would we not shatter it to bits, and then remould it nearer to the heart's desire!"

Also depicted on this stained glass window were Sidney Webb and George Bernard Shaw, two of the society's prominent leaders in its early days, each striking a globe with a hammer, obviously molding it closer to the heart's desire of Fabianism. Also depicted on this window was the official Fabian crest, or coat of arms, which pictured a wolf in sheep's clothing. How fitting!

You will recall our discussion earlier, under False Belief #1, of how many have been led to falsely believe that the United States is a democracy. The globalists' use of this term is simply their way of disguising their socialist agenda, and to make it sound more appealing. But the truth is that there is precious little difference between democracy and socialism. *Webster's New International Dictionary* defines socialism as follows: "A political and economic theory of social organization based on collective or governmental ownership and democratic management of the essential means for the production and distribution of goods." A socialistic government can be said to be "democratic" because it manipulates the masses by engineering consensus through propaganda. In this regard, it is significant to notice the following mission statement of the World Socialist Movement, which is yet another globalist front organization: "The WSM consists of ordinary people who have organized themselves democratically with one objective: to bring about a complete change in world society" [Endnote 48].

False Belief #12: The law requires everyone to join Social Security and pay Social Security taxes, and no one could possibly ever quit Social Security.

This is perhaps the biggest deception of all. Walter E. Williams, distinguished Professor of Economics at George Mason University, wrote: "All we have to do now is to inform the public that the payment of social security taxes is voluntary and watch the mass exodus" [Endnote 49].

The reality is that there isn't even any "security" anymore in this "retirement plan." The funds have basically already been depleted, having been illegally used to help bring down the national debt and to balance the budget. Payments of Social Security benefits today come primarily from further loans that the government gets from the Federal Reserve, thus creating more debt. This pattern simply cannot go on for much longer. People who depend on Social Security today for their future retirement are in for a miserable disappointment. Notice what the former Commissioner of Social Security, Dorcas Hardy, said in the December 1995 issue of *Reader's Digest*: "There is no prospect that today's younger workers will receive all the Social Security and Medicare benefits currently promised them."

This was one of the main reasons, by the way, for the Bush Jr. privatization plan for social Security--to transfer responsibility for these funds away from the government, so that when the bubble inevitably bursts, nobody will figure out that the government had looted the public's retirement money(411)[Endnote 50].

False Belief #13: All U.S. citizens must produce their books and records when summoned to appear before the IRS for an audit.

Not so! On July 28, 1969, Judge Cummings of the 7th Circuit Court of Appeals stated, in the case of U.S. vs. Dickerson: "Only the rare taxpayer would be likely to know that he could refuse to produce his records to IRS agents....Who would believe the ironic truth that the cooperative taxpayer fares much worse than the individual who relies upon his constitutional rights?" - 413 F.2d 1117.

The fact is that the 4th and 5th Amendments to the U.S. Constitution protect your right to privacy in your books and records, as well as your right to not be compelled to be a witness against yourself in a criminal action (but who's the real criminal here, anyway?). Notice the proceeding fascinating admission that the IRS made in this regard: "An individual may refuse to exhibit his books and records for examination on the ground that compelling him to do so violates his right against self-incrimination under the Fifth Amendment and constitutes an illegal search and seizure under the Fourth Amendment"(85).

False Belief #14: The IRS has the lawful authority to press criminal charges against a U.S. citizen who refuses to pay the income tax.

Once again, not so! The Internal Revenue Manual, chapter 1100, titled "Organization and Staffing," states in section 1132.75: "The Criminal Investigation Division enforces the criminal statute applicable to income, estate, gift, employment, and excise tax laws (other than those excepted in IRM 1112.51) involving United States citizens residing in foreign countries and nonresident aliens subject to Federal income tax filing requirements."

* * * * * * *

So what does all of this mean? It means that our constitutional rights have been trampled underfoot, with the consent and blessing of our political leaders. You see, the Founding Fathers wrote the Constitution in such a way as to protect us from the very type of economic servitude that we are now living under. The reality is that we are no longer a free people. We have become slaves to an oppressive, pocket-picking system that has no interest in our rights or freedoms as individuals. As the life continues to be sucked out of hard-working Americans across this country, destroying the American dream, the string-pullers, working behind the scenes, become ever more wealthy, and thus ever more powerful. Can you not see what is happening here? Our beloved country is falling (or already has fallen) into the hands of a hostile power, and almost nobody is even aware of it. But fasten your seatbelt, for you are in for an increasingly bumpy ride as we reveal more and more pieces of the ugly globalist puzzle.

"The most secret knowledge, a science which outdates history, is the science of control over the people, governments and civilizations. The foundation of this ultimate discipline is the control of wealth. Through the control of wealth comes the control of public information and the necessities of life....Through the control of basic necessities comes direct control of people. A significant portion of the American public is yet to become aware of the Invisible Government of Monetary Power. Americans still believe that they are working toward a better way of life. [But] social customs and forms of administration in the United States are being carefully and gradually modified. The change from one type of culture to another is thus accomplished without arousing serious public challenge. The stark truth is that America is now passing from a constitutional republic into a totalitarian, worldwide government." - Former Lieutenant Colonel Archibald E. Roberts of the U.S. Army and director of the Committee to Restore the Constitution, testifying before a special joint committee of the Wisconsin State Legislature(86).

"History records that the money changers have used every form of abuse, intrigue, deceit, and violent means possible to maintain their control over governments by controlling money and its issuance." - James Madison(396).

"When a government is dependent upon bankers for money, they and not the leaders of the government control the situation, since the hand that gives is above the hand that takes....Money has no Motherland; financiers are without patriotism and without decency; their sole object is gain." - Napoleon Bonoparte(396).

"Little wonder that the elite hated the middle class which challenged them in the name of God-given liberty. And little wonder that this hatred grew deeper as the middle class became stronger and imposed restrictions through which all the people, including the most humble, had the right to rule their own lives and keep the greater part of what they earned for themselves. Clearly, if the elite were to rule again, the middle class had to be destroyed so despotism and the system of tribute could be returned, and grandeur and honor and immense riches of the elite--assuring their monopoly rule of all the world." - Taylor Caldwell (a novelist). As quoted in *The New American*, May 1, 1995.

"The financial New World Order is the creation of an elite system of interconnected governments and bureaucrats which conspire to tax, regulate, and inflate the wealth held by the middle class peoples of countries around the world, in the name of global democracy." - Representative Ron Paul(87).

"Behind the ostensible government sits enthroned an invisible government owing no allegiance and acknowledging no responsibility to the people. To destroy this invisible government, to befoul the unholy alliance between corrupt business and corrupt politics is the first task of the statesmanship of the day." -Theodore Roosevelt, April 19, 1906. As quoted by the *Guardian*, January 12, 2002.

"Now, to bring about government by oligarchy masquerading as democracy, it is fundamentally essential that practically all authority and control be centralized in our National Government." - Franklin Roosevelt, as quoted in "Roosevelt Decries Waning State Rule," *New York Times*, March 3, 1930, p. 1.

"In a small Swiss city [Basle] *sits an international organization so obscure and secretive....Control of the institution, the Bank for International Settlements* [the prototype of a planned future central bank of the world's central banks], *lies with some of the world's most powerful and least visible men: the heads of 32 central banks, officials able to shift billions of dollars and alter the course of economies at the stroke of a pen."* - Keith Bradsher, *New York Times*, August 5, 1995.

"Business elites who are working so feverishly to transform the planet into a hard-charging global economy demand an unquestioning obedience to the laws of the marketplace. To that end, they are committed to the manipulation of taste and the engineering of consensus. The last thing they want is a searching discussion of the meaning of life, its highest values and ethical responsibilities. In effect, they cannot afford wisdom." - Theodore Roszak, *America the Wise*. Boston, MA: Houghton Mifflin, 1998.

"[T]he Hegemony of World Finance should reign supreme over everyone, everywhere, as one whole supernational control mechanism." - Montagu Norman, governor of the Bank of England from 1920-1944(320).

"For more than a century, ideological extremists at either end of the political spectrum have seized upon well-publicized incidents to attack the Rockefeller family for the inordinate influence they claim we wield over American political and economic institutions. Some even believe we are part of a secret cabal working against the best interests of the United States, characterizing my family and me as 'internationalists' and of conspiring with others around the world to build a more integrated global political and economic structure--one world, if you will. If that's the charge, I stand guilty, and I am proud of it." - David Rockefeller, *Memoirs*. Random House, 2002, p. 405.

"In all developed countries a new way of life--a severely regimented way--will have to be imposed by a ruthless authoritarian government." - Arnold Toynbee (former director of studies at the Royal Institute of International Affairs [the British equivalent of the CFR] from 1925 to 1955). As quoted by Takashi Oka, "A Crowded World: Can Mankind Survive?," *Christian Science Monitor*, February 10, 1975, pp. 5, 6.

"When all government, domestic and foreign, in little as in great things, shall be drawn to Washington as the center of all power, it will render powerless the checks provided of one government on another and will become as venal and oppressive as the government from which we separated." - Thomas Jefferson. *The Writings of Thomas Jefferson*, Albert Ellery Bergh, ed., Vol. 15. Washington, D.C.: Thomas Jefferson Memorial Association, 1907, p. 278.

"Single acts of tyranny may be ascribed to the accidental opinion of a day; but a series of oppressions, begun at a distinguished period, and pursued unalterably through every change of ministers [presidents], too plainly prove a deliberate systematical plan of reducing us to slavery." - Thomas Jefferson(35 p. 71).

"None are more hopelessly enslaved than those who falsely believe that they are free." - Johann W. von Goethe (1749-1832).

A couple more puzzle pieces

So far we have primarily been looking at how the world government conspirators have been using economic control to bring about their twisted objective. But there are several other important pieces of the puzzle that we have not yet examined. For example, in order to effectively execute the take-over of a nation, without arousing the suspicions of its citizens as to what is really going on, gaining control of that nation's news media and educational system are absolute musts. Not so surprisingly, Karl Marx placed a high priority on control of both of these "propaganda machines," especially education, as a powerful means, not only of suppressing the truth, but of conditioning the masses into willingly accepting changes in the way that their government is run--changes that they otherwise would never accept.

Are you a victim of such propaganda? No doubt, since you first began reading this study you have probably been saying to yourself, "If this were all true, the media would have sounded the warning bell a long time ago." You may also have been asking yourself, "If any of these things were really happening, how come I was never told about them in any of my economics or political science classes?" Here lies the crux of the whole problem, and this is what has given the world government conspirators a big edge over us: The general population tends to believe whatever it is told by its leaders (through the media and educational system). This is how it has always been throughout history--corrupt leaders have ever been able to easily manipulate the masses by falsely winning their trust through propaganda. The world government conspirators know this, and have taken full advantage of it. They are all-too-familiar with the age-old art of mass deception, which was best expressed by Hitler's chief of propaganda, Josef Goebbels: "If you tell a lie big enough and keep repeating it, people will eventually come to believe it"(88, p. 251). George Bush Jr., by the way, was in total agreement with this philosophy. During a speech he delivered on May 24, 2005, in Rochester, New York, he said: "See, in my line of work you got to keep repeating things over and over and over again for the truth to sink in, to kind of catapult the propaganda"(470).

As far as our media go, here in the U.S., the reality of the situation is that ABC, CBS, NBC, CNN, Fox, the *Wall Street Journal*, the *New York Times*, *U.S. News and World Report*--indeed, ALL major avenues of our media--are funded and controlled by the globalist boys. Not only that, but nearly all U.S. journalists and reporters in the big media business are members of either the Trilateral Commission, the Council on Foreign Relations, or the Bilderbergers. They certainly aren't going to bite the hands that feed them, not to mention the fact that most of them favor a world government themselves [Endnote 51]. Sound hard to believe? Surely most everything in this study is hard to believe. But this is just what the conspirators are counting on. All that I ask you to do is consider the evidence herein presented--evidence which will demonstrate that, in regards to what is REALLY going on in our economy and government, we are being lied to. In some instances, the truth is merely withheld from us. But the withholding of truth can be even more devious than telling outright lies. For it is far more subtle, and thus tends to be more difficult to detect [Endnote 52].

The misinformation that permeates our media today is not always sold to us willingly by journalists and reporters. There are some who work in the media business who know what is going on, and do not like it [Endnote 53]. It's for this very reason that the globalists have devised a safety mechanism to be sure that their agenda is kept hidden--it's called job security. Notice what former Harvard business professor David C. Korten wrote along this line: "Millions of thoughtful, intelligent people who are properly suspicious of big government...are being deceived by the false information and distorted...logic repeated constantly in the corporate media. They are being won over to a political agenda that runs counter to both their values and their interests. Those who work within our major corporate, academic, political, governmental, and other institutions [including the media themselves, of course] find...that they dare not speak out in opposition for fear of jeopardizing their jobs and their careers"(53, p. 92).

In the book *Into the Buzzsaw*--a stunning work that exposes media censorship/suppression in the U.S. and the consequences for nonconformists--Kristina Borjesson, the book's editor who was once an Emmy and Murrow Award-winning investigative reporter for CBS, made the following remarks in the introduction: "The buzzsaw is a powerful system of censorship in this country that is revealed to those reporting on extremely sensitive stories, usually having to do with high-level government and/or corporate malfeasance. It often has a fatal effect on one's career. I don't want to mix metaphors here, but a journalist that has been through the buzzsaw is usually described as 'radioactive,' which is another word for unemployable"(90, p. 12).

Later in this same book, in a chapter that she contributed, Borjesson described in detail, speaking from experience, what it is like to go through the "buzzsaw": "The buzzsaw is what can rip through you when you try to investigate or expose anything this country's large institutions--be they corporate or government--want kept under wraps. The system fights back with official lies, disinformation, and stonewalling....Your car is broken into and the thief takes your computer and your reporter's notebook and leaves everything else behind. You feel like you're being followed everywhere you go....The sense of fear and paranoia is, at times, overwhelming. Walk into the buzzsaw and you'll cut right to this layer of reality. You will feel a deep sense of loss and betrayal. A shocking shift in paradigm. Anyone who hasn't experienced it will call you crazy. Those who don't know the truth, or are covering it up, will call you a conspiracy nut"(90, pp. 103, 104).

In his book *Necessary Illusions*, MIT professor Noam Chomsky made these similar, relevant comments: "In short, the major media--particularly, the elite media...--set the agenda that others generally follow....It would hardly come as a surprise if the picture of the world they present were to reflect [their] perspectives and interests....Concentration of ownership of the media is high and increasing [Endnote 54]. Furthermore, those who occupy managerial positions in the media, or gain status within them as commentators, belong to the same privileged elites, and might be expected to share the perceptions, aspirations, and attitudes of their associates, reflecting their own class interests as well [Endnote 55]. Journalists entering the system are unlikely to make their way unless they conform to these ideological pressures, generally by internalizing the values; it is not easy to say one thing and believe another, and those who fail to conform will tend to be weeded out by familiar mechanisms"(91, p. 8). So much for "freedom of the press"!

In addition to lying and withholding truth, the media also manufacture and manipulate the general public's thoughts, opinions, and values. From Edward Bernays' book *Propaganda*, we read: "Propaganda is the executive arm of the invisible government....The conscious and intelligent manipulation of the organized habits and opinions of the masses is an important element in democratic society. Those who manipulate this unseen mechanism of society constitute an invisible government which is the true ruling power of our country....We are governed, our minds are molded, our tastes formed, our ideas suggested, largely by men we have never heard of....It is they who pull the wires which control the public mind, and who harness old social forces and contrive new ways to bind and guide the world....To deplore the existence of such a mechanism is to ask for a society such as never was and never will be. To admit that it exists, but expect that it shall not be used, is unreasonable"(92, pp. 20, 9, 10, 18).

Ben H. Bagdikian, dean emeritus of the Graduate School of Journalism at the University of California at Berkeley, wrote: "[P]ower over the American mass media is flowing to the top...with devouring speed....[T]he country's most widespread news, commentary, and daily entertainment are controlled by...the world's largest corporations.

"[T]he controlling handful of American and foreign corporations now exceed in their size and communications power anything the world has seen before. Their intricate global interlocks create the force of an international cartel.

"There are pernicious consequences. While excessive bigness itself is cause for economic anxieties, the worst problems are political and social. The country's largest media giants have achieved alarming success in writing the media laws and regulations in favor of their own corporations and against the interests of the general public. <u>Their concentrated power permits them to become a larger factor than ever before in socializing each generation with entertainment models of behavior and personal values</u>"(93, p. viii).

In a similar vein of thought, here's what author Benjamin Ginsberg had to say in his book *The Captive Public*: "[W]estern governments have used market mechanisms to regulate popular perspectives and sentiments. The 'marketplace of ideas'...effectively disseminates the beliefs and ideas of the upper classes while subverting the ideological and cultural independence of the lower classes. Through the construction of this marketplace, western governments forged firm and enduring links between socioeconomic position and ideological power, permitting upper classes to use each to buttress the other....In the United States, in particular, the ability of the upper and upper-middle classes to dominate the marketplace of ideas has generally allowed these strata to shape the entire society's perception of political reality and the range of realistic political and social possibilities. While westerners usually equate the marketplace with freedom of opinion, the hidden hand of the market can be almost as potent an instrument of control as the iron fist of the state"(94, pp. 86, 89).

Now take a look at what Ramsey Clark, U.S. Attorney General under L.B.J., had to say about the media and those who control them: "We are a plutocracy, we ought to face it--a country in which wealth controls. That may be true of all countries, but it's uniquely true of ours because of our materialism and concentration of wealth here. Even our democratic processes are hardly that because money dominates politics, and we know it. Through politics it dominates government and it dominates the media. We really need desperately to find new ways to hear independent voices and points of view. It's the only way we're going to find the truth"(95).

There have been many books written over the years that talk of how there is a pervasive bias in the media, enforced at the highest levels of corporate control of the major journals and news reporting agencies across the country. While there is no question that this bias does indeed exist, it is often misidentified, and thus mislabeled. So let us call it by its proper name--globalist. It is a bias that frowns upon loyalties to the Constitution and traditional American values, while favoring all ideologies opposed thereto--a bias that serves to advance the cause of the very powerful and wealthy globalist elites.

Back in 1992, CBS correspondent Bernard Goldberg, who years later authored *Bias: A CBS Insider Exposes How the Media Distort the News*, stated that "We in the press like to say we're honest brokers of information and it's just not true. The press does have an agenda"(96).

Now can you see why the media haven't been ringing the warning bell about what has really been going on in our government and economy? Their job is not to reveal, but to conceal the true nature of politics and economics. As author Thomas A. Lane wrote: "The real political process is hidden from public view by a concert of news media which conceals the true sources of political power"(74, p. 72).

So how did the globalist conspirators first begin to gain significant control of our media? Back in 1917, Congressman Oscar Callaway made this revealing statement: "In March 1915, the J.P. Morgan interests...got together 12 men high up in the newspaper world and employed them to select the most influential newspapers in the U.S. and [a] sufficient number of them to control generally the policy of the daily press of the United States. These 12 men worked the problem out by selecting 179 newspapers, and then began, by an elimination process to retain only those necessary for the purpose of controlling. They found it was necessary to purchase control of 25 of the greatest papers. The 25 papers were agreed upon; emissaries were sent to purchase the policy, national and international of these papers; an agreement was reached; the policy of the papers was bought, to be paid for by the month, an editor was furnished for each paper to properly supervise and edit information regarding the questions of preparedness, militarism, financial policies, and other things of national and international nature considered vital to the interests of the purchasers....This policy also included the suppression of everything in opposition to the wishes of the interests served"(75).

The manipulation of our media actually dates back even before 1917, although it wasn't as coordinated or pervasive. Nevertheless, its effects were serious enough for some to voice their concerns, sometimes quite graphically; especially those who actually worked in the media and had a conscience. For instance, in 1902, W.J. Ghent, former editor of the *American Fabian*, published his book *Our Benevolent Feudalism*, in which he quoted John Swinton, former editorial page editor of the *New York Times*, as saying: "There is no such thing in America as an independent press, unless it is out in the country towns. I am paid for keeping honest opinions out of the paper I am connected with. Other editors are paid similar salaries for doing similar things....The business of a New York journalist is to distort the truth, lie outright, to pervert, to vilify, to fawn at the feet of mammon, and to sell his country and his race for his daily bread, or for about the same thing, his salary. We are the tools for vassals of the rich men behind the scenes. We are jumping-jacks. They pull the strings, and we dance. Our time, our talents, our lives, our possibilities, are all the property of other men. We are intellectual prostitutes."

Suppression of information is one of the most important functions of our modern mainstream media. For a good example of such suppression, consider this: In June of 1991, the Bilderbergers held their annual meeting for that year in Baden-Baden, Germany. During a speech given by David Rockefeller at that meeting, he stated: "We are grateful to the New York Times, the Washington Post, Time magazine, and to many others whose directors have attended our meetings and respected our promise of discretion for almost forty years [referring back to the founding of the Bilderbergers in May of 1954]. It would have been impossible for us to develop our plan for the world if we had been subject to the bright lights of publicity during those years. But the world is now more sophisticated and prepared to march towards a world government. The supranational sovereignty of an intellectual elite and world bankers is surely preferable to the national autodetermination practiced in past centuries"(78)[Endnote 56].

Do you see what Rockefeller was saying here? He was thanking major media representatives for not reporting what had been going on at Bilderberger meetings over the years. So much for investigative, trustworthy journalism. Like it or not, I'm afraid that our media have sold out. Indeed, they have been sold out for a long time.

One media representative, in particular, who has respected the Bilderberger's "promise of discretion" is Paul Gigot of the *Wall Street Journal*. A Bilderberger himself, Gigot attended the 1996 Bilderberger conference near Toronto, Canada, and when asked to comment about the happenings at this conference, he replied: "The rules of the conference, which we all adhere to, are that we don't talk about what is said. It is all off the record. The fact that I attend is no secret"(76).

The Bilderbergers do indeed have a "rule" of silence. After the June 2000 Bilderberger meeting in Brussels, Belgium, for example, a deliberately-vague press release was issued which ended with this statement: "Participants have agreed not to give interviews to the press during the meeting. In contacts with the news media after the conference it is an established rule that no attribution should be made to individual participants of what was discussed during the meeting."

Even on the rare occasions that an honest journalist desired to report on a Bilderberger conference, such a thing was soon found to be impossible. In 1971, for example, the Bilderberger conference for that year took place at the Laurence Rockefeller Woodstock Inn in Woodstock, Vermont. Speaking of this upcoming conference, the Rutland, Vermont, *Herald* reported in its April 20 issue: "A rather tight lid of secrecy is being kept on the conference....The Woodstock Inn will apparently be sealed up like Fort Knox....No press coverage will be allowed, with the exception of issuing a statement at the end of the meeting [which, as always, revealed absolutely nothing]...."

At this time it is appropriate to take a second look at a quote cited earlier from former Georgetown professor Dr. Carroll Quigley: "The powers of financial capitalism had...[a] far-reaching aim, nothing less than to create a world system of financial control in private hands able to dominate the political system of each country and the economy of the world as a whole. This system was to be controlled in a feudalist fashion by the central banks of the world <u>acting in concert, by secret agreements arrived at in frequent private meetings and conferences</u>"(28, p. 324). Can you not see that the Bilderberger meetings (amongst other similar groups and their respective private meetings), along with their "secret agreements" that they arrive at during such meetings, are an exact fulfillment of what Quigley was talking about?

The same veil of secrecy upheld by the Bilderbergers, as you might expect, is also enforced by the Council on Foreign Relations. Compare this next quote with the similar Bilderberger policy of silence cited above: "It would not be in compliance with the organization's non-attribution rule for a meeting participant a) to publish a speaker's statement in attributed form in a newspaper; b) to repeat it on television or radio, or on a speaker's platform, or in a classroom; or c) to go beyond a memo of limited circulation, by distributing the attributed statement in a company or government agency newsletter....A meeting participant is forbidden knowingly to transmit the attributed statement to a newspaper reporter or other such person who is likely to publish it in a public medium. The essence of the Rule...is simple enough: participants in Council meetings should not pass along an attributed statement in circumstances where there is substantial risk that it will promptly be widely circulated or published"(77).

Can you now see why these organizations are called "secret societies"? They obviously have a lot of secrets to hide.

Incidentally, the globalists also fund and control our entertainment media, which have much to do with the moral breakdown in this country. And why would they want to deprive us of our national moral standards? The answer is summed up in the following quote from an article that appeared in *Psychiatry* back in 1946: "The re-interpretation and eventual eradication of the concept of right and wrong...[is] the belated objective...for charting...changes in human behavior....<u>Freedom from moralities means [to be] free from outmoded types of loyalties</u>"(79). (More is said about the globalists' deliberate destruction of our society's moral standards in Appendix 6.)

But let us now move on to the subject of education. Have the globalists really gained control of this avenue of information as well?

In 1953, Congress established the Reece Committee to investigate external agencies (tax exempt foundations, such as the Rockefeller Foundation) that had been exerting an influence upon the U.S. and its public institutions. What follows is an excerpt from a report that this committee presented before Congress: "In the international field, foundations, and an interlock among some of them and certain intermediary organizations, have exercised a strong effect upon our foreign policy and upon public education in things international....The net result of these combined efforts has been to promote 'internationalism' in a particular sense--a form directed toward 'world-government' and a derogation of American 'nationalism'"(14, p. 105).

There was good reason for the Reece Committee to draw this conclusion. By that time, and even for a considerable amount of time before then, evidence that the globalists were controlling education in the U.S. was everywhere present. To illustrate this, shortly after the founding of the United Nations in 1945, President Truman asked for a commission to be formed to report on education in America. Volume One of this report, which was printed in 1947, stated: "The dramatic events of the last few years have tended to focus our attention on the need for a world view, for global vision, for international-mindedness...

"Education for peace is the condition of our survival, and it must have a high priority in all our programs of education. In the words of the constitution of the United Nations Educational, Scientific, and Cultural Organization (UNESCO)...'it is in the minds of men that the defenses of peace must be constructed...'

"The task is to secure recognition and acceptance of this [global] oneness in the thinking of the people, so that the concept of one world may be realized psychologically, socially, and in good time politically. It is this task in particular that challenges our scholars and our teachers to lead the way toward a new way of thinking...

"East and West are coming together in one world order....It remains for the peoples of the world to make the United Nations work--by insisting that their governments shall use it and shall strengthen it step by step, supporting it by international law and international courts to which all nations, the strong as well as the weak, shall be subject.

"Toward achievement of this ultimate goal UNESCO promises much...for human betterment and world brotherhood [Endnote 57]...

"There is urgent need for a program of education for world citizenship that can be made a part of every person's general education...it must be done"(99).

The push for a "new way of thinking," mentioned in the above quote, is something that all globalists have called for through the years. It simply refers to the brainwashing that must take place in order to deceive people into accepting their new global slave masters, with special attention being focused on the U.N. as the main source of global authority. Just look at what Mikhail Gorbachev wrote in his book *Perestroika*: "[W]e know that we in this world are, on the whole, now linked by the same destiny....All of us...need to learn...to work out a new mode of thinking....[T]he role of the United Nations with its experience of streaming international cooperation is more important than ever before...[and] is essential for the stability of the world. It is necessary to think and act in a new way....[This] can and must rally mankind, and facilitate the formation of a global consciousness....Humanity must evolve a new mode of political thought, a new concept of the world....[A] new way of thinking is taking shape...[but] these principles are not new--we have inherited them from Lenin....[P]erestroika is a revolution...a direct sequel to the great accomplishments started by the Leninist Party in the October days of 1917 [meaning the Bolshevik Revolution]. And not merely a sequel, but an extension and a development of the main ideas of the Revolution"(83, pp. 123-144).

Please notice how Gorbachev credited Lenin as being the inspiration for the "new way of thinking" that is taking shape in the world. These chilling words of Gorbachev, a powerful leader in the globalist movement, should serve as a wake-up call for all who are even mildly acquainted with Lenin's political philosophy, which is perhaps best summed up in the following words of Lenin himself: "Our power does not know liberty or justice. It is entirely established on the destruction of the individual will. We are the masters. Complete indifference to suffering is our duty. In the fulfillment of our calling, the greatest cruelty is a merit....Through a systematic terror, during which every breach of contract, every treason, every lie will be lawful, we will find the way to abase humanity down to the lowest level of existence. That is indispensable to the establishment of our dominance"(97, pp. 115, 11). Another quote that we should look at, which is of great significance here, is one made by U Thant, a former Secretary General of the U.N.: "Lenin was a man with a mind of great clarity and incisiveness and his ideas have had a profound influence on the course of contemporary history....His ideals of peace and peaceful coexistence among states...are in line with the aims of the UN charter"(98).

Coming back to Gorbachev for a moment, and his push for a new way of thinking, take note of this next statement he made at the Middle East peace talks in Madrid, Spain, on October 30, 1991: "We are beginning to see practical support [for globalism]. And this is a very significant sign of the movement toward a new era....We see both in our country [Russia] and elsewhere...ghosts of the old thinking....When we rid ourselves of their presence we will be better able to move toward a new world order..."(18, p. 174).

The emphasis upon a "new way of thinking," specifically in the realm of education, can be traced back to John Dewey, the "father of progressive education," and his disciples like Dr. Harold Ruggs, who wrote back in 1933: "A new public mind is to be created. How? Only by creating tens of millions of individual minds and welding them into a new social mind. Old stereotypes must be broken up and 'new climates of opinion' formed in the neighborhoods of America....[T]hrough the schools of the world we shall disseminate a new conception of government--one that will embrace all the activities of men, one that will postulate the need of scientific control and operation of economic activities..."(139, pp. 32, 271).

It should not be surprising to discover that the NEA--the National Education Association (the nation's largest teacher union)--heavily endorses UNESCO and its push for a "new way of thinking" through education. Notice, for instance, what the April 1946 NEA Journal, p. 175, had to say on this matter: "Nations that become members of UNESCO accordingly assume an obligation to revise the textbooks used in their schools...

"The universal rededication of minds, the guidance of will and purpose and the desires of the peoples and nations of the world must begin in the schools of each nation." The NEA has also stated: "In much of the world the press is on for education to be employed...for molding people to...particular ways of thinking and feeling...recognizing it as a powerful instrument for shaping the minds and hearts of people"(100).

And why does the NEA want to mold people? Another NEA Journal article provides us the answer to this question: "In the struggle to establish an adequate world government, the teacher can do much to prepare the hearts and minds of the children for global understanding. At the very top of all the agencies which will assure the coming of world government must stand the school...the teacher"(101)[Endnote 58].

To aid teachers in this task, a later NEA Journal article supplied them with the following instructions: "As you teach about the United Nations, lay the ground for a stronger United Nations by developing in your students a sense of world community. The United Nations should be transformed into a...world government. The psychological foundations for wider loyalties must be laid....Teach about the various proposals that have been made for strengthening the United Nations and the establishment of world law. Teach those attitudes which will result ultimately in the creation of a world citizenship and world government. We cannot directly teach loyalty to a society that does not yet exist, but we can and should teach those skills and attitudes which will help to create a society in which world citizenship is possible"(102).

The view of the globalists who control education is that there is something wrong with children who do not think the way they desire them to. Thus there has been an ongoing push to correct their "improper" thoughts and ideas in the classroom setting. Speaking on this issue at a childhood education seminar in Denver back in 1973, Dr. Chester Pierce, Professor of Education and Psychiatry at the Faculty of Medicine and Graduate School of Education, Harvard

University, made these shocking remarks: "Every child in America entering school at the age of five is mentally ill, because he comes to school with certain allegiances toward our founding fathers...toward his parents, toward a belief in a supernatural Being, toward the sovereignty of this nation as a separate entity. It's up to you teachers to make all of these sick children well by creating the international children of the future"(17, p.135)[Endnote 59]. This sounds so much like the educational philosophy of UNESCO (surprise, surprise!): "The kindergarten or infant school has a significant part to play in the child's education. Not only can it correct many of the errors of home training but it can also prepare the child...on his way to membership in the world society"(104)[Endnote 60].

Back in 1953, Senator William Jenner, then the chairman of the Senate Internal Security Subcommittee, addressed the following questions to the entire Senate: "How many of you Senators know what the UN [through UNESCO] is doing to change the teaching of the children in your own home town? The UN is at work there, every day and night, changing the teachers, changing the teaching materials, changing the very words and tones--changing all the essential ideas which we imagine our schools are teaching to our young folks.

"How in the name of Heaven are we to sit here, approve these programs, appropriate our own people's money--for such outrageous 'orientation' of our own children, and of the men and women who teach our children, in this nation's schools?"(105)

Though Washington officials will often give assurance that citizens have local control over their children's education, their legislative actions betray such claims. For example, on February 27, 2001, President George W. Bush, in an address to Congress, affirmed his support of "local control of schools." In addition, he declared that "We should not, and we will not, run all schools from Washington, D.C." But then, not even a full year after making this education promise, George W. signed the "No Child Left Behind Act," which the December 19, 2001 *New York Times* correctly referred to as a move "to expand [the] federal role in public education." In fact, this law was said by the *Los Angeles Times* to be "the most important piece of education legislation passed in Washington since 1965" [Endnote 61]. It called for, amongst other things, the nationalization of testing standards for children grades 3 through 8, and mandated that children in this grade-range be tested on a yearly basis, at the end of each school year. Are nationalized testing standards what George W. considered a fulfillment of his promise to "not run all schools from Washington, D.C."?

Another example of this type of legislation was Clinton's "Goals 2000: Educate America Act," which was signed into law on March 31, 1994. And then, on May 4 of the same year, Clinton succeeded in getting another socialist piece of federal education legislation passed through Congress--the "School-to-Work

Opportunities Act" [Endnote 62].

Does the federal government have the constitutional authority to legislate, or in any way direct, educational policies?   Absolutely not!   In fact, the Constitution denies the federal government such authority.   Amendment 10 clearly states: "The powers not delegated to the United States [federal government] by the Constitution, nor prohibited by it to the states, are reserved to the states respectively, or to the people" [Endnote 63]. Yet, despite this clear wording of the Constitution, off runs the federal government on its education legislation campaign. And it is precisely through this medium that much of the globalist agenda has been imposed upon school children across this country.

Robert Holland, editorial page editor for the *Richmond Times-Dispatch*, wrote a letter on October 6, 1994, to Richard Riley, former U.S. Secretary of Education, regarding the "Goals 2000" legislation. In this letter, he stated: "I have today obtained a copy of the 'Community Action Toolkit' of the National Education Goals Panel, of which you are a member....The kit makes this statement: 'Only by changing the attitudes and behaviors of community members will it be possible to reach the National Education Goals.' With all due respect, sir, that does not sound like the government believes that we citizens have any choice regarding the shape education reform will take.   In fact, isn't such a government-directed propaganda campaign unprecedented in America's history? Some of the topics in this kit [include]: Describe Allies and Opponents. Identify Change Agents. Trouble-shooting in the Event of Opposition. And Avoid the Term Outcome-Based Education....Finally, sir, what is your authority under the United States Constitution to conduct a campaign aimed at rigging the outcomes of the education debate in every local community in America?"(107, pp. 45, 46)

Regarding federal education "reforms" and the push for national standards, particularly during the Reagan-Bush Sr.-Clinton years, Kenneth Goodman, former president of the International Reading Association, wrote in the September 7, 1994 issue of *Education Week*: "I accuse the politicians and technicians of the standards movement of using standards as a cover for a well-orchestrated attempt to centralize power and thus control who will teach, who will learn, what will be taught in the nation's schools, and who will determine the curriculum for schools and for teacher education....The standards movement promises the political power brokers that by controlling outcomes they can control schools while appearing to support local control."

Yes, the forces behind education today are after only one thing--power. But it is important to remember that the vast majority of modern teachers have no clue of what is going on with education at the highest levels of administration. The globalists know this, and couldn't be more happy because of it. However, they also have been aware, from the time they first began sabotaging education, that there would inevitably be some teachers who would become wise to them, and that out of this group there would be some who would not value their jobs more than a clear conscience. Thus it has been the aim of the globalists, for a long time, to weed out existing non-compliant teachers and to prevent non-compliants from entering the profession. The NEA, and many of its leaders, have readily admitted this on numerous occasions over the years. The next two quotes vividly illustrate this: "NEA will become a political power second to no other special interest group....NEA will have more and more to say about how a teacher is educated, whether he should be admitted to the profession, and depending on his behavior and ability whether he should stay in the profession" - NEA Journal(108). "[A] good deal of work has been done to begin to bring about uniform certification controlled by the unified profession in each state. A model Professional Practices Act has been developed, and work has begun to secure passage of the Act in each state where such legislation is needed. With these new laws, we will finally realize our 113-year-old dream of controlling who enters, who stays in, and who leaves the profession. Once this is done, we can also control the teacher training institutions." - George Fischer, former NEA president(109). And you thought that teacher certification/licensure was about ensuring high standards for teachers?

How, you may ask, does the certification/licensure requirement for teachers determine who gets a job? In most states (destined to go national), the prospecting teacher is given a test (supposedly to evaluate whether he/she is skilled enough to enter the profession) in which a passing grade is the deciding factor. The problem with the test is that the questions are so subjective and murky that ten different people correcting the same test independently could easily assign ten different grades. As if this isn't bad enough, anyone who fails the test is not able to contest his/her grade, since the test-taker never sees the test again once it is handed in. All that he/she receives is a percentile grade in the mail. With such a system in place, nonconformists can easily be prevented from entering the teaching profession by being assigned a failing grade [Endnote 64], without the test even having to be corrected. After all, how would anyone know? But the sad fact is that even if the failing grade was contestable, the subjective and murky nature of the questions on the test make it impossible for the failed test-taker to know with any degree of certainty if the assigned grade is inaccurate enough to be contested. In time, such a rigged testing game will be used nationally for recertification/license-renewal purposes, to decide whether an already-credentialed teacher has his/her contract renewed.

As far as how determination is made as to who is a conformist and who is not, all that needs to be done is to ask a few probing essay questions on the test (which they do), and/or to contact the college or university that the prospecting teacher attended, and make a few personal inquiries (which they also do). Or, in the future, when tests will be given for recertification/licence-renewal, the teacher's current employer will be contacted.

As you can see, the teacher testing requirement serves globalist interests quite well. But in addition to the above-mentioned "benefits," there is also a money-making aspect involved here. The test is usually in two parts, costing, on the average, about $100 each. Therefore, there is an obvious great advantage to a person failing the test (or tests) at least once or twice before finally getting a passing grade (which is usually what happens), even if the person is deemed a conformist candidate for teaching. (Many non-conformist prospects usually give up after failing the rigged test for the third time, which is just what the globalists want.) But even when a person finally passes the test, the game is not yet over. Passing the test merely "qualifies" a person for their license/certification. From there, the prospecting teacher must apply for his/her license/certification, a process that requires--you guessed it--another $100 or so. Oh, and let's not forget that this teacher license/certification is only good for about five years, after which time another $100 must be shelled out for renewal [Endnote 65].

Not only is our educational system controlled at kindergarten, grade school, and high school levels, but at college and university levels as well, as the following authoritative personal testimony of former Representative Larry Bates will demonstrate: "During my three terms in the Tennessee House of Representatives, I became chairman of the powerful banking and commerce committee. That was when my eyes were first opened to some of the devious schemes being hatched by our so-called leaders. That was also when I learned that most of what I had been taught about economics was not too reliable.

"I can truthfully say my own biggest obstacle to understanding economics was my formal training in it. Now don't get me wrong; I'm still loyal to the University of Tennessee. I'm a past president of the national alumni association and a former member of its board of governors, but I can't endorse the economics education I received there.

"I learned that the economy was supposed to function based on several 'natural laws'...that everything happening in the markets--all the head-spinning twists and turns--were 'natural phenomena' caused by all the different factors 'impacting' the economy, such as supply, demand, etc. Boy, was I naive! I bought it--all of it. But now I know better"(110, p. 11).

And how, you may ask, did the globalists first begin to gain control of our institutions of higher learning? Rene Wormser, Counsel for the Reece Committee (which we discussed earlier), wrote: "Research and experimental stations were established at selected universities, notably Columbia, Stanford, and Chicago. Here some of the worst mischief in recent education was born. In these

71

Rockefeller-and-Carnegie-established vineyards worked many of the principal characters in the story of the suborning of American education. Here foundations nurtured some of the most ardent academic advocates of upsetting the American system and supplanting it with a Socialist state"(80).

It's actually not very difficult to fathom how the globalists have maintained control over higher education. Like so many other avenues that they exert control over, the mechanism has almost always been money. Any college or university that strays from the program, or allows a significant number of its professors to stray, will quickly find out that its federal grant money supply will suddenly dry up. And, as you might guess, few, if any, of such institutions are willing or able to withstand this type of coercion.

Not only do the globalists control public education institutions around the country (and around the world), but private ones as well, through "accreditation" standards imposed upon them. It's all made to look good on paper, but what is really going on behind the scenes is a hijacking, on a global scale, of all educational establishments, regardless what banner they operate under. Yet this isn't enough--the globalists are also hijacking the homeschooling efforts of parents around the globe, through the United Nations. This was brought out, for instance, by the June 20, 2006 edition of *The Brussels Journal*, which stated: "In today's Belgian newspaper Gazet van Antwerpen Bob Van de Voorde, the spokesman of Frank Vandenbroucke, the minister of Education, says: 'One of the conditions [for homeschooling] is that the homeschoolers must sign a document in which they promise to rear their children along the lines of the UN Convention on Children's Rights [more on this later]. [Some] parents have not done this. This is why the ministry has started an inquiry'"(526).

Earlier we talked about secret societies and their role in the formation of world government. Another such society, not previously mentioned, which has operated particularly in the fields of our media and our educational institutions, is the collective group of recipients of Rhodes scholarships. It was always the intention, from the beginning, of Cecil John Rhodes, the creator of this scholarship at Oxford University, to utilize his "scholars" to assist the globalist cause. Note, for example, the following excerpt from a letter he wrote to his close friend, W.T. Stead, in the autumn of 1890: "The key of my idea discussed with you is a Society, copied from the Jesuits as to organization...an idea which ultimately [leads] to the cessation of all wars [don't be fooled by this noble-sounding goal!]....The only thing feasible to carry this idea out is a secret one [secret society][Endnote 66] gradually absorbing the wealth of the world to be devoted to such an object [there you have it--picking people's pockets in the name of "peace"!]....Fancy the charm to young America...to share in a scheme to take the government of the whole world [here's the real goal--power!]"(112, p. 13).

In 1951, sixty-one years after Rhodes wrote this letter, the *Chicago Tribune* printed a series of articles in the month of July, which revealed that Rhodes' dream of utilizing his scholars to advance the world government agenda was in full swing. The first excerpt we will examine appeared in the July 15 edition: "Today many American Rhodes Scholars are working assiduously to make the dream of their imperial patron come true....More than a third of the 1,185 living American scholars are in the educational field....Rhodes Scholars also command posts in the United Nations and economic cooperation administration. The returning savants are active in the field of opinion molding with a large sprinkling among the eastern internationalist press, magazines, and radio."

On the front page of the July 21 *Tribune*, a feature article appeared, entitled "Rhodes' Wards Head Global Foundations: Dole Out Cash to One Worlders." And then we find, in the July 22 edition, an article written by William Fulton, which stated: "[T]he American Rhodes Scholars network in the United States...is completed and glued together by their numbers in the field of molding public opinion....Rhodes Scholars in the public opinion field constitute a faithful clique for their colleagues in the government, primarily in the State Department which they dominate....With this tie-in, they're attempting to bring about the fulfillment of the lifelong ambitions held by their educational benefactor, Cecil John Rhodes."

Finally, on July 31, in an article called "OWI [Office of War Information] Propaganda Machine Linked to Rhodes Men," the *Tribune* stated: "Those who absorbed the [Elmer] Davis [Rhodes Scholar and head of OWI] training have pushed the...concept of policing the world with American soldiers and economic aid and have fought for a world federation under which the United States would surrender its sovereignty"(112, pp. 83-86).

Yes, Rhodes Scholars have been working quite busily toward the fulfillment of Cecil's goal of world government, often employing the most unscrupulous tactics with every forward step that they have taken, just like any other globalist front organization or secret society. Here's another quote revealing the insidious workings of Rhodes Scholars: "[Frank] Aydelotte [American Secretary to the Rhodes Trustees]...became known as a sort of 'kingmaker' of college presidents. He believed that the best way to promote academic excellence was to appoint Rhodes Scholars to every vacancy for college presidencies or deanships. Whenever he heard that a university was seeking a new executive or dean, he worked his private networks to ensure that Rhodes Scholars received serious consideration. Though no selection committee would ever admit it, it was widely believed that dozens of college presidents and deans owed their new jobs to his cloakroom lobbying....In the world of business, Rhodes

Scholars have occupied virtually every level of every field,....Nearly every field in the world of business has, at one time or another, had a Rhodes Scholar at or near its pinnacle....The huge investment banking firm of Goldman Sachs has included dozens of [Rhodes] scholars over the past half century, but never as many as in the 1990s, when at any given moment at least a half dozen have been partners....Many [Rhodes] scholars agree that there is one area in which a strong Oxford network does seem to operate: government"(113)[Endnote 67].

The Rhodes Scholarship clan is not the only globalist secret society that has set up its base of operation on the campus of a prominent academic institution. Later on we will be looking at another one--Yale's Order of Skull and Bones.

It should go without saying that the Council on Foreign Relations has also exerted a powerful influence on education and the media, for the advancement of global government. Congressman John R. Rarick is one of many government officials who have pointed this out. Back in 1972, he stated before Congress: "The Council on Foreign Relations--dedicated to one-world government, funded by a number of the largest tax-exempt foundations, and wielding such power and influence over our lives in the area of finance, business, labor, military, education, and mass communication media--should be familiar to every American concerned with good government and with preserving and defending the U.S. Constitution and our free-enterprise system.

"Yet the nation's 'right-to-know-machinery'--the news media--usually so aggressive in exposures to inform our people, remain conspicuously silent when it comes to the CFR, its members, and their activities. And I find that few university students and graduates have even heard of the Council on Foreign Relations.

"The CFR is 'the establishment.' Not only does it have influence and power in key decision-making positions at the highest levels of government to apply pressure from above, but it also finances and uses individuals and groups to bring pressure from below, to justify the high level decisions for converting the United States from a sovereign constitutional republic into a servile member state of a one-world dictatorship"(115).

The CIA is one of the primary means through which the CFR has worked over the years to exercise its control over education and the media. This fact became public knowledge in 1975 through the findings of a Senate committee headed by Frank Church (the Church Committee, which exposed, for example, the Operation Mockingbird plot). In fact, former CIA director William Colby, whose efforts inspired the formation of the Church Committee, had this to say about CIA influence in the media: "The Central Intelligence Agency owns everyone of any significance in the major media"(114, p. 13).

And as far as the CIA's influence in our education system goes, the Church Committee Report declared: "The CIA is now using several hundred American academics (administrators, faculty members, graduate students engaged in teaching) who, in addition to providing leads and, on occasion, making introductions for intelligence purposes, write books and other material to be used for propaganda purposes abroad....These academics are located in over 100 American colleges, universities and related institutions. At the majority of institutions, no one other than the individual concerned is aware of the CIA link. At the others, at least one university official is aware of the operational use of academics on his campus"(314).

As you may have guessed, nothing has changed since this information came to light in 1975, except that the degree of control by the CFR/CIA over our media and education system has actually increased.

What an incredibly sad state of affairs this all is! But what's even more sad is the fact that the propaganda of the media and educational system in this country is so potent a force that, even when presented with a wealth of evidence, most people still refuse to believe or acknowledge that they are being deceived. And the same is true, of course, in most other countries around the world. Thus the globalist plot marches on, with virtually no opposition. This is just what H.G. Wells predicted would happen in his book *The Shape of Things to Come*, where he wrote: "There was nowhere any immediate uprising in response to the proclamation of a World Government. Although it had been plainly coming for some years, although it had been endlessly feared and murmured against [by some, anyway], it found no opposition prepared anywhere."

* * * * * * *

"There are legions of conspirators. Their lives have become revolutions. They are in every town and village and institution in America. These are more involved in education than any other category of work. Education is humanistic. Its humanistic methods are linking in national networks across the nation." - Marilyn Ferguson, *The Aquarian Conspiracy*. Los Angeles, CA: J.P. Tarcher, 1980.

"We must win the common people in every corner. This will be obtained chiefly by means of schools..." - Adam Weishaupt(1, p. 111).

"[A] pervasive system of thought control exists in the United States....The citizenry is indoctrinated by employment of the mass media and the system of public education....People are told what to think about....The old order is

crumbling....Nationalism should be seen as a dangerous social disease....A new vision is required to plan and manage the future, a global vision that will transcend national boundaries and eliminate the poison of nationalistic 'solutions.'...A new Constitution is necessary....Americans really have no choice, for constitutional alteration will come whether or not it is liked or planned for....Ours is the age of the planned society....No other way is possible." - Arthur S. Miller, *The Secret Constitution and the Need for Constitutional Change,* 1987(112, p. 134).

"Pravda and Isvestia [propaganda newspapers] *in the former Soviet Union would have been hard-pressed to surpass the American media in their subservience to the official agenda....They have abandoned the notion of objectivity or even the idea of providing a public space where problems are discussed and debated....It's a scandal that reveals the existence of a system of propaganda, not of serious media so essential in a democratic society."* - Edward Herman, Professor Emeritus of Finance at the Wharton School, University of Pennsylvania (Philadelphia). As quoted by Olivier Pascal-Moussellard in *Telerama* (French paper), January 30, 2002.

"The nation's immediate problem is that while the common man fights America's wars, the intellectual elite sets its agenda. Today, whether the West lives or dies is in the hands of its new power elite: those who set the terms of public debate, who manipulate the symbols, who decide whether nations or leaders will be depicted on 100 million television sets as 'good' or 'bad.' This power elite sets the limits of the possible for Presidents and Congress. It molds the impressions that move the nation, or that mire it." - Richard Nixon, *The Real War.* New York: Warner Books, 1980.

"[T]he picture of the world that's presented to the public has only the remotest relation to reality. The truth of the matter is buried under edifice after edifice of lies upon lies....It's...necessary [for our globalist-controlled government] *to completely falsify history...to make it look as if when we attack and destroy somebody we're really protecting and defending ourselves against major aggressors and monsters....When you have total control over the media and the educational system and scholarship is conformist, you can get that across."* - Noam Chomsky, *Media Control: The Spectacular Achievements of Propaganda.* New York: Seven Stories Press, 1997, pp. 32, 30, 31.

"It's easy to imagine an infinite number of situations where the government might legitimately give out false information. It's an unfortunate reality that the

issuance of incomplete information and even misinformation by government may sometimes be perceived as necessary to protect vital interests." - Ted Olson, Solicitor General under Bush Jr.'s administration, *Washington Post*, March 21, 2002.

"There are some things the general public does not need to know and shouldn't. I believe democracy flourishes when the government can take legitimate steps to keep its secrets and when the press can decide whether to print what it knows." - Katharine Graham, CFR member and former chairman of the board of The Washington Post Company(397).

"Lies are the order of the day for policy implementors....Political words have never matched political deeds. Why not?...The center of political land [base of operation] has been elsewhere than with elected and presumably responsive representatives in Washington, and this power elite has its own objectives ["vital interests"], which are inconsistent with those of the public at large." - Anthony Sutton, *Wall Street and the Rise of Hitler*. Seal Beach, CA: '76 Press, 1976, p. 172.

"[I]t is a matter of public record that a tiny portion of the population controls the lion's share of the wealth and most of the command positions of state, manufacturing, banking, investment, publishing, higher education, philanthropy, and media. And while not totally immune to popular pressures, these individuals exercise a preponderant influence over what is passed off as public information and democratic discourse." -Michael Parenti, *History As Mystery*. San Francisco, CA: City Lights Books, 1999, p. 5.

"The American people should be made aware of the trend toward monopolization of the great public information vehicles and the concentration of more and more power over public opinion in fewer and fewer hands." -Spiro Agnew (Nixon's vice president), in a speech he gave in Des Moines, Iowa, November 13, 1969. (The speech itself was written by Pat Buchanan.)

"The press...traditionally sides with authority and the establishment." - Sam Donaldson, ABC correspondent(215, p. 77).

"Politicians spin the truth--that is what they do for a living. The news media's job is supposed to be unscrambling that spin, separating truth from lies....But it's just not working anymore. The public simply doesn't know what's going on much of the time. They don't know who to trust and what to believe. The one thing the

public does seem to agree on more and more consistently, alas, is that the news media can't be fully trusted." - Tom Fenton, *Bad News*(463, p. 82).

"[I]mpersonal forces over which we have almost no control seem to be pushing us all in the direction of the Brave New Worldian nightmare; and this impersonal pushing is being consciously accelerated by representatives of commercial and political organizations who have developed a number of new techniques for manipulating, in the interest of some minority, the thoughts and feelings of the masses." - Aldous Huxley, *Brave New World Revisited*, 1959(412).

"[The importance of mass psychology] has been enormously increased by the growth of modern methods of propaganda. Of these the most influential is what is called 'education.' Religion plays a part, though a diminishing one; the press, the cinema, and the radio play an increasing part." - Bertrand Russell, *The Impact of Science on Society*(154).

"[T]he creators of false images are operating today...full time, festooned about the White House and on Capitol Hill, busy creating 'managed news'...even withholding some news." - Curtis B. Dall, *FDR: My Exploited Father-in-Law*, p. 157.

"Let us enter the living room and we can enter the mind. It's power, our power. Public opinion is crucial. Someone must use a guiding hand. I've been hired, financed,....the names don't matter, though you might recognize some of them. Let's just call them an elite of power, or maybe an influential elite who understand the value of manipulating public opinion....The public wants to be led. It needs to be led. We have long term plans." - Robert Mitchum playing the part of "Mr. Quinn" in the 1981 film *Agency*.

"[O]ne of the best kept secrets is the degree to which a handful of huge corporations control the flow of information in the United States. Whether it is television, radio, newspapers, magazines, books or the Internet, a few giant conglomerates are determining what we see, hear and read." - Representative Bernie Sanders (Independent, VT)(549).

The other half of the puzzle

Marx and Weishaupt had both called for the abolition of all religion. This may yet be a latent goal of the globalists, to be implemented after their world government is completely in place. But for the time being, they recognize that abolishing all religion would arouse far too much resistance, and would thus threaten to destroy their plans for world domination. Not to mention that they see religion as a powerful unifying factor that can actually aid them in bringing about their designs. So their tactic has been to embrace the concept of a single, unified system of world religion that will serve as their partner in power. As H.G. Wells put it in his 1939 book, *The New World Order*: "The reorganisation of the world has at first to be mainly the work of a 'movement' or a Party or a religion or cult....[T]hey [members of this world religion] will do all they can to spread and perfect this conception of a new world order..."(148).

Which religious institution do you suppose will serve as the head of this emerging global religious system? It would obviously have to be one that is already universal in nature, with adherents the world over. It would also have to be one that plays good politics and could thus win the acceptance of all the world's major religions. Can you guess by now which religious institution this could be? Rest assured that no other religious organization in the world could meet these requirements more effectively than the Roman Catholic Church [Endnote 68]. Indeed, in order for the emerging world government system to work, the cooperation of the Vatican, the most wealthy and most powerful religious institution on the globe, whose tentacles reach deep into every nation, is imperative.

This is not to imply that everyone on earth will be forced to convert to Catholicism--only that the papacy will be recognized as a unifying, global religious authority whose decisions on religious matters will be final and universally accepted. Such decisions, of course, will be tailored to appeal to the "herd mentality" of the world's masses, and will be carefully presented in such a way that most will be unable to recognize the manipulation that is taking place.

Before continuing, it is of absolute necessity that the reader be aware that the following information is not being presented for the purpose of "Catholic bashing," as some will imply. The problem that we will be dealing with does NOT involve Catholic people themselves, but the system of Catholicism--the hierarchical structure of this institution. Please understand that there are many, many sincere Catholic people who would not support what their leaders are up to, if they were to become aware of what has been going on. The reality is that they have no clue of what their leaders are seeking to accomplish. And what is it that they are seeking to accomplish? Absolute power [Endnote 69].

Is it possible, you may ask, that this could really be happening? Is the Vatican really interested in a partnership in power in the coming New World Order? Well, perhaps this should be answered with another question: Do you really suppose that the Vatican would NOT be interested in such power? You see, the Catholic Church, for roughly 90% of its history, was the uncontested spiritual master of the entire known world, persecuting, through the hand of the state, anyone who dared question its "divine authority." This institution is well-acquainted with power--totalitarian power. And it wants nothing more than to regain that power that it once had. Don't be fooled by its prestige and pageantry--it is NOT what it appears to be. The reality is that the Catholic Church is nothing more than a despotic, power-hungry system under the guise of a "godly" religion. If you doubt this, please continue reading...

In its efforts to unite all religions under its umbrella, one of the biggest challenges that the papacy encountered, and one upon which it focused much attention, was the problem of how to break down Protestant "prejudice" against itself, while at the same time alleviating any suspicions that Protestants might develop as its power increased (remember that Protestantism had traditionally been vehemently opposed to Catholicism's claim to religious primacy, hence the name "Protestant"). Today, however, for the most part, Protestant "prejudice" and suspicion are no longer concerns of the papacy, primarily because of the "neutralizing" effect of the ecumenical movement. Over the years, since the 1960s, this movement has been so successful, in uniting Protestants back with Rome, that most Protestants are no longer protesting the pretentious authority of this "church." They have been seduced by the stated goal of the ecumenical movement, which is to "break down the barriers that divide." Though this certainly sounds noble enough, it only serves to conceal Rome's dark agenda. Sound crazy? Well, I hope that you are more willing to swallow the bitter truth than a sweet lie.

Is Rome really interested in "breaking down the barriers that divide," as it claims? Or is it simply seeking to bring Protestant "rebels" under its thumb? Let's let Rome answer this for itself, from one of its periodicals: "They [Protestants] conveniently forget that they separated from us [the Catholic Church], not we from them; and that it is for them to return to unity on Catholic terms, not for us to seek union with them, or to accept it, on their terms....Protestantism is rebellion against the authority of Christ vested in His Church. It neither possesses authority or has any desire to submit to authority....Protestantism has really proved to be the ally of paganism....All forms of Protestantism are unjustified. They should not exist"(119).

Here's another quote that carries the same message, from the May 31, 1995 edition of the *San Francisco Chronicle*: "Pope John Paul II said yesterday that he is willing to seek agreement with other Christian denominations on the future role of the papacy. The pope made his offer in a 115-page encyclical, 'That They All May Be One,' which is dedicated to the search for unity among Christian churches that split from each other during the past thousand years....The pope made clear he would not accept a symbolic papacy without teeth and that Rome would have to hold the primary place among Christians. He also said a pope should have the authority to make infallible declarations regarding the basic tenets of faith."

As you can see, the Catholic Church defines "unity" with other churches as the practice of them submitting to its alleged authority. But what about those non-conformist churches that don't want unity with Catholicism--that don't agree to submit to its authority? How does the Catholic Church view such "rebellious" churches? To answer this question, all we need do is look at Catholic/Protestant relations in Third World countries, where Protestant endorsement of ecumenism has not been successful like it has been in the United States (people in the Third World are obviously not as gullible as they are here). In the May 1994 issue of *Charisma* magazine, for example, we find these interesting comments: "Stunned by the staggering growth of evangelical [Protestant] 'sects' in Brazil, leaders of the Roman Catholic church have threatened to launch a 'holy war' against Protestants unless they stop leading people from the Catholic fold....At the 31st National Conference of the Bishops of Brazil...Bishop Sinesio Bohn called evangelicals a serious threat to the Vatican's influence in his country. 'We will declare a holy war; don't doubt it,' he announced, 'the Catholic Church has a ponderous structure, but when we move, we'll smash anyone beneath us.' According to Bohn, an all-out holy war can't be avoided unless the 13 largest Protestant churches and denominations sign a treaty...that would require Protestants to stop all evangelism efforts in Brazil. In exchange, he said Catholics would agree to stop all persecution directed toward Protestants. Bohn called his proposal an 'ultimatum,' and said it would leave no room for discussion."

So, there you have it--churches are either to join with Rome and ultimately submit to papal authority (as has been happening in the United States), or face retribution (as has been happening in Third World countries).

Today, the Protestant churches who have been shaking hands with Rome have no idea (on the laity level, that is) where the road that they are on is leading them [Endnote 70]. If only they would read such books as *The Keys of This Blood*, where the late Jesuit Malachi Martin, who was a foremost authority on Vatican affairs, informs us of the belief of Pope John Paul II that all religious groups "are destined to undergo a series of severe shocks and mutations as...they adapt themselves to the new globalism emanating from more powerful groups. There is no way that any one of them will be able to maintain itself in any vibrancy and progressive strength unless it allows--or suffers--its provincialism to be enlarged beyond the confines it traditionally observed. Individuals among them may for a while maintain themselves within those confines. But, inevitably, as groups they will have to face dire alternatives. Either they will become thoroughly and realistically globalized and therefore capable of collaborating in the building of a geopolitical structure. Or, as groups, they will remain in place, diminish in numbers and influence, and finally lose their identity as operative parts in a new world order"(120, pp. 291, 292).

Besides the ecumenical movement, to further aid in the process of uniting all churches (at least all Protestant churches, for starters), the globalists created institutions like the World Council of Churches and the National Council of Churches. In addition to uniting churches, these organizations, it goes without saying, have also enticed member churches into embracing the concept of world government. In this regard, a March 1942 *Time* article spoke about the recommendations of the National Council of Churches on how to bring about world government: "[A] world government...[requires] [s]trong immediate limitation on national sovereignty. International control of all armies and navies. A universal system of money. Worldwide freedom of immigration. Progressive elimination of all tariff and quota restrictions on world trade. A democratically controlled international bank.

"A new order of economic life is both imminent and imperative through voluntary cooperation within the framework of democracy or through explosive political revolution"(121).

Please notice the proposed tactical options listed here for achieving acceptance of global government and economics: either through "cooperation" or "explosive political revolution." In other words, either by consent or FORCE.

Can you not see that the purpose of uniting all churches is to assist in bringing about the New World Order? This type of globalist propaganda has been echoed in the religious world, at the highest levels, for a long time now. Just after WW I, for instance, in 1919, the American Baptist Publication Society published a book fittingly called *The New World Order*, written by Samuel Zane Batten, which contained these revealing statements: "Men must learn to have world patriotism. World patriotism must be a faith....There is no more justice for the claim of absolute sovereignty on the part of a nation than on the part of an individual....The only alternative is World Federation...with a world parliament, an international court, and an international police force....Men must have an international mind before there can be a world federation....Internationalism must first be a religion before it can be a reality and a system."

The next quote is another example of globalist propaganda emanating from the religious world. It is an excerpt from *A Memorial to be Addressed to the*

House of Bishops and the House of Clerical and Lay Deputies of the Protestant Episcopal Church in General Convention (October 1940): "The term Internationalism has been popularized in recent years to cover an interlocking financial, political, and economic world force for the purpose of establishing a World Government. Today Internationalism is heralded from pulpit and platform as a 'League of Nations' or a 'Federated Union' to which the United States must surrender a definite part of its National Sovereignty. The World Government plan is being advanced under such alluring names as the 'New International Order,' 'The New World Order,' 'World Union Now,' 'World Commonwealth of Nations,' 'World Community,' etc. All the terms have the same objective; however, the line of approach may be religious or political according to the taste or training of the individual."

Here's yet another example of globalist propaganda that has been pawned off on the religious world over the years: In 1971, a book called *Christian Biopolitics* was published in which the author, Kenneth Cauthen, wrote: "The task to which I would like to see Christians the world over commit themselves during the next three decades is to formulate visions of a good future in the light of which believers can learn to...cope with change. The changes are coming. Believers need to be at work causing changes that direct men toward the promise of the new world. The changes are coming. Christians need to learn to live with the new, to welcome it, and to be open to it. The changes are coming"(330, p. 153). Yes, the changes sure are coming. And, unfortunately, many unsuspecting church-goers have already learned to "live with the new," to be "open to it," and to "welcome it."

One final piece of globalist religious propaganda that we will look at is a book that was published back in 1958. Called *If the Churches Want World Peace*, it was written in order to take advantage of well-meaning, yet ignorant Christians who, after witnessing the ravages of two World Wars and the more recent Korean War, were desperate to see an end to all the fighting. The solution that this book offered was for the churches to "come together as one," and put pressure on the government to endorse the United Nations and its policies as our only hope for world peace. On page 133 we find the following astonishing statement: "Of potential significance to the future of international relations is the ecumenical movement of our times. Prior to the Reformation, Christianity in the Western world was a unified movement, held together by the organization of the Catholic Church. The Reformation ended all this, splitting Christendom into fragments and leading in some cases to the establishment of national churches. The universal quality of the Christian faith was thus destroyed"(122).

Did you catch that? This quotation calls for a return to the Dark Ages! The authors of this book would have us believe that the Protestant Reformation, which freed the world from the death grip of papal tyranny, was a big mistake, and that our only hope for world peace is to be united with Rome! Rome has been the greatest threat to freedom that the world has ever known, and has thus been the most formidable barrier to peace. The only reason why there was "unity" in the Western world prior to the Reformation was because the Catholic Church, through the power of the state, ruthlessly executed anyone who dared even question its policies or dogmas. Is this the New World Order that we are headed for? It would appear so, when reading books like *National Patriotism In Papal Teaching*, written in 1942 by John J. Wright, who at that time was serving as Bishop of Worcester, Massachusetts. In this book, Wright discussed the dominant role that the papacy intended to play in the emerging world government: "[M]odern obligations of patriotism ended with the consideration of the great emphasis placed by the last four Popes on the patriotic obligation to promote a world order...

"Over all the nations of the earth, regardless of their political organization or differences, whether or no [sic] they are in point of present fact in union with the Holy See [the Vatican], the...authority of the Roman Pontiff acts as a bond transcending all national lines and constituting men and nations without exceptions 'sons of a common father...sheep and lambs of the same fold.'

"In order that the Church may accomplish her work of disposing men and nations as well as make her positive contribution of a world code and a world moral tribunal, two conditions are manifestly essential, the first as a point of practical necessity, the second as an ideal goal to be attained: (1) the nations of the world must guarantee the absolute independence of the Holy See in the exercise of its mission of teaching men and nations; (2) all men desirous of lasting social union must seek, as an indispensable condition of that union in any perfect degree, religious unity in submission to the Divine authority of the Holy See..."(118, pp. 195, 249, 316).

To illustrate just how dangerous the call for unity with Rome is, we only need look at how thoroughly opposed it has been (and still is) to the cause of liberty, and how hungry it has been (and still is) for power. To accomplish this task, let's take a look, for starters, at some very revealing statements made by Pope Pius IX, in his Encyclical Letter of August 15, 1854: "The absurd and erroneous doctrines or ravings in defense of the liberty of conscience are a most pestilential error--a pest, of all others, most to be dreaded in a state." This same pope, in his Encyclical Letter of December 8, 1864, anathematized those who "assert the liberty of conscience and of religious worship," as well as those who "maintain that the church may not employ force."

Well over a hundred years after the above-cited statements were penned by Pius IX, Vatican sentiments about freedom, as well as its own lust for power, had not changed. In his book *Vicars of Christ: The Dark Side of the Papacy*, Catholic author Peter DeRosa, speaking specifically in reference to Pope John Paul II's attitude toward the predominantly liberal Catholic laity in America, wrote: "The chief reason the pope has targeted the American church for his missiles is this: an absolute monarchy of the Vatican variety is in direct conflict with the basic ideals of the first and greatest republic in the world. America prides itself on being the land of the free; and certain forms of freedom are alien to the pontiff's notion of Christian faith. For him, Catholic truth is absolute and obedience to it a vital necessity. He, as God's Anointed Spokesman, is obliged to demand instant and unwavering obedience of all, from the humblest parishioner to the most astute theologian"(123, p. 145).

Please don't let this last quote fool you into thinking that the Vatican, or any pope at any given time, are only interested in religious power, or in the suppression of religious freedom alone. The Vatican and its heads of state (the popes) also lust after political power, and the suppression of political freedom. This is to be expected, since the papacy is, by nature, a totalitarian system that has always operated as much in the political sphere as in the religious, if not more so.

Looking at the U.S. State Department's website gives us a very revealing glimpse into the nature of the Vatican as a political entity. On the webpage that deals with the Vatican, under the heading "Government and Institutions," we read: "The Pope exercises supreme legislative, executive, and judicial power over the Holy See and the State of the Vatican City." In other words, the pope is an absolute dictator.

Under "Foreign Relations," we read: "The Holy See conducts an active diplomacy....[I]t maintains formal diplomatic relations with 174 nations; 68 of these maintain permanent resident diplomatic missions accredited to the Holy See in Rome. The rest have missions located outside Italy with dual accreditation. The Holy See maintains 106 permanent diplomatic missions to nation-states. Furthermore, The Holy See has two separate permanent diplomatic missions: one to the European Union, another to the Russian Federation." Here we can see that the papacy is in bed with nearly every nation on earth.

We further read, under the heading "Foreign Relations": "The Holy See is especially active in international organizations. The Holy See...is a permanent observer of the United Nations Organization (UN), Organization of American States (OAS) in Washington, Organization of African Unity (OAU),...World Trade Organization (WTO), World Health Organization (WHO), World Food Programe (WFP), United Nations Educational, Scientific and Cultural Organization (UNESCO), United Nations Environment Programme (UNEP), United Nations International Drug Control Programme (UNDCP), United Nations Center for Human Settlements (UNCHS),...and the United Nations Food and

Agriculture Organization (FAO)"(329).

What we find here is that the papacy is an intimate partner with the United Nations and other globalist front organizations. Surprised?

Let us now review some interesting Catholic quotes that more fully reveal the papacy's lust for political power and suppression of civil and religious liberties:

- "Because the [Catholic] Church is universal and has members in every country, even though it be pagan or non-Catholic she finds it advisable to come to some agreement with the governments of countries....Hence she arranges concordats, receives diplomatic representatives from various countries, sends legates and nuncios to deal with foreign governments on her behalf....The dictum that 'The Church should not interfere in politics' is an easy and quite misleading phrase. Politics is bound up with human acts, with which the Church is very much concerned; she is therefore liable to have to interfere in politics at any time..." - *A Catholic Home Encyclopedia*(328), under the heading, "Politics and Religion."

- "Liberalism [is] a group of errors regarding the relation between Church and state, divine law, ecclesiastical law and various articles of belief. In various forms it contends that all laws are derived from the authority of the state; or, while granting a juridical authority to the Church, it denies that the Church is in any way supreme or superior to the state and, maintaining that her authority is over consciences only, lays down that she has no external or social authority; or, granting the Church's independence and supremacy, it lays down that her power should not be pressed....It has been frequently condemned by a succession of popes from Pius IX to Benedict XV..." - Ibid., under the heading, "Liberalism."

- "The Roman Catholic Church, convinced, through its divine prerogatives, of being the only true Church, must demand the right to freedom for herself alone, because such a right can only be possessed by truth, never by error. As to other religions...she will require that by legitimate means they shall not be allowed to propagate false doctrine. Consequently, in a state where the majority of people are Catholic, the Church will require that legal existence be denied to error, and that if religious minorities actually exist, they shall...[be] without opportunity to spread their beliefs. If, however, actual circumstances, either due to government hostility or the strength of the dissenting groups, makes the complete application of this principle impossible, then the [Catholic] Church will require for herself all possible concessions, limiting herself to accept, as a minor evil, the...toleration of other forms of worship. In some countries Catholics will be obliged to ask full religious freedom for all, resigned at being forced to cohabitate where they alone should rightfully be allowed to live....The Catholic Church would betray her trust if she were to proclaim, theoretically and practically, that error can have the same rights as truth..." - F. Cavalli, S. J., in *La Civilta Catholica*(124).

- "Some people would deviously have you believe that religion has nothing to do with 'politics,' that you should only be informed about prayer and happy events so as not to trouble you. You see how crafty the enemy is. And yes, sadly some very good souls have been mesmerized into believing that....We are aware that in high places in the Church, and in the governments of the free world, there are those followers of Satan, the secular humanists, who refuse to acknowledge the rights of God in society and public life, as well as those false Christians who claim to love Jesus Christ and His Mother but who really deny them the right to rule the Church and its leaders and who deny them the right to have the rulers of society obey Jesus our King and Mary our Immaculate Queen [via the Catholic Church, of course]..." - *The Fatima Crusader*(125).

- "We have no right to ask reasons of the [Catholic] church, anymore than of Almighty God, as a preliminary to our submission. We are to take with unquestioning docility, whatever instruction the church gives us." - *The Catholic World*(126).

Yes, Rome lusts after both political and religious power, and it despises both political and religious freedom. In the coming New World Order, since the papacy will obviously be influencing all policy-making decisions--political, religious, and otherwise--this will indeed result, if all goes according to plan, in a return to the Dark Ages, or something in close proximity thereto.

Some Catholic apologists have tried to convince detractors that Catholicism has changed since the Council of Vatican II, arguing that it no longer lusts for power and control. But the truth is, the only change made by the papacy since Vatican II has been to put on a friendlier-looking mask so that it could more subtly carry out its quest for global power and control.

However, this post-Vatican II power and control quest has not always been quite so subtle, especially under John Paul II, who supported the New World Order agenda more aggressively than any pope since the days of Weishaupt. Throughout his entire pontificate, his aim was to assert himself as a key player, if not THE key player, in global religio-political affairs. In *The Keys of this Blood*, Malachi Martin wrote: "In essence Pope John Paul seems to perceive what the New World Order should be. The Pontiff is not only a calculated blueprint for the New World Order but it is determined that he shall lead it....[He] is determined to endure his Pontificate with an international profile and among leaders and nations indicating a position for himself as a special leader among leaders because in the competition he plans to emerge the victor." Martin later went on to say that John Paul II "insists that men have no reliable hope of creating a stable geopolitical system unless it is on the basis of Roman Catholic Christianity"(120, p. 492).

Speaking about the view of Pope John Paul II regarding the two different models for a New World Order, one held by Russia (this book was written before the fall of the Iron Curtain)[Endnote 71], and the other by the U.S., Martin wrote: "The primary difficulty for Pope John Paul II in both of these models for the New World Order is that neither of them is rooted in the moral laws of human behavior revealed by God through the teaching of Christ, as proposed by Christ's Church [meaning, of course, the Catholic Church]. He is adamant on one capital point: No system will ensure and guarantee the rights and freedoms of the individual if it is not based on those laws. This is the backbone principle of the New World Order envisaged by the Pontiff"(120, p. 19).

On October 28, 1978, during his ceremonial coronation, John Paul II addressed the world in ten different languages with the following message: "'Open wide the doors of Christ. To His saving power open the boundaries of states, economic and political systems, the vast fields of culture and civilization and development. Do not be afraid....I want your support in this, my mission.'

"It quickly became clear [commented Malachi Martin]...that John Paul would not confine his message, his influence or his leadership to ecclesiastical matters. Those who had begun to worry that His Holiness intended to insert himself into their temporal affairs were apparently right to do so"(120, pp. 63, 67).

Not long after his coronation, John Paul II drew up a 24,000-word document called *Redemptor Hominis*. Speaking of this document, Martin wrote: "Indeed, the note that dominated and animated that encyclical document was John Paul's insistence that the hard, intractable problems of the world--hunger, violation of human dignity and human rights, war and violence, economic oppression, political persecution--any and all of these can be solved only by acceptance and implementation of the message of Christ's revelation announced by the papacy and the Roman Catholic Church"(120, p. 74).

John Paul II never wavered in his support of the New World Order or the United Nations. As late as January 1, 2004, over 25 years after his coronation, CNN's website carried an article entitled "Pope Calls for a New World Order," which stated: "Pope John Paul II rang in the New Year on Thursday with a renewed call for peace in the Middle East and Africa and the creation of a new world order....[H]e stressed that to bring about peace, there needs to be a new respect for international law and the creation of a 'new international order' based on the goals of the United Nations"(127). Benedict XVI, John Paul II's successor, as you should come to expect, expressed the same warm sentiments about creating a New World Order. For instance, according to Yahoo News on Christmas Day in 2005, he urged humanity to "unite against terrorism, poverty and environmental blight and called for a 'new world order' to correct economic imbalances"(520)[Endnote 72].

Malachi Martin did not mince words in describing just how pervasive the control that this emerging New World Order (influenced heavily by the papacy) will have over our lives (unless a stop is put to it): "Willing or not, ready or not, we are all involved in an all-out, no-holds-barred,...global competition...about who will establish the first one-world system of government that has ever existed in the society of nations. It is about who will hold and wield the dual power of authority and control over each of us as individuals and over all of us together as a community; over the entire 6 billion people.

"Now that it has started, there is no way it can be reversed or called off....[O]nce the competition has been decided, the world and all that's in it--our way of life as individuals and as citizens of the nations; our families and our jobs; our trade and commerce and money; our educational systems and our religions and our cultures; even the badges of our national identity,...all will have been powerfully and radically altered forever. No one can be exempted from its effects. No sector of our lives will remain untouched"(120, p. 15).

Will history repeat itself? Will we really return to the Dark Ages, with church and state becoming fully reunited? Apparently so, if Rome has its way [Endnote 73].

The funny thing about the intermingling of church and state, en route to global government, is that we're seeing a cooperative, mutually beneficial relationship emerging between these two entities, where both of them are taking turns scratching each other's back, and each is using the other's power to buttress its own. And never has this relationship been more brazenly flaunted than under the Bush Jr. administration, through its intimate love affair with the Religious Right. For here we had the Bush crowd promising gullible parishioners, in both the Catholic and Protestant worlds, a "moral" America in exchange for their support--support that they secured in a most anti-constitutional manner. As the *New York Times* reported on August 9, 2004: "The Bush campaign sent Mr. [Ralph] Reed to recruit pastors at the annual meeting of the conservative Southern Baptist Convention. According to campaign memorandums, it has asked 'people of faith team leaders' to help identify thousands of 'friendly congregations' around the country. It asked religious outreach volunteers to petition their pastors to hold voter registration drives, and to speak on behalf of the campaign to Bible studies and church groups.

"The campaign has asked volunteers to send in copies of congregational directories for comparison with voter registration rolls--a move some conservative religious leaders have denounced as a violation of the privacy of the church and its members."

As far as securing support from the Catholic Church went, the July/August 2004 issue of *Church and State* reported: "In mid-June,...during his trip to Rome Bush sought help from Vatican officials in urging more American bishops to rally to his side in the political arena.

"...[A] Vatican official stated that Bush made the request in a June 4 meeting with Vatican Secretary of State Angelo Sodano....[O]ther officials who attended the meeting confirmed that Bush pledged he would wage a robust battle this election season on touchy cultural issues, and he requested the Vatican's help in spurring more American bishops to join his cause."

At the same time, measures were taken under Bush Jr.'s watch (through the introduction of H.R. 235) to enable churches and other religious organizations to endorse political candidates from the pulpit, without jeopardizing their tax exempt status (as long as they were the "right" candidates, of course).

It need not even be mentioned that a very dangerous precedent has been set here. The toxic blend of church and state that came to the fore under Bush Jr. shows just how close we are to a literal return to the Dark Ages.

The treasonous, anti-constitutional nature of blending church and state was bad enough, but Bush Jr.'s claim to be a "compassionate conservative Christian," deeply concerned with upholding the highest moral standards, was a disgusting display of blatant hypocrisy (in light of his endorsement of torture, for example-- more on this later)[Endnote 74]. Furthermore, his religious and moral rhetoric sounded so frighteningly similar to an old brainwashing technique used by despots in the past.

One good example of this was Adolf Hitler, who found the religious and moral trump card to be a most effective manipulation tool for bending the public's will to line up with his own. Here are a few interesting quotes from him that illustrate how he utilized this strategy:

- "May God Almighty give our work His blessing, strengthen our purpose, and endow us with wisdom and the trust of our people, for we are fighting not for ourselves but for Germany." - From a speech delivered in Berlin, February 1, 1933.

- "I believe that I am acting in accordance with the will of the Almighty Creator..." - *Mein Kampf*(438).

- "The Government, being resolved to undertake the political and moral purification of our public life, are creating and securing the conditions necessary for a really profound revival of religious life....The National Government regard the two Christian Confessions [Protestant and Catholic] as the weightiest factors for the maintenance of our nationality....It will be the Government's care to maintain honest co-operation between Church and State; the struggle against materialistic views and for a real national community is just as much in the interest of the German nation as in that of the welfare of our Christian faith. The Government of the Reich, who regard Christianity as the unshakable foundation of the morals and moral code of the nation, attach the greatest value to friendly relations with the Holy See and are endeavoring to develop them." -From a speech at the Reichstag, March 23, 1933.

There's another motive that lies behind politicians professing to be religious, aside from gaining political support--that as long as they claim to be pious, they can get away with the most atrocious abuses of power. In fact, notice what Pat Robertson said about Bush Jr. in this regard: "The Lord has just blessed him. I mean, he could make terrible mistakes and comes out of it. It doesn't make any difference what he does, good or bad, God picks him up because he's a man of prayer and God's blessing him"(439).

The power of the Religious Right movement grew exponentially under George W. Bush. And the Religious Right certainly didn't hide, nor did it blush over, that fact. One Religious Right organization, in particular, that exerted a powerful influence in the Bush administration, posing a serious threat to our rights and liberties, is a group called the Council for National Policy (CNP). On May 2, 2001, ABC News described this "private club" as "the most powerful conservative [and religious] group you've never heard of." It is, in fact, yet another globalist front organization that seeks world domination. As ABC further reported, it "has deservedly attained the reputation for conceiving and promoting the ideas of many who in fact do want to control everything in the world" [Endnote 75].

The CNP, like any other globalist organization, is a secret society. And, as such, it strictly adheres to a familiar membership requirement policy of total silence regarding what transpires at its meetings. As the Americans United for the Separation of Church and State website reported in October 2004: "'The media should not know when or where we meet or who takes part in our programs, before or after a meeting,' reads one of the cardinal rules of the organization. The membership list of this group is 'strictly confidential.' Guests can attend only with the unanimous approval of the organization's executive committee. The group's leadership is so secretive that members are told not to refer to it by name in e-mail messages. Anyone who breaks the rules can be tossed out." This article later reported that "Back when the CNP was founded [in 1981], it was a little less media shy. In the summer of 1981, Woody Jenkins, a former Louisiana state lawmaker who served as the group's first executive director, told Newsweek bluntly, 'One day before the end of this century, the Council will be so influential that no president, regardless of party or philosophy, will be able to ignore us or our concerns or shut us out of the highest levels of government'"(440).

Despite its secrecy, it is known to have had many prominent figures attend its meetings over the years, either as members or at least as guest speakers. Among them have been Tim LaHaye, John Ashcroft, Ed Meese, Ralph Reed, Pat Robertson, Jerry Falwell, John Ankerberg, Grover Norquist, Oliver North, James Dobson, Jay Sekulow, Clarence Thomas, Alberto Gonzales, Donald Rumsfeld, George W. Bush, etc.

No wonder the CNP has the power it does!

Another dangerous Religious Right "ally" of the Bush Jr. administration was the Unification Church, or the Moonies. The founder of this organization, Reverend Sun Myung Moon, has been a close friend of the entire Bush family for many years, and was a major contributor to both presidential campaigns of Bush Jr. George Bush Sr. once said of him: "I want to salute Reverend Moon. He's the man with the vision"(444).

With all this in mind, let us take a look at the religious and political philosophy of Mr. Moon, in his own words: "You must realize that America has become the kingdom of Satan. Americans who continue to maintain their privacy and extreme individualism are foolish people. The world will reject Americans who continue to be so foolish....

"We must have an autocratic theocracy to rule the world. So we cannot separate the political field from the religious. My dream is to organize a Christian political party including the Protestant denominations, Catholic and all religious sects. We can embrace the religious world in one arm and the political world in the other"(444). He's the "man with the vision" alright.

Do not underestimate the threat that the Religious Right poses, through its blind religious zeal coupled with totalitarian political power, to bring about hell on earth. Indeed, to a large degree, it already has done just that. Notice what Bob Woodward wrote in his book *Bush At War*: "The President was casting his mission and that of the country in the grand vision of God's Master Plan," in which Bush, in his own words, promised "to export death and violence to the four corners of the earth in defense of this great country and rid the world of evil"(308).

* * * * * * *

"[Soon] the whole world will be brought to adoration of our Eucharistic Lord and obedience to His Vicar the pope." - *The Fatima Crusader*, Issue 38, Fall 1991, p. 55.

"From Rome to Washington, geopolitical analysts are talking about a 'new alliance' between the world's chief military power, the U.S., and the world's chief spiritual leader, the pope." - *Inside the Vatican*, October 1993, p. 37.

"I believe that in the twenty-first century human life is going to be a unity in all its aspects and activities. I believe that, in the field of religion, sectarianism is going to be subordinated to ecumenicalism, that in the field of politics, nationalism is going to be subordinated to world government." - Arnold Toynbee, *Experiences*, Oxford University Press, 1969.

"[W]e may well be circling back to the kind of world system that existed before industrialism....This is an immense leap that carries us forward and backward at the same time, and propels religion once more to the center of the global stage...a case in point is the growing global power of the Catholic Church." - Alvin Toffler, *Power Shift*. New York: Bantam Books, 1990, pp. 451, 452.

Deadly oaths

To demonstrate just how devious the mind-set of Weishaupt was (as well as that of his modern globalist followers), we will now scrutinize some rather enlightening excerpts from the Extreme Oath of the Jesuits, given during the Ceremony of Induction, when a Jesuit is about to enter a position of command. Weishaupt himself was sworn in with this oath, as are all top-ranking Jesuits. The ceremony begins with the superior officer reading the following words: "My son, heretofore you have been taught to act as the dissembler [one who acts like your friend, but isn't], among the Roman Catholics to be a Roman Catholic,...to be a spy even among your own brethren. To believe no man, to trust no man. Among the reformers, to be a reformer, among the Protestants to be a Protestant, and obtaining their confidence, to seek even to preach from their pulpits, and to denounce with all the vehemence in your nature, our holy religion, and the pope...that you might be able to gather together all information for the benefit of your order as a faithful soldier of the pope.

"You have been taught to insidiously [or secretly] plant the seeds of jealousy and hatred between states that were at peace, and incite them to deeds of blood, involving them in war with each other, and to create revolutions and civil wars in countries that were at peace.

"To take sides with the combatants and to act secretly in concert with your brother Jesuit...who might be engaged on the other side, but openly opposed to that with which you might be connected. Only that the church might be the gainer in the end, in the conditions fixed in the treaties for peace...and that the end justifies the means.

"You have been taught your duty as a spy, to gather all statistics, facts, and information in your power from every source; to ingratiate yourself into the confidence of the family circle of Protestants and heretics of every class and character, as well as that of the merchant, the banker, the lawyer, among the schools and universities, in parliaments and legislatures,...and in the councils of state, and to be all things to all men, for the pope's sake, whose servants we are unto death.

"You have received all your instructions heretofore as a novice and a neophyte,...but you have not yet been invested with all that is necessary to command in the army of Loyola [the founder of the Jesuits] in the service of the pope.

"You must serve the proper time as the instrument and executioner as directed by your superiors; For none can command here who has not consecrated his labors with the blood of the heretic; For without the shedding of blood no man can be saved.

"Therefore, to fit yourself for your work and make your own salvation sure, you will, in addition to your former oath of obedience to your order and allegiance to the pope, repeat after me:

"'I, _____, now, in the presence...of all the apostles and saints and sacred hosts of heaven,...declare that I will, when opportunity presents, make and wage relentless war secretly or openly, against all heretics, Protestants, and liberals, as I am directed to do; to extricate, and to exterminate them from the face of the whole earth; and that I will spare neither age, sex, or condition; and that I will hang, burn, waste, boil, flay, strangle and bury alive these infamous heretics; rip up the stomachs and wombs of their women and crush their infant's heads against the walls, in order to annihilate forever their execrable race.

"'When the same cannot be done openly, I will secretly use the poisoned cup, the strangulating cord, the steel of the poniard, or the leaden bullet, regardless of the honor, rank, dignity or authority of the person or persons, whatever may be their condition in life, either public or private, as I at any time may be directed so to do by any agent of the pope or superior of the Brotherhood of the holy faith of the Society of Jesus [Jesuits]'"(131).

"The Jesuits are a military organization, not a religious order. Their chief is a general of an army, not the mere father abbot of a monastery. And the aim of this organization is Power. Power in its most despotic exercise. Absolute power, universal power, power to control the world by the volition of one man...The General of the Jesuits insists on being master, sovereign, over the sovereign." - Napoleon Bonoparte, *Napoleon's Memoirs.* New York: Howard Fertig, 1988.

"To arrive at the truth in all things, we ought always to be ready to believe that what seems to us white is black if the hierarchical Church so defines it." -Ignatius Loyola (founder of the Jesuits), *Spiritual Exercises*, originally written in 1548.

Weishaupt required new recruits of his Bavarian Illuminati to swear an oath similar to that of the Jesuits, with each one vowing "to perpetual silence and unshakable loyalty and submission to the Order...[and] here making a faithful and complete surrender of my private judgment, my own will, and every narrow-minded employment of my own power and am ready to serve it with my fortune, my honor and my blood....The friends and enemies of the Order shall be my friends and enemies; and with respect to both I will conduct myself as directed by the Order...[and] devote. myself to its increase and promotion, and therein to employ all my ability...without reservation"(1, p. 71).

It is this precise "blind loyalty" mentality that serves as the driving force behind all of the minions of the globalist elites.

Another good example of such secret society "blind loyalty" oaths is the Masonic Oath for the Entered Apprentice Degree. Here are some disturbing excerpts from it: "I, _____, of my own free will and accord...most solemnly and sincerely promise and swear, that I will always hail, ever conceal, and never reveal, any of the arts, parts or portions of the hidden mysteries of ancient Freemasonry....All this I most solemnly, sincerely promise and swear...binding myself under no less penalty than that of having my throat cut across, my tongue torn out from its roots, and my body buried in the rough sands of the sea...should I ever knowingly violate this my Entered Apprentice obligation"(132, pp. 34, 35).

From the Masonic Oath for the 28th Degree of the Scottish Rite, we read: "I, _____, promise and swear...[n]ever to reveal any of the secrets of the degree....And should I willfully violate this my obligation, may my brethren seize me and thrust my tongue through with a red hot iron, to pluck out my eyes...to cut off my hands and expose me in that condition in the field to be devoured by...voracious animals, and if none can be found, may the lightning of heaven execute on me the same vengeance"(133, 2:217).

Just what do you suppose it is that Masonry is hiding, which requires such repulsive oaths of silence and secrecy? Could it be that they don't want people to know their evil plan to tyrannically rule the world, in cooperation with other secret societies? Here are a couple authoritative Masonic quotes which demonstrate that this is indeed their big secret:

- Masonic author H.L. Haywood wrote: "It [Masonry] is a world law, destined to change the earth into conformity with itself, and as a world power it is something superb, awe-inspiring, godlike"(134, p. 90).

- J. Blanchard, another Masonic author, made this similar remark: "If then we wish order and peace to prevail on earth, we must be united; we must have but one will, but one mind....Masonry, victorious over all adverse circumstances, will become the honored medium of uniting all mankind in one vast brotherhood"(133, 2:277, 299).

- Manly P. Hall (1901-1990), who we quoted from earlier, further confirmed the nature of Masonry's secrecy when he encouraged aspiring Masons in his book, *The Lost Keys of Freemasonry*, to "join those who are really the living powers behind the thrones of modern national and international affairs"(63, p. 78).

In addition to this, Mr. Hall once wrote a book called *The Secret Destiny of America*, wherein he documented how Masonry has been using the U.S. government, pretty much from the beginning, to advance its agenda of world government. Here's one particularly enlightening statement he made therein: "There exists in the world today...a body of enlightened humans united in what might be termed, an Order of the Quest. It is composed of those whose intellectual and spiritual perceptions have revealed to them that civilization has a secret destiny..."(414).

In another one of his books, *The Secret Teachings of All Ages*, Hall further stated: "Not only were many of the founders of the United States government Masons, but they received aid from a secret and August body existing in Europe which helped them to establish this country for a peculiar and particular purpose known only to the initiated few"(454).

- The Masonic Bible makes this similar boast: "[F]or well over one hundred and fifty years [as of 1951], the destiny of this country [the U.S.] has been determined largely by men who were members of the Masonic Fraternity"(135, p. 49).

- Ebenezer Sibly, a prominent 18th century English Mason, wrote in his 1784 book *A New and Complete Illustration of the Occult Sciences*: "I shall now call the attention of my reader to that remarkable era in the British history, which gave independence to America, and reared up a new Empire, that shall soon or late give laws to the whole world"(458).

So, can there be any doubt as to what the REAL purpose is of Freemasonry, and other such "secret societies"? Can there be any doubt as to what their "secret" is?

Since the days of Weishaupt, such secret societies have hand-picked individuals that they felt had just the right qualifications (usually the ability to craftily lie, cheat, and murder without a conscience) to help advance the globalist agenda. After recruiting such individuals, secret societies, especially those based on university campuses like Skull and Bones at Yale, then groom these new recruits to think and act in accordance with "the plan," promising to pay for their education and guaranteeing them a good job once they graduate (usually a governmental position), as long as they swear by oath to serve the globalist interests of their Order.

Although this game of filling government positions with secret society insiders is essentially ignored by the mainstream media, there have been a few notable exceptions. One such occasion was on February 7, 1995, when Rush Limbaugh stated on his show: "You see, if you amount to anything in Washington these days, it is because you have been plucked or handpicked from an Ivy League school--Harvard, Yale, Kennedy School of Government--you've shown an aptitude to be a good Ivy League type, and so you're plucked so-to-speak, and you are assigned success. You are assigned a certain role in government somewhere, and then your success is monitored and tracked, and you go where the pluckers and the handpickers can put you."

George Bush Sr., of course, was one of these "plucked" or "handpicked" people (for that matter, so was his son, George W. Bush). A member of Skull and Bones (which is a kindred "fraternity" of Masonry), he (Bush Sr.) served the globalist agenda of his secret society most faithfully. We find confirmation of this from a 1991 *Washington Post* article: "What he [Bush Sr.] may be guided by is a thread that runs deep through his own life and times. Like the 'wise men' chronicled by authors Walter Isaacson and Evan Thomas in their 1986 study of six influential men who shaped American policy [*The Wise Men*--a book about secret societies and their influence and control in the U.S. government], Bush can trace his own roots back to bastions of the establishment such as...Yale [where Bush was inducted into Skull and Bones in 1947]. His father, Prescott Bush, was a friend and business associate of these men....They were an elite group who helped shape a New World Order....They steered the United States...toward a new and difficult international role..."(129).

Now let's look at an illuminating statement made by Bush Sr. himself, just before the outbreak of the 1991 Persian Gulf War with Iraq: "For two centuries [referring back to the days of Weishaupt], we've done the hard work of freedom [the push for world government]. And tonight, we lead the world in facing down a threat to decency and humanity. What is at stake is more than one small country; it is a big idea: a New World Order....

"We have within our reach the promise of a renewed America. We can find meaning and reward by serving some higher purpose than ourselves--a shining purpose, the illumination of a thousand points of light....Join the community of conscience...[and] the world can therefore seize this opportunity to fulfill the long-held promise of a New World Order..."(130).

Did you notice Bush's mention of "a thousand points of light" in this last quote? The significance of this statement cannot be over-stressed. It is an "insider" term that has been used by members of secret societies for the past two-hundred-plus years, referring to the various conspiring groups around the world that are all working together toward the same goal of world government. Bush Sr. himself pointed this out during his acceptance speech at the Republican Convention in New Orleans, back in 1988, when he said: "This is America: the Knights of Columbus, the Grange, Hadassa,...the Order of Ahepa,...LULAC [all of which are secret societies]...--a brilliant diversity spread like stars, like a thousand points of light in a broad and peaceful sky"(87, p. 78).

Now let's notice a statement made by H.G. Wells, a 33rd-degree Mason, from his 1934 book *Experiment in Autobiography*: "I believe this idea of a planned World-State is one to which all our thought and knowledge is tending....It is appearing partially and experimentally at a thousand points...its coming is likely to happen very quickly....Plans for political synthesis seem to grow bolder and more extensive....The New Plan in America [meaning F.D.R.'s New Deal] and the New Plan in Russia [meaning Stalinism] are both related to the ultimate World-State."

How interesting! And here is something else interesting: You may recall how earlier we had discussed the "Great Seal" on the back of our one dollar bill (which shows the symbol of an uncapped pyramid with the "all-seeing-eye" on top). We talked about how the Latin words *Novus Ordo Seclorum*, meaning "New World Order," are written underneath this pyramid. Well, as it turns out, this seal is saturated with Masonic symbols that have been used by this Order since at least 1782, back in the days of Weishaupt. It was under F.D.R., by the way, a 32nd-degree Mason, that its inclusion on the dollar bill, back in 1935, had come about.

But getting back, for a moment, to the Order of Skull and Bones and the power it wields in the push for world government, it is appropriate that we take a look at a few more fascinating quotes.

In the March 27, 2000 issue of the *New York Observer*, Ron Rosenbaum wrote an article called "Inside George W.'s Secret Crypt," in which he discussed the headquarters of Skull and Bones at Yale as "the secret citadel, the sanctum sanctorum,...the place of weird, clandestine, occult bonding rituals that has shaped the character of American ruling class figures." He also stated that "the mission of Skull and Bones, which is--depending on how you look upon it--a kind of enlightened...elitism, or a secret conspiracy to rule the world"(18, p. 270).

In May of 2000, *Atlantic Monthly* published an article called "George W., Knight of Eulogia" by Alexandra Robbins, in which she described the Skull and Bones clan and George W.'s involvement therein. She then went on to say that "Ron Rosenbaum [cited above], the author of a 1977 *Esquire* article on Skull and Bones, wrote that a Bonesman warned him not to get too close: 'The alumni still care,' the source warned. 'Don't laugh. They don't like people tampering and prying. The power of Bones is incredible. They've got their hands on every lever of power in the country. You'll see--it's like trying to look into the Mafia'"(18, pp. 277, 278).

A couple years later, on September 30, 2002, Robbins, during an interview on Radio Liberty about her book *Secrets of the Tomb: Skull and Bones, the Ivy League, and the Hidden Paths of Power*, told Dr. Stan Monteith: "I want them [readers of her book] to learn that Skull and Bones exists. It is real. It has much more power within America and within the world scene than people believe. And the reason I wrote the book is to get the message out to mainstream America that

Skull and Bones is something that we should be fearful of and disturbed by, and only by spreading the truth about this organization will we be able to tear it down."

It is vitally important to note that the two major candidates for the 2004 election, George W. Bush and John F. Kerry, were both Skull and Bones members, and when asked by Tim Russert on NBC's "Meet the Press" about their involvement with this organization, they refused to provide any information, giving the same vague, scripted responses. Let us look at some excerpts from these two interviews, beginning with the Kerry one:

Tim Russert: "You both were members of Skull and Bones, the secret society at Yale. What does that tell us...?"

John Kerry: "Not much because it's a secret..."(300).

And now the excerpts from the Bush interview:

Tim Russert: "You [and Kerry] were both in Skull and Bones, the secret society."

President Bush: "It's so secret we can't talk about it"(301).

Do you not see a problem here? Isn't it clear that presidential candidates are indeed hand-picked, so that the globalist agenda will always march forward, regardless which party they represent? And isn't it obvious that all of this is due to the treacherous workings of globalist secret societies?

* * * * * * *

"I want to talk about our common responsibilities in the face of a common danger....[T]he dimensions of its threat have loomed large on the horizon for many years. Whatever our hopes may be for the future--for reducing this threat or living with it--there is no escaping either the gravity or the totality of its challenge to our survival and to our security--a challenge that confronts us in unaccustomed ways in every sphere of human activity....
<u>*The very word 'secrecy' is repugnant in a free and open society; and we are as a people inherently and historically opposed to secret societies, to secret oaths and to secret proceedings....*</u>
Today no war has been declared--and however fierce the struggle may be, it may never be declared in the traditional fashion. Our way of life is under attack. Those who make themselves our enemy are advancing around the globe. The survival of our friends is in danger. And yet no war has been declared, no borders have been crossed by marching troops, no missiles have been fired.
If the press is awaiting a declaration of war before it imposes the self-discipline of combat conditions, then I can only say that no war ever posed a greater threat to our security. If you are awaiting a finding of 'clear and present danger,' then I can only say that the danger has never been more clear and its

presence has never been more imminent.

It requires a change in outlook, a change in tactics, a change in missions--by the government, by the people, by every businessman or labor leader, and by every newspaper. For we are opposed around the world by a monolithic and ruthless conspiracy that relies primarily on covert means for expanding its sphere of influence--on infiltration instead of invasion, on subversion instead of elections, on intimidation instead of free choice, on guerrillas by night instead of armies by day. It is a system which has conscripted vast human and material resources into the building of a tightly knit, highly efficient machine that combines military, diplomatic, intelligence, economic, scientific and political operations.

Its preparations are concealed, not published. Its mistakes are buried, not headlined. Its dissenters are silenced, not praised. No expenditure is questioned, no rumor is printed, no secret is revealed. It conducts the Cold War, in short, with a war-time discipline no democracy would ever hope or wish to match." - J.F.K., speaking before the American Newspaper Publishers Association , New York City, April 27, 1961.

What next?

So what happens next? What sinister plans do the globalists have in mind to finally ring in their era of complete world domination? And how will the masses accept, without question, their oppressive, dark agenda? The answer is quite simple--it's the oldest trick in the book: Simply create a major crisis, and then come along with a drastic solution to the problem (the Hegelian Dialectic process--thesis, antithesis, synthesis, or problem, reaction, solution). Because of this "crisis," the people will be so desperate for a solution that they will be willing to resort to ANYTHING, including giving up their rights and freedoms (the few that remain), in order to restore "peace" [Endnote 76]. And all of this will be done covertly, so that the people will have no idea that the whole thing was set up. Indeed, a major crisis is exactly what our globalist buddies have been busily planning for a long time.

MIT professor and CFR member Lincoln P. Bloomfield is one globalist, specifically, who taught the importance of a planned crisis as a means of bringing about desirable changes leading to world government. In 1962, the U.S. State Department contracted (No. SCC 28270) with him to write *A World Effectively Controlled by the United Nations*, in which he stated: "[W]ould the United States itself seriously consider disbanding its own armaments and abrogating to an international authority beyond its direct control...?...Would the United States Senate ratify such a scheme?...The quick answers to these questions, so put, tend to be negative. [How could we therefore bring about] a sudden transformation in national attitudes?...[A] crisis, a war, or a brink-of-war situation so grave or commonly menacing that deeply-rooted attitudes and practices are sufficiently shaken to open the possibility of a revolution in world political arrangements"(331, p. 103).

Further along this line, CFR member James MacGregor Burns stated back in 1987: "I doubt that Americans under normal conditions could agree on the package of radical and 'alien' constitutional changes that would be required [to set up world government]. They would do so, I think, only during and following a stupendous national crisis"(138).

In 1993, CFR member Herman Kahn, in conjunction with Anthony J. Wiener, wrote an essay called "World Federal Government," which stated that world government requires "intense external danger" and that "a world government could only be created out of war or crisis--an emergency that provided an appropriate combination of the motivations of fear and opportunity"(338, p. 306).

David Rockefeller, speaking at the Business Council for the U.N. on September 14, 1994, declared: "We are on the verge of a global transformation.

All we need is the right major crisis, and the nations will accept the New World Order"(17, p. 95).

Creating a world government will involve, of course, the creation of a fully-functioning world central bank. With this thought in mind, consider this statement from the Human Development Report, a report released by the Social and Economic Council of the United Nations in June of 1994: "It will take some time and probably some <u>international financial crisis</u> before a full-scale world central bank can be created"(p. 84).

Yes, a major crisis--most likely a rigged economic collapse--is headed our way. When it comes, rest assured that it will be no accident! [Endnote 77] And in its wake, expect to see a world system of government being set up.

One of the many benefits that an economic collapse will bring the globalists will be a cashless society, where all financial transactions will be conducted electronically. The potential that this will have for total domination of every aspect of every person's life, everywhere in the world, will be enormous. Early stages of this are already in place, and are being sold to people as convenient luxuries--even necessities. One measure being undertaken is the smart card, which has been pushed in countries around the globe, under the guise of making shopping easier and quicker. Not only are these cards being used to replace cash and credit cards, but ID cards as well. And, having a microchip planted within these cards, they don't just identify you--they contain volumes of updatable information about you that is instantly retrievable by a card-reader device.

But these cards are only the beginning. The ultimate goal is to have every person injected with a microchip that will serve the same functions, and even more. This technology is already in use, and discussion of it has become commonplace in the mainstream media. One particularly revealing article on this subject was written by *WorldNetDaily* on May 14, 2003, which had this to say: "Applied Digital Solutions, a technology development company, yesterday said it has created and successfully field-tested a prototype of a GPS [global positioning satellite] implant for humans.

"The dimensions of this initial 'personal location device,' or PLD, prototype are said to be 2.5 inches in diameter by 0.5 inches in depth, roughly the size of a pacemaker. Once inserted into a human, the device can be tracked by Global Positioning Satellite technology and the information relayed wirelessly to the Internet, where an individual's location, movements and vital signs can be stored in a database for future reference....

"As the process of miniaturization proceeds in the coming months, the company said it expects to be able to shrink the size of the device to at least one-half and perhaps to as little as one-tenth the current size....

"Applied also markets the implantable VeriChip, a radio frequency identification chip that can carry an individual's unique identification number as well as store personal data"(452).

A satellite-trackable chip implant that stores personal data and a personal, unique identification number? [Endnote 78] It goes without saying that what we are dealing with here has tremendous potential to become the most serious affront to personal liberties the world has probably ever seen [Endnote 79].

As it stands right now, receiving an implantable chip is purely voluntary. However, the day is not far off when people will be compelled by law to receive such implants [Endnote 80]. With this very nightmarish thought in mind, take note of what Senator Joseph Biden asked Judge John Roberts during his Supreme Court confirmation hearings on September 12, 2005: "Can a microscopic tag be implanted in a person's body to track his every movement? There's actual discussion about that. You will rule on that--mark my words--before your tenure is over"(527).

And when will this day come, when we will be forced to receive an implantable microchip? It will surely arrive in the wake of the coming planned crisis--a subject on which we will now return our focus.

Though an economic collapse is, without a doubt, the main crisis that is being planned, it is certainly not the only one. Another one that has been under consideration is an environmental disaster on a global scale, which this next quote elaborates on: "In 1963, 15 CFR leaders in the Kennedy administration met at Iron Mountain, New York, to formulate...and promote the goal of world government....This special study group worked for two years to produce a document called 'The Report From Iron Mountain [Endnote 81].' On page 66 of this document, they wrote: 'It may be, for instance, that gross pollution of the environment can eventually replace the possibility of mass destruction by nuclear weapons as the apparent threat to the survival of the species....It constitutes a threat that could be dealt with only through social organization and political power. But...it will be a generation, to a generation and a half before environmental pollution, however severe, will be sufficiently menacing on a global scale, to offer a possible basis for solutions'"(140, p. 310).

Now let's look at a quote from UNCED (United Nations Conference on Environment and Development, Rio de Janeiro, 1992), in a report this Conference produced entitled "In Our Hands, Earth Summit '92" (which was drafted up, by the way, roughly "a generation, to a generation and a half" after the Report From Iron Mountain): "The world community now faces together greater risks to our common security through our impacts on the environment than from traditional military conflicts with one another....We must now forge a new 'Earth Ethic' which will inspire all peoples and nations to join in a new global partnership of

North, South, East, and West"(140, p. 311)[Endnote 82].

Do you see the connection between these last two quotes? Are the globalists planning a major, world-wide environmental crisis (or planning to escalate the existing one) to help facilitate their global domination scheme?

It is highly possible that the coming rigged crisis might be both economic and environmental in nature, perhaps being triggered by a phony terrorist attack involving some type of "weapon of mass destruction." In this regard, the NewsMax website, on Friday, November 21, 2003, covered a story about an interview with General Tommy Franks (the man who led out in the 2003 military campaign against Iraq), which was to appear (and did appear) in the upcoming December issue of *Cigar Aficionado*, a men's lifestyle magazine. This article reported: "Gen. Tommy Franks says that if the United States is hit with a weapon of mass destruction that inflicts large casualties, the Constitution will likely be discarded in favor of a military form of government [a police state!]....

"...[Franks] warned that if terrorists succeeded in using a weapon of mass destruction (WMD) against the U.S. or one of our allies, it would likely have catastrophic consequences for our cherished republican form of government....

"If that happens [a WMD attack], Franks said, '...the Western world, the free world, loses what it cherishes most, and that is freedom and liberty we've seen for a couple of hundred years in this grand experiment that we call democracy....

"It means [we have] the potential of a weapon of mass destruction and a terrorist, massive, casualty-producing event somewhere in the Western world--it may be in the United States of America--that causes our population to question our own Constitution and to begin to militarize our country in order to avoid a repeat of another mass, casualty-producing event. Which in fact, then begins to unravel the fabric of our Constitution....'

"Franks ended his interview with a less-than-optimistic note. 'It's not in the history of civilization for peace ever to reign. Never has in the history of man....I doubt that we'll ever have a time when the world will actually be at peace'"(165).

Indeed, how could peace ever reign when corrupt power mongers don't want it? There simply has to be war and terrorism to convince the masses that they need oppressive government measures to "protect" them.

Another person who talked about martial law coming in the wake of another terrorist attack in the U.S. was retired Army General Wayne Downing, who had served as Bush Jr.'s deputy national security advisor for counterterrorism until July 8, 2002. He told the *Washington Post* in late 2002: "The United States may have to declare martial law someday, in the case of a devastating attack with weapons of mass destruction causing tens of thousands of casualties. This could mean that the military would be given the authority to impose curfews, protect businesses and communities, even make arrests"(457).

Just how, exactly, after the coming manufactured crisis, will the government set up a police state in this country? What agency will it work through to accomplish this? Many think that FEMA (Federal Emergency Management Agency) is a people-friendly government organization that was created to help victims recover from a disaster. But the real truth is that FEMA was created ultimately for the purpose of taking over the functions of government during a national emergency, in a major crackdown that will involve policing the streets with tanks and imposing a very strict curfew. This, of course, will instantly nullify the U.S. Constitution, at the drop of a dime, without inciting a great deal of public protest, as it will be done in the name of "crisis management" or "emergency management." It will be suggested that, because of the out-of-control looting and rioting, drastic measures (martial law--a police state) will have to be resorted to in order to get things back under control [Endnote 83]. When this happens, things will be so chaotic at first that it will be very easy for the "new government" to round up all those who oppose this self-appointed power structure (because they recognize it for what it is), and cart them off to concentration camps [Endnote 84].

If the idea of concentration camps in the U.S. sounds impossible to believe, take note of what we find in the article "Camps for Citizens: Ashcroft's Hellish Vision," from the August 14, 2002 edition of the *Los Angeles Times*: "Atty. Gen. John Ashcroft's announced desire for camps for U.S. citizens he deems to be 'enemy combatants' has moved him from merely being a political embarrassment to being a constitutional menace.

"Ashcroft's plan...would allow him to order the indefinite incarceration of U.S. citizens and summarily strip them of their constitutional rights and access to courts by declaring them enemy combatants.

"The proposed camp plan should trigger immediate congressional hearings and reconsideration of Ashcroft's fitness for this important office....Ashcroft has become a clear and present threat to our liberties....

"...If we cannot join together to fight the abomination of American camps, we have already lost what we are defending."

Commenting further on this issue, CNN/FindLaw declared: "We now are faced with a scary prospect--indefinite detentions of multiple citizens because the government decides they are dangerous. The mere suggestion of camps or group detention facilities implies that the Executive is, in fact, considering using its newfound citizen-combatant detention program on a broader scale....[I]f this sounds frightening, that's because it is"(167).

We find these additional shocking revelations in the February 4, 2008 edition of the *San Francisco Chronicle*: "Since 9/11, and seemingly without the notice of most Americans, the federal government has assumed the authority to institute martial law, arrest a wide swath of dissidents (citizen and noncitizen alike), and detain people without legal or constitutional recourse in the event of [an emergency]...

"Beginning in 1999, the government has entered into a series of single-bid contracts with Halliburton subsidiary Kellogg, Brown and Root (KBR) to build detention camps at undisclosed locations within the United States. The government has also contracted with several companies to build thousands of railcars, some reportedly equipped with shackles, ostensibly to transport detainees....

"What could the government be contemplating that leads it to make contingency plans to detain without recourse millions of its own citizens?

"The Constitution does not allow the executive to have unchecked power under any circumstances. The people must not allow the president to use the war on terrorism to rule by fear instead of by law"(572).

What follows is a frightening list of Executive Orders that will be implemented under FEMA's direction in the case of a national emergency, from FEMA's own documents (recorded in the Federal Register), which call for, amongst other things, the detention of dissenters in government "work brigades" (concentration camps):

10995 provides for the takeover of all communications media.
#10997 calls for the takeover of all electric power, petroleum, gas, and minerals.
#10998 calls for the seizure of all food resources and farms.
#10999 calls for the suspension of all modes of transportation--highways, seaports, airports, etc.
#11000 calls for the mobilization of all civilians (who resist) into work brigades under government supervision (i.e. concentration camps!).
#11001 calls for the complete takeover of all health and education functions.
#11002 designates the Postmaster General to operate a national mandatory registration of all citizens (to make an assessment of who the "rebels" are).
#11004 provides for the Housing and Finance Authority to relocate communities, designate areas to be abandoned, and establish new locations for populations [Endnote 85].

Incidentally, it was Colonel Oliver North, back in the early 1980s in the basement of the White House, who drafted up this set of FEMA Executive Orders. Several years later, during the Iran/Contra Hearings, which were broadcast on national television, this question was addressed to Colonel North by

Representative Jack Brooks (D-TX): "Colonel North, in your work at the NSC [National Security Council], were you not assigned at one time to work on plans for the continuity of government in the event of a major disaster?" Immediately Senator Inouye, Chairman of the Senate Iran/Contra Committee, interjected with the following comment: "I believe that question touches upon a highly sensitive and classified area. So may I request that you not touch upon that, Sir?" Rep. Brooks then responded by saying: "I was particularly concerned, Mr. Chairman, because I read in Miami papers, and several others, that there had been a plan developed..., a contingency plan in the event of an emergency, that would suspend the American Constitution. And I was deeply concerned about it, and was wondering if that was the area in which he had worked." Suddenly Inouye interrupted Brooks by saying: "May I most respectfully request that this matter not be touched upon at this stage. If we wish to get into this, I'm certain arrangements can be made for an executive session." Do you smell something foul here? [Endnote 86]

If the globalists have their way and martial law is introduced here in the wake of a staged crisis, who do you suppose it will be that will enforce Oliver North's Executive Orders, under FEMA's direction? The plan is to utilize our own military, in cooperation with U.N. foreign troops [Endnote 87]. In this regard, Harvard professor and CFR member Joseph S. Nye remarked, in the January 27, 1992 edition of the *New York Times*, that there is a need for a "U.N. rapid deployment force [for use in time of a crisis]--led by the U.S.--for the coming New World Order." This U.N./U.S. rapid deployment force will be dispatched to various places around the world, of course, wherever needed, and not just in the United States.

The only things that have prevented U.S. military forces from being able to police our streets have been the Posse Comitatus Act, signed into law by Congress in 1878, and the Insurrection Act of 1807. The Insurrection Act limits a president's use of the military for domestic law enforcement, whereas the Posse Comitatus Act forbids it altogether. But both of these laws, especially Posse Comitatus, have come under attack, beginning in the mid-1990s and escalating in the wake of the 9-11 terrorist attacks. For example, Air Force General Ralph E. Eberhart, who Bush Jr. chose to lead the military's Northern Command (NORTHCOM), stated in the July 21, 2002 edition of the *New York Times* that he favored changes in existing law to give increased domestic powers to the military, to protect the nation against terrorist attacks. He then went on to say, "We should always be reviewing things like Posse Comitatus and other laws if we think it ties our hands in protecting the American people." This same article proceeded to talk about how Eberhart's opinion is shared by other senior military officials, and represents a "shift in thinking" at the Pentagon which historically has resisted involvement in domestic law enforcement operations.

Speaking before the Sixth Defense Ministerial of the Americas in Quito, Ecuador, on November 17, 2004, Secretary of Defense Donald Rumsfeld (CFR member) echoed the same sentiments. He said that since the September 11, 2001 terrorist attacks, "we have had to conduct an essential reexamination of the relationships between our military and our law enforcement responsibilities in the U.S. The complex challenges of this new era and the asymmetric threats we face require that all elements of state and society work together"(406).

Perhaps you will not be shocked to discover that the safeguards of the Posse Comitatus Act and the Insurrection Act of 1807 have actually already been officially removed, leaving us wide open to the possibility of a police state being set up in the U.S., whenever our globalist-controlled government decides to do so. This was revealed in a February 19, 2007 *New York Times* article called "Making Martial Law Easier," which stated: "A disturbing recent phenomenon in Washington is that laws that strike to the heart of American democracy have been passed in the dead of night. So it was with a provision quietly tucked into the enormous defense budget bill at the Bush administration's behest that makes it easier for a president to override local control of law enforcement and declare martial law.

"The provision, signed into law in October, weakens two obscure but important bulwarks of liberty. One is the doctrine that bars military forces, including a federalized National Guard, from engaging in law enforcement. Called posse comitatus, it was enshrined in law after the Civil War to preserve the line between civil government and the military. The other is the Insurrection Act of 1807, which provides the major exemptions to posse comitatus. It essentially limits a president's use of the military in law enforcement to putting down lawlessness, insurrection and rebellion, where a state is violating federal law or depriving people of constitutional rights.

"The newly enacted provisions upset this careful balance. They shift the focus from making sure that federal laws are enforced to restoring public order. Beyond cases of actual insurrection, the president may now use military troops as a domestic police force in response to a natural disaster, a disease outbreak, terrorist attack or to any 'other condition.'

"Changes of this magnitude should be made only after a thorough public airing. But these new presidential powers were slipped into the law without hearings or public debate. The president made no mention of the changes when he signed the measure, and neither the White House nor Congress consulted in advance with the nation's governors"(563).

The law mentioned in this article, passed by Bush Jr. on October 17, 2006, is known as Public Law 109-364, or the "John Warner Defense Authorization Act of 2007" (H.R. 5122), which gave him, or any other president, the ability to declare a "public emergency" and station troops anywhere in America, which will take control of state-based National Guard units without the consent of the governor or any other local authorities, in order to "suppress public disorder"(564).

Section 1076 of this massive Authorization Act is entitled "Use of the Armed Forces in Major Public Emergencies" (i.e. "Setting Up a Police State"). Section 333, "Major Public Emergencies; Interference with State and Federal Law," states that "the President may employ the armed forces, including the National Guard in Federal service, to restore public order and enforce the laws of the United States when, as a result of a natural disaster, epidemic, or other serious public health emergency, terrorist attack or incident, or other condition in any State or possession of the United States, the President determines that domestic violence has occurred to such an extent that the constituted authorities of the State or possession are incapable of maintaining public order, in order to suppress, in any State, any insurrection, domestic violence, unlawful combination, or conspiracy."

In preparation for the coming police state, local and state police forces, who will obviously be called upon to assist U.N. and U.S. military troops in the imposition of martial law, have been arming themselves to the teeth (at the behest of Washington) with military equipment and weapons, and some have even received military training. If you doubt that these things have indeed been happening, check out, for starters, the two quotes that follow:

- "Many Cold War military suppliers are converting to civilian law enforcement. The Department of Justice, the CIA and the Pentagon are quietly taking an active and coordinated role in marketing defense-related technologies to law enforcement agencies." - National Criminal Justice Commission, 1996(114).

- "Throughout the nation, paramilitary, SWAT or tactical policing--that is, law enforcement that uses the equipment, training, rhetoric and group tactics of war-- is on the rise. According to a study by sociologist Peter Kraska, the nation has more than 30,000 such heavily-armed, militarily trained police units....Between 1995 and 1997 the DOD (U.S. Department of Defense) gave local police departments more than 3,800 M-16 automatic assault rifles, 2,185 M-14 semiautomatic rifles, 73 M-79 grenade launchers and 112 armored personnel carriers--1.2 million pieces of military hardware in 1997 alone." - *The Nation*(168).

Is it not painfully apparent what is going on here?

But we are not just dealing with military weapons stockpiling and military training exercises within local and state police forces across the country. There have actually been real military-style raids, utilizing military weapons and equipment, that have been conducted in neighborhoods and housing facilities all over the nation, involving local, state, and federal personnel.

A good case in point was the incident in Waco, Texas, back in 1993. While some have argued that the Branch Davidians (the followers of David Koresh at the Waco compound) got what they deserved because they were "crazy cultists," the reality is that, whether crazy cultists or not, they had their rights trampled underfoot by the Gestapo-like FBI and BATF, along with local and state officials, on the TV screens of millions of Americans, and almost nobody raised a voice in protest against this atrocity.

David Koresh was the only one that government officials wanted, and they could have easily arrested him, without incident, during one of his morning jogs. Yet the government seized the entire facility and terrorized all of its occupants, including 17 children. Why?

For six hours prior to the blaze that later destroyed the Waco compound and its residents on April 19, 1993, the government pumped a CS/MeCl gas mixture into the facility, supposedly for the purpose of forcing the Davidians to surrender. But this was a blatant lie. The truth is that this gas mixture paralyzes its victims and, having been fired along with pyrotechnic rounds at the end of this six-hour period, the entire edifice easily went up in violent flames.

The whole Waco fiasco was so completely mismanaged, and government authorities were so blatantly abusive of their power, right from the word go, that many have concluded that complete destruction of the Davidians and their compound was intended from the very beginning. Some had drawn this conclusion even before the Davidians met their tragic fate. One such person was the former McLennan County district attorney, Vic Feazell, who was quoted in the March 2, 1993 edition of the *Houston Chronicle* as saying: "The feds are preparing to kill them. That way they can bury their mistakes....It's sad for the Davidians. And it's sad for our government."

All during the standoff, which began on February 28, government agents taunted the occupants of the compound with blaring music, day and night, to prevent them from sleeping and to psychologically break their will (Was this a military experiment in psychological warfare?). On one occasion, most interestingly, federal agents blasted Nancy Sinatra's song "These Boots are Made for Walkin'," which contains the following lyrics that were obviously intended by the feds to serve as a taunting premonition of what was to come: "You keep thinkin' that you'll never get burned. I just found me a brand new box of matches....Well these boots are made for walkin', and that's just what they'll do.

And one of these days these boots are gonna walk all over you."

None of the government's accusations made about Koresh, by the way, were ever substantiated, such as "illegal" weapons stockpiling and child abuse. In fact, a 1996 congressional investigation concluded that the BATF's investigation of the Davidians "was grossly incompetent [and that] the affidavit filed in support of the warrants contained an incredible amount of false statements..."(169, p. 94).

Maybe now you can understand why the FBI prevented fire trucks from gaining access to the Waco compound until long after it collapsed into a pile of ashes; there was to be no discovery of incriminating evidence at their crime scene--evidence such as the front door, which showed that the first shots fired in the initial siege had come from outside, and were not from the Davidians within the compound, as was falsely claimed.

One obvious purpose of this whole operation was to send a message to other radical religious groups, that a similar fate will await them unless they keep their mouths shut (Koresh, for years, had been very outspoken about his adversity toward government abuse of power). Another obvious purpose was to condition the public, as well as those who work in law enforcement, to accept such tyrannical police raid tactics as the norm. As Clinton said during an April 21, 1993 White House press conference, in regards to Waco: "There is unfortunately a rise in this sort of fanaticism all over the world. And we may have to confront it again."

Waco, of course, was not a unique incident of this sort. As another example, consider the 1992 Ruby Ridge tragedy in Idaho, where Randy Weaver's young teenage son was shot in the back by a federal agent, and was killed instantly. Later, after a standoff at the Weaver home, another federal agent fatally shot Weaver's unarmed wife, Vicki, in the face while on their front porch, holding their ten-month-old baby daughter in her arms. The next morning, agents taunted Randy by yelling out to his dead wife, "Good morning, Mrs. Weaver. We had pancakes for breakfast. What did you have?"(339) Later, Vicki's murderer was awarded a medal for "valor."

And what, exactly, was Weaver's crime? He refused to be an informant for the feds who were investigating some of his neighbors. After his refusal to cooperate, they decided to "punish" him by setting him up through entrapment, sending an undercover agent to his home to petition him to saw off some shotguns. Though Weaver refused, the agent persisted relentlessly until Weaver finally gave in. As a result of this "illegal" firearms transaction, Weaver was served a court order with a wrong date on it (which, as you might guess, was later said to have been a "mistake"). When Weaver didn't show up in court on the earlier date than what was on his court order, the feds began their war on the Weaver family.

Another good example of American Gestapoism took place on October 2, 1992, just outside Malibu, California, when recently-retired Donald Scott was shot to death in his own home by federal and state agents who broke in without a search warrant, in the middle of the night, while Scott was sound asleep. This action took place, according to its perpetrators, as part of the "war on drugs." Supposedly, a federal agent had previously spotted from a plane a crop of marijuana growing on Scott's 200-acre property. Of course, there turned out to be absolutely no marijuana anywhere on the premises and, prior to launching the deadly assault, no attempt had been made to definitively determine the accuracy of the allegation that there was.

So what was the real reason for this travesty? Federal personnel had recently tried to purchase Scott's valuable and scenic property to expand the adjacent Santa Monica Mountains National Recreation Area. When Scott refused to sell, the decision was made to take advantage of new asset forfeiture laws and seize the property under the premise that it was being used to conduct illegal drug dealing activities (this law stated that any property raided for drugs could be seized, even if no drugs were found). Scott's big "mistake" was grabbing a handgun and coming out of his bedroom to hopefully frighten off what he thought were burglars (well, burglars without a badge, that is).

Yet another similar incident occurred on April 22, 2000, when heavily-armed federal agents marched on the home of some relatives of six-year-old Elian Gonzalez in Miami, Florida, to forcefully take him and send him back to Cuba. Though nobody was injured in this particular incident, it served to further demonstrate that a dangerous pattern exists of overly-zealous, power-hungry federal agencies that seem to enjoy terrorizing and brutalizing innocent American citizens.

One final example we will look at occurred in the pre-dawn hours of October 17, 2002. Approximately fifty law enforcement officers (from the Oregon State Police, Eugene and Springfield Police Departments, Portland Police Bureau, Oregon National Guard, the Lane County Sheriff, etc.) swarmed a residential neighborhood in Eugene, armed with automatic assault rifles and accompanied by a National Guard military Light Armored Vehicle, which looked like an army tank. The purpose of this raid was to supposedly bust up a marijuana-growing operation, but no evidence of such an operation was ever found in the three homes that were raided (what a familiar pattern).

The whole densely-populated neighborhood was awakened that morning by "flash bang" grenades being hurled into the back yards of the three target homes. Without knocking, masked and armored SWAT police smashed in the doors of the three residences. They forced the occupants from their beds and would not allow them to get dressed. Even though no evidence was found after ransacking these homes for hours, in a pathetic attempt to justify this outrageous invasion, several individuals were arrested anyway, thereby exposing them to the possibility of having their homes forfeited under Oregon drug laws. The victims were later released without any charges (after all, what could they have been charged with?), but were left with deep emotional scars and severe damage to their properties.

One neighbor--a schoolteacher--who was trying to get to her car to leave for work that morning, called out to an officer standing nearby, to ask if it was permissible for her to leave. The only reply she got was, "I haven't shot anyone in two weeks"(340). This should help you to understand the kind of mentality that many in "law enforcement" have in this country today. Welcome to the new American Tyranny! It would appear that we don't even have to wait for martial law to be officially declared, in order for this country to become a full-fledged police state.

In the wake of the Hurricane Katrina disaster that wiped out most of New Orleans in late August 2005, martial law was actually declared in this city, in the name of "maintaining law and order." As the Yahoo News website reported on September 2, 2005, in an article called "Troops Deployed in Anarchic New Orleans with Shoot to Kill Orders": "New Orleans was primed for all-out combat, as Iraq-tested troops with shoot-to-kill orders moved into the hurricane-devastated city to quell rioters and looters.

"The deployment of 300 members of the Arkansas National Guard came ahead of a tour of the affected region by President George W. Bush, who vowed 'zero tolerance' for the armed gangs terrorising the flooded city.

"Louisiana Governor Kathleen Blanco said the guardsmen had been authorized to open fire on 'hoodlums' profiteering from the destruction wrought by Hurricane Katrina, which is believed to have left thousands dead.

"'These troops are fresh back from Iraq, well trained, experienced, battle tested and under my orders to restore order in the streets,' Blanco said.

"'They have M-16s and they are locked and loaded.

"'These troops know how to shoot and kill and they are more than willing to do so if necessary and I expect they will,' she said"(511).

Along this same line, the *Army Times* website reported on September 30, 2008: "The 3rd Infantry Division's 1st Brigade Combat Team has spent 35 of the last 60 months in Iraq patrolling in full battle rattle, helping restore essential services and escorting supply convoys.

"Now they're training for the same mission--with a twist--at home.

"Beginning Oct. 1 for 12 months, the 1st BCT will be under the day-to-day control of U.S. Army North, the Army service component of Northern Command, as an on-call federal response force for natural or manmade emergencies and disasters, including terrorist attacks....

"...[T]his new mission marks the first time an active unit has been given a dedicated assignment to NorthCom, a joint command established in 2002 to provide command and control for federal homeland defense efforts and coordinate defense support of civil authorities....

"They may be called upon to help with civil unrest and crowd control or to deal with potentially horrific scenarios such as massive poisoning and chaos in response to a chemical, biological, radiological, nuclear or high-yield explosive...attack....

"The 1st BCT's soldiers also will learn how to use "the first ever nonlethal package that the Army has fielded," 1st BCT commander Col. Roger Cloutier said, referring to crowd and traffic control equipment and nonlethal weapons designed to subdue unruly or dangerous individuals without killing them"(556).

As you can see, we are heading into a police state without even necessarily having a major crisis befall us to precipitate it. In fact, notice what the February 6, 2005 *Toronto Sun* had to say about this: "This week, former military intelligence analyst William Arkin revealed a hitherto unknown directive, with the Orwellian name 'JCS Conplan 0300-97' [also known as the Strategic Support Branch], authorizing the Pentagon to employ special, ultra-secret 'anti-terrorist' military units on American soil for what the author claims are 'extra-legal missions'[that is, missions outside the law]. In other words, using U.S. soldiers to kill or arrest Americans, acts that have been illegal since the U.S. Civil War"(459).

Even in light of such revelations as these, there are still those who will insist that our leaders, especially in the military, would never turn on us and betray the Constitution. But what they don't realize is that a tremendous shift has been taking place among many of our military leaders in recent decades, in regards to their attitude toward patriotism. Former deputy chief of staff for intelligence at the Pentagon, Major Ralph Peters, is one such example. In 1994, he wrote a position paper called "Warrior Class," in which he stated: "The desire for patriotism is considered an enemy doctrine. The U.S. armed forces must be prepared to fight against all those who oppose the New World Order and who are holding out for nationalism....

"This new warrior class is most dangerous because they consist of those who fight out of strong religious beliefs [principles of freedom, equality, justice, etc.]....

"There is a world-wide class of patriots who number in the millions, and if the current trend continues, there may be more of these who love freedom and are now the target of the New World Order....

"You cannot bargain and compromise with these warriors....We, as the military, need to commit more training time to counter these threats. [Who poses the real threat here?] We must have an active campaign to win over the populace....This must be coupled with irresistible violence"(170, p. 7).

James J. Schneider, a professor of military theory at the School of Advanced Military Studies at the U.S. Army Command and General Staff College in Fort Leavenworth, Kansas, is another example of prominent individuals in our military who have expressed such treasonous sentiments. In an April 1995 article called "Ambushing the Future," which appeared in *Special Warfare*, a publication of the U.S. Army JFK Special Warfare Center, he declared: "The future will be dominated by a resurgent force that will change the nature of both the nation-state and the national security system....We have yet to divine the full implications of the revolution in geopolitics euphemistically called the new world order. For the Army, and for Special Forces, the future will be a period of global reconstruction. But, there is another aspect of reconstruction that anticipates the future--the army's unique relationship to the U.S. Constitution. As an army we are fortunate to have such a rich historical tradition. But, this experience is of little use if it cannot be interpreted in the light of future operations. In other words, to learn from the past we must anticipate the future. And, the future will be dominated by a single overwhelming presence--the United Nations....The U.N.'s central role in shaping the future during global reconstruction will persist, and its geopolitical influence will...increase"(171, pp. 65, 66).

General Colin Powell, upon receiving the Global Leadership Award from the United Nations Association--USA, on April 21, 1993, while still serving as Chairman of the Joint Chiefs of Staff, stated: "[T]he principles of the United Nations Charter are worth our lives, our fortunes, and our sacred honor"(112, p. 155).

It's very clear where the loyalties of our military leaders lie. And our media, expectedly, are following right behind them. In October of 1993, for example, the *San Francisco Chronicle* reported: "The UN now has multinational foreign troops, peace keeping troops stationed in fourteen countries around the world. They all have one thing in common--The international soldiers are there to bring tranquility and safety [WHAT PROPAGANDA!][Endnote 88] to places who cannot do so on their own. So, perhaps there is one more place a UN multinational force is desperately needed, the United States of America"(172)[Endnote 89].

Since 1993, when the above quote was written, U.N. troops have indeed been coming to this country, and in very large numbers. As *The Spotlight* reported in late 1994: "Thomas Pickering, the U.S. ambassador to Russia, admitted on November 5, 1994, that, 'Yes, foreign troops are being based here, from Russia and from some other countries....[T]here will be brigade-sized units coming from Russia, and maybe other UN nations, to familiarize them here'"(173)[Endnote 90].

On September 2, 1992, George Bush Sr., speaking before the U.N., said: "The U.S. is prepared to make available our bases and facilities for multi-national training and field exercises. One such base nearby with facilities is Fort Dix"(17, p. 59).

So why the big push to train so many foreign troops on American soil? Well, think about it for a moment: Wouldn't foreign soldiers be much more reliable to comply, when told to fire at American citizens who resist the New World Order, than domestic soldiers? [Endnote 91]

Because the globalists realize that many U.S. soldiers will never fire on fellow Americans, and fearing a possible rebellion from them, they have taken precautions to prevent an unwanted situation from arising. Their main course of action has been to ship U.S. soldiers overseas that they suspect might be a problem, and to keep the ones here that they believe can be trusted to sell out their country. But how, you may ask, have the globalists been able to tell the difference, in the U.S. military, between those whom they can and can't trust to betray their fellow countrymen? In some cases, simply by asking them, upon recruitment. At the Twenty-nine Palms Marine Base near San Diego, California, for instance, an eye-opening survey was given to Marine recruits on May 10, 1994. This same survey was also given, around the same time, to U.S. Army Special Operations recruits. In this "Combat Arms Survey," recruits were asked if they agreed to the following:

45. I am a United Nations fighting person [What gives the military the right to use U.S. soldiers to fight for a foreign entity?]. I serve in the forces which maintain world peace and every nation's way of life. I am prepared to give my life in their defense [That's funny--I thought our soldiers were supposed to defend the U.S. ALONE!].

46. The U.S. government declares a ban on the possession, sale, transportation and transfer of all non-sporting firearms. A thirty (30) day amnesty period is permitted for the firearms to be turned over to the local authorities. At the end of this period, a number of citizen groups refuse to turn over their firearms. Consider the following statement: I would fire upon U.S. citizens who refuse or resist confiscation of firearms banned by the U.S. government(175).

While we're on the subject of banning firearms, you may be interested to know that another factor which Marx stressed was the establishment of gun control laws, ultimately leading to the confiscation of all weapons out of the hands of the people. Why? To prevent them from defending themselves against government tyranny. And isn't this just what is happening in this country today? Under the pretext of "making our streets safer," our government is seeking to disarm us through increasingly restrictive gun control laws (there goes yet another one of our constitutional rights!), thus leaving us defenseless against the coming martial law that is being planned. This Hitlerian strategy is precisely what gave the Nazis the edge over their domestic opponents.

Amendment 2 of the U.S. Constitution states: "A well regulated militia, being necessary to the security of the free state, the right of the people to keep and bear arms shall not be infringed." Despite this clear wording of the Constitution, however, U.S. citizens today are being arrested for possessing a gun without a permit (the Constitution is their permit!). And then we had the Clinton administration pushing so vigorously to establish a national gun registration law, and the Bush Jr. administration pushing for a national assault weapons ban [Endnote 92]. Can you see the war that our globalist-controlled government is waging against the 2nd Amendment?

Hitler fought for, and succeeded in establishing, the same thing that Clinton pushed for--a national gun registration law. And this is what Hitler had to say about it, back in 1935: "This year will go down in history. For the first time, a civilized nation has full gun registration. Our streets will be safer, our police more efficient, and the world will follow our lead into the future"(17, p. 51). Here's what *The Communist Rules of Revolution* states on this matter: "Register all firearms, under any pretext, as a prelude to confiscating them"(140). Now compare this last quote with the next two astonishing quotes:

- "Waiting periods are only a step. Registration is only a step. The prohibition of firearms is the goal." -Attorney General Janet Reno(141).

- "Our main agenda is to have all guns banned. We must use whatever means possible. It doesn't matter if you have to distort facts or even lie. Our task of creating a Socialist America can only succeed when those who would resist us have been totally disarmed." - Sarah Brady, Chairman, Handgun Control, Inc.(142)

Yes, the goal of gun registration is to ultimately disarm the people. Once you know who has the guns, you know where to go to get them. Thus, as stated before, you leave the people defenseless against government tyranny. And, no surprise, it has been the U.N. behind the push for disarmament around the world, not only of nations (which is quite obvious), but of individual citizens as well.

The proceeding excerpt from an article in a 1994 edition of the *Washington Times* confirms this point: "So quietly that even the gun lobby hasn't noticed, the United Nations is beginning to set its sights on global gun control. The U.N. Disarmament Commission has adopted a working paper...that proposes tighter controls on the gun trade in the United States and other member nations as a way of combating international arms trafficking"(143).

Later on, in a related article on the same page of this same edition of the *Washington Times*, we read: "The Clinton administration has agreed to participate in a discussion of ways for the United Nations to control the manufacture of guns and their sales to civilians. This represents the first U.N. effort to foster regulation of the multi-million-dollar trade in small arms....The U.N. working paper [mentioned in the above quote] declares that governments individually are 'impotent' to deal with global arms trafficking and proposes 'harmonization' of gun control standards around the world to make trafficking easier to spot and prevent. 'The arms permitted for civilian use...should be subject to controls at all points in the chain, from production and/or acquisition up to the time they are sold to an individual. From then on they should remain subject to monitoring and control,' the paper says. Any 'harmonization' would inevitably mean tightening controls on the loosely regulated U.S. gun business..."(144).

Further in this vein of thought, on September 25, 1999, the BBC aired "UN Targets Small Arms," in which it was reported that U.N. Secretary General Kofi Annan "told a special meeting of the Security Council...that member states should...adopt gun control laws including a prohibition of...private ownership of small arms." Do you not see the connection between the U.S. government and the U.N. pushing for gun control?

The whole purpose for the 2nd Amendment, in addition to enabling "we the people" to defend ourselves against government abuse, was to serve as a buffer to prevent the government from becoming abusive in the first place. We see this point echoed numerous times in the writings of the Founding Fathers. Here are a couple examples:

- "Before a standing army can rule, the people must be disarmed, as they are in almost every kingdom in Europe. The Supreme power in America cannot enforce unjust laws by the sword, because the whole body of the people are armed, and can be, on any pretense, raised in the United States." - Noah Webster(145).

- "Americans never need fear their government because of the advantage of being armed, which the Americans possess over the people of almost every other nation." - James Madison(146).

Are you now starting to better understand the grave implications that gun control laws can have for us?

Besides leaving people defenseless against the government itself, another obvious reason for the government wanting to take guns away from people is to make them defenseless against the rioters and looters that will spring up after the coming planned crisis. Being desperate from their inability to protect themselves and their families, the people will cry out to the government for help. "Of course we'll help you," the government will tell them. "However, we first need to suspend the Constitution." Get it?

To justify its war on gun ownership, the government has often advanced the idea, echoed frequently in the media, that taking guns away from people will stop (or greatly reduce) crime in this country. But do you buy this propaganda? Consider Washington, D.C., for example. This city has the toughest gun control laws in the country, and yet it also has the highest rate of gun-related crimes. Obviously criminals are more likely to commit their crimes in areas where they know that most of the people are disarmed. Thus the government's push for "gun control" actually increases crime, instead of curtailing it.

The truth is, the government wants to disarm law-abiding citizens, not criminals. If you have any doubts about this, just look at how local police departments around the country have been conducting gun drives, promising that no questions will be asked if people simply turn in their "illegal" handguns. Some districts are even offering cash in return for compliance with such voluntary confiscation programs. But who is it that actually turns in their weapons during these drives? Is it Billy the burglar or Robby the rapist? Of course not! It's the law-abiding citizens who comply.

Whether it's gun drives, gun permits, or gun registration, none of these measures stop criminals from getting guns and committing gun-related crimes. Criminals get their guns, of course, on the street, through the underground, without any "waiting periods." The government actually loves it when criminals obtain guns and commit gun-related crimes, since these crimes are easily seized upon as justification for implementing more strict gun control laws.

It goes without saying that the reason the government wants law-abiding citizens disarmed, instead of criminals, is because law-abiding citizens are more likely to resist an outlaw government than those who are already outlaws themselves. Thus law-abiding citizens are actually considered by our globalist-controlled government to be its enemies, or at least its potential enemies, which pose the greatest threat to its attainment of totalitarian power. With this thought in mind, here's an important question to ponder in regards to the push for increasingly stringent gun control laws in this country: Should we feel secure in giving up our arms, leaving ourselves defenseless against a power-hungry government that has already proven itself to be untrustworthy through such incidents as Waco and Ruby Ridge?

Now I am not suggesting that we run down to our local gun shop and begin stocking up a huge supply of weapons. The gun seizure issue was simply brought up to further illustrate how our government has been covertly working to remove our freedoms and increase its power, in order to set up the New World Order.

Yes, the globalists are well aware that they don't have all of the people fooled, and that they will indeed have to contend with those who will not give in to their twisted designs, who might even pose a threat to their rise to absolute power if they are in possession of self-defensive weapons. Thus there is a tremendous contempt, on the part of the globalists, for such "non-compliant," patriotic citizens. We see this contempt vividly portrayed in the writings of authors like Sharif M. Aboullah. In his book *The Power of One*, a masterpiece of globalist propaganda designed to make the general public believe that the emerging world government system will be an absolute paradise, he wrote: "In this country, one of the signs of the coming new world order is the breakdown of large institutions, including banking, business and government. Once-mighty brokerage houses are failing; accounting firms are facing bankruptcy; banks are on the auction block; even the former pillars of commerce like Sears have fallen on hard times.

"Many people treat these signs with alarm. However, Barbara Marx Hubbard talks about being able to recognize what is breaking through from what is breaking down. In his book *Voluntary Simplicity*, Duane Elgin has a graph that shows the stages of civilizational decline. As one civilization falls, there is a rising curve for the new order. The decline actually sows the seeds for a new civilizational order. Our question is: Which slope will we devote our attention to--the declining or the one advancing?

"...I am seeing that indeed the old society is continuing its collapse, making space for the new to emerge. I can feel hopeful about what is breaking through, by looking at what is breaking down...

"For those who want to lock into the old society, who want to revive the dinosaur [patriots who will resist the New World Order], it appears that the world is coming to an end. Jump out the windows, slit your wrists, drink the poison Kool-Aid: there is nothing left to live for.

"As for me, I say let the old society die. It will turn into the humus for a new civilization...

"[T]he leaders of the new society must prepare for an abrupt shift in economic, social and political patterns. The changes could take as long as twenty years to fully manifest. On the other hand, the old society could unravel very swiftly, almost overnight.

"There are several quick change scenarios which could bring the old society to a grinding halt. Most of the scenarios involve shortages of oil, money, or both [artificial, manufactured shortages, of course]. One way or another, it could all be over in three weeks"(147, pp. 67-69)[Endnote 93].

Well, how about it--are you feeling "hopeful" about what is soon to "break through"? And do you feel good about what is "breaking down"?

The contempt that the globalists have for patriotic citizens runs far deeper than mere emotions. Their ultimate goal is to completely annihilate them [Endnote 94]. One author who brought this out most profoundly, referred to in the above quote, was New Age occultist Barbara Marx Hubbard, a former advisor to presidents Bush Sr. and Reagan, and a U.S. vice-presidential candidate in 1984. In her unpublished manuscript, *The Book of Co-Creation: An Evolutionary Interpretation of the New Testament*, which she claimed was directly channeled to her by her "spirit guides," she described the agenda for anyone who resists the coming world government as follows: "'No worldly peace can prevail until the self-centered members of the planetary body [opposers and resisters of the New World Order] either change, or die. That is the choice....This act is as horrible as killing a cancer cell. It must be done for the sake of the future of the whole. So be it; be prepared for the selection process which is now beginning.

"'We, the elders [supposed "spirit guides"], have been patiently waiting until the very last moment before the quantum transformation, to take action to cut out this corrupted and corrupting element in the body of humanity. It is like watching a cancer grow; something must be done before the whole body is destroyed.

"'Now as we approach the quantum shift from creature-human to co-creative human...the human who is an inheritor of godlike powers...the destructive one-fourth must be eliminated from the social body. We have no choice, dearly beloveds. It is a case of the destruction of the whole planet, or the elimination of the ego-driven godless one-fourth who, at this time of planetary birth, can, if allowed to live on to reproduce their defective disconnection, destroy forever the opportunity of Homo Sapiens to become Homo Universalis, heirs of God'"(149, p. 308).

For a brief glimpse at what the globalists intend for our lives to be like under their coming despotic system, once all the dust of resistance has settled, consider this: In 1959, an organization was formed by the globalists called The World Constitution and Parliament Association. The intended purpose of this organization is obvious from its title--to draft up an international constitution for the emerging world government. And in June of 1977, their dream was finally realized with the completion of a document titled *The Constitution for the Federation of Earth*, which was signed by 135 participants from 25 different countries. Here are a few examples of policies/laws that this document proposes:

- Article I, point 4 reveals that the (socialist/communist) world government will regulate and control nearly every aspect of the lives of all citizens of the world (except for those in control, of course).
- Article II, points 4-7 reveal that the world will be divided into 20 World Electoral and Administrative Regions and 10 Magna-Regions. This, of course, will mean the end of all present national boundaries, as well as all present forms of government.
- Article III, point 2 calls for the seizure of all personal weapons of self-defense.
- Points 14 and 17 tell us that the world government will have total control of all international trade, banking, and finance.
- Point 21 talks about plans for controlling population growth and solving problems of population distribution.
- Point 37 talks about designating a world language.
- Article V, section A, point 3 permits the World Parliament to "reject the international laws developed prior to the advent of world government."
- Article IX tells us that the World Judiciary branch of the world government will interpret the rights of world citizens and would issue rulings regarding the sentencing of those who refuse to submit to the demands of the world system.
- Article X covers the Enforcement System of the world government, which will enforce the decisions of the World Judiciary and other governing bodies. One means of enforcement that is discussed would include the denial of financial credit to those who fail to comply with world law (section D, point 2)(416).

Another revealing glimpse into what life will be like under the emerging New World Order comes from the globalist and Fabian socialist English philosopher, Bertrand Russell: "The [New World Order] System, one may surmise, will be something like this: Except...[for] the governing aristocracy, all but 5 percent of males and 30 percent of females will be sterilized....As a rule, artificial insemination will be preferred to the natural method. The unsterilized, if they desire the pleasures of love, will usually have to seek them with sterilized partners [Endnote 95].

"Children will be taken from their mothers and reared by professional nurses....The laboring class [meaning all those but the "aristocracy"] will have such long hours of work and so little to eat that their desires will hardly extend beyond sleep and food...[there will be] abolition of the family [Endnote 96]...[and a] supreme duty of devotion to the state.

"Gradually, by selective breeding, the congenital differences between the rulers and the ruled will increase until they become almost different species. A revolt of the plebs [the ruled masses] would become as unthinkable as an organized insurrection of sheep against the practice of eating mutton.

"Even if all are miserable, all will believe themselves happy, because the government will tell them that they are so"(154).

Compare this last forecast with the next one, made by Aldous Huxley back in 1959: "And it seems to me perfectly in the cards that there will be within the next generation or so a pharmacological method of making people love their servitude, and producing...a kind of painless concentration camp for entire societies, so that people will in fact have their liberties taken away from them but will rather enjoy it, because they will be distracted from any desire to rebel by propaganda, brainwashing, or brainwashing enhanced by pharmacological methods"(413)[Endnote 97]. Does the word Prozac ring a bell? [Endnote 98] Perhaps not so coincidental, Prozac has the very same numbing effect on people that "Soma" did in George Orwell's novel, *1984*.

A rather ugly picture, wouldn't you say? This Orwellian "Big Brother" nightmare [Endnote 99] is destined to become a reality if we don't wake up, and fast! In fact, as we have seen, almost every piece of the globalist puzzle is already in place. There isn't much left to do.

To help you to put into better perspective just how far down the road to ruin the globalists have taken us, check out the following 1902 globalist forecast of what life would become like in this country, as we moved progressively closer toward world government. And notice, specifically, how nearly all of what it predicted has already come about: "[The] coming status...will be something in the nature of a Benevolent Feudalism....Group ' fidelity...is already observable....The autocrats...will distribute benefits to the degree that makes a tolerant, if not satisfied people....

"A person of offensive activity [non-compliant] may be denied work in every feudal shop and on every feudal farm from one end of the country to the other....His actions will be promptly communicated to the banded autocracy...of industries....The individual security of place and livelihood of its members will then depend on the harmony of their utterances and acts with the wishes of the great nobles; and so long as they rightly fulfill their functions their recompense will be generous....

"A host of economists, preachers and editors will be ready to show indisputably that the evolution taking place is for the best interests of all....What the barons will most dread will be the collective assertion of the villains at the polls; but this, from experience, they will know to be a thing of no immediate danger. By the putting forward of a hundred irrelevant issues they can hopelessly divide the voters at each election; or, that failing, there is always to be trusted as a last resort the cry of impending panic....

"Two divisions of the courtier class are the judges and the politicians....They must satisfy the demands of the multitude, and yet, on the other hand, they must obey the commands from above....The nobles will have attained to complete power, and the motive and operation of Government will have become simply the registering and administering of their collective will....

"Armed force will, of course, be employed to overawe the discontented and to quiet unnecessary turbulence. Unlike the armed forces of the old feudalism, the nominal control will be that of the State....

"When the new order is in full swing...so comprehensive and so exact will be the social and political control that it will be exercised in a constantly widening scope....Peace [absence of all opposition] will be the main desideratum....

"A happy blending of generosity [bribery] and firmness [outright tyranny] will characterize all dealings with discontent....[To] the prevention of discontent...the teachings of the schools and colleges, the sermons, the editorials...and even the plays at the theaters will be skillfully and persuasively molded." - *The Independent*, April 3, 1902(179).

Jimmy Carter's National Security Advisor, Zbigniew Brzezinski, projecting into the future in his book *Between Two Ages*, stated: "As one specialist [Gordon J.F. McDonald] noted, 'By the year 2018, technology will make available to the leaders of the major nations a variety of techniques for conducting secret warfare....Techniques of weather modification could be employed to produce prolonged periods of drought or storm, thereby weakening a nation's capacity and forcing it to accept the demands of the competitor [Endnote 100].'...Before long the social elites of most of the more advanced countries will be highly internationalist or globalist in spirit and outlook....Deliberate management of the American future will become widespread....The function of sovereignty...is clearly no longer compatible with reality..."(48).

Here is yet another interesting globalist projection into the future, from back in the early 1950s: "When we have definite international laws and an army to enforce them, we shall have international peace. When atomic bombs are made only by a world government and used only by a world army, who could resist?...

"Give the U.N. absolute power to regulate international trade and commerce....

"Immigration control now handled by each country would be relinquished to the U.N. along with the power to arbitrarily remove people from one part of the world and settle them in a place a U.N. planner determines their skills, etc., are needed....

"Establish an international police force strong enough that no nation can resist its orders....

"Give the U.N. power of taxation....

"Place control [in the U.N.'s hands] of broadcast stations, press, speech, etc...to ensure development [coercion] of 'cooperative' public opinion." -F.A. Magruder's *American Government* (textbook), 1952 edition.

H.G. Wells gave some very upsetting forecasts of living conditions under the coming world government (which, again, he strongly favored). In his 1901 book *Anticipations of the Reactions of Mechanical and Scientific Progress Upon Human Life and Thought*, he wrote: "In its more developed phases I seem to see the new republic as a sort of outspoken secret society, with which even the prominent men of the ostensible state may be openly affiliated....In all sorts of ways they will be influencing and controlling the apparatus of the ostensible governments....

"[T]he ethical system which will dominate the world state...will be shaped...to check the procreation of base and servile types....

"The method that must in some cases still be called in to the help of man is death...the merciful obliteration of weak and silly and pointless things. The new ethic will hold life to be a privilege...and the alternative in right conduct between living fully, beautifully, and efficiently, will be to die....The men of the new republic will have little pity and less benevolence....The men of the new republic will not be squeamish either in facing or inflicting death....They will have an ideal that will make killing worth the while....

"The state will be the reserve guardian of all children. If they are being undernourished, if their education is being neglected, the state will step in, take over the responsibility of their management, and enforce their charge upon the parents....

"The new republic will aim to establish...a world state with a...common rule. All over the world its...control will run."

In 1907 Wells published *New Worlds for Old*, in which he gave this forecast: "The broad lines of the process of transition from the present state of affairs to the Socialist state of the future as they are developed by administrative Socialism lie along the following lines. The peaceful and systematic taking over from private enterprise...of the great common services....Systematic expropriation of private owners by...increased taxation. The building up of a great scientifically organized administrative machinery to carry on these enlarging public functions. A steady increase and expansion of public education, research...and all such public services. The systematic promotion of measures for...the public feeding of school children....The systematic creation of a great service of public health....The recognition of the claim of every citizen to welfare....The...establishment of a legal minimum wage....These are the broad forms of the Fabian Socialist's answer to the question of how [the socialist state of the future will be run]....

"From saying that the unorganized people cannot achieve Socialism, they passed to the implication that organizations alone, without popular support, might achieve Socialism. Socialism was to arrive as it were insidiously....Socialism ceased to be an open revolution, and became a plot. Functions were to be shifted, quietly, unostentatiously, from the representative to the official he appointed; a bureaucracy was to slip into power....Essentially the Socialist attitude is this, an insistence that parentage can no longer be regarded as an isolated private matter; that the welfare of the children is of universal importance, and must, therefore, be finally a matter of universal concern. The State...is now every year becoming more and more their Guardian, their Over-Parent."

The final H.G. Wells forecast we will look at comes from a book he published in 1928, called *The Open Conspiracy: Blue Prints for World Revolution*, in which he stated: "This open and declared intention of establishing a world order...[is] a scheme for all human conduct....The form in which the Open Conspiracy will first appear will certainly not be that of a centralized organization. Its most natural and convenient method of coming into being will be the formation of small groups of friends....Fundamentally important are...the entirely provisional nature of all loyalties associated with existing governments, and the supreme importance of population control....The production and distribution of staple necessities is apprehended as one world business....This large loose assimilatory mass of groups and societies will be definitely and obviously attempting to swallow up the entire population of the world and become the new human community."

In his famous 1932 book *Brave New World*, Aldous Huxley foresaw that "The twenty-first century...will be the era of World Controllers....Under a scientific dictatorship education will really work--with the result that most men and women will grow up to love their servitude and will never dream of revolution. There seems to be no good reason why a thoroughly scientific dictatorship should ever be overthrown"(pp. 25, 116).

Back in 1962, another globalist, former Israeli prime minister David Ben-Gurion, provided his own foresights, which, though off a bit on the timing, were otherwise strikingly accurate: "The image of the world in 1987 as traced in my imagination: The Cold War will be a thing of the past....[There will be] a gradual democratization of the Soviet Union....[T]he United States [will transform] into a welfare state with a planned economy. Western and Eastern Europe will become a federation of autonomous States having a Socialist and democratic regime"(180).

One final globalist forecast that we will look at was written by Alice Bailey, wife of Foster Bailey, a famous 33rd-degree Mason. She, being a Co-

Mason herself, was quite familiar with the secrets of Masonry, and was keenly aware of, and supportive of, its hidden (yet not-so-hidden) globalist agenda [Endnote 101]. In her book *Externalization of the Hierarchy*, she talked about "points of light" (recall how we quoted earlier from George Bush Sr., where he talked about "a thousand points of light") in connection with a "New Group of World Servers" engaged in the effort of "group work of a new order...the world of the Brotherhood...the Forces of Light," and that "out of the spoliation of all existing culture and civilization, the new world order must be built." She then went on to forecast that "[G]reat changes will take place...national currencies will...[be] largely superseded...by a universal monetary exchange....National material assets and the needed commodities will all be provided for under an entirely new system [world socialism].

"Private enterprise...will be regulated; the great public utilities, the major material resources and the sources of planetary wealth--iron, steel, oil and wheat, for instance--will be owned...by a governing, controlling international group...under international direction [Endnote 102].

"This moment is symptomatic of a change in the orientation of man's thinking...foundational to the new world order which will emerge...

"In the preparatory period for the new world order there will be a steady and regulated disarmament. It will not be optional. No nation will be permitted to produce and organize any equipment for destructive purposes....One of the first tasks of any future peace conference will be to regulate this matter and gradually see to the disarming of the nations"(182).

So, do you have any doubt that a massive conspiracy exists, and has existed for a long time, to rule over every individual in the world, with an iron fist of tyranny?

* * * * * * *

"An international government, with police power over <u>every individual</u> citizen in the nations belonging to it...is the only way [to world peace]." - Supreme Court Justice Owen J. Roberts, *The Philadelphia Inquirer*, May 2, 1943.

"[T]he UN must be given the constitutional authority to maintain security through laws which call for obedience from the <u>individual</u> inhabitants of the world as their first duty and which no national government can override..." - Cord Meyer Jr. (CFR member and CIA employee from 1951-1977), *Peace or Anarchy.* Boston: Little, Brown and Co., 1948.

"In 1931, when Brave New World was being written, I was convinced that there

was still plenty of time. The completely organized society, the scientific caste system, the abolition of free will by methodical conditioning, the servitude made acceptable by regular doses of chemically induced happiness...--these things were coming all right, but not in my time....Twenty-seven years later,...I feel a good deal less optimistic....In the West,...individual men and women still enjoy a large measure of freedom. But...this freedom and even the desire for this freedom seem to be on the wane." - Aldous Huxley, *Brave New World Revisited*, 1959(412).

"It is time to tell the world's people not what they want to hear but what they ought to hear. What they ought to hear is that if we really want to promote peace and justice, we must...strengthen the UN....The UN must have taxing power....It must have a large peacekeeping force....It must be able to make and enforce law on the individual." [Endnote 103] - John Logue, vice-president of the World Federalist Association. Spoken before a subcommittee of the House Foreign Affairs Committee on December 4, 1985. See U.S. Congress, House, Foreign Affairs Committee, Subcommittee on International Operations, U.S. Policy in the U.N., 99 Congress, 1st Sess., December 4, 1985. Washington, D.C.: Government Printing Office, 1985, pp. 152-157.

"To achieve world government, it is necessary to remove from the minds of men their individualism, loyalty to family,...[and] national patriotism." - G.B. Chisholm, former executive director of the World Health Organization, *The Utah Independent*, September 1977.

"World federal enforcement should...be a coercion of law operating on individuals whoever they are and wherever they may be..." - Edith Wynner, *World Federal Government, Why? What? How?*, 1954.

"[T]he capacity to assert social and political control over the individual will vastly increase. It will soon be possible to assert almost continuous control over every citizen..." - Zbigniew Brzezinski, *Between Two Ages.*

"Our power does not know liberty or justice. It is entirely established on the destruction of the individual will." - Vladimir Lenin. As quoted by Michael Sturdza in *Betrayal by Rulers.*

"We need a program...for political control of our society. The purpose is...control of the mind. Everyone who deviates from the given norm can be surgically mutilated. The individual may think that the most important reality is his own existence, but this is only his personal point of view....Man does not have

the right to develop his own mind. We must electronically control the brain.
Some day armies and generals will be controlled by electronic stimulation of the
brain [microchip implants?]." - Dr. Jose M.R. Delgado, former Director of
Neuropsychiatry, Yale University Medical School, and a former researcher for the
CIA's MK Ultra mind control experimental program, *Congressional Record*, No.
26, Vol. 118, February 24, 1974.

Conclusion

It should be obvious to the reader by now that the box-cover puzzle picture of our modern society presented to us by our government, educational system, and media does not match up with the picture that emerges once we undertake the effort of assembling all the jumbled puzzle pieces for ourselves. It should thus also be obvious, even to the most staunchly skeptical reader, that there truly is a grand-scale conspiracy for world government that has been in the works for over two centuries, involving a multiplicity of interwoven networks that are all laboring covertly toward this enslaving goal.

Inevitably, there will always be those readers who will still wish to deny, against all the undeniable evidence presented herein, that such a conspiracy does indeed exist. But there is one thing that they simply cannot deny: We are definitely headed for disaster if the present pattern of corruption, resulting from concentrating too much power and money in the hands of too few individuals in government, as well as in the realms of finance and big business, does not cease. The truth is, if the constitutional system of checks and balances continues to be ignored, this country will unavoidably wind up a dictatorship, even if there wasn't a conspiracy to make it such. And, on the global level, the same holds true, of course, for the United Nations and other global institutions, where power and money are also dangerously concentrated in the hands of a few. And just think: Should we wind up under a global dictatorship, where could any dissidents possibly go in order to find refuge? There will simply be no place to run--a very frightening prospect indeed!

Though the majority of people around the world today do not realize that there is a widespread conspiracy for world government, there are, encouragingly, many who at least are aware of certain aspects of it, such as the WTO, for example, against which they have admirably and loudly voiced their protests. However, because such people are oblivious to the big picture--failing to understand just how extensive the control of the enemy really is--they have often wound up ignorantly fighting on the wrong side. Let us examine, therefore, a couple of the most prominent misconceptions that have plagued such people, with the hope of clearing up the confusion that these misconceptions have engendered:

- There are some people who, disgusted with the abuses of power in the U.S. government, look to the U.N. as the only hope for reforming Washington. However, what such people fail to recognize is that the boys who control U.S. foreign and domestic policies are the same ones who hold the reins of power at the U.N.--primarily the CFR crowd. These misguided would-be reformers should instead be focusing on pressuring Congress to restore constitutional law and order, and to make all branches of government accountable to the people, whose interests they are supposed to serve. They should also be pressuring Congress to pull us out of the U.N.

Some have objected to the notion that the U.N. and U.S. are conspiring partners working for world government, citing the fact that the U.S. has often ignored U.N. resolutions and has sometimes failed to pay its yearly "membership dues." But this is exactly how a conspiracy works. Conspiring groups must *appear* to be opposed to one another, at least on occasion, so that their hidden mutual agenda will not so easily be detected, or so that, if detected, claims of a conspiracy can be refuted on this very *apparent* oppositional basis.

- There are others who, disgusted with the abuses of monopolistic capitalism and the unfair distribution of wealth, look to socialism, or even communism, as the answer. This raises a very important point. Regardless what some may think about communism and/or socialism being the salvation of the downtrodden masses, let's just say that such forms of government, or any other forms of government under any other names, if controlled by the globalists, will always lead to the concentration of money and power in the hands of a few, at the expense of the many. In this sense, perhaps the best name for the form of government favored by the globalists would be fascism. But these terms-- fascism, communism, socialism, for the most part, don't really matter in the globalist context, as they can be adjusted (and have been adjusted) to mean whatever the power elites want them to mean. And the same can be said about all other political terms and labels, such as liberal, conservative, democrat, republican, left, right, patriotism, etc.--these terms and labels often amount to nothing more than different masks for the same face. Even national flags are often misused to rally support for globalist causes that have nothing to do with genuine national interest. Therefore, to avoid the twisted web of confusion that the misuse of these terms, labels and symbols can create, we should hold fast to just one principle: removing control from the rich and powerful and restoring it to the people. For us, here in the United States, this means, once again, restoring the Constitution. Rallying behind any other cause, under any number of names it might go by, may very well wind us up on the side of the globalists, without us even realizing it.

This is what wound up happening to many black civil rights activists back in the 1960s. To prove this point, I will here provide an excerpt from a testimony by Jerry Kirk (a student at the University of Chicago who was active in the Communist Party up till 1969), which he delivered in 1970 before the House and Senate Internal Security Committees: "Young people have no conception of the conspiracy's strategy of pressure from above and pressure from below....They have no idea that they are playing into the hands of the Establishment they claim to hate. The radicals think they're fighting the forces of the super rich, like Rockefeller and Ford, and they don't realize that it is precisely such forces which are behind their own revolution, financing it, and using it for their own purposes"(532).

It is truly a tragedy that many people, though rightly opposed to the abuses of the elites around the world (or to the few abuses that they are aware of, anyway), frequently wind up arguing amongst themselves over illegitimate issues, such as left vs. right or democrat vs. republican government, and wind up playing right into the hands of the globalists who want the public divided and ignorant of their manipulation of all the major, seemingly different political parties and schools of thought. The point is this: Regardless what differences people may have (or think they have) in their political points of view, such differences must be laid aside so that everyone can unite against a common enemy that seeks to enslave us all.

Let us look at an example of what is being discussed here, so that we can better understand how the globalists mislead so many people through false paradigms: Whenever the globalists pull a stunt through one of their republican presidential puppets, the liberal democrats will cry foul, but their claims will be written off by conservative republicans as "left wing propaganda." On the other hand, whenever the globalists pull a stunt through one of their democratic presidential puppets, it's the republican conservatives that will cry foul, but their claims will be written off by democratic liberals as "right wing propaganda." And all the while that the masses are pointing fingers back and forth at each other's parties, the globalist agenda is able to march on, unrecognized for what it is, and thus unchecked. It's all nothing but a massive mind manipulation game.

But the question still remains: What can we do about all of this? The first step is to arm ourselves with knowledge. As would be the case with any war--and this surely is a war--we need to know our enemy. I believe that there is truth in the saying "Ignorance is bliss." But in this case, it is our ignorance that is their bliss. As long as we are ignorant, their plan marches on. However, if we, after educating ourselves, could unite and let them know that we are aware of what they are doing, and that we are not going to stand for it, we may yet halt, or at least slow down, their progress. Good luck in your endeavors!

* * * * * * *

"We stand today at a critical juncture. If we do nothing, if we do not challenge the Silent Takeover, do not question our belief system, do not admit our own

culpability in the creation of this 'New World Order,' then all is lost." - Noreena Hertz, *The Silent Takeover*(341, p. 12).

"If you will not fight for right when you can easily win without blood shed; if you will not fight when your victory is sure and not too costly; you may come to the moment when you will have to fight with all the odds against you and only a precarious chance of survival. There may even be a worse case. You may have to fight when there is no hope of victory, because it is better to perish than to live as slaves." - Winston Churchill.

"The history of liberty is a history of limitations of government power, not the increase of it. When we resist, therefore, the concentration of power, we are resisting the powers of death, because concentration of power is what always precedes the destruction of human liberty." - Woodrow Wilson(227, p. 22).

"The exercise of leadership often brings out the worst in men. Ideals and noble aims are forgotten as leaders, driven by vanity and egoism, become entrapped by the temptations of power." - Suzanne Keller, *Beyond the Ruling Class*(20, p. 274).

"...Governments are instituted among men, deriving their just powers from the consent of the governed, that whenever any form of government becomes destructive of these ends, it is the right of the people to alter or abolish it, and to institute new government." - Declaration of Independence.

Appendix 1

The game of staging wars

By at least the close of the first decade of the 20th century, globalist institutions were busy planning for WW I. Several decades later, the U.S. House of Representatives established the Committee to Investigate Tax Exempt Foundations (the Reece Committee), headed up by Norman Dodd. As a part of the investigations of this Committee, an examination of the meeting minutes of the Carnegie Endowment for International Peace (what a misleading name!) was conducted. Based on this aspect of its investigation, the Committee stated that "The trustees of the Foundation brought up a single question: If it is desirable to alter the life of an entire people, is there any means more efficient than war?...They discussed this question for a year and came up with an answer [in 1911]: There are no known means more efficient than war"(183). Thus we see that the globalists had indeed planned WW I years in advance, and had intended to utilize it, amongst other purposes, to "alter the life" of the American people, i.e. to mold them into being more open to the concept of world government.

In regards to WW II and the Korean War, check out this quote from an article on the Council on Foreign Relations, which appeared in the December 9, 1950 edition of the *Chicago Tribune*: "The members of the Council are persons of much more than average influence....They have used the prestige that their wealth, their social position, and their education have given them to lead their country toward bankruptcy and military debacle. They should look at their hands. There is blood on them--the dried blood of the last war [WW II] and the fresh blood of the present one [the Korean War]." Here's a related quote, dating back a few years earlier, from the *Saturday Evening Post*: "The Rockefeller Foundation and the Council on Foreign Relations...intend to prevent, if they can, a repetition of what they call in the vernacular 'the debunking journalistic campaign following World War I.' Translated into precise English, this means that the Foundation and the Council do not want journalists or any other persons to examine too closely and criticize too freely the official propaganda and official statements relative to 'our basic aims and activities' during World War II. In short, they hope that, amongst other things, the policies and measures of Franklin D. Roosevelt will escape in the coming years the critical analysis, evaluation and exposition that befell the policies and measures of Woodrow Wilson and the Entente Allies after World War I"(184). If only our media were this straight-forward today. What a different world it would be.

How exactly have the globalist boys created wars? Well, in the case of WW I, they began by encouraging European nations to establish alliances with each other (i.e. the Triple Alliance: Germany, Italy, Austria/Hungary and the Triple Entente: England, Russia, France), presenting such pacts as being a safeguard against war, when in reality they accomplished the very opposite. For as one nation attacked another, all of the allied nations were inevitably dragged into the conflict. Europe, at this time, was especially susceptible to a grand-scale war breaking out, since there was tremendous economic tension between several European nations. Germany, particularly, was seen as a threat, since its economy was rapidly growing by leaps and bounds. Just one incident, therefore, was all that was needed as an excuse for belligerence, and that incident happened to have been the assassination of Austria's archduke, Francis Ferdinand. From there, the globalists simply made sure that each combatant nation received all the loans that were needed to carry on an effective war campaign.

Just after this war, the globalists then took measures to set the stage for a possible second global conflict, if deemed necessary, by drafting up the Versailles Treaty. This treaty made Germany responsible for WW I, and imposed upon it a heavy burden of reparation payments. As the twenties rolled on, and it became clear that the League of Nations was failing, the globalists, realizing that a second global conflict would indeed be necessary, tweaked Germany's economy to drive it further down the road to ruin. By the end of 1923, the value of the German mark had sunk to one twenty-billionth that of the English pound. In this time of desperation, the fiendish globalist bankers stepped forward to "help" Germany by offering "financial aid" programs like the Dawes Plan and the Young Plan. These plans involved loans that were designed to give the appearance of providing relief, while in reality worsening Germany's predicament. And worsen it they did! By 1931, Germany had paid out 10.5 billion marks in reparations, but had borrowed 18.6 billion marks. This, coupled with the effects of the rigged 1929 stock market crash, had brought the German people to the point where they were all-too-eager to embrace the radical fanatic Hitler, who promised to provide them relief from the oppression of the Versailles Treaty. When he came through with his promise, the German people shouted his praises. But there was another group of people who were quietly hailing him as well--the banksters, who knew that he was just the man they needed to set into motion their next planned global conflict.

Astonishingly, Marshal Ferdinand Foch of France, supreme commander of all allied forces at the end of WW I, saw the Versailles Treaty for what it was, right from the very start. Not only did he correctly predict that another war would result from this "peace treaty," but he foresaw exactly how long it would take for this conflict to break out. He said: "This is not a peace treaty, it's a twenty years armistice"(305). Strangely enough, Lenin had made some similar remarks about this treaty: "What is the Versailles Treaty? This unheard of, predatory peace, enslaves tens of millions of people....This is not a treaty but dictates imposed by robbers with a knife in hand on a defenseless Germany....[T]his international order, which rests on the Versailles Treaty, rests in reality on a volcano"(343, pp. 353, 354).

Even after the next planned universal war (WW II), the globalists set the stage for a possible third world war, should the United Nations fail, by establishing the state of Israel, and then getting the U.S. to become its ally. Why? So that in case the Arab world should attack it (or be deliberately provoked into attacking it), the U.S. and most of Europe (ultimately through NATO) would be drawn into the conflict and break up this last-remaining stronghold of resistance against the emerging New World Order.

Yes, history is not a bunch of freak chance happenings, as many falsely believe, but is instead made up of a series of well-planned events. This point has been recognized and expressed by numerous authoritative sources over the years. One such source is a famous international investment advisor and former U.S. Air Force instructor pilot, R.E. McMaster Jr., who had this to say: "There are two views of history: (1) History happens by accident or (2) It is planned. The general public is taught that history happens by accident. However, the upper echelons...know that history is planned"(185). In this same regard, we find in a publication called *The New Group of World Servers*, produced by World Goodwill, a United Nations NGO (non-governmental organization), the following enlightening statement: "Humanity is not following a haphazard or uncharted course--there is a Plan"(4).

Before WW II even ended, the globalist boys at the CFR were busy planning U.S. post-war foreign policy, intending to use the U.S. as a war-waging machine for world-wide political and financial conquest purposes. A big problem they faced, however, was how to get around a certain constitutional restraint that made such war-waging policies very difficult to execute--the problem of the Constitution only allowing Congress to declare war (Article 1, Section 8). But it wasn't long before the CFR clan finally came up with the cunning, yet illegitimate solution, two-fold in nature, that they had been looking for: a) War would be waged without war actually being declared, thus bypassing Congress (recall that every U.S. military campaign since WW II was, in fact, carried out without war being officially declared by Congress); b) It would be falsely claimed that treaties supersede the Constitution (recall that this claim has been made many times over the years to justify U.S. enforcement of U.N. resolutions and participation in U.N. "peacekeeping" operations abroad). This two-fold solution was included in a 1944 confidential memorandum presented by the CFR to the U.S. State Department, which was worded thusly: "[A] possible...difficulty was cited, namely,...the constitutional provision that only Congress may declare war. This argument was countered with the contention that a treaty would override this barrier, let alone the fact that our participation in such police action as might be recommended by the international security organization [which, of course, later became known as the U.N.] need not necessarily be construed as war"(190).

Once the globalists found a way to get over this constitutional hurdle, it didn't take them long to begin their worldwide war-staging frenzy. Their first major undertaking was the Korean War. Did you ever wonder why this war dragged on for so long (1950-1953), and what it was really all about?$? Ever wonder what the REAL reason was for General Douglas MacArthur being fired? Though he has often been faulted for China's entry into this war, with the claim that his cocky attitude caused him to underestimate the risks of pushing to the Yalu, this simply was not the case. Under the pretext of avoiding inciting China, the U.S. Navy was ordered by CFR-controlled Truman to protect the mainland from Chiang Kai-shek's troops on Taiwan (Formosa). But all that this action accomplished was to free up the communist Chinese armies for their strike across the Yalu. In order to halt this strike, MacArthur ordered the bombing of the Yalu's bridges, but within hours his order was countermanded by General George C. Marshall (CFR member, who at that time was serving as Secretary of Defense). Speaking of this incident, MacArthur later remarked: "I realized for the first time that I had actually been denied the use of my full military power to safeguard the lives of my soldiers and the safety of my army. To me, it clearly foreshadowed a future tragic situation in Korea, and left me with a sense of inexpressible shock"(186, p. 402).

American planes were not allowed to strike supply depots across the Yalu, or to attack MIGs whenever they retreated across the Chinese border. Though the reason given for this was, once again, to prevent "a wider war," it was these very restrictions, along with the blockade of Taiwan ordered by Truman, that gave the Chinese their boldness to attack. In fact, notice what General Lin Piao, commander of the Chinese forces, had later stated: "I never would have made the attack [across the Yalu] and risked my men and my military reputation if I had not been assured that Washington would restrain General MacArthur from taking adequate retaliatory measures against my lines of supply and communication"(187, p. 375). General Mark W. Clark, who later signed the Korean armistice, wrote that it was "beyond my comprehension that we would countenance a situation in which Chinese soldiers killed American youth in organized, formal warfare and yet we would fail to use all the power at our command to protect those Americans"(188, p. 315).

The simple fact is that American soldiers were deliberately sacrificed through intentionally bad war strategies, in order to give the appearance that China was a major threat. Why? President Truman himself provided the best answer to this question when, in late November of 1950, he stated during a secret meeting of the National Security Council: "If the Chinese threat evaporates, the President doubts that you could go ahead with a $45 billion program [the prewar military "program" had been under $14 billion]"(189, p. 117).

The Korean War had ended in a stalemate, with nothing having been accomplished except a huge death toll and a fat wad of cash for the globalists. This war also gave clout to the newly-born, CFR-founded U.N., under whose aegis the Korean War was fought.

But let's now move on to Vietnam. Ever wonder why this war also dragged on for so long, and cost so many lives (on both sides of the conflict)? Ever wonder why we were even there in the first place?$? This war was not intended to be won--only to drag on, like Korea (although Vietnam, of course, dragged on for much longer). In support of this assertion, look at what Lieutenant General Ira C. Eaker said in the March 1968 issue of *Science & Mechanics*: "Our political leaders elected to fight a land war, where every advantage lay with the enemy, and to employ our vast sea and air superiority in very limited supporting roles only. Surprise, perhaps the greatest of the principles of war...was deliberately sacrificed when our leaders revealed our strategy and tactics to the enemy....The enemy was told...that we would not bomb populated areas, heavy industry, canals, dams, and other critical targets--and thus sanctuaries were established by us along the Chinese border and around Haiphong and Hanoi. This permitted the enemy to concentrate antiaircraft defenses around the North Vietnamese targets that our Air Force was permitted to attack--greatly increasing our casualties. Missiles, oil and ammunition were permitted to enter Haiphong harbor unmolested and without protest"(14, pp. 122, 123).

To disguise the otherwise obvious global imperial aims of this war, the U.S. hid behind the facade of a "coalition effort," which gave the impression that the world, as a whole, approved of its military conquests. Eisenhower brought this very point out in his memoirs. When considering intervention in Vietnam in 1954, he recognized that the main burden of the operation would fall upon the U.S., but that "the token forces supplied by these other [coalition] nations, as in Korea, would lend real moral standing to a venture that otherwise could be made to appear as a brutal example of imperialism"(575).

Interestingly, during the heat of the fighting in Vietnam, from 1966 to 1967, the Soviet Union sold to the United States over $2 million worth of magnesium--a metal vital in military aircraft production--when there was a shortage of it in the United States. This occurred at a time when Washington maintained an embargo on supplying communist countries with certain alloys of the same metal.

At about the same time, China sold several thousand tons of steel to the

United States in South Vietnam, for use in the construction of new Air and Army bases. This was at a time when Washington maintained a boycott on all Chinese products(216, pp. 130, 131). Can you not see that the U.S. was actually covertly in partnership with the very countries that it openly appeared to be opposed to? Does this not tell you a little something about the true nature of the Cold War-- that the whole thing was a colossal fraud?

The wars in Korea and Vietnam were only two links in a long chain of U.S. military and CIA campaigns conducted after WW II, launched under the guise of "containing communism," which served only to advance globalist financial and political goals. In the course of these campaigns, scores of legitimately-elected leaders of various countries around the world (primarily in South America, Asia, and Africa) were ousted from power and replaced with unscrupulous puppets who could be trusted to sell their countries out to the exploitations of globalist corporations, the World Bank, the IMF, the U.N., etc. Not one of these conflicts was brought on by an attack on the United States, or even the threat of an attack. As you can see, warfare has become our national policy--a way of life. It is, in fact, big business--very big business.

As the post-WW II decades marched on, in order to justify their trail of Cold War crimes, to win the support of the public, and, most importantly, to create a diversion, the globalists, through their control of our government and media, pumped us with Cold War propaganda that the enemy--Soviet communism--was spreading abroad, when in reality the real enemy was right here in our midst [Endnote 104]. Observe what George Kennan, the State Department official who fathered the U.S. "containment" policy that was designed to prevent Soviet influence from expanding, had to say on this matter: "I sometimes wonder what use there is in trying to protect the West against fancied external threats when the signs of disintegration within are so striking"(191).

The Cold War was truly nothing but a bunch of hype. Here's a most revealing admission of this ugly reality from a 1956 panel report (a panel dominated, by the way, by CFR members who helped create and direct the Cold War) which was sponsored by none other than the Rockefeller Brothers' Fund, entitled "Prospects for America": "It has been necessary to drum up support for United States [foreign] policy by stressing the imminent threats and crisis and by harping on...communism..."(192, p. 293). In this same vein of thought, Pierre Mendes-France, French executive director of the World Bank in the early post-WW II years, once said of the "communist threat": "The Communists are rendering a great service...[b]ecause we have a 'Communist danger.'...We must keep up this indispensable Communist scare"(193, p. 234). Colonel James A. Donovan, after retiring from the U.S. Marine Corps, further stated back in 1970: "If there were no Communist bloc..., the defense establishment would have to invent one"(194).

Let's look at some of the major U.S. military and/or CIA interventions in foreign sovereign nations since WW II (both during and after the Cold War), involving either aerial bombings, ground wars, CIA-led coups, rigging of elections, assassinations, breaking up of labor unions, etc., to see just how intrusive the globalist-controlled U.S. government has been in the affairs of nations that were essentially minding their own business:

China 1945-1951
Marshall Islands 1946-1958
Philippines 1945-1953, 1970s-1990s
Albania 1949-1953, 1991-1992
Eastern Europe 1948-1956
Korea 1945-1953
Vietnam 1960-1975
Guatemala 1953, 1980s
Laos 1964-1973
Indonesia 1965, 1975
Cambodia 1969-1975
El Salvador 1980-1994
Nicaragua 1978-1990
Iran 1953
Costa Rica 1950s, 1970-1971
Middle East 1956-1958
Haiti 1959, 1987-1994, 2004
British Guiana/Guyana 1953-1964
Iraq 1958-1963, 1972-1975, 1991-2003, 2003-?
Soviet Union 1940s-1960s
Thailand 1965-1973
Ecuador 1960-1963
Congo/Zaire 1960-1965, 1977-1978
Algeria 1960s
Brazil 1961-1964
Peru 1965, 1990s
Dominican Republic 1963-1965
Cuba 1959-?
Ghana 1966
Uruguay 1969-1972
Chile 1964-1973
South Africa 1960s-1980s

Bolivia 1964-1975
Portugal 1974-1976
East Timor 1975-1999
Angola 1975-1980s
Jamaica 1976
Honduras 1980s
Seychelles 1979-1981
South Yemen 1979-1984
South Korea 1980
Chad 1981-1982
Grenada 1979-1983
Suriname 1982-1984
Libya 1981-1989
Fiji 1987
Panama 1989
Afghanistan 1979-1992, 2001-?
Bulgaria 1990-1991
Somalia 1993
Mexico 1990s
Colombia 1990s-?
Yugoslavia 1995-1999

Carefully researching each one of these military/CIA campaigns, from the Cold War period, will reveal that almost none of the targeted countries had anything to do with the Soviet Union, or vice versa. Yet, once again, the excuse given for almost every one of these interventions was Soviet containment. The truth is, we were lied into every one of them.

U.S. intervention in Nicaragua serves as a good illustration of just how devastating this nation's Cold War foreign policy was. In 1979, the Sandinistas (FLSN) ousted the U.S.-backed dictatorship of Anastasio Somoza. The globalist-controlled U.S. government liked Somoza because he kept the people in line, often with brutal force, making it easier for them to be exploited. Thus the Sandinistas were resented by Washington. They were also disliked because they sought political reform on behalf of the oppressed poor of Nicaragua. Consequently, the U.S. government, through the CIA, created and backed the Contras, the opposition movement to the Sandinistas. For the next eleven years, this country was torn apart, and its poverty-stricken population was driven into even worse impoverishment as the two major factions battled it out. The Sandinistas, of course, were labeled as "communists" in order to justify U.S. support for the Contras.

Highlighting the type of horrors that the people of Nicaragua faced during this period of needless turmoil at the hand of the Contras, David Womble wrote in *The CIA in Nicaragua*: "Witness For Peace, an American Protestant watchdog body, collected a list of Contra atrocities in one year, which include murder, the rape of two girls in their homes, torture of men, maiming of children, cutting off arms, cutting out tongues, gouging out eyes, castration, bayoneting pregnant women in the stomach, amputating the genitals of people of both sexes, scraping the skin off the face, pouring acid on the face, breaking the toes and fingers of an 18 year old boy, and summary executions. These were the people Ronald Reagan called the 'freedom fighters' and the 'moral equivalent of our founding fathers'"(515).

The U.S.-induced chaos that broke out in Nicaragua, beginning immediately after the ousting of Somoza, was so bad that even Somoza himself came to the conclusion that the U.S. government had very sinister motives behind its involvement in his country. After much diligent research, he concluded that the United States was being controlled by powerful, corrupt forces which were destroying it from within, and using it to destroy other nations. In 1980, he authored a book called *Nicaragua Betrayed*, in which he stated: "No longer can we afford the luxury of silence....[T]he people of the United States and the free world must know what is happening, events that sooner or later will affect them. With my many years in government, with my military training and background, with my close association with governmental leaders throughout the world, and with intelligence information, I come to one startling conclusion: there is a planned and deliberate conspiracy in the United States of America to destroy that republican form of government....[T]he capitalistic free enterprise system that made the United States the productive wonder of the world is undergoing radical surgery"(197, p. 291, 66)[Endnote 105]. (Note: Somoza was murdered a few weeks after his book was published.)

In the January 9, 1985 edition of London's *Guardian*, former CIA analyst David MacMichael told the real story of why the U.S. had become so involved with Nicaragua. The *Guardian* quoted him as saying: "We have control and we don't want to lose it. The ideology of anti-communism ...provides the rationalization..."

The main reason that Washington reeked so much havoc in Nicaragua and its economy, throughout the decade of the 1980s, was to bring its people to their knees so that they would vote out the Sandinistas. As Edward Herman, author of *Beyond Hypocrisy: Decoding the News in an Age of Propaganda*, put it: "[U.S. policies] devastated the Nicaraguan economy [and] were certainly the primary contributor to a fall in the per capita income of over 50 percent between 1980 and 1990. It seems obvious, therefore, that the United States had purposefully tilted the playing field in a direction unfavorable to the ruling party"(516). Mark Weisbrot, author of *What Everyone Should Know About Nicaragua*, further wrote: "By 1990 the Nicaraguans had suffered more than they could take from the war and economic embargo, so when President George Bush [Sr.] made it clear that their misery would continue until the Sandinistas were voted out of office, a majority cried uncle"(515).

The U.S. campaign in Nicaragua provides us with a good glimpse at how the CIA typically operates. To aid the Contras in their fight against the Sandinistas, the CIA distributed a manual entitled *Psychological Operations in Guerrilla Warfare*, which gave instructions on how to effectively carry out political assassination, blackmail, kidnaping, mob violence, and the blowing up of public buildings. It later stated that "if...it should be necessary...to fire on a citizen who was trying to leave the town," guerrillas should explain that "he was an enemy of the people"(199).

The CIA also produced a comic book for the Contras to distribute to the citizens of Nicaragua, called *Freedom Fighters Manual*--a 16-page booklet which informed the reader on how to "liberate Nicaragua from oppression and misery" by "a series of useful sabotage techniques." Some examples of the techniques listed were: "stop up toilets with sponges...pull down power cables...put dirt into gas tanks...put nails on roads and highways...cut down trees over highways...[use the] telephone to make false hotel reservations and false alarms of fires and crimes...hoard and steal food from the government...leave lights and water taps on...steal mail from mail boxes...go to work late...call in sick...short circuit electricity...break light bulbs...spread rumors...threaten supervisors and officials over the phone"(200).

Edgar Chamorro, a former colonel with the Contras, later gave the following testimony before the World Court about the CIA's operation in Nicaragua: "We were told that the only way to defeat the Sandinistas was to use the tactics the agency [the CIA] attributed to Communist insurgencies elsewhere: kill, kidnap, rob, and torture....Many civilians were killed in cold blood. Many others were tortured, mutilated, raped, robbed, or otherwise abused. When I agreed to join...I had hoped that it would be an organization of Nicaraguans....[It] turned out to be an instrument of the U.S. government"(314, p. 585).

No wonder Harry Truman said, in 1963: "Those fellows in the CIA don't just report on wars and the like, they go out and make their own, and there's nobody to keep track of what they're up to....It's become a government all of its own and all secret. They don't have to account to anybody. That's a very dangerous thing in a democratic society, and it's got to be put a stop to"(293, p. 392)[Endnote 106].

Such murderous and sabotaging behavior was not, and still is not, the exception in U.S. foreign interventions, but is instead, unfortunately, the rule. Most Americans have a fairy tale view of our government being the world's champion of human rights, freedom, and justice. But this rhetoric does not match up with the facts. Another typical case scenario of outrageous abuse of power and total disregard for human rights during U.S. foreign interventions was the CIA's Operation Phoenix, which resulted in the murder of tens of thousands of innocent Vietnamese civilians that were "suspected" of being communist sympathizers. As part of this Operation, many U.S. soldiers were sent on "search and destroy" missions, being ordered to "shoot anything that moves." Of particular noteworthiness was the famous My Lai massacre, during which hundreds of unarmed villagers, including women, children, and the elderly, were shot in cold blood, and at least one woman in this village was raped before being killed. Others were ordered into a ditch where rapid-firing machine guns were unleashed upon them. Still others were sadistically tortured by applying electric shocks to the genitals of both male and female victims [Endnote 107]. Such behavior, it goes without saying, is horrifyingly reminiscent of Hitler's Nazi Germany.

Regarding the Cold War crimes of the U.S., in general, here's what MIT professor Noam Chomsky had to say: "Parliamentary governments were barred or overthrown, with US support and sometimes direct intervention, in Iran in 1953, in Guatemala in 1954...and [again] in 1963..., in the Dominican Republic in 1963 and 1965, in Brazil in 1964, in Chile in 1973....Our policies have been very much the same in El Salvador and in many other places across the globe. The methods [were] not very pretty. What the US-run Contra forces did in Nicaragua, or...our terrorist proxies...in El Salvador or Guatemala, [wasn't]...ordinary killing. A major element [was] brutal, sadistic torture--beating infants against rocks, hanging women by their feet with their breasts cut off and the skin of their face[s] peeled back so that they...[bled] to death, chopping people's heads off and putting them on stakes. The point [was] to crush independent nationalism and popular forces that might bring about meaningful democracy....[T]here's a very solid case for impeaching every American president since the Second World War. They've all been either outright war criminals or involved in serious war crimes"(198, pp. 21, 22, 32).

Former Attorney General Ramsey Clark summed this whole mess up rather succinctly: "The greatest crime since World War II has been U.S. foreign policy"(114).

To help you better understand the complete psychopathic mentality that has underpinned U.S. military interventions abroad since WW II, here are several upsetting quotes to ponder:

- "It is now clear that we are facing an implacable enemy [meaning the Soviet

Union] whose avowed objective is world domination by whatever means and whatever cost [hopefully you can see this for what it is--pure propaganda!]. There are no rules in such a game. Hitherto acceptable norms of human conduct do not apply. If the United States is to survive, long-standing American concepts of 'fair play' must be reconsidered. We must develop effective espionage and counterespionage services and must learn to subvert, sabotage and destroy our enemies [i.e. those who refuse to be exploited] by more clever, more sophisticated, and more effective methods than those used against us. It may become necessary that the American people be made acquainted with, understand and support this fundamentally repugnant philosophy." - From a 1954 White House commission report (the Doolittle Report) on CIA covert activities(156, p. 42).

- "The fact that some elements [of the U.S. government] may appear to be potentially 'out of control' can be beneficial to creating and reinforcing fears and doubts within the minds of an adversary's decision makers....That the U.S. may become irrational and vindictive if its vital interests are attacked should be a part of the national persona we project to all adversaries....It hurts to portray ourselves as too rational and cool-headed." - U.S. Strategic Command (STRATCOM), "Essentials of Post-Cold War Deterrence," 1995(114, p. 162).

- "[T]o put it in a terminology that harkens back to the more brutal age of ancient empires, the three grand imperatives of imperial geostrategy are to prevent collusion and maintain security dependence among the vassals, to keep tributaries pliant and protected, and to keep the barbarians from coming together." - Zbigniew Brzezinski(204, p. 40).

- "Kissinger counseled his aides that deviousness was part of their job....He told one of them, 'This is not an honorable business conducted by honorable men in an honorable way. Don't assume I'm that way and you shouldn't be.'...
    "In [Gen. Alexander] Haig's presence, Kissinger referred pointedly to military men as 'dumb, stupid animals to be used' as pawns for foreign policy." - *The Final Days: The Classic Behind-the-Scenes Account of Richard Nixon's Dramatic Last Days in the White House*(208, pp. 194, 195).

    For further insight into the mind-set of people like Kissinger, here's another helpful quote: "In *Without Conscience*, renowned criminologist Dr. Robert Hare identified the key emotional traits of psychopaths. Included in what he called 'The Psychopathy Checklist' were the inability to feel remorse, a grossly inflated view of oneself, a pronounced indifference to the suffering of others, and a pattern of deceitful behavior"(209, p. 6).

Are you beginning to understand that the scoundrels who run our government, at the highest levels of power, truly are absolute psychopaths?

And then there's the problem of the damage done by our military and intelligence establishments to our economy. The U.S. government spends more on its military and intelligence than all other government programs combined. Not only that, but the United States' military and intelligence budget is larger than the next 60 largest military and intelligence budgets in the world combined. This should help you to understand where our scandalously outrageous national debt primarily came from, as well as the record-high deficits we have been facing.

As if swallowing the biggest piece of the national budget pie isn't enough, the Pentagon admitted in 2001 that it couldn't even account for where a great portion of the money given to it actually went. In fact, it stated that it "lost" over a trillion dollars. In May 2001, the deputy inspector general at the Pentagon confessed that "$4.4 trillion in adjustments to the Pentagon's books had to be cooked to compile...required financial statements and that $1.1 trillion...was simply gone and no one can be sure of when, where or to whom the money went"(302). By January 2002, the amount of money missing from the Pentagon had jumped up to $2.3 trillion(456).

With all of the foregoing in mind, the proceeding remarks made by President Eisenhower during his farewell address on January 17, 1961, should send shivers down your spine: "[W]e have been compelled to create a permanent armaments industry of vast proportions....We annually spend on military security more than the net income of all United States corporations. This conjunction of an immense military establishment and a large arms industry is new in the American experience. The total influence--economic, political, even spiritual--is felt in every city, every Statehouse, every office of the Federal government....[W]e must not fail to comprehend its grave implications. Our toil, resources and livelihood are all involved; so is the very structure of our society. In the councils of government, we must guard against the acquisition of unwarranted influence, whether sought or unsought, by the military-industrial complex. The potential for the disastrous rise of misplaced power exists and will persist. We must never let the weight of this combination endanger our liberties or democratic processes. We should take nothing for granted. Only an alert and knowledgeable citizenry can compel the proper meshing of the huge industrial and military machinery of defense with our peaceful methods and goals, so that security and liberty may prosper together." What a solemn warning. Yet it has obviously gone unheeded.

Perhaps unheeded isn't strong enough of a word--Eisenhower's warning has been outright shunned, especially in regards to the havoc that the "military-industrial complex" has reeked on our economy. To demonstrate this point even further, let's take a look at a few resumés of prominent government officials and Pentagon-contracting corporate chieftains over the years:

- Robert McNamara was president of the Ford Motor Company before becoming Secretary of Defense under Kennedy and Johnson.
- George Schultz was Secretary of the Treasury and chairman of the Council on Economic Policy under Nixon. He later became the president of Bechtel, and then served as Secretary of State under Reagan.
- Casper Weinberger was vice president of Bechtel, and later became Reagan's Secretary of Defense.
- Dick Cheney, who was Secretary of Defense under Bush Sr., later became chairman and CEO of Halliburton, and then vice president under Bush Jr.
- George Bush Sr., the founder of Zapata Petroleum Corp., later became ambassador to the U.N., CIA director, vice president under Regan, president, and then became an important advisor to the Carlyle Group, an international equity firm that owns United Defense. This company has also employed Frank Carlucci as its chairman and managing director. Carlucci had previously served as CIA deputy director and Secretary of Defense under Reagan, replacing Weinberger. Bush Jr. and James Baker (Bush Sr.'s Secretary of State) have also worked for Carlyle.

While this list doesn't even scratch the surface, it should be enough to demonstrate the enormity of the problem we are faced with.

Now back to our discussion of the Cold War.

In spite of the obvious scandalous nature of this "war," many have attempted to "prove" the legitimacy of the "Soviet threat" by pointing to the Cuban Missile Crisis. But the Cuban Missile Crisis itself was a scandal. The globalist-controlled U.S. government was simply trying to stir up more fear of the Soviets, in order to gain public support for involvement in Vietnam, by blowing out of proportion Soviet activities in Cuba. For years, the U.S., at that time, had been maintaining military bases and nuclear missile silos near the Soviet border. Thus, in attempting to set up a nuclear missile base in Cuba, near the U.S., the Soviets were merely trying to "even the score." Khrushchev himself made this very point, stating: "Since the Americans have already surrounded the Soviet Union with a ring of...military bases and...missile launchers, we must pay them back in their own coin...so they will know what it feels like to live in the sights of nuclear weapons"(189, p. 221).

Rest assured that the Soviets were not trying to "provoke" the U.S. during the Cuban Missile Crisis (or at any other time, for that matter). As London's

Guardian reported on January 1, 1999: "The Soviet Union had no intention of launching a military attack on the West..., in stark contrast to what Western politicians and military leaders were saying in public about the 'Soviet threat.'"

The Soviets were well aware that their nuclear capabilities nowhere near matched ours (at least not until the 1980s, by which time, primarily through their immense military budget, their economy was in ruins, leading ultimately to the Soviet Union's collapse in December 1991). So the Soviets were quite obviously not interested in provoking the U.S. The real instigator in the Cuban Missile Crisis (and throughout the whole Cold War) was the arrogant, globalist-controlled U.S. government, which had the audacity to demand that the Soviets turn back from simply trying to give the U.S. a taste of its own medicine [Endnote 108].

The truth is that, from the end of World War II until the collapse of the Soviet Union, the U.S., for the most part (particularly through its military-intelligence apparatus), did all it could to perpetuate bad relations with the Soviets, even while appearing to work toward healthy relations with them. For example, on May 1, 1960, a U.S. U-2 spy plane was shot down by the Soviets for trespassing 1,200 miles into their airspace. The timing of this event was most interesting, being just two weeks before peace talks in Paris began between the U.S., the Soviets, France, and England--peace talks that utterly failed because of the U-2 incident. Thus the order to send in this spy plane at that particular time can only be explained as either a very stupid move, or else it was a mission of sabotage to perpetuate the politically and financially profitable "Cold War." Which do you suppose it was?

But coming back to the Cuban Missile Crisis for a moment, there is one final important point worth noting: Though Kennedy obviously began his presidency as a staunch Cold Warrior, and thus taking a firm stand against the Soviets during the Cuban Missile Crisis, he later changed his position on this matter, probably realizing how scandalously exaggerated the whole "Soviet threat" actually was. So much had he changed his position, in fact, that he later sought peaceful relations with the Soviets, and even with Cuba, which caused many of his enemies to call him a "communist" [Endnote 109].

* * * * * * *

"War is the parent of armies; from these proceed debts and taxes; and armies, and debts, and taxes are the known instruments for bringing the many under the domination of the few." - James Madison, April 20, 1795.

"Wars are not fought to defeat an enemy; wars are fought to create a condition." - Edwin Stanton (Abraham Lincoln's secretary of war), *Mr. Secretary.*

"In Europe, the view that America is part of what has gone wrong in our world, rather than a force to help make it right, has become all too common. In America, there are voices that deride and deny the importance of Europe's role in our security and our future. Both views miss the truth--that Europeans today are bearing new burdens and taking more responsibility in critical parts of the world; and that just as American bases built in the last century still help to defend the security of this continent, so does our country still sacrifice greatly for freedom around the globe.

Yes, there have been differences between America and Europe. No doubt, there will be differences in the future. But the burdens of global citizenship continue to bind us together. A change of leadership in Washington will not lift this burden. In this new century, Americans and Europeans alike will be required to do more-- not less. Partnership and cooperation among nations is not a choice; it is the one way, the only way, to protect our common security and advance our common humanity." - Senator Barack Obama, during a speech he delivered in Berlin, Germany, on July 24, 2008.

Appendix 2

Creating poverty

The days of single income families for average wage earners are gone in this country. In order for the average family to get by today, both father and mother must work full-time jobs (often including overtime as well). At the same time, most average families no longer have any emergency savings that they can fall back on. In fact, far from having any surplus cash, a great many average families are loaded down with heavy credit card debts. And all the while, as each year goes by, the gap between their wages and their living costs continues to widen.

Between 1970 and 2000, for example, the average take-home pay increased about 300%, whereas the cost of the average home rose over 1,500%. Do you suppose this was accidental? It certainly was not! To prove this point, we need look no further than globalist Zbigniew Brzezinski, who, in his book *Between Two Ages*, wrote: "In the economic-technological field some international cooperation has already been achieved, but further progress will require greater American sacrifices. More intensive efforts to shape a new world monetary structure will have to be undertaken with some consequent risk to the present relatively favorable American position"(49, p. 300).

A similar statement was made by John Foster Dulles, a CFR member who became Secretary of State under Dwight D. Eisenhower: "Some dilution or leveling off of the sovereignty system as it prevails in the world today must take place...to the immediate disadvantage of those nations which now possess the preponderance of power....The United States must be prepared to make sacrifices...in setting up a world politico-economic order which would level off inequalities of economic opportunity with respect to nations"(201).

The decades-old plan has been to gradually reduce the U.S. economy, along with the economies of all other First World nations around the globe, to Third World status. In 1972, the Club of Rome (a globalist front group) basically admitted this very thing in a study it produced called *The Limits to Growth*. This study declared that "Entirely new approaches are required to redirect society toward goals of equilibrium rather than growth." This report further pointed out that, in order to "save the earth," "joint long-term planning will be necessary on a scale and scope without precedent." Finally, this study talked about the need for a "supreme effort" by everyone to "organize [a] more equitable distribution of wealth and income worldwide"(337, p. 196). In other words, desperate poverty for the masses, and enormous wealth for the elites.

In 1975, the CFR drafted up a similar study--a series of economic policy blueprints for the coming decade of the 1980s. These blueprints stated: "A degree of 'controlled dis-integration' in the world economy is a legitimate objective for the 1980s"(487, p. 55).

Would you not agree that the diminishing of our economy, as well as other First World economies, is all happening according to plan?

Speaking of reducing all First World nations to Third World status, let's talk for a moment about the nations that are already at that level. How do you suppose they got into the mess that they are in? Is their plight their own doing? Is it their own fault that their situation perpetuates? If you stop and think about it, you'll realize that most of these countries should actually be quite wealthy.

Many African countries, for instance, have the finest diamond and gold mines in the world. They could and should be among the richest of countries. Yet they rank, instead, among the most impoverished on the planet. But obviously SOMEONE is benefiting from the untold riches that are made from the mining of gold and diamonds in these countries.

Another good example is Brazil, which has some of the world's largest vital mineral deposits. Yet this is also a very poor country.

And how about Haiti, which possesses the most fertile soil on earth, but is again one of the poorest of countries?

Do you think this is all accidental? Are we to believe that these countries are incapable of helping themselves? Or can it be that they are being PREVENTED from helping themselves, because their mines and rich croplands are owned by globalist institutions? Can it be that these institutions fear that these countries would pose a serious threat to their globalist agenda if they were ever to regain control of their own resources? Indeed, if this ever happened, these countries would gain economic independence, and with that would come political independence as well. Thus global government would never be possible. Not to mention the fact that the globalists want the resources of these nations for their own greedy selves, to fatten their own wallets. Are you getting the picture?

The same holds true, of course, for the problem of world hunger. Why do you suppose that we have so many people starving in the world today? Is starvation unavoidable? Accidental? Author Susan George, in her book *How the Other Half Dies*, tells us that "Hunger is not an unavoidable phenomenon....Today's world has all the physical resources and technical skills necessary to feed the present population of the planet or a much larger one....Hunger is not a scourge but a scandal"(202, p. 3).

Though this book was written back in 1977, its message holds as true today as it did back then--that starving countries would be able to grow and/or buy their own foodstuffs if they were allowed to utilize their own natural resources for themselves. But, of course, the globalists would never allow this. If anything, their aim has been to drive poor and starving countries further in the hole, in order to maintain their global financial and political monopoly.

The globalists also use food as a mechanism of coercion, cutting off supplies to countries that refuse to comply with their demands (like the U.N.-imposed, U.S.-enforced sanctions on Iraq from 1991 to 2003, which caused the deaths of 1.5 million Iraqis)[Endnote 110]. Commenting on this tactic of food deprivation, Catherine Bertini, former U.S. Assistant Secretary of Agriculture and former Executive Director of the United Nations World Food Program, made these cold remarks: "Food is Power! We use it to control behavior. Some may call it bribery. We do not apologize"(348).

So, if you want to better understand where the globalists intend to take us all, study starving Third World countries.

But simply controlling the natural resources of Third World countries is sometimes not enough to keep them poor and compliant. Often it has happened that such countries have tried to rise up and take back what belongs to them, and to regain their independence. Whenever this has occurred, the globalists found it necessary to employ U.S. military and/or CIA covert operations to whip the dissidents back into submission. This is not to imply that all military or CIA operations had purely economic motives behind them. In fact, most were dual in nature--having both political and economic objectives. But nearly every such intervention had some sort of economically exploitatious agenda behind it. And, conveniently, this economic motive has always been easily hidden behind false cloaks like "containing communism," "spreading freedom and democracy," or "fighting terrorism."

Many of these globalist-launched U.S. operations, especially those that were purely economically-motivated, were indirect interventions. That is to say, they were coordinated by the CIA and other U.S. government agencies, which utilized rebel groups in target countries to do their dirty work for them, providing these groups with training, weapons, and financial assistance. Here's what political analyst Michael Parenti had to say about this: "With the financial and technical assistance of the U.S. Central Intelligence Agency...and other such units, military and security police throughout various client states are schooled in the fine arts of surveillance, interrogation, torture, intimidation, and assassination. The U.S. Army School of the Americas (SOA) at Fort Benning, Georgia, known throughout Latin America as the 'School of the Assassins,' trains military officers from U.S. client states in the latest methods of repression....

"In countries that have had...revolutionary governments, which redistributed economic resources to the many rather than the few, such as Nicaragua, Mozambique, Angola, and Afghanistan, the U.S. national security state has supported antigovernment mercenary forces in wars of attrition that destroy schools, farm cooperatives, health clinics, and whole villages....

"These wars of attrition extract a horrific toll on human life and eventually force the revolutionary government to discard its programs....

"Why has a professedly peace-loving, democratic nation found it necessary to use so much violence and repression against so many peoples in so many places? An important goal of U.S. policy is to make the world safe for *Fortune 500* and its global system of capital accumulation. Governments that strive for any kind of economic independence or any sort of populist redistributive politics, that attempt to take some of their economic surplus and apply it to not-for-profit services that benefit the people--such governments are the ones most likely to feel the wrath of U.S. intervention or invasion....No country that pursues an independent course of development shall be allowed to prevail as a dangerous example to other nations"(203, pp. 24, 25, 39, 43).

Have Third World nations ever asked for, desired, or even needed U.S. intervention in their affairs? General David Sharp, former U.S. Marine Commandant, provided a good answer to this question, back in 1966: "I believe that if we had and would keep our dirty, bloody, dollar soaked fingers out of the business of these [Third World] nations so full of depressed, exploited people, they will arrive at a solution of their own....And if unfortunately their revolution must be of the violent type because the 'haves' refuse to share with the 'have-nots' by any peaceful method, at least what they get will be their own, and not the American style, which they didn't want and above all don't want crammed down their throats by Americans"(114, p. 175).

But despite what Third World nations might want or need, the globalist-controlled U.S. government has always pushed its own agenda in these countries. The quotes that follow should suffice to provide a crystal clear glimpse into the twisted, economically-motivated thinking behind Washington's (Wall Street's) shameless, ravenous, and parasitic policies toward Third World countries over the years:

- "[T]o maintain this position of disparity [in poor countries]...we will have to dispense with all sentimentality and day-dreaming....We should cease to talk about vague and...unreal objectives such as human rights [and] the raising of the living standard [actually, they never did stop *talking* about these things--what they did do was stop *upholding* them]....The day is not far off when we are going to have to deal in straight power concepts. The less we are then hampered by idealistic slogans, the better." - U.S. State Department Policy Planning Study #23, 1948(114, p. 169).

- "The hidden hand of the market will never work without a hidden fist--

McDonald's cannot flourish without McDonnell Douglas, the designer of the F-15." - *New York Times Magazine*(205).

- "Our first objective is to prevent the...emergence of a new rival...we must maintain the mechanisms for deterring potential competition from even *aspiring* to a larger regional or global role" [Endnote 111]. - From a 1992 Defense Department planning paper(206).

A good case study of corrupt economic motives behind U.S. foreign interventions, where a poor country was prevented from trying to get ahead while bringing the poorest of its population along with it, is the U.S.-backed 1973 overthrow of the president of Chile, Salvador Allende, which was masterminded by Henry Kissinger. On this matter, Michael Parenti wrote: "It was not Allende who wrecked the Chilean economy....If anything, in two short years, his Popular Unity Government brought about a noticeable shift...away from the wealthy elites who lived off interest, dividends, and rents, and toward those who lived off wages and salaries.

"In Allende's Chile there was a small but real modification of class power....What alarmed leaders like Kissinger was not that Allende's social democratic reforms were failing but that they were succeeding. The trend toward politico-economic equality had to be stopped. So Kissinger, the CIA, the White House, and the U.S. media went after the Popular Unity Government tooth and nail. In the name of saving Chile's democracy, they destroyed it, instituting a fascist dictatorship under General Augusto Pinochet, one that tortured and executed thousands, disappeared thousands more, and suppressed all opposition media, political parties, labor unions, and peasant organizations.

"Immediately after the military coup, General Motors, which had closed its plants when Allende was elected, resumed operations, demonstrating how [monopolistic] capitalism is much more comfortable with fascism than with social democracy. Far from rescuing the economy, the CIA-sponsored coup ushered in an era of skyrocketing inflation and national debt, with drastic increases in unemployment, poverty, and hunger"(203, pp. 76, 77).

Once again, this same disgusting type of scenario has repeated itself over and over, as the U.S. stuck its nose in the affairs of nations around the world.

It is most appropriate at this time to review Arnold Toynbee's 1961 summation of American foreign policy, which is just as timely now as it was then: "America is today the leader of a world-wide anti-revolutionary movement in the defense of vested interests. She now stands for what Rome stood for. Rome consistently supported the rich against the poor in all foreign communities that fell under her sway; and, since the poor, so far, have always and everywhere been far more numerous than the rich, Rome's policy made for inequality, for injustice and for the least happiness of the greatest number"(292, pp. 92, 93).

Martin Luther King Jr. was very outspoken about the economic exploits of the U.S. military machine (which may have been the real reason for his assassination). During a speech he gave back in 1967, he said: "We have no honorable intentions in Vietnam. Our minimal expectation is to occupy it as an American colony and maintain social stability for our investments. This tells why American helicopters are being used against guerillas in Colombia and Peru. Increasingly the role our nation has taken is the role of those who refuse to give up the privileges and pleasures that come from the immense profits of overseas investment"(326).

Although the practice by the globalists of utilizing the U.S. military (and the CIA) to advance their economic interests certainly escalated after WW II, with the outbreak of the Cold War, this game, of course, began long before that time (minus the CIA, which wasn't created until after WW II, and the OSS [Office of Strategic Services], the CIA's predecessor, which was created during WW II). Referring to pre-WW II U.S. military interventions, former Marine Lieutenant General Smedley Butler, winner of two congressional Medals of Honor, wrote back in 1933: "I spent thirty-three years and four months in active military service....And during that period I spent most of my time as a high-class muscle-man for big business, for Wall Street, and the bankers....Thus, I helped make Mexico and especially Tampico safe for American oil interests in 1914. I helped make Haiti and Cuba a decent place for the National City Bank boys to collect revenues in. I helped in the raping of half a dozen Central American republics for the benefit of Wall Street....In China I helped to see to it that Standard Oil went its way unmolested"(304, p. 2).

Are you getting the picture that U.S. military operations have almost never had anything to do with "keeping us safe" or "spreading democracy"?

And what about the future? Is there any sign that this pattern will change? Of course not! To the contrary, the globalists intend to escalate this pattern, to help rush in their New World Order. In addition to utilizing military and covert CIA operations for dominating other countries' economies, there are other types of warfare that are being developed and employed. One example is the sinister application of advanced weather modification technology. Elsewhere in this study we cited a quote from Zbigniew Brzezinski's book *Between Two Ages*, where he talked about this very thing. We will here repeat an applicable portion of it: "As one specialist [Gordon J.F. McDonald] noted, 'By the year 2018, technology will make available to the leaders of the major nations a variety of techniques for conducting secret warfare....Techniques of weather modification could be employed to produce prolonged periods of drought or storm, thereby weakening a nation's capacity and forcing it to accept the demands of the competitor'"(48). (Note: The subject of hi-tech weather control is elaborated upon in Appendix 9.)

The globalists also plan to utilize U.S. dominance of space technology to maintain their monopoly over the world's economic scene. The U.S. Space Command's policy statement, "Vision for 2020," states that "the globalization of the world economy will continue, with a widening gulf between 'haves' and 'have-nots,'" and that the Pentagon's mission is thus to "dominate the space dimension of military operations to protect U.S. interests and investments." One key policy mentioned was "denying other countries access to space"(303).

With friends like the globalist-controlled U.S. government, who needs enemies? Far from the U.S. being a "beacon of light" and a dispenser of "democracy" around the world, the real consequences of its interventions have brought nothing but darkness, despair, and despotism--the globalists wouldn't have it any other way.

Appendix 3

Globalization--impoverishment in high gear

The push for a global economy, or "globalization," as it is commonly called, is nothing more than globalist corporations recklessly and ruthlessly looting and exploiting the entire planet for their own personal profit and lust for power. The *Chicago Tribune* gave this informative synopsis of globalization: "Global production is not...[employing] the growing number of people who want jobs. Even those with jobs find that the pressures of globalization are pushing wages down....This flow [of money], coupled with the ease with which companies move jobs around the globe, has shattered the ability of national governments to control their own economies....The trends can only accelerate...[resulting in] outrage..., where traditional ways of life are under assault by international forces. This understandable reaction, by people who have lost control of their lives to vast impersonal forces, is not more than a futile gesture in a world where no country can afford the luxury of dropping out"(210).

An even more informative and bold overview of globalization appeared in the November/December 1996 issue of *Society*, in an article by Ian Angell of the London School of Economics and Political Science (established by the Fabian [socialist] Society of England). The title of the article was "Winners and Losers in the Information Age," which stated: "Individuals and companies are setting up large transnational networks that pay absolutely no heed to national boundaries and barriers [Endnote 112]....Those who wrap themselves in the flag can soon expect to be buried in it....We can expect massive civil unrest and disorder....Governments, like all other organizations, will have to survive economically on the efforts of an elite few....Governments will have no other choice other than to acquiesce to the will of global enterprise....That citizens elect their slave masters makes democracy slavery none the less....The masses will not win in the natural selection for dominance of an increasingly elitist world"(112, pp. 176, 177).

The WTO (formerly called GATT)[Endnote 113] and NAFTA are two of the more commonly-known pieces of the globalization puzzle. Let us first look at the WTO and its effects on the U.S. economy, particularly in respect to its push for heightened U.S.-China trade relations.

Speaking on this matter, Senator Paul Wellstone had warned that "the trade deal with China...[is more] about making it easier for U.S. firms to relocate jobs to China, than about exports. U.S. manufacturers who relocate production to China, or outsource to contractors in China, will unquestionably save on labor costs. But what will this mean for their competitors in the United States? If we encourage companies to relocate their production to low-wage China without any minimum standards for labor, the environment, or human rights, we are making domestic firms with higher standards less competitive. Many of them will have to either lower their own standards or get out of the business"(18, pp. 288, 289).

U.S.-China trade deals have been particularly disastrous for job security in the U.S. Between 1992 and 1999, for example, over 870,000 U.S. jobs were lost to Chinese trade relations, according to the Economic Policy Institute. These same trade relations have not done anything for the people of China, either. The National Labor Committee has revealed that Chinese workers in U.S. companies that have relocated to China work "under conditions of indentured servitude, forced to work 12 to 14 hours a day, seven days a week, with only one day off a month, while earning an average of 3 cents an hour"(18, p. 289).

And now for the big question: Why is it that George Bush Sr., Clinton, and Bush Jr. would all be big supporters of China having the most favored nation trading status with the U.S., especially in light of the fact that this country has had a very poor record of human rights violations? Of course, when one considers the U.S. government's own record of human rights violations, this doesn't seem so surprising. Nevertheless, could the reason for Clinton and both Bushes being so supportive of trade with China be the fact that they were (and still are) globalists who have sold us out to their buddies in the GATT/WTO economic death trap? In this vein of thought, during his May 25, 2000 radio program, Rush Limbaugh asked: "How come [George W.] Bush and Clinton are on the same side of the China issue? New World Order?"

Yes, Rush, that's exactly why! George Bush Sr. made this very admission during a press conference back on February 6, 1991, when he stated: "We've left China out of the equation, and we ought not to do that....I took on some shots for trying to keep relations with China....[However, it] is vital to this New World Order"(140, pp. 286, 287).

But make no mistake about it--the global financial elite are after much more than mere killer profits. What they ultimately seek, of course, is absolute power on a global scale. To back up this claim, let me draw your attention to a few key quotes:

- From a book written back in 1974, called *Global Reach*, we read: "The men who run the global corporations are the first in history with the organization, technology, money, and ideology to make a credible try at managing the world as an integrated economic unit....What they are demanding in essence is the right to transcend the nation-state, and in the process, transform it"(211, pp. 13, 15, 16).

- Speaking about the Trilateral Commission in his book *With No Apologies,*

Senator Barry Goldwater penned these words: "What the Trilaterals truly intend is the creation of a worldwide economic power superior to the political government of the nation-states involved. As managers and creators of the system they will rule the world"(46, p. 299).

- Sir James Goldsmith, a member of the European Parliament, stated back in 1994: "What we are witnessing is the divorce of the interests of the major corporations and the interests of society as a whole....We have a system being proposed which will result in massive unemployment, massive hemorrhaging of jobs and capital, but which will increase Corporate profits....There is absolutely no doubt whatsoever that the World Trade Organization is a major diminution of sovereignty....GATT, global free trade, is...Marxism"(212).

- Charles Derber, in his book *Corporation Nation*, declared: "The largest global corporations are swallowing up an ever larger share of the world economy, while also building a new global architecture of governing institutions such as the WTO....The same web of vast global corporations that are helping shape America's destiny are working simultaneously to shape the new global order and govern it in their own interests"(213, p. 213).

- *USA Today*, back in late 1999, reported: "The WTO is but one of a rising number of international organizations that are stripping away our sovereignty. But should we fight them or embrace them as the forerunners of the New World Order?...[W]e had best recognize that there is no way to stop globalism"(214).

- On CNN's Lou Dobbs Show, on January 8, 2007, the following fascinating exchange took place between Dobbs and reporter Bill Tucker:

Dobbs: "Tonight, [we report on] a proposal for an expanded so-called free trade zone from Alaska to the tip of South America. It's a plan from the business elites, the political elites, that will cost more American jobs, cost more American sovereignty, but it would fulfill the president's father's vision [referring to George Bush Sr.'s talk of a New World Order]. Bill Tucker reports."

Tucker: "It's not a new idea. President Bush talked about it back in 1991....Now former United States trade investor Robert Zoellick is talking about it again with renewed vigor. This time, a new world order with business at the helm of trade and economic policy. Advocating what he calls the Association of American Free Trade Agreements, [he speaks of] a separate nongovernment entity which would include North, Central, and South America....

"It's an agenda that goes hand in hand with the United States, Mexico, and Canada, working quietly and behind the scenes to promote a common market with common deregulation for the benefit of multinational corporations. It's an agenda that so far has resulted in an increase in U.S. corporate profits of 45 percent, while wages of American workers have risen only 3 percent in the last five years....

"[This agenda results in] effectively surrendering the sovereignty of the United States.

Dobbs: "You know, talking about Zoellick's proposal, it's not Zoellick's proposal. It's daddy's proposal. And people better understand that they mean exactly what they're saying. It's a new world order they're trying to create. And they're trying to do so not only without approval or consent of the governed of this country, but despite the popular will. This is a straightforward assault by the elitists in this country"(561).

Since Bush Jr. took office, the plan of destroying U.S. jobs, and thereby maximizing corporate profits, had marched forward at an alarmingly rapid pace. In the April 2004 edition of their journal, the AFL-CIO reported: "The United States has lost 2.8 million manufacturing jobs since President George W. Bush took office in January 2001. In fact, manufacturing employment in the United States fell to 14.5 million in December 2003, its lowest level in 45 years, according to the U.S. Bureau of Labor Statistics (BLS). As a share of total U.S. jobs, manufacturing has declined since its peak of 40 percent just after World War II to 27 percent in 1981 and now stands at about 12 percent"(574).

As far as NAFTA goes, what we have here is simply a regionalized version of the more globally-oriented WTO, whose objectives and beneficiaries are the same. Noam Chomsky had this to say about NAFTA: "The only respect in which it is a genuine North American Free Trade Agreement is that it applies to North America: it is not 'free,' it is not about 'trade,' and it is surely not based on an 'agreement' among the irrelevant public. The 'free trade agreements'...[are] designed to keep wealth and power firmly in the hands of the masters of the 'new imperial age'"(45, p. 183).

By the way, what do you suppose the EU (European Union), along with its "Eurodollar," are all about?--They're simply Europe's regional equivalent of NAFTA and other developing North American unifications [Endnote 114].

While we're on the subject of the European Union, I should point out that uniting the nations of Europe had been a goal of the globalists from very early on. In fact, Winston Churchill, during a speech he delivered on May 13, 1947, declared: "Without a united Europe there is no prospect of world government. It is the urgent and indispensable step toward that realization of the goal"(112, p.

74).

Should there be any lingering doubt that programs such as NAFTA are designed to advance the cause of world government, or the New World Order, notice what Henry Kissinger said, just prior to Congress ratifying the NAFTA agreement: "What Congress will have before it is not a conventional trade agreement but the hopeful architecture of a new international system. A regional Western Hemisphere Organization dedicated to democracy and free trade [yah right!] would be a first step towards the New World Order that is so frequently cited but rarely implemented"(217).

To show just how far we have digressed toward losing our national sovereignty and merging with other nations, all we need do is look at the incredibly bold and treasonous moves made in this direction under the Bush Jr. administration. So bold and treasonous were these moves, in fact, that even CNN couldn't keep quiet about it. On June 9, 2005, Lou Dobbs reported: "[A]n astonishing proposal [has been made] to expand our borders to incorporate Mexico and Canada and simultaneously further diminish U.S. sovereignty. Have our political elites gone mad?...

"[A] panel sponsored by the Council on Foreign Relations [produced a May 2006 report called "Building A North American Community," in which it declared that it] wants the United States to focus not on the defense of our own borders, but rather create what effectively would be a common border that includes Mexico and Canada."

Later, a clip was played that featured CFR member Robert Pastor, who made this comment: "What we hope to accomplish by 2010 is a common external tariff which will mean that goods can move easily across the border. We want a common security perimeter around all of North America, so as to ease the travel of people within North America."

Afterward, Dobbs retorted: "Americans must think that our political and academic elites have gone utterly mad at a time when three-and-a-half years, approaching four years after September 11, we still don't have border security. And this group of elites is talking about not defending our borders, finally, but rather creating new ones. It's astonishing"(477, 528).

Yes, it is astonishing. But it's also quite predictable. This is exactly what the globalists have been wanting for a very long time. And now they are licking their chops in anticipation of it. Not only are we looking at a loss of U.S. sovereignty, but maximum profits for globalist corporations, and minimal wages for the slave labor workers. This is precisely what they mean by "free trade" [Endnote 115].

It's most revealing to compare the above CNN report with the following June 17, 2000 Ottawa, Canada, *Citizen* article, called "Border With U.S. 'Likely to Disappear,'" which also talked about the proposed plan to merge the U.S. with Canada and Mexico. This article stated: "An American [globalist] think-tank is calling on Canada, the United States and Mexico to combine customs, immigration and security functions to the point at which borders become almost irrelevant. A study released yesterday by the Carnegie Endowment for International Peace urges the three countries to explore whether a North American 'integration project' is worth pursuing and to develop a strategic plan for rethinking border relationships."

In case you still aren't convinced that the "free trade" farce is an age-old dream come true for the globalists, leading us ever closer to their world government trap, look, for instance, at what Senator George W. Malone, quoting from E.F. Tompkins, an editor of the *New York Journal-American*, stated before Congress back in 1958: "The free-trade movement...is related in this country to the...world government movement"(323).

In this same year, a July *Harper's* article, speaking about the boys at the CFR, said that they "have one objective in common: they want to bring about the surrender of the sovereignty and the national independence of the U.S. They want to end national boundaries and racial and ethnic loyalties supposedly to increase business and ensure world peace. What they strive for would inevitably lead to dictatorship and loss of freedoms by the people. The CFR was founded for 'the purpose of promoting disarmament and submergence of U.S. sovereignty and national independence into an all-powerful one-world government.'"

Going back even further than this, Woodrow Wilson, in an address to Congress on January 8, 1918, outlined his famous Fourteen Points (which were actually written by Colonel House). The very next year, these Fourteen Points became the focus of the Versailles Treaty. Point #14, which called for the formation of the League of Nations, is particularly worth noting. It proposed (amongst other things) that all trade barriers between nations be removed.

Perhaps you are wondering how NAFTA got passed through Congress if it is so blatantly detrimental to our economy. If so, here's your answer: As mentioned earlier, most members of Congress belong to the CFR, and are thus already in favor of such programs before they even come up for vote. But as for those who didn't belong to the CFR at the time of the NAFTA bill vote, the globalists were easily able to silence most of them (as they have done on so many other, similar occasions) by simply calling upon the services of their henchmen, the CIA. This point was brought out in the January 1994 issue of *Worth* magazine, in an article by David Andelman called "The CIA's Trade Secret." Andelman revealed in this article that the CIA had pushed intensely to get NAFTA passed, and had threatened to expose illegal activities of certain members of Congress if they didn't vote in favor of it. Does this not confirm for you, once again, where the CIA's interests and loyalties really lie?

William Blum, in his book *Killing Hope*, provides us with a good overview of the workings of NAFTA, along with the WTO: "[It's now] New-World-Order time....They've got their NAFTA and...their GATT World Trade Organization. They're dictating economic, political and social development all over the Third World and Eastern Europe....Everything in sight is being deregulated and privatized. Capital prowls the globe...with ravenous freedom...operating free of friction, free of gravity"(216, p. 7).

Though not involved directly in the "free trade" movement, the World Bank and the International Monetary Fund are two more important pieces of the globalization puzzle, which the globalists have used throughout the years to create economic havoc all over the planet, and to help set the stage for their planned unified world economy [Endnote 116]. One of the many crimes committed by these institutions against countries abroad, particularly Third World countries, is the manipulative manner in which they deny these countries much-needed loans unless they comply with certain demands. As an example of this, Greg Palast, who writes for London's *Guardian* and *Observer* newspapers, described in his book, *The Best Democracy Money Can Buy*, how he came across an IMF document called "Ecuador Interim Country Assistance Strategy," which was marked "Confidential. Not for distribution." Palast thusly elaborated on the contents of this document: "Ecuador's government was *ordered* to raise the price of cooking gas by 80 per cent by November 1, 2000, it says. Also, the government had to eliminate 26,000 jobs and cut real wages for the remaining workers by 50 per cent in four steps in a timetable specified by the IMF. By July 2000, Ecuador had to transfer ownership of its biggest water system to foreign operators, then Ecuador would grant British Petroleum's ARCO unit rights to build and own an oil pipeline over the Andes. That was for starters. In all, the IMF's 167 detailed loan conditions looked less like an 'Assistance Plan' and more like a blueprint for a financial *coup d'etat*"(218, p. 46).

The Senate Committee on Foreign Relations warned of this very thing happening back in 1977, stating that, for poor countries, "there will be no escaping IMF conditionality, [with] little choice but to accept whatever terms the IMF...choose[s] to lay down"(219).

But the picture is even uglier than this, because the "loans" that the IMF/World Bank hand out are designed to only give the appearance of providing relief to poor countries, while crippling them even further in the long run, just like the Dawes and Young Plans ultimately did for Germany in the 1920s. Palast described how Argentina, for example, was promised, back in September of 2000, an economic "aid" package of $8 billion by the IMF, World Bank, and a few private lenders. However, as Palast revealed, there was "less to this generosity than meets the eye." One of the hidden conditions of this aid package, said Palast, was that "Argentina will continue to 'peg' its currency, the peso, to the dollar at an exchange rate of one to one. The currency peg doesn't come cheap. American banks and speculators have been charging a whopping 16 per cent risk premium above normal in return for the dollars needed to back this currency scheme.

"Now do the arithmetic. On Argentina's $128 billion in debt, normal interest plus the 16 per cent surcharge by lenders comes to about $27 billion a year. In other words, Argentina's people don't net one penny from the $8 billion loan package"(218, p. 60).

In his book *Confessions of an Economic Hit Man*, author John Perkins provides us with a unique former insider's perspective on how the globalists use economics and other tools (of the World Bank and similar institutions) to enslave and destroy. In the Preface, Perkins wrote: "Economic hit men (EHMs) are highly paid professionals who cheat countries around the globe out of trillions of dollars. They funnel money from the World Bank, the U.S. Agency for International Development (USAID), and other foreign 'aid' organizations into the coffers of huge corporations and the pockets of a few wealthy families who control the planet's natural resources. Their tools include fraudulent financial reports, rigged elections, payoffs, extortion, sex, and murder. They play a game as old as empire, but one that has taken on new and terrifying dimensions during this time of globalization.

"I should know; I was an EHM...."

Perkins then went on to give a couple examples of what happens to heads of state who refuse to play the globalists' rigged game: "Jaime Roldos, president of Ecuador, and Omar Torrijos, president of Panama...[were both killed] in fiery crashes. Their deaths were not accidental. They were assassinated because they opposed that fraternity of corporate, government, and banking heads whose goal is global empire. We EHMs failed to bring Roldos and Torrijos around, and [so] the other type of hit men, the CIA-sanctioned jackals who were always right behind us, stepped in....And if the jackal[s] fail[ed]..., then the job [fell] to the military."

A little further on in this book, Perkins wrote: "...My job...was to encourage world leaders to become part of a vast network that promotes U.S. commercial interests. In the end, those leaders become ensnared in a web of debt that ensures their loyalty. We can draw on them whenever we desire--to satisfy our political, economic, or military needs. In turn, they bolster their political positions by bringing industrial parks, power plants, and airports to their people. The owners of U.S. engineering/construction companies become fabulously wealthy."

Perkins did not actually work for the government, at least not directly.

Later, in chapter 2, he explained: "U.S. intelligence agencies--including the NSA--would identify prospective EHMs, who could then be hired by international corporations. These EHMs would never be paid by the government; instead, they would draw their salary from the private sector. As a result, their dirty work, if exposed, would be chalked up to corporate greed rather than to government policy. In addition, the corporations that hired then, although paid by government agencies and their multi-national banking counterparts (with taxpayer money), would be insulated from congressional oversight and public scrutiny, shielded by a growing body of legal initiatives, including trademark, international trade, and Freedom of Information laws"(460).

Coming back to the WTO for a moment, an important development transpired during the public protests against this institution in late 1999 in Seattle, Washington, where it held its annual meetings for that year, which further demonstrates the thorough control that the globalists have over our government. As tens of thousands of peaceful protesters attempted to voice their legitimate concerns in the streets of Seattle, they found their efforts disrupted and severely discredited by an anarchist group known as the Blac Bloc.

With clubs in hand, they mingled in with the legitimate protesters and began smashing storefront windows and car windshields. Strangely, these anarchists didn't seem terribly concerned about being arrested, casually walking down the street as they vandalized all along the way. The peaceful protesters were furious over this outrage, demanding that the vandals leave. Meanwhile, the locals were ringing the Seattle Police Department's phones off their hooks, but there was no response.

Later it was revealed that federal agents had instructed local police to ignore any calls during the protests, and not break ranks around the Convention Center where the WTO meetings were being held. This was covered in the local media in Seattle, but got no attention nationally.

One local reporter who gave good coverage of this fiasco was Meeghan Black of Seattle's KIRO 7 Eyewitness News. On Tuesday, December 7, 1999, she reported live on the scene, stating that the Blac Bloc anarchists "broke windows at The Gap, they're smashing windows at McDonald's, they're dumping over garbage cans, and they are very angry...and hostile. We're seeing more clashes with other [peaceful, legitimate] protesters, telling them to stop because they're giving everyone a bad name. None of the protesters--the legitimate protesters down here--want any of this kind of action, and they are very angry."

Then the host at the studio broke in with a question: "Meeghan, any sign yet of police trying to track them down?" Meeghan then replied: "I don't see police anywhere." Later she commented, during the same broadcast, that "Several police officers have told us, because they were assigned to control the protester crowds, they weren't allowed to break ranks and to stop the Blac Bloc. So the group just continued destroying property."

It wasn't until the next day that the police took action, long after the Blac Bloc group had their fun and left the area. A state of emergency was declared, and the peaceful protesters, receiving the blame for the carnage of the previous day, were, without provocation, teargassed, beaten, and arrested--almost 600 of them--and interred for 180 days thereafter in a federal detention center (Sand Point Brig).

All the while, none of the Blac Bloc members were arrested. On the contrary, it was reported by Christina McKenna of KIRO 7 Eyewitness News the following week that they were placed in rent-free government housing projects. What other conclusion can be drawn from this except that these thugs were being rewarded for their services, having been hired by the federal government, on behalf of their beloved corporate buddies in the WTO, to sabotage the protests?

The obvious intended purpose of this scam was to destroy the credibility of the legitimate protesters by making them look bad, and consequently to make the WTO look good. No wonder these anarchists weren't fleeing from their crime scenes--they were obviously told in advance that the police wouldn't disturb them. These anarchists were, in fact, contracted *agent provocateurs*. Does this help you to understand whose interests our government is really out to protect? [Endnote 117]

A very similar thing took place in late November of 2003, in Miami, where peaceful protesters, protesting against a summit meeting of the Free Trade Area of the Americas (FTAA--another WTO-type globalization body), were abused by police without cause. They were fired upon indiscriminately with skin-piercing rubber bullets, gassed with an array of chemicals, blasted with loud concussion grenades, shocked with stun guns, beaten bloody with batons, etc., and all for having done absolutely nothing except being "audacious" enough to voice their opinion in opposition to the atrocious exploitations of globalist corporations. Just like with the Seattle protests, local police were the means of suppression, inspired and coordinated by the federal government. In fact, the $8.5 million cost of this "security" operation came straight out of Bush Jr.'s $87 billion budget for the "war on terror" in Iraq(415, pp. 29-31)[Endnote 118].

For those who are familiar with the FBI's (and the CIA's) COINTELPRO (counterintelligence program) that ran from 1956 to 1977, this type of despicable government behavior should come as no surprise. As part of this program, the FBI had subverted groups and harassed people it deemed to be threats to national security or to the established social and political order. Speaking on this matter, James Bovard wrote: "Over 2,300 separate [illegal] operations were carried out to incite street warfare between violent [and even non-violent] groups, to wreck marriages, to get people fired, to smear innocent people by portraying them as government informants [who were often consequently murdered], to sic the IRS on people, and to cripple or destroy...[various] other organizations. The FBI let no corner of American life escape its vigilance..." COINTELPRO even targeted Vietnam War protest groups, black civil rights groups, and the women's liberation movement(164, pp. 148-154).

In further regards to COINTELPRO, a Senate committee declared that the purpose of this program was to "exploit conflicts within and between groups; to use news media contacts to disrupt, ridicule, or discredit groups; to preclude 'violence-prone' or 'rabble rouser' leaders of these groups from spreading their philosophy publicly, and to gather information on the 'unsavory backgrounds'-- immorality, subversive activity, and criminal activity--of group leaders....[and to] prevent these groups from recruiting young people"(220).

With the foregoing information in mind, notice this ridiculous remark made by Attorney General John Ashcroft: "In its 94-year history, the FBI has been...the tireless protector of civil rights and civil liberties for all Americans"(221). Yah right!

But as if all of this isn't frightening enough, the Patriot Act now gives the FBI, CIA, and other government agencies the ability, under the color of law, to go back to conducting COINTELPRO-type activities against anyone, anywhere, any time they choose (supposedly in the name of the "war on terrorism"). (Section 802 of the Patriot Act defines "domestic terrorism," in part, as "activities that...appear to be intended...to influence the policy of a government by intimidation or coercion," which can easily be applied to peaceful protests against globalization).

Through the Patriot Act, federal thugs can now come into your home without a warrant, arrest you without charges, and hold you indefinitely without a trial. In conjunction with other anti-Constitutional pieces of legislation passed in the wake of 9-11, like the December 2004 Intelligence Bill, you can be arrested as a "non-material supporter of terrorism" (whatever that means!), be deported to Guantanamo Bay, and then be tortured simply because you attended some type of anti-globalization rally (which they could easily construe as non-material support of terrorism--what a nice vague term).

Thanks to the treasonous Bush Jr. administration, there are absolutely no more protections against unlimited government prying, harassment, and outright oppression. The Constitution has been effectively abolished.

In case you suffer from the delusion that the Patriot Act is only meant for dealing with foreign terrorists, you not only need to read Section 802, but you might also want to check out such articles as "U.S. Uses Terror Law to Pursue Crimes From Drugs to Swindling," *New York Times*, September 28, 2003; "Anti-

Terror Laws Target Americans, Not Just Terrorists," *Capitol Hill Blue*, June 15, 2004; and "Terror Law Nabs Common Criminals," Wired News, September 14, 2003, http://www.wired.com/news/conflict/0,2100,60440,00.html.

One American citizen, in particular, that was arrested under Patriot Act provisions was Jose Padilla. Originally he was arrested in May 2002, supposedly for attempting to build a "dirty bomb," although no evidence was ever presented to prove this allegation, and he was never formally charged with this "crime." After holding him for 4 years without affording him any legal representation or charging him with anything, they finally changed the reason they were detaining him, and formally charged him with "conspiracy to murder, kidnap, and maim persons in a foreign country." Yet, on August 21, 2006, he was acquitted of these charges(533). This man had his Constitutional rights trampled for over 4 years, and he hadn't even done anything! Are you getting the picture of what the Patriot Act is really all about? (More is said about the Patriot Act in Appendix 7.)

Does the government have the authority to suspend our Constitutional rights under any circumstances? Not according to this ruling by Justice David Davis in the 1866 Lambdin Milligan case: "The Constitution of the United States is a law for rulers and people, equally in war and in peace, and covers with the shield of its protection all classes of men, at all times, and under all circumstances," and none of its provisions "can be suspended during any of the great exigencies of government"(498).

Appendix 4

The Kennedy assassination

Many have concluded, and for good reasons, that it was the CIA that actually carried out the treasonous Kennedy assassination. Though space does not permit a lengthy coverage of this subject here, let us examine a few important highlights.

Anyone who is even mildly familiar with the workings of the CIA is aware that, throughout its grotesque history, it has been known as, amongst other things, a professional political assassination squad. It's own documents attest to this fact. Take, for example, the proceeding excerpts from "A Study of Assassination," one of several documents drafted up by the Agency in the early 1950s and released to the public by this "intelligence" organization on May 23, 1997. This particular document, incidentally, was used by the CIA to train participants in the 1954 coup in Guatemala: "For secret assassinations...the contrived accident is the most effective technique. When successfully executed, it causes little excitement and is only casually investigated.

"The most efficient accident...is a fall of 75 feet or more onto a hard surface. Elevator shafts, stair wells, unscreened windows and bridges will serve....The act may be executed by sudden, vigorous grabbing of the ankles, tipping the subject over the edge. If the assassin immediately sets up an outcry, playing the 'horrified witness,' no alibi or surreptitious withdrawal is necessary.

"Drugs can be very effective. If the assassin is trained as a doctor or nurse and the subject is under medical care, this is an easy and sure method. An overdose of morphine administered as a sedative will cause death without disturbance and is difficult to detect. The size of the dose will depend upon whether the subject has been using narcotics regularly. If not, two grains will suffice. If the subject drinks heavily, morphine or a similar narcotic can be injected at the passing out stage, and the cause of death will often be held to be acute alcoholism.

"Edge weapons: Any legally obtained edge devise may be successfully employed. A certain minimum of anatomical knowledge is needed for reliability. Puncture wounds of the body cavity may not be reliable unless the heart is reached. The heart is protected by the rib cage and is not always easy to locate....Absolute reliability is obtained by severing the spinal cord in the cervical region. This can be done with the point of a knife or a light blow of an axe or hatchet. Another reliable method is the severing of both jugular and carotid vessels on both sides of the windpipe"(156, pp. 43, 44).

In 1975, a Senate committee headed by Frank Church (the Church

Committee) revealed that the CIA had been responsible for planning and executing, amongst other sinister things, a number of political assassinations abroad, using everything from poison to machine guns, and had sometimes even employed mob hit men to do their dirty work for them. While this committee didn't mention Kennedy's assassination (it was actually focused on foreign covert activities by the Agency, although it's doubtful that it would have implicated the CIA in Kennedy's assassination, even if it had been focused on domestic Agency activities), nevertheless, it further illustrates the CIA's propensity for ruthless, murderous removal of those it does not want in power.

On this note, consider this next quotation--a personal testimony given by Lieutenant Colonel Daniel Marvin, a veteran of 8 combat campaigns who had earned 21 awards and decorations, a paratrooper for 15 years, and one who served in the elite special forces, the Green Berets. Just a few weeks after Kennedy's assassination, Marvin had volunteered for specialist guerilla training at Fort Bragg. Regarding this training, he stated that "Almost all the instruction in the guerilla war school was classified. The most secret was the top secret training on assassinations and terrorism. At that time we went to a different building that had a double barbed wire fence around it and guard dogs....

"[T]he John F. Kennedy situation...was brought to our attention as a classic example of the way to organize a complete program to eliminate a nation's leader while pointing the finger at a lone assassin. It involved also the coverup of the assassination itself. We had considerable detail. They had a mock layout of the...area, and it showed where the shooters were....They told us that Oswald was not involved in the shooting and...that he was the patsy--the one that was set up....

"[W]e really felt that...one of those instructors may have been involved himself in the assassination of John F. Kennedy"(157).

Now take notice of what the October 3, 1963 *New York Times* had to say about the CIA, just prior to Kennedy's assassination: "Twice the CIA flatly refused to carry out instructions from Ambassador Henry Cabot Lodge brought from Washington because the agency disagreed [with them]. The CIA's growth was likened to a malignancy which the very high official was not sure even the White House could control. If the United States ever experiences an attempt at a coup to overthrow the Government it will come from the CIA. The agency represents a tremendous power and total unaccountability to anyone."

Further proof of the CIA's involvement in J.F.K.'s assassination came in April of 2007. On May 1, Detroit's WXYZ, Channel 7, reported: "An audio file serving as the final testimony of CIA veteran and convicted Watergate conspirator E. Howard Hunt, on the assassination of President John F. Kennedy, has surfaced.

"It has been distilled down from a 20-minute tape made by Hunt at his home in Miami, according to his oldest son with whom E. Howard Hunt had enjoyed a good relationship in later life.

"The unmarked cassette was received in the mail by his oldest son, Saint John Hunt, in January 2004. At the time, the 86-year-old E. Howard Hunt was not well. According to Saint John Hunt, his father's only request was that the information not be released until his death. Shortly thereafter, he recovered from his illness and he would not die until January of 2007. The tape remained in Saint John Hunt's hands the entire time.

"According to Saint John Hunt, the existence of the tape was unknown by his extended family until its broadcast on 'Coast to Coast Live with Ian Punnett' on April 27, 2007. Many of the details of the tape were included in an interview with Rolling Stone magazine published earlier in the month.

"The contents of the tape are consistent with E. Howard Hunt's CIA career. He was a significant team member of many CIA 'wet ops,' that is, bloody operations such as the violent overthrow of the democratically-elected Guatemalan government of Jacobo Arbenz in 1954 and the assassination of Che Guevara. The Guatemalan civil war that resulted from the CIA-backed coup would eventually lead to the deaths of 200,000 people....

"[D]espite many allegations over the years, E. Howard Hunt had always denied...any involvement in the assassination of JFK. In 1978, Hunt testified under oath to Congress that neither he nor the CIA had anything to do with the murder of the president.

"According to this tape, he was only half-lying.

"The 'wet op' that was pulled off in Dealey Plaza on November 22, 1963...was put together by several CIA veterans and contract players-for-fire in a...hit originally 'suggested' by then Vice-President Lyndon B. Johnson. One of the many purposes of this tape, according to E. Howard Hunt, was to make clear...LBJ's involvement in the assassination.

"Perhaps as a way of justifying the assassination, Hunt seems focused on establishing the 'chain of command' to this action that allows him to see himself as following orders toward a greater patriotic goal.

"On the tape, the man Hunt refers to as 'Frank' is, according to written notes taken by Saint John Hunt, CIA Operative and later Watergate co-conspirator Frank Sturgis, sometimes spelled 'Sturgess.' The mastermind appears to be Cord Meyer."

On the tape, Hunt implies that Kennedy's death was the work of a certain faction within the CIA, and not the CIA as a whole. But this only makes sense, since this is how the CIA works--assigning jobs like this to clandestine operatives within the agency, without the bulk of its employees being aware of what is going on. And what was the main motive for this murder? WXYZ went on to say: "They were...resentful of the way that the White House had been treating the CIA through Kennedy's disdainful public posture on intelligence and the firings of many of their former associates.

"In sum, with the permission of LBJ, Cord Meyer, David Phillips, David Morales, [and] E. Howard Hunt conspired to create a...hit 'for the good of the country.'

"And here, finally, is the taped testimony that proves that once and for all"(568).

Of no surprise, the CIA, pretty much from the start, went to great lengths to see to it that all objections raised to the Warren Commission's conclusions were quickly brushed off by the media as paranoid speculations. One of the ways that the CIA did this is best demonstrated in one of its own documents (#1035-960), originally stamped "Top Secret." This document was drafted up in January 1967, and was sent out to CIA media assets at CBS, ABC, NBC, and the *New York Times*. It was also stamped "PSYCH," presumably as part of the CIA's Psychological Warfare Operations, in the CS (Clandestine Services) division. This document stated, in part: "Conspiracy theories have frequently thrown suspicion on our organization, for example by falsely alleging that Lee Harvey Oswald worked for us [he did!]. The aim of this dispatch is to provide material for countering and discrediting the claims of the conspiracy theorists, so as to inhibit the circulation of such claims....

"We do not recommend that discussion of the assassination question be initiated where it is not already taking place [in other words, avoid the issue at all costs]."

The document then went on to instruct that, when discussion became unavoidable, media personnel should "discuss the [Warren Commission's] publicity problem with liaison and friendly elite contacts (especially politicians and editors), pointing out that the Warren Commission made as thorough an investigation as humanly possible, that the charges of the critics are without serious foundation, and that further speculative discussion only plays into the hands of the opposition.

"Point out also that parts of the conspiracy talk appear to be deliberately generated by Communist propagandists. Urge them to use their influence to discourage unfounded and irresponsible speculation." As if the Warren Commission's conclusions themselves weren't "unfounded and irresponsible speculation."

But did you catch how this document urged the media to label opposition to the Warren Commission's conclusions as communist propaganda? Nobody knows propaganda better than the CIA! In fact, notice what this document went on to say: "[E]mploy propaganda assets to answer and refute the attacks of the critics. Book reviews and feature articles are particularly appropriate for this purpose....Our play should point out, as applicable, that the critics are I) wedded to theories adopted before the evidence was in, ii) politically interested, iii) financially interested, iv) hasty and inaccurate in their research, or v) infatuated with their own theories..." [Endnote 119].

It needs to be pointed out that the Warren Report, while we're on this subject, along with its accompanying 26 supplemental volumes, containing altered eyewitness testimonies, ignoring key pieces of evidence, magic bullet proposal (where a single bullet supposedly followed an impossible trajectory, inflicting a multiplicity of wounds along the way)[Endnote 120], etc., was not the result of an "investigation" into Kennedy's assassination, but was instead the result of one of the biggest government coverups in American history. But this shouldn't surprise us, when we consider the fact that Chief Justice Earl Warren (CFR member and 33rd-degree Mason) "just so happened" to appoint Allen Dulles (also a CFR member and a 33rd-degree Mason), the former CIA director that Kennedy fired, to head up this "investigation"? As President Nixon once commented: "[The Warren Report] was the greatest hoax that has ever been perpetuated"(158).

In addition to the CIA media propaganda campaign squashing objections raised against the Warren Commission's conclusions, there was also a massive murder campaign, probably conducted by the CIA as well, involving the death of roughly 200 people who had key information that was very damaging to the validity of the Commission's conclusions. These people--eyewitnesses, investigators, and even a few who were involved to some degree in the assassination plot--were shot, stabbed, bludgeoned, pushed from great heights, or given drugs to induce either a heart attack or an aneurism, to name but a few methods of elimination. But, of course, according to the CIA, this must just be a bunch of "unfounded and irresponsible speculation."

Here's a bit more "speculation" for you to consider:

- Oswald was a poor shot, yet he was supposedly able to pull off what no expert sharpshooter in the world has ever been able to reproduce.
- The view from the Texas Schoolbook Depository window that Oswald supposedly had, when he is said to have discharged the fatal shot, was obstructed by a tree.
- No gun powder residue was found on either of Oswald's cheeks, meaning that he could not have fired a rifle that day.
- The sight on the rifle Oswald allegedly used was not aligned.
- Senator Connally's wrist alone had more bullet fragments found in it than what were missing from the so-called "magic bullet," which was found in nearly pristine condition on a stretcher at Parkland Hospital.

- The Zapruder film clearly shows that the deadly shot came from Kennedy's front, thrusting him violently backward, and not from the back, as the Warren Commission claimed.
- The famous "backyard photo" of Oswald holding the murder weapon, pictured on the front cover of *Life*, was nothing more than a cut-out picture of Oswald's head superimposed on someone else's body (this has been proven on a number of counts, but can easily be seen by comparing the conflicting shadow angle beneath Oswald's nose with that of the one cast on the ground by the feet).
- Oswald was said to have been interrogated for 12 hours, yet there are no transcripts or recordings of this verbal interaction, and he was never afforded legal counsel.
- The motorcade route was changed at the last minute, taking the President into an area where there were conveniently very few eyewitnesses to his murder.
- The limo driver, rather than speeding off to safety when shots were being fired, instead slowed down and turned around to look at the President, seemingly to make sure he was fatally wounded before he finally decided to step on the gas and get out of the danger zone.

It is also pertinent to draw attention to the fact that important pieces of evidence were either destroyed or "misplaced" immediately following the assassination. Here are a few of the more pertinent examples:

- The Lincoln that Kennedy rode in was thoroughly washed down after he was dropped off at Parkland Hospital. It also had its windshield quickly replaced, which had a bullet hole in it that would have shown that the fatal shot came from the front of the car, in the direction of the Grassy Knoll.
- Kennedy's throat wound was altered by a tracheotomy, which was performed in spite of the fact that it was known he was already dead.
- Kennedy's body arrived at the Bethesda Naval Hospital two hours later than it should have, with head wounds that did not match those described by ALL medical personnel who first examined them in Dallas.
- Kennedy's brain was removed and disappeared without a trace.

And then there was the problem of altered testimonies from eyewitnesses, or partial omissions thereof, by the Warren Commission. Many eyewitnesses complained that their printed testimonies in the Commission's report either contained things that they never said, or omitted important things that they did say.

A coverup of this magnitude, involving individuals and institutions at the local, state, and federal levels of government, obviously required top-level planning and orchestration. Can you now understand why the government is keeping thousands of documents relating to this assassination under lock and key until 2038?

* * * * * * *

In the light of the tremendous amount of evidence of government involvement in J.F.K.'s assassination, we should not be shocked to find out that the same is the case with the murder of his brother, RFK.

On June 4, 1968, RFK, destined to become the next president of the United States, shared the same fate as his brother, in the kitchen of the Los Angles Ambassador Hotel.

Sirhan Sirhan, wielding a .22-caliber pistol, seemed the likely assassin. However, Thomas Noguchi, the county coroner who examined RFK's body, stated that the deadly shot was fired from a steep upward angle, less than one inch from the head, just behind the right ear. Sirhan, however, was located no less than 6 feet away, IN FRONT of RFK. So he couldn't have been the murderer. In confirmation of this, NBC reported on March 26, 2008: "New forensics evidence presented Tuesday during a symposium at Foxwoods suggests Sirhan Sirhan did not fire the fatal shots that killed Sen. Robert Kennedy in 1968....

"Dr. Robert Joling, a forensics investigator who has studied the Robert Kennedy assassination for almost 40 years, determined that the fatal shots must have come from behind the senator.

"Sirhan, however, was 4 to 6 feet in front of Kennedy and never got close enough to shoot Kennedy from behind, the investigator said.

"The other evidence was the Pruszynski recording. This is the only audio recording of the assassination. Another scientist analyzed it and concluded that at least 13 shots were fired from two different guns."

There was a person who was in just the right position to have fired the deadly shot that killed RFK--Thane Cesar, a private security guard. As it turned out, he was also touting a .22-caliber pistol at the time. And, according to eye-witness Don Schuman, Cesar did indeed draw his weapon while Sirhan was shooting.

Cesar at first said he had sold his .22 BEFORE RFK's assassination. However, he later changed his story and stated that he sold it AFTERWARD. By the time the new owner was tracked down, he said that the pistol had been stolen.

Another problem is the fact that Sirhan's gun was capable of firing only 8 shots, and yet a total of at least 13 bullets, as stated above, were fired. And then, to make matters worse, the LAPD later admitted that they destroyed the door and ceiling panels that contained the key bullet holes--another case of missing evidence.

Here's another problem: Over 2,500 photos from this crime scene turned up missing, mostly at the hand of the LAPD. Was this a coincidence?

Though Cesar appears to have been the actual murderer of RFK, the whole operation was obviously coordinated by the CIA, as usual. In this regard, the BBC's Newsnight reported on November 21, 2006: "New video and photographic evidence that puts three senior CIA operatives at the scene of Robert Kennedy's assassination has been brought to light.

"The evidence was shown in a report by Shane O'Sullivan, broadcast on BBC Newsnight.

"It reveals that the operatives and four unidentified associates were at the Ambassador Hotel, Los Angeles, in the moments before and after the shooting on 5 June, 1968.

"The CIA had no domestic jurisdiction and some of the officers were based in South-East Asia at the time, with no reason to be in Los Angeles."

Two of these CIA agents were positively identified as David Morales and Gordon Campbell. Regarding Morales, the BBC went on to cite an interview conducted with Robert Waitor, a former friend and lawyer of Morales. He admitted that Morales confided to him that he was involved in the murder of both Kennedys. Waitor said that Morales told him, "I was in Dallas when we got that Mother F___er, and I was in Los Angeles when we got the Little Bastard."

Morales, and indeed the whole CIA, hated Robert, like his brother before him, because, among other things, he wanted to shut down the Vietnam War. He also indicated that he wanted to reopen the investigation of his brother's death, if elected to the presidency.

Appendix 5

The theft of our rights and liberties

Our rights and liberties are under relentless attack by the globalists. Although this is a problem occurring in countries all over the world, we will here be focusing our attention only on some of the more outstanding examples of how this has been happening right here, in the "land of the free":

- The soaring cost of homes in this country is increasingly, subtly, and deliberately robbing us of our "right to property"--something else that Marx had called for. And, no surprise, robbing us of our property rights is also part of the U.N.'s agenda. We will address this issue in more detail in Appendix 15. But for now, notice what "Habitat I," the report of the 1976 U.N. Conference on Human Settlements, had declared: "[P]rivate land ownership is a principal instrument of accumulating wealth and therefore contributes to social injustice....Public control of land is therefore indispensable....Public ownership of land is justified in favor of the common good, rather than to protect the interests of the already privileged"(324)[Endnote 121].

These same sentiments were repeated by "Habitat II" at the June 1996 U.N. Conference on Human Settlements, which were taken right out of Marx's *Manifesto*. And another thing taken from Marx's *Manifesto* is the call for abolition of all rights of inheritance, which is yet one more right that is on its way out in this country. Through the inheritance tax, for example, many can't even afford to inherit a home today, let alone buy one.

For those lucky enough to afford a home in America these days, there are other attacks on property rights to contend with. For instance, to burn leaves on one's own property, add an extension on one's own home, or even to build a shed, one must obtain a permit ($$$) and be sure that he/she isn't violating any "zoning laws."

Once a person decides to undertake building a shed or adding an extension on his/her home, in addition to paying a permit fee, an even greater fleecing will result from the property tax increase that person will suffer. Of course, one need not undertake any such building project in order to suffer a massive increase in property tax. And for some people (especially the elderly on low, fixed incomes), an increase in property tax of just $75 per month (not uncommon) can be enough to force them to sell their homes. Is this freedom?

One particularly disgusting scam related to the loss of our right to property, which resulted in roughly 1.3 million Americans losing their homes, was the mortgage foreclosure crisis under the Bush Jr. administration. It all started in the 1990s, when banks lured many people into getting mortgages with floating interest rates. The rates started out low, so many were easily drawn in. But as the years marched on and inflation set in, coupled with massive job losses and interest rate hikes, many people could no longer afford their mortgage payments and thus lost their homes. This, you can bet, was all by design.

- To get a job in just about any field today, one must be "licensed" or "certified." No longer can a person train on their own as a paid apprentice. Instead, he/she has to go into debt--a debt that bankruptcy will not erase--and sacrifice years of his/her life in an "accredited" school of "higher learning"--so much for the right to contract. People today must literally BUY their jobs. But, in many cases, they can't even find jobs anymore in the fields that they went to school for, once they graduate (because many jobs have gone overseas, or because these graduates don't have the right connections). Thus they find themselves stuck with unaffordable, inescapable student loan debts.

Be assured, this despair is no accident. Indeed, this is all happening according to plan--a very old plan. W.J. Ghent, former editor of the *American Fabian*, writing in 1902 as though he was looking back in time (to our current era) from a distant point in the future, penned these words: "[Banks constituted] one of the most important forces of the Oligarchy [globalist rulers]....The labor castes, the Mercenaries, and the great hordes of secret agents and police...were all pledged to the Oligarchy....The condition of the people of the abyss was pitiable....All their old liberties were gone. They were labor-slaves. Choice of work was denied them. Likewise was denied them...the right to bear or possess arms. They were not land-serfs like the farmers. They were machine-serfs and labor serfs"(350).

When a person is lucky enough to get a decent job these days, his/her stress doesn't end there. On the contrary, a whole new series of stresses take hold: After getting a physical (and, in many cases, an intrusive urine test), the new employee must deal with the hassle of being constantly scrutinized by cameras and supervisors who track his/her every activity on the telephone and the computer, as well as tracking how often he/she uses the bathroom, and how long a period of time he/she spends therein, all in the name of maximizing corporate profits by optimally exploiting the worker. And as if this isn't bad enough, the employee must now work day after day with the anxiety of wondering how long it will be before a layoff is forthcoming. This is pure oppression.

- Because of the outrageous cost of living today, coupled with the scarcity of jobs and lowering of wages, many people are forced into a trap of perpetual credit card debt. Since they often don't have cash on hand to even buy life's basic necessities, they have no choice but to charge such items. At one time this problem wasn't so threatening, as people always had the life-saving option of filing bankruptcy if they got to the point where they absolutely could no longer financially keep their noses above water. But this safety valve was essentially removed by Bush Jr., through his April 2005 bankruptcy law, which now makes it almost impossible for the average person to get out of debt when filing under chapter 7, and it has substantially driven up the cost of filing.

The obvious purpose of this new law was to steer people away from filing a chapter 7 bankruptcy, and push them into chapter 13 instead. This means that the filer is only able to be relieved of a portion of his/her debt. And, to make matters even worse, this bill was passed at a time when credit card companies began to sharply increase the minimum monthly payments they require of their customers (some companies made increases as high as 200%). We can sum this all up in one word: slavery!

- To drive a car, one must first register it ($$$), and then obtain a permit ($$$), then a license ($$$), and in many states the car must also be inspected ($$$), insured ($$$), and an excise tax must be paid on it. From there, as if that isn't enough, the driver must then drive in constant fear of harassment from over-zealous, quota-meeting police who love to hand out state revenue-generating slips for being "estimated" to have driven over the speed limit (and let's not forget that a speeding ticket usually results in an increase in the driver's auto insurance premiums, and, in many states, the amount of the fine now doubles if not paid within twenty days).

- Most people today are not only unable to afford their own healthcare costs, they can't even afford health insurance premiums. But for those who do have health insurance, they are often denied any choice as to what doctor they see, or treatment they receive, and they can scarcely afford their co-payments after their insurance companies pay their share.

The "profit over people" mentality pervades the medical establishment, and its effects have been devastating. The elderly have especially been affected, who are unable to afford much-needed medications, or who die premature deaths because hospitals, under pressure from insurance companies, release them too quickly after major surgeries, denying them a proper recovery time. There have even been many documented cases of elderly patients being taken off life support machines or being given lethal injections of morphine, all because insurance companies want to save money.

Of course, the inability to afford medications, at least in some instances, might be a blessing in disguise, since many medications today are downright health hazards--some are even deadly. Certain depression medications, for example, have been directly linked to many incidents of suicide! [Endnote 122] Other types of medications have been known to cause heart, kidney, and other major organ failures.

In addition to all of this, we also see tremendous pressure being put on people (in many cases, as a prerequisite to getting a job or attending a school) to be immunized with potentially harmful, or even lethal, inoculations (measures are now underway to make vaccinations mandatory in the U.S.).

All-too-often, when harmful effects of certain drugs or inoculations are brought to light through scientific studies, scientists on the payroll of pharmaceutical companies begin a massive propaganda campaign to discredit such studies. And then, with help from their friends at the Food and Drug Administration (FDA), they assure the public that all is well. This trend has gone on successfully for a long time now. The reason for this, of course, is that the FDA, along with a host of other federal and corporate "health-oriented" entities, such as the American Medical Association, Center for Disease Control, Department of Health and Human Services, major pharmaceutical companies, HMOs--you name it--are all controlled by the globalists.

Ever wonder why, despite decades of research and countless billions of dollars, no cures for cancer and other major diseases have ever been found, or even come close to being found? Well, the answer is quite simple, but it has eluded most people because they refuse to believe that things are this bad. Nevertheless, here's the answer: There is no money to be made in cures. The big profits come from continuously-repeated, costly treatments. Such treatments only deal with symptoms, but never address their root causes. This whole system, like everything else in modern society, is set up for profit-making, with no consideration whatsoever for peoples' well-being. Though most people in health-related fields do have a genuine concern for those with health problems, they don't know how, nor are they able, to provide help beyond the limited confines of what is already set in place. Their education has trained them to only accept the profit-driven methodologies, and to reject all else as quackery.

To demonstrate what a fraud the whole health industry is (at the highest levels), we only need to look at the monstrously corrupt marriage that has taken place between big government and big pharmaceutical companies. A good example of how this toxic relationship works was brilliantly illustrated in an article posted on the salon.com website on June 16, 2005, which stated: "When a study revealed that mercury in childhood vaccines may have caused autism in thousands of kids, the government rushed to conceal the data--and to prevent parents from suing drug companies for their role in the epidemic.

"In June 2000, a group of top government scientists and health officials gathered for a meeting at the isolated Simpsonwood conference center in Norcross, Ga. Convened by the Centers for Disease Control and Prevention, the meeting was held at this Methodist retreat center, nestled in wooded farmland next to the Chattahoochee River, to ensure complete secrecy. The agency had issued no public announcement of the session--only private invitations to fifty-two attendees. There were high-level officials from the CDC and the Food and Drug Administration, the top vaccine specialist from the World Health Organization in Geneva and representatives of every major vaccine manufacturer, including GlaxoSmithKline, Merck, Wyeth and Aventis Pasteur. All of the scientific data under discussion, CDC officials repeatedly reminded the participants, was strictly 'embargoed.' There would be no making photocopies of documents, no taking papers with them when they left.

"The federal officials and industry representatives had assembled to discuss a disturbing new study that raised alarming questions about the safety of a host of common childhood vaccines administered to infants and young children. According to a CDC epidemiologist named Tom Verstraeten, who had analyzed the agency's massive database containing the medical records of 100,000 children, a mercury-based preservative in the vaccines--thimerosal--appeared to be responsible for a dramatic increase in autism and a host of other neurological disorders among children. 'I was actually stunned by what I saw,' Verstraeten told those assembled at Simpsonwood, citing the staggering number of earlier studies that indicate a link between thimerosal and speech delays, attention-deficit disorder, hyperactivity and autism. Since 1991, when the CDC and the FDA had recommended that three additional vaccines laced with the preservative be given to extremely young infants--in one case, within hours of birth--the estimated number of cases of autism had increased fifteenfold, from one in every 2,500 children to one in 166 children....

"[I]nstead of taking immediate steps to alert the public and rid the vaccine supply of thimerosal, the officials and executives at Simpsonwood spent most of the next two days discussing how to cover up the damaging data. According to transcripts obtained under the Freedom of Information Act, many at the meeting were concerned about how the damaging revelations about thimerosal would affect the vaccine industry's bottom line....

"[T]he government has proved to be far more adept at handling the damage than at protecting children's health. The CDC paid the Institute of Medicine to conduct a new study to whitewash the risks of thimerosal, ordering researchers to 'rule out' the chemical's link to autism. It withheld Verstraeten's findings, even though they had been slated for immediate publication, and told other scientists that his original data had been 'lost' and could not be replicated. And to thwart the Freedom of Information Act, it handed its giant database of vaccine records over to a private company, declaring it off-limits to researchers. By the time Verstraeten finally published his study in 2003, he had gone to work for GlaxoSmithKline and reworked his data to bury the link between thimerosal and autism....

"The drug companies are also getting help from powerful lawmakers in Washington. Senate Majority Leader Bill Frist, who has received $873,000 in contributions from the pharmaceutical industry, has been working to immunize vaccine makers from liability in 4,200 lawsuits that have been filed by the parents of injured children. On five separate occasions, Frist has tried to seal all of the government's vaccine-related documents--including the Simpsonwood transcripts--and shield Eli Lilly, the developer of thimerosal, from subpoenas. In 2002, the day after Frist quietly slipped a rider known as the 'Eli Lilly Protection Act' into a homeland security bill, the company contributed $10,000 to his campaign and bought 5,000 copies of his book on bioterrorism. Congress repealed the measure in 2003--but earlier this year, Frist slipped another provision into an anti-terrorism bill that would deny compensation to children suffering from vaccine-related brain disorders. 'The lawsuits are of such magnitude that they could put vaccine producers out of business and limit our capacity to deal with a biological attack by terrorists,' says Andy Olsen, a legislative assistant to Frist..."(480).

Does this enrage you? Good, it ought to. And here's something else to boil your blood: These same pharmaceutical companies that are destroying the brains of little infants in the name of killer profits also stand to gain from the behavioral drugs these kids will be put on when they get older, to help them deal with their pharmaceutical company-induced brain disorders. In other words, the pharmaceutical companies are sinisterly creating a market for their products-- creating brain disorders that will later require drug treatments--and all with government assistance and protection.

- It seems no one has the right to healthy food, clear water, or fresh air anymore. In addition to government deregulation allowing corporations, by default, to pump our environment with deadly toxins from industrial waste, there are also toxins winding up in our food, water, and air with the full-sanctioning nod of the government, which falsely labels such toxins as being harmless to humans. For example, over 1,500 food products now contain FDA-approved aspartame--a serious neurotoxin that is responsible for 75% of all food additive complaints made to the FDA. This additive, by the way, was rejected by the FDA until the late 1970s, when Donald Rumsfeld became the CEO of G.D. Searle, the company that once held the patent for this product (it's now held by Monsanto). Obviously Rumsfeld pulled a few strings on behalf of his company.

Another toxin we are exposed to on a daily basis, believe it or not, is fluoride, put into our toothpaste and public water supply. Fluoride is another neurotoxin, which was originally marketed in the 19th century as rat poison! It is so harmful, in fact, that toothpaste companies are required to put the following warning label on their packages: "Keep out of the reach of children under 6 years of age. If you accidentally swallow more than used for bushing, seek professional assistance or contact a Poison Control Center immediately...."

Amazingly, fluoride isn't even good for teeth. Far from strengthening them, it actually weakens them. Fluoride poisoning is known as fluorosis, and the early signs of it are mottling and yellowing of teeth enamel. With this in mind, it only makes sense that fluoride is pushed by the dental industry, seeing how profit-driven it is.

But it's not just dentistry's profits that lie behind the fluoridation of toothpaste and the water supply. Being a neurotoxin, it has great potential for dumbing people down and making them apathetic to government abuses of power. For these very reasons, water fluoridation was popular in Nazi Germany.

Of course, there's also chlorine in today's water supply--another deadly poison. But this doesn't even scratch the surface of the list of all the hazardous substances we take into our bodies on a daily basis. We also have insecticides and artificial colorings in our produce; hydrogenated oils and artificial flavorings in our peanut butter; bleach, chemical softeners, preservatives, synthetic vitamins, and a whole host of other chemicals in our bread; antibiotics and hormones in our milk and meat; sodium nitrite and nitrate preservatives, along with chemical dyes, in our hotdogs and cold cuts...and the list goes on and on. As William Longgood, author of *The Poisons in Your Food*, once wrote: "Virtually every bite of food you eat [has] been treated with some chemical somewhere along the line: dyes, bleaches, emulsifiers, antioxidants, preservatives, flavors, flavor enhancers, buffers, noxious sprays, acidifiers, alkalizers, deodorants, moisteners, drying agents, gases, extenders, thickeners, disinfectants, defoliants, fungicides, neutralizers, artificial sweeteners, anticaking and antifoaming agents, conditioners, curers, hydrolizers, hydrogenators, maturers, fortifiers, and many others.

"These are the tools of the food technician--a wizard who can beguile, deceive, and defraud the [consumer] by making him/her think he/she is getting something that he/she isn't. His alchemy can make stale products appear fresh, permit unsanitary practices, mask inferior quality, substitute nutritionally inferior or worthless chemicals for more costly natural ingredients. These chemicals, almost without exception, perform their mission at the cost of destroying valuable vitamins, minerals, and enzymes, stripping food products of their natural life-giving qualities"(583).

As people get sick from all of these toxins, the solution offered to them is to pop pharmaceutical pills. But these chemical substances only compound people's problems. If nothing else, pharmaceuticals will at least ruin the kidneys when taken over an extended period of time. What should be done, instead of taking pharmaceuticals, is to eat a more healthy diet of organically-grown foods, drink plenty of pure water, and take natural herbal supplements to detoxify the system. But don't expect the FDA, the FTC, or any other government regulatory agency to tell you this. Their loyalties lie with the pharmaceutical companies and their huge profits, and not with public health. Notice, for instance, what the *Natural News* website reported on September 18, 2008: "The Federal Trade Commission (FTC) today launched 'Operation False Cures,' a coordinated scheme to censor natural cancer remedies and financially destroy companies offering them for sale. In doing so, the FTC joins the criminals at the U.S. Food and Drug Administration (FDA) who currently operate an extortion racket that works by threatening health supplement companies with legal action unless they settle with the FDA by paying them millions of dollars. Both the FTC and FDA work to protect the interests of the pharmaceutical companies by discrediting or outlawing competing natural cures that work better, more safely, and more affordably than FDA-approved pharmaceuticals"(584).

Measures are underway by the U.N. to outlaw most herbal and other natural food supplement products, through things like Codex Alimentarius--a regulatory code that is intended by its globalist creators to be enforced universally. Codex is made up of thousands of standards and guidelines. One of them, the Vitamin and Mineral Guideline (VMG), is designed to only permit the sale of ultra-low doses of vitamins and minerals (and, at the same time, to make clinically-effective doses illegal). How will the VMG get away with this? By using risk assessment (toxicology) to assess the nutrient "safety levels"of a given product. The reason the globalists want to do this, aside from protecting their corporate monopolies, is best described in the following excerpt from a globalist document called *The Protocols of the Illuminati*, dating back to at least 1905: "The aristocracy, which enjoyed by law the labour of the workers, was interested in seeing that the workers were well fed, healthy and strong. We [the globalists] are interested in just the opposite--in the diminution, the killing out of the [common people]. Our power is in the chronic shortness of food and physical weakness of the worker because by all that this implies he is made the slave of our will, and he will not find in his own authorities either strength or energy to set against our will. Hunger creates the right of capital to rule the worker more surely than it was given to the aristocracy by the legal authority of kings"(276).

Should present trends continue, we will soon be reduced to under-fed, malnutritioned slaves who are overworked and underpaid (indeed, we're almost there now!).

"If people let the government decide what foods they eat and what medicines they take, their bodies will soon be in as sorry a state as are the souls of those who live under tyranny." - Thomas Jefferson.

- Many parents have been finding it more and more difficult to feed their families, with the cost of food going through the roof. One of the main reasons for such high food costs is the fact that the government, on behalf of the major monopolistic food companies who desire to keep their stock holders happy, has been forcing farmers for years to destroy millions of tons of produce in order to keep food costs artificially high. This same practice is quite common all throughout Europe as well [Endnote 123].

Essentially the same thing was done by F.D.R. through his May 12, 1933 Agricultural Adjustment Act, which dictated what a farmer could and could not produce, and how much he could produce--all on behalf of Wall Street.

By the way, what do you think the so-called "energy crises" of the 1970s were all about? At the end of both of them (one in 1973-'74 and the other in 1978-'79), the massive increases in the cost of oil and gas didn't drop one red cent. Nothing like a good "crisis" to boost profits!

As far as the 1973-1974 "energy crisis" goes, the Yom Kippur War of October 6, 1973, has been cited as its cause. Thus the impression most people have is that this energy crisis was unavoidable. However, what many don't realize is that this war was staged. It probably would never have happened except for the fact that, despite the threat of an imminent Arab attack, the Israelis withdrew a significant number of troops from forward positions. In other words, their guard was deliberately let down so that the Arabs would be enticed to attack. Why would the Israelis do this? Because Henry Kissinger, who at the time was serving as both Secretary of State and National Security Advisor, had assured them that the U.S. would support them with an enormous supply of advanced weaponry, to drive out the Arab invaders should they attack, which is exactly what wound up happening(486, p. 234).

This whole plan was orchestrated at the May 1973 Bilderberg meetings in Saltsjobaden, Sweden. At these meetings, a 400% increase in OPEC petroleum revenues was called for over the following decade, which is just about how much oil prices had risen by the early 1980s. Kissinger, of course, played a key role in these Bilderberg meetings, and was probably the mastermind behind the entire plot(488, pp. 130-138).

Not so surprisingly, in early 1980, British journalist David Frost interviewed the Shah of Iran, who said that it was through tremendous pressure from David Rockefeller and Henry Kissinger that Iran and other OPEC nations had significantly increased the price of oil between 1973 and 1974(486, p. 236).

One of the most incredibly pathetic ironies behind the globalists staging phony oil crises is the fact that the United States doesn't even need to rely on foreign oil suppliers--we have plenty enough petroleum right here to independently supply us for a long time. In a December 1972 report, the National Petroleum Council estimated that there were 810.4 billion barrels of oil within U.S. borders, enough to supply this country for at least 125 years. This same report said that the U.S. also has at least a 100-years supply of natural gas under its soil (see also *U.S. News and World Report*, December 2, 1973).

But here's a far more alarming point to ponder: We don't even need to rely on oil (or natural gas) at all for energy. There are plenty enough alternative energy sources (solar, nuclear, wind, etc.), which could do the job just as effectively and even more cheaply. Yet the government has made very little attempt to switch us over to any alternative energy source. The reason for this is obvious--keeping us dependent on oil allows the globalists to maximize their profits by citing its alleged scarcity as an excuse to jack its cost through the roof.

The reason that U.S. oil reserves (particularly in Alaska) are not tapped, and why we aren't told about how much we actually do have, is because, first of all, the globalists already own it. They want to hoard it for future generations of their greedy offspring to exploit. Second of all, if the market was ever flooded with all the oil under U.S. soil, the price would obviously be driven down. And that, my friend, simply will not be allowed to happen.

The massive hike in gas and oil prices that began in late 2005 and peaked in the summer of 2008, as you might guess, was also a colossal fraud. The claim was made that the old problem of "supply and demand" was the cause of this crisis, or else a lack of refineries. But all of this was nothing but pure rhetoric. Speaking on this situation, the November 28, 2005 edition of the UK's *Daily Mail* reported: "An urgent inquiry has been ordered into the gas supply crisis.

"It will focus on claims that major suppliers are rigging the market to inflate prices and boost their profits.

"Wholesale prices have soared in recent weeks, driven by panic over possible shortages and forecasts of a cold winter"(518).

All the while they were claiming "shortages" in oil refineries, companies like Exxon-Mobil were showing record-high profits during this crisis. And where was the government to stop this monopoly? Well, when we realize that Bush Jr., Dick Cheney (his vice president), and several other administration officials had the bulk of their investments in the oil industry, that should answer the question right there.

To further show what a scam the high oil prices were that arose under

Bush Jr.'s watch, notice what Reuters reported on May 10, 2006: "While U.S. consumers struggle with soaring energy prices, Venezuela's gas is now the world's cheapest at 12 cents a gallon and Washington's regional foe, President Hugo Chavez, vows to maintain subsidies that keep fuel dirt-cheap"(524)[Endnote 124].

- Nowadays we can't even start our own retirement fund without parasitic and despotic government intervention, which dictates, through the IRS, whether we can open an IRA in the first place (through earned income or compensation requirements), how much we can contribute each year, when we can make a withdrawal without incurring a "penalty," and how much we can withdraw. This is outrageous!

- The Bank Secrecy Act of 1986 required banks and other financial institutions to report all financial transactions of $10,000 or more, or a combination of transactions over several days that totaled to this amount, to the IRS (the amount has since been lowered to $3,000, and there is talk of it dropping to as low as $500). And all of this is done without the knowledge or consent of the customer. The reason for this is obvious--the IRS needs help in finding new victims for its harassing audits.

- Today's civil asset forfeiture "laws" have given government agencies such as the FBI, FDA, DEA, the Coast Guard, the Securities and Exchange Commission, the Bureau of Land Management, the Department of Housing--even local police departments--the power to seize the homes, cars, boats, cash, etc., of people who merely "look suspicious" or are "suspected" of being involved in an illegal activity. Worse yet, the new asset forfeiture laws actually allow the seizing agency to keep the booty for supplementary funding, even in the absence of proof of guilt of any wrong-doing.

Only about 20% of the victims of these seizures, by the way, are actually arrested or charged with any crime. But regardless whether they are arrested, or charged with any crime, or neither, the burden is left with them to prove their innocence in court, should they have any hope of retrieving their assets (if they can even afford such proceedings).

Actually, what they really need to prove is the innocence of their assets, since it is their assets alone that usually get "arrested." This is no exaggeration. Examples of such cases that have gone to court (because the victims could actually afford the proceedings) include: United States vs. $405,089.23 U.S. Currency, United States vs. 92 Buena Vista Avenue, and United States vs. One Mercedes 560 SEL. So let's remember the new rule for asset justice: "Guilty until proven innocent."

One family had their property seized because a neighborhood kid used their backyard as a meeting place to make a drug deal.

A small business was "legally" looted because a phone on the premises was used by an employee to solicit a prostitute.

Another person lost $5,000 (his vacation spending money) because police dogs detected cocaine residue on it (cocaine residue is commonly found on money, as addicts often roll up bills to use them as straws for snorting the drug)(313).

So, as you can see, the door is wide open for seizing anything from anyone at any time, and under any pretext. Such abuses happen far more frequently than you may care to know, without the victims being guilty of anything except having in their possession something that some government thug had his eyes on. Forget the 5th Amendment which states that private property shall not "be taken for public use without just compensation," and the 14th Amendment which states, "nor shall any State deprive any person of life, liberty, or property, without due process of law." What we are seeing happening here is the fulfillment of the age-old globalist dream of ultimately stealing everything from the public. As a famous socialist author, Jack London, stated back in 1906: "I believe in...striking between the eyes. There are seven million men, all fighting with hard hands and strong arms, who are ready for the conquest of the wealth of the world and the complete overthrow of existing society. We of the revolution which is at hand want all you possess. We want the power of government to our own strong hands. We are going to take all you have away from you"(351).

- Another serious crime being committed against U.S. citizens by "law enforcement" today is the practice of "entrapment"--literally creating criminals out of law-abiding citizens. For example, many police departments across the country have used undercover female police officers to pose as prostitutes and petition passer-bys on the street to employ their services. Often it happens that these "prostitutes" refuse to take no for an answer, relentlessly pursuing their victims with enticing body language, in order to ensure a catch. On the occasion that the target person finally gives in to temptation and accepts the offer, several armed police officers suddenly emerge from hiding and arrest their unsuspecting prey. Aside from the sheer thrill that such power-trip games provide for the unscrupulous law enforcers who play them, there's a far grander scheme behind these criminal-creating exercises, which the following quotes will reveal:

"In order to cut costs, states have increasingly contracted out to private firms the management of [prison] facilities....As a result, incarceration has become one of

the fastest growing businesses in the U.S.A., generating large profits..." - Amnesty International(159).

"To be profitable, private prison firms must ensure that prisons are not only built but also filled. Industry experts say a 90 to 95 percent capacity rate is needed to guarantee the hefty rates of return needed to lure investors....The private prison business is most entrenched at the state level but is expanding into the federal prison system as well." - CounterPunch(160).

"Some of the country's largest and most profitable corporations have quietly begun to use prison labor forces, at wages up to 80% below the national minimum wage. Among those reportedly contracted to employ prisoners, either directly or through their subsidiaries: AT&T, Bank of America, Boeing, Chevron, Costco, Dell Computers, Eddie Bauer, IBM, Konica Business Machines, Microsoft, Starbucks, Texas Instruments, TWA, and US West." - Michael Moore(161).

A point of great interest here is the fact that the U.S. has only 5% of the world's total population, yet it has 25% of the world's prisoners.

And here's another significant point: During the decade of the 1990s, crime rates around the country dropped by a whopping 40%, according to a study conducted by the University of California at Berkeley(585). Yet, at the same time, the national prison population dramatically increased. According to the February 29, 2008 *Washington Post*: "...the nationwide prison population swelled by about 80 percent from 1990 to 2000, increasing by as much as 86,000 a year"(586). Obviously something is seriously wrong here, wouldn't you say?

- In the name of the so-called "war on drugs," law enforcement officers at all levels of government have been conducting heavily-armed sweep searches in neighborhoods across the country (an example of which we have looked at in the "What next?" section of this study), often without search warrants, and often raiding homes without any evidence that the occupants had been involved in illegal drug dealing or use (such homes usually get raided either because of a false "hot tip" that isn't followed up on first, or because they happen to be in the path of a sweep). There have even been cases where innocent victims of these illegal searches have been killed, either from cardiac arrest or from being shot by eager-for-action "law enforcement" officers who "thought" they saw a gun drawn.

· The "war on drugs," incidentally, has been a fraud from the very outset. Despite all the money and man power that have been invested in this "war," there are more illegal drugs and more drug addicts in this country today than there ever were before this "war" began. And do you know why? Many competent researchers, such as former LAPD narcotics investigator Mike Ruppert, have meticulously documented the fact that the CIA has been running the biggest drug smuggling operation in the U.S. (mostly cocaine and heroine) since the 1950s.

So how does the CIA pull this off? That's simple--this agency is absolutely untouchable. There is essentially no government branch that oversees or overawes it (Congress is supposed to do both, but almost never does--either from fear or from favor, and thus being involved in covering up the CIA's tracks). On the few occasions that Congress has called the CIA to task, the CIA has always been able to pull out the old "It's a matter of national security" trump card to drive away troublesome, prying inquiries.

Nevertheless, Congress has, at times, made some damning, albeit rather non-specific, statements about some of the dark activities of the CIA. For instance, the House Intelligence Committee reported back in 1996 that "The CS [Clandestine Service of the CIA] is the only part of the IC [Intelligence Community], indeed of the government, where hundreds of employees on a daily basis are directed to break extremely serious laws in countries around the world [including the U.S.]. A safe estimate is that several hundred times every day DO [Directorate of Operations] officers engage in highly illegal activities"(162, p. 205).

Rest assured that one of these "highly illegal activities"--a big one--is drug trafficking. Not mincing words like the above-cited congressional report, Michael Levine, a former agent with the DEA (Drug Enforcement Agency), stated back in 1996: "I have put thousands of Americans away for tens of thousands of years...with less evidence than is available against Ollie North and CIA people....I personally was involved in a deep-cover case that went to the top of the drug world in three countries. The CIA killed it"(352).

Most of the people arrested in the "war on drugs" are "small-time" local dealers. These arrests give the American public, as well as the bulk of law enforcement officers (who do not know what is going on), the false impression that the drug problem in this country is being handled aggressively. Yet the drugs keep pouring into the country, creating a whole new "generation" of dealers to be arrested, which helps, of course, to advance the interests of the profit-driven prison industry. And the harder these local dealers are pursued, the higher the drug profits are for the CIA, since each arrest drives up the street value of the narcotics. On the occasion that foreign suppliers are busted by the CIA, this is only because they are presenting a competitive threat to the CIA's market, or because they are no longer cooperating with the CIA as loyal "business partners." (Remember Manuel Noriega?)

The motive behind the CIA's drug trade operation is not just money. It's also about drugging up and dumbing down the population, especially the youth, who fight the government's phony wars. Keeping people on drugs (whether they be labeled "legal" or "illegal") is seen as highly beneficial to the cause of the globalists, since drugs serve as great "pacifiers" that help numb people to the effects of their economic and political oppression.

- Nobody really has any "right to privacy" any longer. The government (or anyone else, for that matter), at any time, particularly through the use of computers, can find out anything about our private lives, such as our medical history, financial transactions, educational background, e-mail correspondences-- you name it.

There are many frightening ways in which the government has been spying on us. Another method kicked into high gear in late 1999, when a satellite surveillance system called Echelon, originally created in the 1970s, was upgraded and put into full operation. Run by the National Security Agency, along with the governments of the United Kingdom, Australia, New Zealand, and Canada, this technologically-advanced spy network scans millions of telephone calls, e-mails, and faxes each hour, searching for key words. Obviously our globalist friends are a bit paranoid, wanting to know who might pose a threat to their quest for power(423).

Bearing this program in mind, observe what Zbigniew Brzezinski wrote in the 1976 edition of his book *Between Two Ages*: "[T]he capacity to assert social and political control over the individual will vastly increase. It will soon be possible to assert almost continuous control over every citizen and to maintain up-to-date files, containing even the most personal details about health and personal behavior of every citizen in addition to the more customary data. These files will be subject to instantaneous retrieval by the authorities. Power will gravitate into the hands of those who control information"(49).

Unfortunately, Brzezinski was correct about where our right to privacy was headed. During a documentary program called "Big Brother," first aired on the Discovery Channel on June 8, 1999, as part of a series titled *On the Inside*, the following sobering observations were made: "As we enter a new millennium, rapid improvements in technology are quickly eroding the privacy and freedoms we've taken for granted for so long.

"To better identify us, more and more of our most intimate details will be captured and catalogued. The nightmare world of 'Big Brother' is creeping up on us--a world where surveillance by the state is the norm, where 'Big Brother' can peer into our homes and our workplaces.

"New surveillance technologies are bringing us closer to a time when our movements are tracked, when we will no longer have any secrets, where there will be no borders, where there will be no place to be free. We are coming to the end of privacy."

Another way in which our right to privacy is being violated is through the installation of surveillance cameras in multitudes of locations around the country--banks, toll booths, public arenas, atop light posts on state highways, etc. Would you call this freedom?

The Echelon system described above, as bad as it is, was far surpassed by the snooping powers seized by the Bush Jr. administration, in the wake of the 9-11 terrorist attacks. One such provision, in particular, was the creation of the Total Information Awareness (TIA) program, which operated under the Pentagon's Defense Advanced Research Projects Agency (DARPA). The *New York Times* described this frightening program in these words: "Every purchase you make with a credit card, every magazine subscription you buy and medical prescription you fill, every Web site you visit and e-mail you send or receive, every academic grade you receive, every bank deposit you make, every trip you book and every event you attend--all these transactions and communications will go into what the Defense Department describes as 'a virtual, centralized grand database.'

"To this computerized dossier on your private life from commercial sources, add every piece of information that government has about you--passport application, driver's license and bridge toll records, judicial and divorce records, complaints from nosy neighbors to the F.B.I., and you have the supersnoop's dream: a 'Total Information Awareness' about every U.S. citizen"(163).

Understandably, many civil rights groups protested this program. One complaint that they voiced involved a very interesting symbol that the TIA office initially posted on its website to represent its mission. Speaking on this matter, James Bovard wrote: "DARPA...responded to the surge of criticism by removing the Information Awareness Office logo from the [its own] website. The logo--a giant eye sitting atop a pyramid [the same Masonic image depicted on the back of a one dollar bill, which we discussed earlier], seeing and pulling in the entire world, accompanied by the motto *Scientia est Potentia* (Knowledge is Power)--made some malcontents fear TIA intended to play God"(164, p. 159)[Endnote 125].

Senator Frank Church really knew what he was talking about when he warned of the intelligence community's ability to monitor all forms of communication, and that if not stopped, "There would be no place to hide. If the government ever becomes a tyranny, if a dictator ever took charge in this country, the technological capacity that the intelligence community has given the government could enable it to impose total tyranny, and there would be no way to fight back...."

"[T]he capacity that is there to make tyranny total in America [is enormous] and we must see to it that [the intelligence agencies] that possess this technology operate within the law and under proper supervision, so that we never cross over that abyss. That is the abyss from which there is no return"(254).

The intelligence community had already proven itself untrustworthy (and that's putting it mildly) because of its many pre-9-11 abuses of power. But since 9-11, the power of the intelligence community has been dramatically increased, creating a much higher potential for abuse. Do you not see what a serious situation this is?

And what's even more troubling is the fact that Bush Jr., who pushed so vigorously to make our lives an open book for the scrutinizing eyes of Big Brother government, took measures, at the same time, to ensure that the skeletons in his own closet (and there are many!), as well as the skeletons in the closets of other presidents, never be made available for public view. For example, on November 1, 2001, he issued an executive order (#13233) allowing presidents to bar the release of records covered by the Presidential Records Act under the following grounds: "military, diplomatic, or national security secrets, presidential communications, legal advice, legal work or the deliberative processes of the president and the president's advisors"(358).

Former presidents used to be able to request that their papers remain secret. Now they can ORDER that their papers remain secret. This is pure totalitarianism!

- Parents can't even spank their children out of discipline anymore in this country, without the fear of having them taken away by the Social Services gestapo, under the pretext of saving them from "abuse."

But it's not just for spanking that parents have had their children abducted by child welfare agencies--there are other reasons that have been used for such legalized kidnapings, which are even more ridiculous. Here are a few notable examples: inadequate finances, homeschooling, domestic disputes (a neighbor-- especially one that doesn't like you--can call the police because of an overheard spousal argument, and make the case that you and your spouse are "unfit parents," which has been a leading cause of state-sponsored child abductions around the country), bruises noticed on your child by a teacher at school, refusing to allow your child to be put on "behavioral medication" like Ritalin, etc.

So what's the real agenda behind this fiasco? Aside from the obvious "power grab" factor, child-snatching at the hand of the state has become quite a lucrative business for the social services "industry." For every child taken, "child protection" agencies can get between $25,000 and $250,000 from the federal government per year (the federal government pays $3 for every dollar a state pays to support such children in its custody).

It's gotten so out of hand that every child in the U.S. today has a one-in-twenty-five chance of being taken from his/her parents (about 3,000 kids are taken by state agencies around the country every day, and 70% of these kids are taken from parents who have never abused them or neglected them in any way).

And, even more sickening, children placed in state custody are two to three times more likely to be abused than if left in their homes. So bad is the abuse, in fact, that roughly thirty children die while in state care each year. Many others are victimized by beatings, shakings, scaldings, maimings, deprivations, and sexual abuse. Some states, like Florida, can't even keep track of how many kids they have in custody, or of where they have all been sent(531).

Sometimes children in state custody are put up for adoption while their parents are being led to believe that they will get their kids back if they "cooperate," which usually involves "confessing" to something they aren't guilty of, and then signing up for "psychological help" from the state. Often their children are allowed periodic weekend visits at home, but only in the company of a social worker who is present in the home AT ALL TIMES, watching EVERY MOVE the parents make. If the social worker doesn't like the parents, he/she can write them up for ANYTHING that can be twisted to give the impression that they don't deserve to get their kids back.

While it is true that some parents do abuse their children, requiring some type of intervention, it's obvious that the child welfare system is completely out of control, and that it does not operate in the interests, or rarely operates in the interests, of the children and families it is supposed to be "serving" [Endnote 126].

- Whereas U.S. citizens have traditionally enjoyed the right to pursue legal action in a court of law against anyone or any group that they felt had wronged them, this is now no longer an option for most Americans. As legal fees have risen over the years, nearly everyone has been craftily robbed of this right. This has helped, of course, to ensure that the power of our oppressors, who have rigged the system, will remain unchecked.

Actually, today the globalists run our court system anyway, so that it really doesn't even matter anymore whether or not "we the people" can afford legal fees. As Gerry Spence put it: "[T]he rights of the people...exist mostly in myth....[T]rials have become mere window dressing and mockeries of justice"(58, p. 104).

To demonstrate just how far we have strayed from the constitutional ideal of a fair judicial system, we only need look at the Military Commissions Act of 2006. This gruesome piece of medieval-type legislation grants absolute dictatorial powers to the president, which render the Constitution and the Geneva Conventions totally null and void. The September 28, 2006 *New York Times* stated that this law gives the president "the power to jail pretty much anyone he wants for as long as he wants without charging them, to unilaterally reinterpret the Geneva Conventions, to authorize what normal people consider torture, and to deny justice to hundreds of men captured in error."

Elaborating on some of the biggest problems with this legislation, the *New York Times* continued: "Enemy Combatants: A dangerously broad definition of 'illegal enemy combatant'...subject[s] legal residents of the United States, as well as foreign citizens living in their own countries, to summary arrest and indefinite detention with no hope of appeal. The president could give the power to apply this label to anyone he wanted [including U.S. citizens].

"The Geneva Conventions: [This law] repudiate[s] a half-century of international precedent by allowing Mr. Bush [or any other president] to decide on his own what abusive interrogation methods he considered permissible. And his decision could stay secret--there's no requirement that this list be published.

"Habeas Corpus: Detainees in U.S. military prisons would lose the basic right to challenge their imprisonment....

"Judicial Review: The courts...have no power to review any aspect of this new system, except verdicts by military tribunals. The [law]...limit[s] appeals and bar[s] legal actions based on the Geneva Conventions, directly or indirectly. All Mr. Bush would have to do to lock anyone up forever is to declare him an illegal combatant and not have a trial.

"Coerced Evidence: Coerced evidence would be permissible if a judge considered it reliable--already a contradiction in terms--and relevant. Coercion is defined in a way that exempts anything done before the passage of the 2005 Detainee Treatment Act, and anything else Mr. Bush chooses.

"Secret Evidence: American standards of justice prohibit evidence and testimony that is kept secret from the defendant, whether the accused is a corporate executive or a mass murderer. But [this law] seems to weaken protections against such evidence.

"Offenses: The definition of torture is unacceptably narrow, a virtual reprise of the deeply cynical memos the administration produced after 9/11. Rape and sexual assault are defined in a retrograde way that covers only forced or coerced activity, and not other forms of nonconsensual sex. [This law] effectively eliminate[s] the idea of rape as torture"(553).

On September 17, 2006, when Bush signed this legal chicanery, Keith Olbermann of MSNBC had this to say about it: "[O]n this first full day that the Military Commissions Act is in force, we now face what our ancestors faced, at other times of exaggerated crisis and melodramatic fear-mongering: A government more dangerous to our liberty, than is the enemy it claims to protect us from."

* * * * * * *

Clearly, our rights and freedoms are going out the window. And as time continues, it's obvious that things are only going to get worse. Today we are paying a high price (in more ways than one) for forgetting, as Thomas Jefferson said, that "a government governs best which governs least." This "land of the free and home of the brave" of ours is rapidly becoming the land of the fee and home of the slave. As James Madison once said: "I believe there are more instances of the abridgment of freedom of the people by gradual and silent encroachments of those in power than by violent and sudden usurpations."

Every year in this country, hundreds of new laws and regulations are passed that further restrict our rights and freedoms. Most of these laws and regulations, particularly at the federal level, are pushed for and paid for (through generous campaign contributions--bribe money), if and whenever such pushes and briberies are necessary, by lobbyists acting on behalf of their Wall Street globalist masters, who benefit money-wise and power-wise from these "political favors."

Notice the relevant warning George Washington gave us in his farewell address of September 17, 1796: "[C]ombinations and associations...are likely in the course of time...to become potent enemies by which cunning, ambitious, and unprincipled men will be able to subvert the power of the people and usurp for themselves the reins of government....One method of assault may be to effect in the forms of the Constitution alteration which will impair the energy of the system, and thus to undermine what cannot be directly overthrown" [Endnote 127].

* * * * * * *

"There is no crueler tyranny than that which is exercised under cover of law, and with the colors of justice..." - United States vs. Jenottie, 1982.

"In questions of power...let no more be heard of confidence in man, but bind him down from mischief by the chains of the Constitution." -Thomas Jefferson, Kentucky Resolutions, 1798.

Appendix 6

The NEA: sabotaging education

Reader's Digest, back in 1984, revealed that the NEA had been wreaking tremendous havoc on education, when it carried an article entitled "Guess Who Spells DISASTER for Education?" by Eugene H. Methvin. In this article, the answer to the question posed by the article's title was given in these words: "[N]one other than the powerful National Education Association, as it plays politics and fights to block much-needed reform in our nation's schools."

And how exactly does the NEA spell disaster for education? Professor Chester E. Finn Jr. of Vanderbilt University, after carefully examining the NEA's publications, had concluded that its agenda is driven by a "cohesive radical strategy [which]...includes the delegitimizing of all authority, save that of the state, the degradation of traditional morality, and the encouragement of citizens in general and children in particular to despise [traditional] rules and customs....The NEA is drifting into exceedingly dangerous waters, and probably carrying more than a few teachers and pupils with it"(149, p. 22).

The NEA knows exactly what it is doing, and it is doing it most effectively. Its main aim is to destroy the morals and family loyalties of our youth, in order to make them more easily moldable. This philosophy was graphically illustrated in the book *The Temporary Society: Under the Impact of Accelerating Change*, which stated: "One cannot permit submission to parental authority if one wishes to bring about profound social change....In order to effect rapid changes, any...centralized regime must mount a vigorous attack on the family lest the traditions of present generations be preserved. It is necessary, in other words,...to create...[a] chasm between parents and children to insulate the latter in order that they can more easily be indoctrinated with new ideas. The desire may be to cause an even more total submission to the state....One must teach them not to respect their tradition-bound elders, who are tied to the past and know only what is irrelevant"(222, p. 31)[Endnote 128].

The NEA actually spells disaster for education in many different ways. Let us now look at a quote from an NEA report entitled "Education for the 70s," to show how other major problems with so-called "public education" today had originated with the NEA, which planned these things decades ago: "Schools will become clinics whose purpose is to provide individualized, psycho-social treatment for the student, and teachers must become psycho-social therapists. This will include biochemical and psychological mediation of learning, as drugs are introduced experimentally to improve in the learner such qualities as personality, concentration and memory. Children are to become objects of experimentation"(107, p. 24).

Drugs? Experimentation? [Endnote 129] Does the word Ritalin ring a bell? Do understand that everything in this last quote has already been implemented. The NEA has truly been quite busy.

In regards to "psycho-social therapy" and "psychological mediation" being used in the "education" process, notice what globalist Bertrand Russell wrote back in 1953, in his book *The Impact of Science on Society*: "It is to be expected that advances in psychology will give governments much more control over individual mentality than they now have....

"Education should aim at destroying free will, so that, after pupils have left school they shall be incapable, throughout the rest of their lives, of thinking or acting otherwise than as their school master would have wished....

"[Students should be directed] from a very early age to produce the sort of character and the sort of beliefs that the authorities consider desirable,...[thus] serious criticism of the powers that be will become psychologically impossible....

"I think the subject which will be of most importance politically is mass psychology....Although this science will be diligently studied, it will be rigidly confined to the governing class. The populace will not be allowed to know how its convictions were generated. When the technique has been perfected, every government that has been in charge of education for a generation will be able to control its subjects secretly without the need of armies or policemen....Educational propaganda, with government help, could achieve this result in a generation"(154).

In case you are unaware of just how accurately the last two quotes describe what is going on in education today, take notice of the proceeding quotes, which clearly reveal that the modern focus of education is not so much on teaching facts and information, but on behavior, thought, and attitude modification (through advanced psychological manipulation techniques, of course):

- "[T]he purpose of education and the schools is to change the thoughts, feelings and actions of students." - Benjamin Bloom, a "founding father" of Outcome-Based Education(223, p. 180).

- "The basic goal of education is change--human change--in desirable directions. This issue...focuses attention upon the school as a change agent..." - Harold Drummon, former president of ASCD--Association for Supervision and Curriculum Development(224).

- "We know we can modify human behavior. We're not scared of that. This is the biggest thing that's happening in education today." - James Guines, former Associate School Superintendent for Washington, D.C.(225).

- "[E]ducation should aim not so much at acquisition of knowledge....[Today] there is less need to know the content of information....[There should be a] transformation of life in its totality." - *Foundations of Lifelong Learning*, a 1976 UNESCO publication(107, p. 30).

- "[A] large part of what we call 'good teaching' is the teacher's ability to attain effective objectives through challenging the student's fixed beliefs." - *Taxonomy of Educational Objectives*(226, p. 55).

- "A revolutionary organizer must...agitate, create disenchantment and discontent with the current values to produce a passion for change" [Endnote 130]. - Saul Alinsky (former trainer of NEA staff members), *Rules for Radicals*, 1971.

A typical example of mind manipulation in "education" today is when students are given "reflection questions" with hidden agendas, usually found at the end of an article in a textbook or other scholastic publication. After reading an article on, say, the dropping of the atomic bomb on Hiroshima, students might be asked, "Do you think it's acceptable, under extreme conditions, to give military orders that you know could potentially cost tens of thousands of innocent lives?" or, "How would you justify dropping the atomic bomb, knowing how it would most likely kill and maim many civilians?" or even, "Do you think it is always wrong to kill?" Such questions as these are designed to craftily alter students' perceptions of morality, and have absolutely nothing to do with educating them.

Here's another example of this type of mind manipulation: Perhaps an article on the German conquest of France in 1871 might be assigned, with reflection questions such as, "What does Germany's desire for expanding its power say about the hazards of national sovereignty?" or, "Can you name some examples of how nations abuse their sovereignty today?" or even, "Can you think of some good arguments against modern national sovereignty?" Questions like these are used as lead-ins to discussions about the U.N.

Can't you see how kids' minds are being diabolically toyed with through these types of questions? Very often, to be sure that the desired response is achieved, teacher's manuals will instruct teachers to break the class up into four or five groups, each containing four to five students. The instructions then call for the students to arrange their desks so as to face one another in a circle (cooperative learning), after which time they are to discuss the reflection questions until they can reach a "consensus." This puts tremendous pressure on any potential "nonconformist" or independently-thinking student to change his/her opinion on a matter, in order to meet with the approval of the rest of the group. This pressure becomes all the more intense when, as is often the case, it is told to the class that each group will be assigned a collective grade for the exercise. The result of all of this is nothing but pure brainwashing and mind control.

These mental manipulation classroom exercises, and others like them, are the culmination of decades of research and development of psychological programs. They were actually in use back in the early 1970s, as can be seen from a September 1971 *Psychology Today* article entitled "Persuasion That Persists," written by Milton Rokeach, which stated: "Suppose you could take a group of people, give them a twenty-minute pencil-and-paper task, talk to them for ten or twenty minutes afterward, and thereby produce long-range changes in core values and personal behavior in a significant portion of this group. For openers, it would of course have major implications for education, government, propaganda, and therapy....My colleagues and I have in the last five years achieved the[se] kinds of results....It now seems to be within man's power to alter...another person's values, and to control the direction of the change"(112, p. 115).

The next few quotes will hopefully serve as powerful "smelling salts" to further assist in the task of waking up the reader to what is really going on in our schools:

- "The simple truth is American classrooms have become places where intense psychological warfare is being waged against all traditional values. A child in America is little more than a guinea pig in a psych lab, manipulated by a change agent. All of this is being done with billions of federal dollars in the greatest scam in human history. If Americans put up with it much longer they will deserve the ruin they are paying for." - *N.E.A.: Trojan Horse in American Education*(231).

- "The techniques of brainwashing developed in totalitarian countries are routinely used in psychological conditioning programs imposed on American school-children. These include emotional shock and desensitization,...stripping away defenses, manipulative cross-examination of the individual's underlying moral values, and inducing acceptance of alternative values by psychological rather than by rational means." - *Forbes*(232).

- In 1974, the U.S. Senate Judiciary Committee presented the document *Individual Rights and the Federal Role in Behavior Modification: Report of the*

201

Subcommittee on Constitutional Rights, in which it was stated that "Technology has begun to develop new methods of behavior control capable of altering not just an individual's actions but his very personality and manner of thinking as well. Because it affects the ability of the individual to think for himself, the behavioral technology being developed in the United States today touches upon the most basic sources of individuality, and the very core of personal freedom"(112, pp. 120, 121).

And what is the ultimate agenda behind all of these mind games in education? It's the same agenda that lies behind all globalist endeavors--the advancement of world government, as the next couple quotes will clarify:

- "[A] new world order is necessary if we are to live in harmony with each other....The task of reordering our traditional values and institutions should be one of the major educational objectives of our schools." - *Global Mandate: Pedagogy for Peace*(228).

- "Enlightened social engineering is required to face situations that demand global action now....Parents and the general public must be reached also, otherwise, children and youth enrolled in globally oriented programs may find themselves in conflict with values assumed in the home. And then the educational institution frequently comes under scrutiny and must pull back." - *Schooling for a Global Age*(229, pp. xxiii, xvii).

It is important to point out that most teachers are completely unaware that they are taking part in the manipulation of their student's minds. But the truth is that they don't need to be aware of it in order for it to happen. The way that they are instructed to teach, the manner in which most curricula are set up, the way that the pre-written tests are designed, and the manner in which the textbooks are written automatically ensure that such mind manipulations will take place, with or without the teacher's knowledge or consent (not to mention that of the parents and the students themselves).

In addition to this, teachers are required to declare a "behavioral objective" for each lesson plan they write up. Few teachers stop to ask what this really means. But just by being exposed to this term on a daily basis, they are becoming conditioned to accept their individual roles as behavior modifiers, or "change agents."

Though most teachers can't be blamed for what is going on, many of them have been enticed over the years by various globalist, teacher-oriented publications, which have encouraged them to take hold of the reins of power and assume roles for themselves that are not their place to assume. Here's one such example of what teachers are being told: "[T]he teachers should reach for power and then make the most of their conquest....To the extent that they are allowed to fashion the curriculum and procedures of the schools they will definitely and positively influence the social attitudes, ideals and behavior of the coming generation." - Dr. George Sylvester Counts, *Dare the School Build a New Social Order?*(327)

As you might expect, all that has been said herein about the NEA also holds true for the AFT (American Federation of Teachers), which is globalist-controlled as well. And it is significant to bear in mind that both of these powerful teacher unions are aggressively politically active and, naturally, they both have the same anti-constitutional bias, just like their globalist propaganda counterparts, the media, as we discussed earlier.

* * * * * * *

"Nations that stick to stale old notions and ideologies will falter and fail. So I'm here today to say, America will move forward....New schools for a new world....Reinvent--literally start from scratch and reinvent the American school....Our challenge amounts to nothing less than a revolution in American education." - President George Bush Sr.(230)

Appendix 7

A brief history of U.S. government-rigged crises (Hegelian Dialectic), with a special emphasis on 9-11 and its aftermath

The U.S. government has been well-acquainted with the Hegelian Dialectic process for a long time--planning foreign and domestic crises in order to manipulate the public, although such plans have not always been put into action. One good example of this is found in this next quote: "According to secret and long-hidden documents...the Joint Chiefs of Staff drew up and approved plans for what may be the most corrupt plan ever created by the US government. In the name of anticommunism, they proposed launching a secret and bloody war of terrorism against their own country in order to trick the American public into supporting an ill-conceived war they intended to launch against Cuba. Codenamed Operation Northwoods, the plan, which had the written approval of the Chairman and every member of the Joint Chiefs of Staff, called for innocent people to be shot on American streets; for boats carrying refugees fleeing Cuba to be sunk on the high seas; for a wave of violent terrorism to be launched in Washington, DC, Miami, and elsewhere. People would be framed for bombings they did not commit; planes would be hijacked. Using phony evidence, all of it would be blamed on Castro, thus giving [Joint Chiefs Chairman Lyman] Lemnitzer and his cabal the excuse, as well as the public and international backing, they needed to launch their war." - James Bamford, *Body of Secrets*(233, p. 82). The only reason why this plot was not carried out was that Kennedy forbade it.

Not necessarily does the Hegelian Dialectic involve the direct planning or carrying out of a crisis. Sometimes it merely involves allowing an impending crisis to occur, or else instigating one. For instance, in order to gain public support for entrance into WW I, the U.S. government, in cooperation with the British government, arranged treacherous setups for several passenger and merchant ships. These ships were stocked up, before leaving U.S. harbors, and before being boarded by passengers and crews, with military supplies bound for England and France. They were then sent off on a course that deliberately took them into dangerous waters where many of them were sunk by German U-boats. (Most notably of these was the Lusitania, with 1,198 passengers, 128 of which were U.S. citizens.) And all the while that this was being done, the U.S. was claiming to be neutral in this war.

As the Germans began to torpedo these non-combatant vessels, the U.S. anti-German propaganda machine started demonizing the Germans as vile enemies that needed to be destroyed. In time, the staunchly pacifist/isolationist

American public, viewing the infamous Zimmermann Telegraphs as the final straw, at last agreed to enter the war. Notice what Winston Churchill, who at that time was First Lord of the Admiralty, had written in this regard: "The first British countermove, made on my responsibility,...was to deter the Germans from surface attack. The submerged U-boat had to rely increasingly on underwater attack and thus ran the greater risk of mistaking neutral for British ships and of drowning neutral crews and thus embroiling Germany with other Great Powers [i.e. the U.S.]"(234, p. 300).

The same thing took place during WW II. The U.S. government, knowing a full three days in advance that the Japanese planned to attack Pearl Harbor, having cracked their "Purple Code" at that time, allowed this disaster to happen in order to gain public support for entrance into this war.

Actually, the U.S. initially provoked Germany, in the exact same manner it had done during WW I, through Roosevelt's lend-lease plan of supplying military equipment to aid England and France against Hitler, all the while claiming, once again, as Wilson had done, to be neutral [Endnote 131]. Speaking on this matter, Churchill stated: "The President [Roosevelt]...said...he would become more and more provocative. If the Germans did not like it, they could attack American forces. Everything was to be done to force an 'incident' that could lead to war"(235).

But since Hitler wasn't adequately taking the bait, the U.S. began focusing its lend-lease program more on China, to aid in its war against Japan. At the same time, stringent trade sanctions were imposed on Japan by the U.S., demanding that the Japanese withdraw from China and Indochina if they wanted to have the sanctions lifted. These tactics, of course, proved far more effective for involving the U.S. in the war, instigating the Japanese to strike.

To demonstrate that instigating Japan was indeed the plan, consider this: After meeting with President Roosevelt on October 16, 1941, Secretary of War Henry Stimson (Skull and Bones and CFR member) wrote in his diary: "We face the delicate question of the diplomatic fencing to be done so as to be sure Japan is put into the wrong and makes the first bad move--overt move"(236, pp. 275, 276). Then, on November 25th, Stimson wrote in his diary: "The question was how we should maneuver them [the Japanese] into the position of firing the first shot...."(237, p. 76).

In further reference to the staged involvement of the U.S. in WW II, *WorldNetDaily* reported on May 20, 2005: "For those of us who have invested our time to research world events and what FDR did domestically, that man is hardly someone to admire or hold in high regard. Not only did FDR stomp on the U.S. Constitution, he wanted the Japanese to attack America while concealing his plans from the American people.

"One shouldn't believe everything they read in a book, but in the case of 'Day of Deceit: The Truth about FDR and Pearl Harbor' by Robert B. Stinnett, there can be no denying the awful truth that FDR not only knew the Japanese were going to attack, but official documents prove FDR wanted them to strike America first."

The author of this article, Dewy Kidd, then went on to make this most astonishing admission: "While I'm certain many will disagree, I don't believe the White House and our State Department did everything in their power diplomatically to garner the immense forces in Europe to stand against Hitler without war because it wasn't in the best interests of the international banking cartel who have owned Washington, D.C., since 1913 [referring to the establishment of the Federal Reserve]"(469).

As early as 1898 it appears that this crisis-creating game was being implemented by corrupt U.S. officials. On the night of February 15, 1898, a U.S. warship, the USS Maine, lying in Havana Harbor, suffered a violent explosion, killing over 250 men on board. This incident was quickly seized upon as an excuse to wage war against Spain, even though no evidence existed to show that this nation was in any way involved in this blast.

As a result of this war with Spain, the U.S. had annexed the Philippines, Puerto Rico, Guam, Hawaii, and, at least for a time, Cuba. There's your motive.

Years later, in 1976, a Congressional investigation concluded that there had been no evidence of an external cause for the explosion that started this war. Instead, said Congress, it was probably due to a coal dust explosion in a coal bunker imprudently located next to the ship's magazines. Was this event staged? If not, it was at least unwarrantedly exploited for imperialistic purposes.

Here is yet another instance where the U.S. government employed the Hegelian Dialectic: The Vietnam War shifted into high gear on August 2, 1964, when North Vietnamese torpedo boats attacked the American destroyer *Maddox* in the Gulf of Tonkin. It was also claimed that another attack was launched by North Vietnamese forces two days later. President Johnson referred to these attacks as "open aggression on the high seas," adding that "the attacks were unprovoked"(189, p. 238). But this claim later turned out to be a blatant lie. During congressional hearings four years later, Robert McNamara admitted that North Vietnam had attacked in retaliation for U.S. forces assisting South Vietnamese strikes against the North. It also came to light that the second attack in the Gulf had probably never actually occurred(239).

As it turned out, beginning in February 1964, U.S. forces had been conducting clandestine attacks on North Vietnam, including parachuting sabotage teams, commando raids, and bombings of coastal installations. The resulting Gulf of Tonkin attacks (the real one and the alleged one) had achieved the desired effect--justification for a grand-scale military engagement with North Vietnam. Johnson immediately ordered U.S. planes to bomb the north's ships and bases. He then asked Congress to pass the Gulf of Tonkin Resolution, which enabled him "to take all necessary measures to repel any armed attack against the forces of the United States and to prevent further aggression"(238, p. 606).

Can you think of any other such examples of our globalist-controlled government creating or allowing disasters to occur, in order to gain public support for war-waging schemes (amongst other things)? How about the terrorist attacks on the World Trade Center (WTC) towers and the Pentagon, on September 11, 2001?

The impression was given that the government was caught totally off guard when these attacks struck, and that everything conceivable would have been done to prevent them if it was known in advance that they were coming. However, there are some very serious problems with these claims.

For example, it's well documented that very specific details of these attacks were known a good many years ahead of time, going back to Clinton's first term. Notice what columnist Robert Novak wrote on this matter, in the September 27, 2001 issue of the *Chicago Sun Times*: "The FBI had advance indications of plans to hijack U.S. airliners and use them as weapons, but neither acted on them nor distributed the intelligence to local police agencies. From the moment of the September 11th attacks, high-ranking federal officials insisted that the terrorists' method of operation surprised them. Many stick to that story. Actually, elements of the hijacking plan were known to the FBI as early as 1995..."

So if the FBI had advance knowledge of these terrorist attacks, dating back to 1995, why didn't they follow up on it? Greg Palast, who we quoted from earlier, authored a chapter in the book *Into the Buzzsaw*, in which he pondered this same question thusly: "A simple question [about the terrorist attacks] nagged at me: not the grandly philosophical *why*? but *how*? How had the FBI, CIA, America's zillion-dollar intelligence apparatus missed this one? Over the next two months, I found a frightening answer: *They were told not to look* [italics in original]....

"Working with the *Guardian* and the National Security News Service of Washington, we got our hands on documents that...[revealed] that FBI and CIA investigations [of the bin Laden family] had been slowed by the Clinton administration, then killed by Bush Jr.'s [yes, there are SOME CIA and FBI agents who actually do the job of intelligence gathering that they're supposed to do--or at least they try to]....

"The story made the top of the news--in Britain. In the U.S., one television reporter picked up the report. He was called, he says, by network chiefs, and told to go no further. He didn't"(90, p. 75).

Bush stopped this investigation of the bin Laden family through Executive Order W199i WF213589, which actually called for the arrest of any agent that continued this investigation against orders to stop.

The Bush Jr. administration, particularly, had very specific prior knowledge of the attacks, which it did absolutely nothing about. We offer here but a few of the many sources that confirm this very upsetting revelation:

- "As of Sept. 10th, each of us knew everything we needed to know to tell us there was a possibility of what happened on Sept. 11th." - Assistant Attorney General Michael Chertoff(240).

- "They [members of the Bush administration] don't have any excuse because the information was in their lap and they didn't do anything to prevent it." - Senator Richard Shelby(241).

- "I don't believe any longer that it's a matter of connecting the dots. I think they had a veritable blueprint, and we want to know why they didn't act on it." - Senator Arlen Specter(242).

- "White House officials acknowledged last week that President Bush was provided a written briefing on August 6 [of 2001] stating that bin Laden and his followers had discussed the possibility of hijacking airplanes." - *Washington Post*, May 19, 2002.

- "Because Bush has long insisted he had no inkling of the attacks, the disclosures [that he did indeed know about them in advance] touched off a media stampede....The fact that the nation's popular war president might have been warned a little over a month before September 11 [his August 6 presidential daily briefing]--and that the supposedly straight-talking Bushites hadn't told anyone about it--opened up a serious credibility gap..." - *Newsweek*, May 27, 2002.

- On the PBS website on September 18, 2002, an article was featured with the title "U.S. Had 'Steady Stream' of Pre-9/11 Warnings." This article stated, in part: "Eleanor Hill, staff director for the joint House-Senate inquiry into alleged intelligence failures ahead of the Sept. 11 attacks, released a 30-page statement Wednesday that found information on possible terrorist strikes [that] continued to filter through the nation's intelligence system in the months directly before the attacks. Hill's report details a July 2001 briefing for senior government officials that said a review of five months of intelligence information indicated 'that [Bin

Laden] will launch a significant attack against U.S...interests in the coming weeks....The attack will be spectacular and designed to inflict mass casualties against U.S. facilities or interests'"(360).

Then there were these strange reports, and others like them, that began surfacing after 9-11, which also clearly revealed prior knowledge of the attacks:

- The September 27, 2001 London *Times* reported that Willie Brown, the Mayor of San Francisco, said he was warned by "airport security people" not to fly on September 11.

- Salman Rushdie, who for years has been a target of Muslim fundamentalists for his book *Satanic Verses*, told the same edition of the London *Times* that he was banned by the U.S. government (via the FAA), a week prior to 9-11, from flying into the U.S. or Canada on that fateful day. All that he was told was that there was "something out there." The FAA had confirmed for the London *Times* that it stepped up security prior to 9-11, but would say nothing more.

- The September 24, 2001 issue of *Newsweek* reported: "On Sep. 10th, *Newsweek* has learned, a group of top Pentagon officials suddenly canceled travel plans for the next morning, apparently because of security concerns."

- The CBS News website, on July 26, 2001, featured an article titled "Ashcroft Flying High," which reported: "In response to inquiries from CBS News over why Ashcroft was traveling exclusively by leased jet aircraft instead of commercial airlines, the Justice Department cited what it called a 'threat assessment' by the FBI, and said Ashcroft has been advised to travel only by private jet for the remainder of his term"(359).

- On June 20, 2002, the *Washington Post* revealed that the NSA (National Security Agency) had intercepted Afghani communications on September 10, 2001, regarding the upcoming attacks, but that nothing was done to follow up on this.
   After the release of this story, the White House immediately began insisting that an investigation be launched to discover who had leaked out this story at the NSA, so that he/she could be tried for treason.

- Insider stock trading took place just prior to 9-11, reflecting an obvious foreknowledge of what was coming, since this trading concerned the airlines that were involved in the attacks (and even some of the businesses that were located inside the WTC).

For example, 4,744 put options were placed on United Airlines against only 396 call options at the Chicago Board Options Exchange between September 6th and 7th. Three days later, 4,516 put options were purchased on American Airlines on the exchange and only 748 call options. This represented six times the usual number of put options, and trading in other airlines did not follow this pattern. None of the earnings from any of these trades, by the way, were ever collected.

- A FEMA rescue team "just so happened" to have been deployed in New York City the night before the attacks. On the evening of 9-11, Tom Kennedy, a FEMA official, told Dan Rather on CBS News: "We're...one of the first teams that was deployed to support the City of New York in this disaster. We arrived on late Monday night and went right into action on Tuesday morning."

The question now begs an answer: If there was indeed specific prior knowledge of the 9-11 attacks, why wasn't anything done to prevent them? Did Bush Jr.'s administration actually want these terrorist attacks to occur? To play it fair, let's allow Bush and his globalist buddies to answer this question for us:

- On the evening of 9-11, during a meeting with the National Security Council, George W. said that the attacks provided "a great opportunity"(308, p. 32).

- Secretary of Defense Donald Rumsfeld said that 9-11 "created the kind of opportunities that World War II offered, to refashion the world"(353).

- National Security Advisor Condoleezza Rice (CFR member) asked senior members of the National Security Council, shortly after the 9-11 attacks, to "think about 'how do you capitalize on these opportunities?'"(354).

- In *The National Security Strategy of the United States of America*, issued by the Bush administration in September 2002, we find this similar statement: "The events of September 11, 2001, opened vast new opportunities."

And what were some of these "opportunities" that the 9-11 attacks provided the Bush administration and its globalist comrades? Well, for starters:

- They united the people behind the president and his administration, where previously Bush's approval ratings were very low.

- They stimulated certain sectors of the economy (filled the globalists' pockets) through military build-up and post-war unbidded rebuilding contracts. They also enabled the oil-invested Bush regime, along with friends in the major oil companies, to remove major competitors in the oil price-setting market (Saddam and the Taliban), so that they could charge whatever price they wanted for oil and gas, without having to worry about being undersold.

- They convinced skeptics in Congress that the Pentagon should get massive increases in its budget, particularly for the funding of hi-tech projects that would enable the U.S. to militarily control the realm of space.

In fact, let me draw your attention to a most astonishing document that will shed some very important light on this issue. Produced on January 7, 2001, it's called "Report of the Commission to Assess United States National Security Space Management and Organization," and its purpose was to make proposals regarding U.S. Space Command. This report pointed out that its proposals would most likely meet with great resistance, since they carried an enormous price tag. Then it went on to make this incredible statement: "The question is whether the U.S. will be wise enough to act responsibly and soon enough to reduce U.S. space vulnerability. Or whether, as in the past, a disabling attack against the country and its people--a 'Space Pearl Harbor'--will be the only event able to galvanize the nation and cause the U.S. government to act"(467).

Now look at what Donald Rumsfeld, who served as the head of the commission that wrote this report, said to Senator Carl Levin on the evening of 9-11: "Senator Levin, you and other Democrats in Congress have voiced fear that you simply don't have enough money for the large increase in defense that the Pentagon is seeking, especially for missile defense....Does this sort of thing [the 9-11 attacks] convince you that an emergency exists in this country to increase defense spending, to dip into Social Security, if necessary, to pay for defense spending--increase defense spending?"(468)

Did you catch that? Before 9-11, Rumsfeld's committee called for a "Space Pearl Harbor" to increase defense spending. And then 9-11 just happened to conveniently come along to provide the needed justification for such budget increases. Though it wasn't a "Space Pearl Harbor," it certainly was another Pearl Harbor of sorts. (In the next Appendix, when we discuss the 2003 Iraq campaign, we shall look at another startling pre-9-11 document that called for a "New Pearl Harbor.")

- They united many nations (initially, anyway) in a cooperative effort to defeat a common enemy, bringing them a step closer toward the globalist "utopia." (Though this union turned sour later on, this souring still served the interests of the globalists, as it drove many to look to the U.N. as the only hope for checking the U.S. government's abuses of power in its "war on terrorism," such as its unprovoked and unjustified war on Iraq, and its abuse of Iraqi prisoners of war.)

- They focused public attention on an overseas enemy (created a distraction), so that the real enemy, the globalists, could do their dirty work of sending millions more of our jobs overseas, driving up the national debt, creating new record-high deficits [Endnote 132], and leaving our borders wide open (which by itself is a globalist dream come true, to bring in cheap labor and further dilute patriotism). (For more information on the wide-open border fiasco, see Appendix 16.)

- They provided an excuse to invade countries that had been completely resistant to the New World Order agenda. As it turns out, the primary countries named by Bush as members of the "axis of evil" were the few remaining nations left in the world that could not be bribed into adopting a central bank--Iraq, Iran, Syria, North Korea, and the Sudan.

- They made it possible for the CIA's highly-profitable opium-trafficking business in Afghanistan to be revived, once the Taliban was removed from power (which had outlawed opium farming).

- They resulted in a massive increase in government power (which meant the loss of yet more freedoms/rights for Americans), all under the guise of providing the American people with greater "security."
     At the same time, all of this additional "security" helped to condition Americans, getting them used to seeing federal agents and military personnel policing airports and other public sites, heading us toward a police state. (Of course, many other countries around the world had likewise capitalized on the 9-11 attacks by restricting their citizens' freedoms.)

     One measure, in particular, that Bush took to bring us more "security" in his "war on terrorism," which poses a serious threat to our rights and freedoms, was the passage of H.R. 3162 (also known as the USA Patriot Act), which expanded federal government powers of surveillance, search, and arrest, as touched upon earlier, in Appendix 3. Speaking of this piece of legislation, Representative Ron Paul (R-TX) stated: "I do not believe that our Constitution permits federal agents to monitor phones, mail, or computers without a warrant....History demonstrates that the powers we give the federal government today will remain in place indefinitely....Every 20th century crisis...led to rapid expansions of the federal government. The cycle is always the same, with temporary crises used to justify permanent new laws, agencies, and programs. The cycle is [now] repeating itself"(243).

In the context of this last quote, compare the next two quotes very carefully, the first one originating over two years before the 9-11 terrorist attacks, the second one originating just thereafter:

- "We need greater intelligence and that means not only foreign-gathered intelligence but here at home. This is going to put us on a collision course with rights of privacy. And it's something that...[we] are going to have to come to grips with--how much are we going to demand of our intelligence agencies and how much are we willing to give up in the way of intrusion into our lives? That is a trade-off that is going to have to come." - Secretary of Defense William Cohen(244).

- CFR member Morton H. Halperin stated, just after the fateful 2001 terrorist attacks: "The intelligence agencies have a long list of things they want done. They've been waiting for an event to justify them"(245).

Could anything be said to make it more clear that the government had wanted the powers granted to it in the Patriot Act since long before 9-11, and that the Patriot Act has absolutely NOTHING to do with "keeping us safe"? These very points were brought out by Representative Ron Paul, who said: "I think there is a strong determination on the part of government to know everything about everybody, and fighting terrorism is the excuse, not the reason. All of these laws have been in the mill for years, and everything now is in place for what some people describe as a police state. I think we're on the verge of a very, very tough police state in this country"(246).

Shortly after the 2001 terrorist attacks, Supreme Court Justice Sandra Day O'Connor stated: "We're likely to experience more restrictions on our personal freedom than has ever been the case in our country"(247). Unfortunately, she has turned out to be correct. But rest assured that it was not "necessary" for us to lose our rights in order for the government to "protect" us from foreign threats. As James Madison said on June 29, 1787: "The means of defense against foreign danger have been always the instruments of tyranny at home."

When one considers the tremendous power-grab that began to take place immediately following the 9-11 attacks, the proceeding words of George W. don't seem so surprising: "If this were a dictatorship, it'd be a heck of a lot easier, just so long as I'm the dictator"(307). Bush also told *Washington Post* editor Bob Woodward, "I'm the commander--see, I don't need to explain--I do not need to explain why I say things. That's the interesting thing about being president.

Maybe somebody needs to explain to me why they say something, but I don't feel like I owe anybody an explanation"(308, pp. 145, 146).

Coming back to the so-called "Patriot Act," on September 5, 2002, the Associated Press gave an analysis of this piece of legislation, in an article called "Overview of Changes to Legal Rights." According to this article, some of our rights that this Act tramples are: "Freedom of Association: Government may monitor religious and political institutions without suspecting criminal activity to assist terror investigation....

"Freedom of Information: Government has closed once-public immigration hearings, has secretly detained hundreds of people without charges, and has encouraged bureaucrats to resist public records requests.

"Freedom of Speech: Government may prosecute librarians or keepers of any records if they tell anyone that the government subpoenaed information related to a terror investigation.

"Right to Legal Representation: Government may monitor federal prison jailhouse conversations between attorneys and clients, and deny lawyers to Americans accused of crimes.

"Freedom from Unreasonable Searches: Government may search and seize Americans' papers and effects without probable cause, to assist terror investigation.

"Right to a Speedy and Public Trial: Government may jail Americans indefinitely without a trial" [Endnote 133].

Does this sound like the government is interested in targeting foreign terrorists? Or can it be that "we the people" are the targets? Before you answer this question, check this out: Speaking before the Senate Judiciary Committee on December 6, 2001, Attorney General John Ashcroft stated: "To those who scare peace-loving people with phantoms of lost liberty, my message is this: Your tactics only aid terrorists--for they erode our national unity and diminish our resolve....Charges of 'kangaroo courts' and 'shredding the Constitution' give new meaning to the term, 'the fog of war.'...My message to America...is this, 'If you fit this definition of a terrorist, fear the United States, for you will lose your liberty'"(294).

His message to WHO? Can you not see that the definition of a "terrorist" is here broadened to include anyone who questions the government's liberty-trampling policies?

Similar to Ashcroft's draconian threat, White House spokesman Ari Fleischer, shortly after 9-11, warned "all Americans...to watch what they say [and] watch what they do"(248).

Isn't it painfully obvious that the real war that our globalist-controlled government is waging is targeted against us--"we the people"?

In view of the fact that Ashcroft was most instrumental in pushing for the Patriot Act, his above-cited treasonous comments aren't so unexpected. And since this scoundrel has had such a profound ongoing love affair with totalitarian power, it is of paramount interest to give careful consideration to this next bone-chilling forewarning about where we were headed with the appointment of Ashcroft as Attorney General: Speaking before the Senate Judiciary Committee on January 16, 2001, Dr. Debra Freeman, national spokesperson for presidential candidate Lyndon LaRouche, said that Ashcroft would bring about, under the guise of "crisis management," a "form of brutal bureaucratic fascism on the United States that bears striking similarities to the conditions under which Adolf Hitler seized power in Germany in 1933." She went on to say that it was her aim to present the "strongest possible opposition" to Ashcroft's appointment, because "he would only augment...horrible abuses of power and criminal tyranny..." She then stated: "What you're going to get with...[the] Bush administration, if it's determined to prevent itself from being opposed...[is] crisis management, where...[they] will set off provocations which will be used to bring about dictatorial powers...in the name of crisis management"(295).

Initially, Ashcroft, in order to silence complaints in Congress about the unconstitutional nature of the Patriot Act, had promised that there would be congressional oversight as to how the new powers granted the federal government therein would be handled. But this was a blatant lie. On June 13, 2002, several congresspeople submitted a list of 50 questions to Ashcroft, asking him how the Patriot Act was being implemented. For instance, they inquired, "How many times has the department requested records from libraries, bookstores and newspapers? How many roving wiretaps has the department requested?" Ashcroft refused to answer these and many other questions, even though he was legally required to do so(296). Senate Judiciary Committee Chairman Patrick J. Leahy failed to receive any response to dozens of letters he wrote to Ashcroft, and other senators complained of a complete stonewall(297). In March of 2003, senators continued to complain that Ashcroft still had not provided oversight information about the Patriot Act(298)[Endnote 134]. It simply cannot escape the notice of even the most clumsy of observers what was going on here. The Patriot Act clearly never had anything to do with "fighting terrorism."

Like so many other pieces of unconstitutional legislation that the globalists have gotten passed over the years (such as the 1933 Emergency Banking Relief Act, which we discussed earlier), the Patriot Act was also passed in a most dubious fashion. In fact, as with the Banking Relief Act, it was forced through Congress without anyone even seeing it, let alone reading it. Here's what some Congressmen had to say about the underhanded manner in which this law was passed:

- Representative Ron Paul: "[T]he bill wasn't printed before the vote"(164, p. 76).

- Rep. Jerrold Nadler: "We're told we should vote right now before we've had a chance to read the bill. Well, why didn't we take up the committee bill on the House floor earlier this week?"(164, p. 76)

- Rep. Pete Stark: "Most members, in fact, don't even know what the bill contains"(249).

- Rep. Barry Frank (D-Mass.): "What we have today is an outrageous procedure: A bill, drafted by a handful of people in secret, comes to us without a committee review and immune to amendment." Frank then went on to proclaim that the manner in which the Patriot Act was passed was "the least democratic process for debating questions fundamental to democracy I have ever seen"(164, p. 77).

- Rep. David Obey criticized this legislation as a "back-room quick fix....Why should we care? It's only the Constitution"(249).

- Rep. John Dingell: "I find this a distressing process...denigrating basic constitutional rights, and I find it to have been done in a sneaky, dishonest fashion"(249).

As if the Patriot Act wasn't frightening enough, there was also Patriot Act II, which contains even more shocking provisions than its predecessor. Speaking on this matter, Molly Ivins and Lou Dubose wrote in *Bushwhacked*: "The Department of Justice secretly drafted a sweeping sequel to the Patriot Act. The draft was discovered on February 2, 2003, by the Center for Public Integrity, which posted the plan on its website. This plan was prepared by Ashcroft's staff and has not been officially released; elected officials were not informed. Among its provisions, PATRIOT II would
- "empower the government to strip Americans of their citizenship if they participate in the *lawful* activities of any group the attorney general labels 'terrorist.'
- "no longer require the government to disclose the identity of anyone, even an American citizen, detained in connection with a terrorist investigation--until criminal charges are filed, no matter how long that takes. Thus, an American suspected of being part of a terrorist conspiracy could be held by investigators without anyone being notified. He could simply disappear.

- "repeal current limits on local police spying on religious and political activity, reactivating the old Red Squads that used to do such useful things as spying on Unitarians in Dallas....
- "allow government to obtain credit records and library records without a warrant.
- "permit wiretaps without a court order for up to fifteen days after a terror attack.
- "restrict release of information about health or safety hazards posed by chemical and other plants.
- "expand the reach of the already overbroad definition of terrorism--individuals engaged in civil disobedience could lose their citizenship, and their organizations could be subjected to wiretapping.
- "permit the extradition, search, and wiretapping of Americans at the behest of foreign nations, whether or not treaties allow it.
- "strip lawful immigrants of the right to a fair deportation hearing, and bar federal courts from reviewing immigration rulings.
- "authorize a DNA database of 'suspected terrorists'--a group so broadly defined it could include anyone associated with 'suspected' groups, and any 'noncitizen suspected of certain crimes or having supported any group designated as terrorist'"(299, pp. 279, 280).

On Saturday, December 13, 2003, Bush passed into law a section of Patriot Act II which gives the FBI the power to check the financial records of ANYONE, without that person even being suspected of having committed any crime (let alone a terrorist act). It was most unusual for a piece of legislation to be signed into law on a Saturday. But even more unusual (or perhaps not so unusual for the powerfully-deceptive Bush regime) was the fact that, on the very next day, it was announced that Saddam Hussein had been captured. Thus attention was conveniently focused away from the passage of this part of Patriot Act II [Endnote 135]. There was consequently almost no mainstream media coverage whatsoever of this ramrodding of legislation giving the FBI such intrusive, unconstitutional powers.

Most of the rest of Patriot Act II was passed on December 7, 2004 (right after the presidential election, conveniently), as part of the so-called "9-11 bill," or the "intelligence bill." As you should come to expect by now, no one in Congress read the thing before signing it into law (it was over 3,000 pages long). Speaking of the passage of this bill, the December 10, 2004 *Washington Post* reported: "The intelligence package that Congress approved this week includes a series of little-noticed measures that would broaden the government's power to conduct terrorism investigations, including provisions to loosen standards for FBI surveillance warrants and allow the Justice Department to more easily detain suspects without bail.

"Other law-enforcement-related measures in the bill--expected to be signed by President Bush next week--include an expansion of the criteria that constitute 'material support' to terrorist groups and the ability to share U.S. grand jury information with foreign governments in urgent terrorism cases....

"But civil liberties advocates and some Democrats said the measures would do little to protect the public while further eroding constitutional protections for innocent people caught up in investigations....

"Sen. Russell Feingold (D-Wis.) said that while he voted for the bill because of its intelligence reforms, he opposed much of the expansion of law enforcement power.   Most of it was not part of the Sept. 11 panel's recommendations.

"'I am troubled by some provisions that were added in conference that have nothing to do with reforming our intelligence network,' Feingold said. He later added: 'This Justice Department has a record of abusing its detention powers post-9/11 and of making terrorism allegations that turn out to have no merit.'

"Charlie Mitchell, legislative counsel for the American Civil Liberties Union, said the law enforcement measures are 'most troubling in terms of the trend they represent.' He added: 'They keep pushing and pushing without any attempt to review what they've done.'...

"Some of the changes [called for in the "9-11 bill"] were originally part of a legislative draft drawn up by Justice prosecutors in 2002 as a proposed expansion of the USA Patriot Act, administration and congressional officials said. The draft, leaked to the media and dubbed 'Patriot [Act] II' by critics, was never introduced as a bill in its entirety. But portions were introduced as stand-alone legislation....

"One key change [in the bill] is a provision in the new intelligence package that targets 'lone wolf' terrorists not linked with established terrorist groups such as al Qaeda. In language similar to earlier Senate legislation, the bill would allow the FBI to obtain secret surveillance and search warrants of individuals without having to show a connection between the target of the warrant and a foreign government or terrorist group..."(409).

In light of the onslaught of vigorous attacks launched by the Bush administration against our civil liberties after 9-11, the following hypocritical "double speak" words of George W. are most disgusting, which he voiced before a joint session of Congress on September 20, 2001: "Americans are asking, why do they [the 9-11 terrorists] hate us? They hate...our freedoms..."(361). Who hates our freedoms, George?

The WTC/Pentagon attacks served yet another important function for the globalists. After the collapse of the Soviet Union, the globalist boys had been at a loss to find an effective replacement global threat that could be used to justify an ongoing, long-term war-waging campaign against nations and organizations resistant to their agenda. The quotes that follow will illustrate just how desperate the globalists actually were after the end of the Cold War:

- CFR member Colin Powell (then serving as Bush Sr.'s Chairman of the Joint Chiefs of Staff) thusly complained about the end of the Cold War: "I'm running out of demons. I'm running out of villains. I'm down to Castro and Kim Il Sung"(315).

- In his 1996 book *Winning the Peace*, globalist John Gerard Ruggie wrote: "The core problem [globalist] American leaders faced in...1945 [after WW II] once again has become pressing: devising a coherent rationale to ensure continuous and active international engagement by the United States in support of a stable international order [i.e. New World Order]"(250, p. 6).

- Early in 1992, shortly after the Cold War had ended, Colonel Dennis Long, director of "total armor force readiness" at Fort Knox, stated: "For 50 years, we equipped our football team, practiced five days a week and never played a game [with the Soviets]. We had an enemy with demonstrable qualities, and we had scouted them out. [Now] we will have to practice day in and day out without knowing anything about the other team. We won't have his playbook, we won't know where the stadium is, or how many guys he will have on the field. That is very distressing to the military establishment, especially when you are trying to justify the existence of your organization and your systems"(251).

- NATO had lost its purpose for existence at the end of the Cold War. Thus the globalists, who created NATO, were desperate to find a reason to keep it alive. And the 9-11 attacks provided just what they were looking for. This was revealed when the CFR's website featured an article called "NATO After 9/11: Crisis or Opportunity?" on March 4, 2002, which stated: "The central question of the day in the trans-Atlantic relationship [NATO] is whether the U.S. and Europe will be able to fashion a common strategy for a global war on terrorism. Will we stand shoulder to shoulder just as we confronted the Soviet Union during the Cold War? Are our political leaders on both sides of the Atlantic willing to make the same kind of political commitment to hammer out common objectives and policies and recast our institutions to meet this challenge? We must look in the mirror and ask ourselves whether we as leaders are prepared to draw the right conclusions and do what we can now to reduce that threat, or whether it will take another, even deadlier attack to force us into action"(355).

- The end of the Cold War also brought sorrows to the U.S. intelligence community, particularly the CIA, which had lost its mission. It, too, needed a new enemy to justify its existence. As the *New York Times* put it, on February 4, 1992: "[I]n a world where the postwar [Cold War] enemy has ceased to exist, the CIA and its handful of sister agencies, with their billion-dollar satellites and mountains of classified documents, must somehow remain relevant in the minds of Americans."

With the new "war on terrorism" in the wake of the 9-11 attacks, the globalists could once again utilize our military and CIA to wage overt and covert wars anywhere they desired. All that they needed to do was to convince the American people, who, for the most part, would fight and fund such wars, that these wars were necessary to help stamp out terrorism. The 9-11 attacks, therefore, truly were the answer to globalist prayers. In his 1997 book, *The Grand Chessboard*, Zbigniew Brzezinski expressed this globalist prayer request in living color, stating that in America it is "difficult to fashion a consensus on [globalist] foreign policy issues [war-waging], except in the circumstances of a truly massive and widely perceived direct external threat"(204, p. 211)[Endnote 136]. In chapter 2 of this same book, Brzezinski had this to say: "It is also a fact that America is too democratic at home to be autocratic abroad. This limits the use of America's power, especially its capacity for military intimidation....[T]he pursuit of power is not a goal that commands popular passion, except in conditions of a sudden threat or challenge to the public's sense of domestic well-being."

Yes, the globalists had been WANTING a crisis to strike, to manipulate the public into going to war, and to curtail civil liberties (or ensure that we not remain "too democratic at home" in America).

Pertinent to our discussion of the public being manipulated into going to war after 9-11, let us look at a quote from another contributing author to the book *Into the Buzzsaw*. The author this time is Robert McChesney, a research professor with the Institute of Communications Research at the University of Illinois, who wrote: "Journalists had every reason to be skeptical about the rush to war immediately following September 11 [of 2001]. Since the late nineteenth century, the U.S. government has worked aggressively to convince the citizenry of the necessity of going to war in numerous instances. In cases like World War I, Korea, Vietnam, and the Gulf War, the government employed sophisticated propaganda campaigns to whip the population into a suitable frenzy. It was well understood within the establishment at the time--and subsequently verified in historical examinations--that the government needed to lie in order to gain support for its war aims. The media system, in every case, proved to be a superior propaganda organ for militarism and empire. This is the context for understanding the media coverage since September 11. The historical record suggests we should expect an avalanche of lies and half-truths in the service of power, and that is exactly what we have gotten. Our news media have played along in toto, having learned nothing from history....No skepticism was shown toward U.S. military, political, and economic interests that might benefit from militarism and war"(90, pp. 378, 379).

Regarding the particularly obvious degree of media control exerted by the Bush administration in the wake of the 9-11 attacks, perhaps no one has made statements more revealing than the following ones by Dan Rather, while being interviewed on the BBC's "Newsnight" on May 16, 2002: "The belief runs so strong in both the political and military leadership of the current war effort [in Afghanistan] that those who control the images will control public opinion. They realize what an entertainment-oriented society ours has become. Therefore...they would say to themselves: 'Hey, we've had the Hollywoodization of the news, we have had the Hollywoodization of almost everything else in society, why not the Hollywoodization of the war?' And I want to say quietly but as forcefully as I can that I hope this doesn't go any further; it has gone too far already. I am appalled by it, I do think it is an outrage--this is a personal opinion....

"What's going on...is a belief that the public doesn't need to know...the belief that there does not have to be a high degree of communicable trust between the leadership and the led....Limiting access, limiting information to cover the backsides of those who are in charge of the war, is extremely dangerous and cannot and should not be accepted. And I am sorry to say that up to and including the moment of this interview, that overwhelmingly it has been accepted by the American people. And the current administration [of Bush Jr.] revels in that, they relish that, and they take refuge in that....

"It is an obscene comparison--you know, I am not sure I like it--but, you know, there was a time in South Africa that people would put flaming tires around people's necks if they dissented. And in some ways the fear is that you will be necklaced here, you will have a flaming tire of lack of patriotism put around your neck. Now it is that fear that keeps journalists from asking the toughest of the tough questions, and to continue to bore in on the tough questions so often. And..., I am humbled to say, I do not except myself from this criticism."

It is very important to highlight a particular pertinent point from this interview: Mr. Rather was speaking so freely here because he was being interviewed on a *foreign* news broadcast, and would never, for obvious reasons, have been so candid over American airwaves.

One of the biggest lies propagated by the U.S. government and media regarding the 9-11 attacks was the claim that the motive for these attacks was an extremist Muslim hatred for, and resentment of, our freedoms and our way of life. Hogwash! The motive behind any alleged Islamic fundamentalist terrorist attack in this country would be retaliation for years and years of outrageous U.S.-orchestrated and/or sponsored acts of aggression and terror in the Muslim/Arab world. This is not to exonerate any supposed fanatic Muslim terrorist plotters against America. Killing innocent people can never be excused on any grounds. Nevertheless, there are reasons why Middle East extremists would want to attack us, which our government does not want us to contemplate. One very observant author, William Blum, gives us some clear insights into Muslim/Arab terrorist motives against the U.S.: "The shooting down of two Libyan planes in 1981; the bombardment of Beirut in 1983 and 1984; the bombing of Libya in 1986; the bombing and sinking of an Iranian ship in 1987; the shooting down of an Iranian passenger plane in 1988; the shooting down of two more Libyan planes in 1989; the massive bombing of the Iraqi people in 1991; the continuing bombings and sanctions against Iraq; the bombing of Sudan and Afghanistan in 1998; the habitual support of Israel despite its belligerence and routine torture, and condemnation of Arab resistance to it; the double standard applied to Israeli terrorism, such as the wilful massacre of 106 Lebanese at the UN base at Qana in 1996; the continued persecution of Libya, now nearing the end of its second decade; the abduction of wanted men from Muslim countries, such as Malaysia, Pakistan, Lebanon and Albania; the large military and hi-tech presence in Islam's holiest land, Saudi Arabia, and elsewhere in the Persian Gulf region...these are some of the American actions that can turn an Arab or a Muslim into a fanatic, into a terrorist, into a decrier of 'America, the Great Satan'"(156, p. 30). Will the real terrorists please stand up?

Not only has the globalist-controlled U.S. government supported and orchestrated terrorist activities in the Middle East, but pretty much everywhere else in the world. For example, our government has been training South American rebel forces in terrorism tactics for decades, not just through the CIA, as we discussed earlier, but also through the School of the Americas (SOA, which we also discussed earlier, in Appendix 2), located at Fort Benning, Georgia. In 2000, this training school changed its name to the Western Hemisphere Institute for Security Cooperation (WHISC), in a lame attempt to improve its image and avoid a congressional order to shut it down. But its function and tactics have remained unchanged. Speaking about this literal terrorist training camp, Chalmers Johnson wrote in his book *The Sorrows of Empire*: "Over the years it has trained well over 60,000 Latin American military and police officers, significant numbers of whom have been implicated in cases of torture, rape, massacre, and assassination. Among them was Roberto D'Aubuisson, the leader of El Salvador's right-wing death squads. Lower-level SOA graduates have participated in human rights abuses that include the March 24, 1980, assassination of El Salvador's Archbishop Oscar Romero (in which the CIA may have been implicated) and the December 1981 El Mozote massacre of 900 Salvadoran civilians. As of late 2002, civil war-torn Columbia's army includes some 10,000 SOA/WHISC graduates"(306, p. 136).

Would you not agree that the United States is guilty of massive hypocrisy, professing to be fighting a "war on terrorism" when all the while it has been one of the world's biggest propagators of such activities?

Let us now look at one final manner in which the WTC/Pentagon terrorist attacks served the interests of the globalists, particularly the ones in the oil business: UNOCAL, a giant American-based oil conglomerate, had wanted, several years before 9-11, to build a 1,000-mile-long pipeline from the Caspian Sea (an area very rich in oil and natural gas--trillions of dollars worth) through Afghanistan to the Arabian Sea. This oil conglomerate (which worked in conjunction with Enron and Halliburton) spent $10 billion on geological surveys for this pipeline's construction. All of the leading Taliban officials came to Texas in 1998 to negotiate the terms of the agreement for this pipeline with UNOCAL. But then, between 1998 and 1999, the Taliban started changing its mind, considering instead to award the pipeline project to Bridas, a company from Argentina. Prior to this time, the Taliban was heavily supported by the U.S. But with the souring of the UNOCAL deal, it suddenly became viewed by U.S. officials as the most evil entity on the planet.

Interestingly, the leader of the new Afghan government set up by the U.S. after ousting the Taliban from power, Hamid Karzai, had formerly worked for UNOCAL. In addition to this, Bush later appointed Lakhdar Ibrahimi, formerly the chief consultant to UNOCAL, as a special envoy to represent the U.S. to this new Afghan government. It should thus come as no shock to discover that on January 31, 2002, it was announced that the construction of the Trans-Afghan pipeline was fully underway, with full U.S. government support(422). UNOCAL and Haliburton were jointly awarded the contract, of course [Endnote 137].

Globalist U.S. foreign policy planners actually had their eyes on Afghanistan's natural resources at least four years before 9-11. Our good friend, Mr. Brzezinski, wrote in his *Grand Chessboard* in 1997 that Central Asia was "a potential economic prize: an enormous concentration of natural gas and oil reserves is located in the region, in addition to important minerals, including gold"(p. 124). Then, just three months prior to 9-11, an article from the Foreign Military Studies Office of Fort Leavenworth stated: "The Caspian Sea appears to be sitting on yet another sea--a sea of hydrocarbons. Western oilmen flocking to the area have signed multibillion-dollar deals. U.S. firms are well-represented in the negotiations, and where U.S. business goes, U.S. national interests follow....

"The presence of these oil reserves and the possibility of their export raises new strategic concerns for the United States and other Western industrial powers. As oil companies build oil pipelines from the Caucasus and Central Asia to supply Japan and the West, these strategic concerns gain military implications....The uninterrupted supply of oil to global markets will continue to be a key factor in international stability"(342).

Given the information in the last few paragraphs, we should expect to find evidence that the Bush administration was planning to attack Afghanistan before the 9-11 tragedy. And indeed, that's just what we find. One such piece of evidence turned up on September 18, 2001, before the plan to attack Afghanistan was even made known to the American public. On this day, Pakistan's former Foreign Secretary, Niaz Naik, told the BBC's George Arney that he was informed by American officials at a meeting in Germany two months earlier, in mid-July, that an invasion on Afghanistan was being planned sometime before the mid-October snows began(424). The CBS News website additionally reported on May 17, 2002: "Shortly before the Sep. 11 attacks on the United States, U.S. security officials prepared a presidential order to dismantle the al Qaeda network later blamed for the attacks, the White House said Friday"(357). Also, the Inter Press Service, in reference to meetings between Taliban and U.S. officials during the summer of 2001, stated on November 15, 2001: "At one moment during the negotiations, the U.S. representatives told the Taliban, 'either you accept our offer of a carpet of gold, or we bury you under a carpet of bombs.'" How convenient that 9-11 came at just the right time! Now we know what Britain's prime minister, Tony Blair, meant when he said: "To be truthful about it, there was no way we could have got the public consent to have suddenly launched a campaign on Afghanistan but for what happened on September 11"(356).

Stan Goff, retired Master Sergeant in U.S. Special Forces who formerly taught courses in military science at the U.S. military academy at West Point, New York, made the following fascinating observations on October 10, 2001: "Given this evidence that a military operation to secure at least a portion of Afghanistan has been on the table, possibly as early as five years ago, I can't help but conclude that the actions we are seeing put into motion now are part of a pre-September 11th agenda. I'm absolutely sure of that, in fact. The planning alone for operations of this scale, that are now taking shape, would take many months. And we are seeing them take shape in mere weeks. It defies common sense. This administration is lying about this whole thing being a 'reaction' to September 11th. That leads me, in short order, to be very suspicious of their yet-to-be-provided evidence that someone in Afghanistan is responsible. It's just too damn convenient. Which also leads me to wonder--just for the sake of knowing--what actually did happen on September 11th, and who actually is responsible"(464).

The oil motive behind the war on Afghanistan is one of the main reasons why the Bush administration fought so eagerly to prevent any attempt at a serious investigation into the events of 9-11, or an investigation into the failure of U.S. intelligence to prevent the attacks. Notice what Joseph Trento wrote about this in the Introduction to the book *Forbidden Truth*: "The day after the 9-11 attacks vice-president Cheney call[ed] the senate majority leader Tom Daschle trying to talk him out of any major investigation into the intelligence failure. There could be no serious investigation because a serious investigation in the end would reveal that money and oil were more important than protecting...the United States"(252, p. xii).

We also need to point out that, at the time of the post-9-11 U.S. attack on Afghanistan, some of the largest defense contractors, including United Defense, were owned by the Carlyle Group, with one of its top advisors being George Bush Sr.(425), who later retired from this position in late 2003. While on this train of thought, notice the following chilling forewarning given by Charles Lewis, executive director of the Center for Public Integrity, as quoted in the *New York Times* in the early days of Bush Jr.'s presidency: "Carlyle is as deeply wired into the current administration as they can possibly be. George H. W. Bush is getting money from private interests that have business before the government, while his son is president. And, in a really peculiar way, George W. Bush could, some day, benefit financially from his own administration's decisions, through his father's investments. The average American doesn't know that and, to me, that's a jaw-dropper"(253).

Should you have any lingering doubts, against all the existing evidence, that the U.S. government, at best, sat back on 9-11 and allowed the attacks on the Pentagon and the WTC to take place, you might want to take note of the fact that this was exactly what happened at the time of the first terrorist strike on the WTC, on February 26, 1993. Emad Salem, an FBI informant, had infiltrated the terrorist group that organized the bombing. According to the October 28, 1993 *New York Times*, Salem offered to replace the deadly explosives with a harmless powder, but the FBI refused his offer. On October 29, 1993, *New York Newsday* further reported that "'Instead of trying to stop it [the bombing], they [the FBI] just waited for it to happen, then swooped in and arrested everyone,' said an investigator. 'It was incredible.'" Here again we can see the government's dirty fingerprints all over an alleged "terrorist attack." This is a pattern that has become all-too-familiar, unfortunately. (Oh, incidentally, the FBI got a huge budgetary increase after this attack, in the name of "counterterrorism.")

There is actually a significant amount of convincing evidence to suggest that 9-11 resulted from more than just deliberate government negligence, simply allowing the attacks to have occurred. A careful examination of the events of 9-11, as well as many of the facts surrounding those events, reveals something even more sinister--that the whole operation may have been an inside job, or that the government at least played a significant role in what happened on that fateful day.

For starters, there has never been any evidence found or presented to show that Afghanistan was in any way involved in the attacks of 9-11. This point was admitted by Robert Mueller, the head of the FBI, on April 19, 2002, while speaking at the Commonwealth Club of California in San Francisco. He said: "In our investigation, we have not uncovered a single piece of paper--either here in the U.S. or in the treasure trove of information that has turned up in Afghanistan and elsewhere--that mentioned any aspect of the September 11th plot"(362).

What about Osama bin Laden? Was he really responsible for the 9-11 terrorist attacks, as we have been told? He certainly had the lack of scruples to pull off something like 9-11. But where is the proof that he did it? Forget citing the videos that appeared in the media, where Osama supposedly claimed responsibility for the attacks, as there are far too many problems with them, which indicate that they are most likely CIA-orchestrated forgeries. For example, the one released on December 9, 2001, shows "Osama" gesturing with his right hand, when the real Osama is left-handed, according to the FBI's website; the quality of the tape was very poor, so that "Osama's" lips could not be seen well (thus a false audio recording could have easily been dubbed over the video, if the video itself was real); "Osama's" facial features on this tape, particularly his nose, looked very different from previously-released Osama videos, etc.

Then there was the video released on October 29, 2004, in which "Osama" again took credit for the 9-11 attacks. However, there were several problems with this tape as well, such as the fact that he was supposed to be addressing U.S. citizens therein, and yet was speaking in Arabic. Why would he have done this, when he is able to fluently speak in English? Another problem with this tape is the timing of its release--just 4 days before the presidential election. Speaking on this matter on CNN's Larry King Show, on the same day that this tape was released, Walter Cronkite said: "So now the question is basically right now, how will this [video tape] affect the election? And I have a feeling that it could tilt the election a bit. In fact, I'm a little inclined to think that Karl Rove, the political manager at the White House, who is a very clever man, he probably set up bin Laden to [do] this thing"(434)[Endnote 138].

On September 17, 2001, CNN reported that bin Laden told Al Jazeera: "I would like to assure the world that I did not plan the recent [9-11] attacks..." Could this be the same "bin Laden" who appeared in the videos mentioned above? Why would he initially deny responsibility for the 9-11 attacks, only to turn around later and boast that he was behind them?

It's awful strange how bin Laden was never actually caught. Was it ever even the intention of the Bush crew to catch him in the first place? On September 15, 2001, President Bush said of him: "If he thinks he can hide and run from the United States and our allies, he will be sorely mistaken"(366). Two days later, he stated: "I want justice. And there's an old poster out West, I recall, that says, 'Wanted: Dead or Alive'"(367). But then his rhetoric started to change. On December 28, 2001, a few weeks after the Afghanistan war "officially" ended, Bush said: "Our objective is more than bin Laden"(368). His focus then started to shift. In his January 2002 State of the Union address, Bush described Iraq as part of an "axis of evil," and failed to mention bin Laden at all. But then on March 8, 2002, Bush caught himself, and vowed: "We're going to find him [Osama]"(369). But only a few days later, on March 13, Bush, completely changing his rhetoric again, said of Osama: "He's a person who's now been marginalized....I just don't spend that much time on him....I truly am not that concerned about him." Instead, Bush was "deeply concerned about Iraq"(370). The rhetorical shift was completed when Joint Chiefs of Staff Chairman Myers (CFR member) stated on April 6, 2002: "The goal has never been to get bin Laden"(371). This only makes sense, since the Bush and bin Laden families had been friends for years, dating back long before the 9-11 attacks, and they were also close business partners in the Carlyle Group [Endnote 139].

To top it off, the FBI's bin Laden webpage, containing a rap sheet of all the crimes he is wanted for, does not mention the 9-11 attacks at all(538). When asked to explain this dilemma, the FBI's chief of investigative publicity, Rex Thomb, stated: "The reason why 9/11 is not mentioned on Osama Bin Laden's Most Wanted page is because the FBI has no hard evidence connecting bin Laden to 9/11"(539).

It actually gets even crazier than this. According to the July 11, 2002 *New York Times*, "Osama bin Laden is dead. The news first came from sources in Afghanistan and Pakistan almost six months ago: the fugitive died in December and was buried in the mountains of southeast Afghanistan. Pakistan's president, Pervez Musharraf, echoed the information. The remnants of Osama's gang, however, have mostly stayed silent, either to keep Osama's ghost alive or because they have no means of communication"(540).

As if the lack of evidence to connect bin Laden and Afghanistan to 9-11 isn't problematic enough, there has also never been any evidence offered to prove that any of the 19 listed hijackers boarded any of the four planes involved in the 9-11 attacks. Consider the fact that there are absolutely NO surveillance camera pictures of any of these 19 individuals from either the Boston or Newark airports, which Flights 11, 175, and 93 left from on 9-11. This includes the airport parking lot cameras, those at the departure terminals, and all of the ones in between.

There should literally be hundreds of such pictures. But, again, there are none [Endnote 140].

Stranger still, it's been reported that at least 8 of the 19 alleged hijackers were still alive after 9-11(496), most notably Mohamed Atta, the one who was supposed to be the ringleader of the whole 9-11 plot, who helped fly Flight 11 into the WTC's North Tower. He was said to be living in Morocco, according to the September 2, 2002 edition of London's *Guardian*(427), as well as other sources. Also, absolutely none of the names of the alleged 19 hijackers were found on the official passenger manifests from any of the four planes involved in the attacks. Not only that, but none of these manifests even contained Arab-sounding names(428)[Endnote 141].

A moment ago (in Endnote 140) we talked about the surveillance camera pictures from Dulles Airport on the morning of 9-11, and how they are most likely fakes. Here is another reason for making this assertion: One of the hijackers identified in these pictures was Salem al-Hamzi, a man whom the September 21, 2001 *Guardian* confirmed to still be alive, and thus had nothing to do with the 9-11 attacks. Said the *Guardian*: "The FBI acknowledged yesterday that some of the terrorists involved in the attacks last week were using false identities, as it emerged that at least two men had been wrongly implicated. After analysis of the passenger lists of the four hijacked flights and other immigration documents, investigators identified Salem Al-Hamzi and Abdulaziz Al-Omari as two of the terrorists. The real Salem Al-Hamzi, however, is alive and indignant in Saudi Arabia, and not one of the people who perished in the American Airlines flight that crashed on the Pentagon. He works at a government-owned petroleum and chemical plant in the city of Yanbu. He said yesterday he had not left Saudi Arabia for two years, but that his passport had been stolen by a pickpocket in Cairo three years ago"(426).

In regards to Flight 77, specifically, another major problem arises pertaining to the total lack of evidence that there actually were Arab terrorists involved in the 9-11 attacks. In late November of 2001, the FBI announced that it had identified all but one of the non-hijacker passengers of Flight 77, but it said that the identities of the hijackers had not been confirmed through their remains(494). Over a year later, in February 2003, it was reported that the FBI still had not given DNA profiles to medical examiners so that the hijacker remains could be positively identified(495). Isn't it strange that only the non-hijacker remains were said to have been identified? Why do you suppose this was the case? Let me boldly proclaim that the FBI has never given DNA profiles of the Flight 77 hijackers to medical examiners--and never will--because it simply doesn't have such profiles, and because there were no Arab hijackers on that plane. That's right, NONE!

One of the many reasons for making this assertion was just mentioned--the fact that Salem Al-Hamzi, one of the supposed Flight 77 hijackers--was found to still be alive after 9-11. But here's yet another compelling reason: On July 6, 2003, the *Sierra Times* posted an article called "Autopsy: No Arabs on Flight 77." It was written by Thomas R. Olmsted, a psychiatrist and former Naval line officer who obtained, through a Freedom of Information Act request, an official Flight 77 passenger autopsy report from the Armed Forces Institute of Pathology. This report, as you might guess, did not mention any Arab names whatsoever, let alone the names of the alleged Flight 77 hijackers.

Curiously, the report contained 3 new names--Robert and Zandra Ploger, and Sandra Teague--that were not listed on the official passenger manifest released by American Airlines to the media. Why didn't American include these names on its list?

Another curious point about this autopsy report is that it only mentions one Flight 77 victim that could not be identified--a toddler, Dana Falkenberg. Why is this curious? It's strange enough that no hijacker remains from this plane were ever found. But why didn't this autopsy report mention the fact that hijacker remains couldn't be identified, like it did for the toddler?(497) Can't you see what a fraud this whole thing is?

So who hijacked the planes on 9-11, if the named hijackers didn't board them? Well, perhaps it's not a question of *who*, but *what*. Many researchers have concluded that the planes were probably overtaken from the ground, via remote control. Interestingly, an episode of Fox TV's *Lone Gunmen* (a short-lived spin-off of the X-Files show), aired on March 4, 2001, a half year before the 9-11 attacks, was about a passenger plane being remotely controlled by the government in a phony terrorist attack stunt, which was to crash into--you guessed it--the World Trade Center. Such an undertaking is well within the technological capabilities of the government, and it need not even be said that our globalist-controlled government definitely has the lack of scruples required to pull off such an operation.

On August 3, 2002, a Portuguese newspaper reported on an independent inquiry into 9-11 by a group of military and civilian U.S. pilots that had challenged the official version of events that transpired on that fateful day. The group's press statement included the proceeding pertinent remarks: "The so-called terrorist attack was in fact a superbly executed military operation carried out against the USA, requiring the utmost professional military skill in command, communications and control. It was flawless in timing, in the choice of selected aircraft to be used as guided missiles and in the coordinated delivery of those missiles to their preselected targets." A member of the inquiry team, a U.S. Air Force officer who flew over 100 sorties during the Vietnam war, stated: "Those birds [airliners] either had a crack fighter pilot in the left seat, or they were being maneuvered by remote control"(429).

Another indication of total government complicity in the 9-11 attacks is the obvious military stand-down that occurred on that morning. How could it be, for instance, that from 8:15 (the time it was known that Flight 11 was hijacked) until about 9:40 (the time that the last designated target was hit--the Pentagon), a period of almost an hour-and-a-half, there was no intercept of any of the hijacked planes? To put into perspective just how ridiculous this total lack of response was, one only need realize that there are very specific, legally-binding protocols that are to be followed during a crisis, or even a suspected crisis situation of this nature. Notice what the October 27, 2002 edition of London's *Observer* newspaper had to say in this regard: "By law, the fighters [fighter planes] should have been up at around 8:15. If they had, all the hijacked planes might have been diverted or shot down....Certainly, the one-hour 20-minute failure to put fighter planes in the air could not have been due to a breakdown throughout the entire Air Force along the East Coast. Mandatory standard operational procedure had been told to cease and desist...." MSNBC reported on September 12, 2001: "Pilots are supposed to hit each fix with pinpoint accuracy. If a plane deviates by 15 degrees, or two miles from that course, the flight controllers will hit the panic button. They'll call the plane, saying, 'American 11, you're deviating from course.' It's considered a real emergency, like a police car screeching down a highway at 100 miles an hour."

None of these procedures were followed on 9-11. And, to make matters worse, not one person--in either NORAD, the Air Force, or any other government agency--was so much as scolded for failure to act defensively that morning. The reason for this is quite obvious: they were responding in the exact manner that they were told to. These attacks were simply not to be thwarted, period.

NORAD, in particular, has no excuse for its lack of effective action on 9-11. On the contrary, it was extra prepared that morning for a preventative response, because it was in the midst of conducting a week-long semiannual exercise called "Vigilant Guardian"(579). NORAD was thus fully staffed and alert, and senior officers were manning stations throughout the U.S. The entire chain of command was in place and ready when it was first known that Flight 11 was hijacked(580). ABC News made mention of this on September 14, 2002, stating that NORAD was "conducting training exercises [and] therefore had extra fighter planes on alert."

To further demonstrate the ridiculousness of the total lack of a preventative military response on 9-11, ponder this: No airplane flying over any United States air space can get any more than 10 minutes out of reach of an Air Force jet intercept. But when we're talking about the Washington, D.C. and New

York City areas, the response time is even quicker, since there are so many air bases near these cities. The mystery deepens even more when we consider that, at top speed, military aircraft can fly over 1,800 mph. At this speed, jets from the west coast could have at least intercepted Flight 77. This is one of the biggest smoking guns, revealing definite government complicity on 9-11.

The lack of response to Flight 77 is particularly alarming. This plane was known to have been hijacked early on, and yet was allowed to head toward Washington without an intercept, or even an attempt at one, for over 40 minutes, and all of this occurred AFTER the two towers in New York had already been hit. How was this possible? You're going to tell me that the Pentagon, the most powerful military headquarters in the world, protected by Andrews Air Force Base, was unable to stave off this attack? This incredible lack of response tells us that there obviously had to be stand-down orders given that morning. In fact, this point was indirectly admitted by Secretary of Transportation Norman Mineta, during his testimony before the 9-11 Commission on May 23, 2003. Mineta said that he arrived at the Presidential Emergency Operating Center (PEOC) at 9:20 a.m. on 9-11, at which time "There was a young man who had come in and said to the vice president, 'The plane is 50 miles out. The plane is 30 miles out.' And when it got down to, 'The plane is 10 miles out,' the young man also said to the vice president, 'Do the orders still stand?' And the vice president turned and whipped his neck around and said, 'Of course the orders still stand. Have you heard anything to the contrary?' Well, at the time I didn't know what all that meant. And..." Suddenly, commission member Lee Hamilton broke in to ask exactly which plane Mineta was referring to, and Mineta replied with this confirmation: "[It was] [t]he flight that came into the Pentagon." But please take notice of this most important aspect of Mineta's testimony: When Cheney was asked, "Do the orders still stand?", what exactly do you suppose these orders were? They certainly weren't shoot-down orders, that's for sure. For Mineta went on to make that point clear, after which time Hamilton repeated his comment, for clarification purposes, saying: "And so there was no specific order there to shoot that plane down." Mineta then replied: "No, sir."

Do you see the problem here? Since there were no orders to shoot down Flight 77, the orders that Cheney was being asked to confirm must have been stand-down orders. Why else would Cheney's aide have kept asking him if the orders still stood? Wouldn't he have carried them out immediately, if these orders were in fact shoot-down orders? It's awful funny how Hamilton didn't ask Mineta any further questions about what he thought these orders may have been. Instead, he changed the subject.

Another major problem is the fact that there was no general evacuation called for, as Flight 77 headed toward Washington for 40 minutes, either at the

Pentagon, the White House, or the Capitol. Pentagon Spokesman Glenn Flood, when asked why there was no Pentagon evacuation, gave this ridiculous reply: "[T]o call for a general evacuation...would have been just guessing....We evacuate when we know something is a real threat to us"(430). "We evacuate when we know something is a real threat to us"? Oh, and when was that--when the plane actually hit the Pentagon? Please remember that two hijacked planes had already hit the towers in New York at this point, and a third hijacked plane was known to be heading for Washington. Yet this man said that an evacuation would have been "just guessing"?

There's even a question as to whether or not it was Flight 77 that actually hit the Pentagon. One problem is the fact that very little plane debris was ever found in or around the building (and of the small amount that was found, none of it looked like it came from a Boeing 757). As CNN's Jamie McIntyre put it, as he reported live from the Pentagon on 9-11, shortly after this facility was attacked: "From my closeup inspection, there's no evidence of a plane having crashed anywhere near the Pentagon. The only [crash] site is the actual side of the building that's crashed in....The only pieces left that you can see are small enough that you can pick up in your hand. There are no large tail sections, wing sections, fuselage, nothing like that anywhere around, which would indicate that the entire plane crashed into the side of the Pentagon and then caused the side to collapse...almost about 45 minutes later."

A further problem is that there was no damage on either side of the Pentagon's impact hole from the wings of the plane, or above this same hole from the tail (the impacting craft actually went through a fairly large window, without doing any damage to the frame). The hole looked far more consistent with what would be expected from a missile strike (or a missile with wings, modified to look like a plane, as some have speculated). Congruent with this assertion is the startling testimony given by Don Perkal, a Pentagon official whose office was located just around the corner from the impact zone: "The airliner crashed between two and three hundred feet from my office in the Pentagon, just around a corner from where I work. I'm the deputy General Counsel, Washington Headquarters Services, Office of the Secretary of Defense. A slightly different calibration and I have no doubt I wouldn't be [alive]....My colleagues felt the impact, which reminded them of an earthquake. People shouted in the corridor outside that a bomb had gone off upstairs on the main concourse in the building. No alarms sounded. I walked to my office, shut down my computer, and headed out. Even before stepping outside I could smell the cordite. Then I knew explosives had been set off somewhere"(546). Cordite, of course, is an explosive used in missiles.

Then there was the mysterious claim initially made by the Pentagon that the impacting aircraft was not captured on tape, even though there are literally hundreds of cameras all over the premises. Later, in March of 2002, the Pentagon changed its story, admitting that one camera (just one?) caught this event, but only five unrevealing frames were released from this film. All that these frames showed was the explosion, but none of them featured the aircraft itself.

Later, on May 16, 2006, it was admitted that a second Pentagon camera had caught the strike on tape, but nothing was revealed in this footage either--no hint that it was actually a Boeing that trekked across the Pentagon's lawn on 9-11.

It was most convenient that the Pentagon was struck in an area where there were no important personnel stationed. It was also convenient that this same area of the building was the only part of the entire complex that had recently undergone renovations that were designed to enable this part of the structure to withstand a direct hit by a missile, or the blast of a bomb. Funny that the alleged terrorists, who supposedly had carefully planned out these attacks years in advance, would not have known that the maximum "bang for the buck" would have been achieved by targeting the other side of the facility. It's also funny that Pentagon officials would choose to reinforce such an unimportant portion of this building, rather than the opposite side, wouldn't you say?

We also have the equally-disturbing question about what really brought the Twin Towers of the World Trade Center down on 9-11. Strong and abundant evidence exists that they came down via explosives planted in the buildings (controlled demolitions).

For instance, there are multiple and highly credible eye-witness testimonies from firemen, reporters, and various civilians who reported hearing "bombs" or "multiple explosions" going off as the towers came down. One reporter said she saw flames coming out of the base of the North Tower as it began to collapse.

Then there were the seismograph readings from Columbia University, which showed significant tremors occurring at the moment the towers began to fall, followed by several smaller tremors as they continued falling. This is exactly what happens during a controlled demolition--a massive explosion is set off at the base of a building, followed by several smaller explosions that are triggered in sequence, to ensure that most of the edifice crumbles to dust and falls straight down.

Additionally, we have the personal testimony of Larry Silverstein, the owner of the complex, admitting on a PBS documentary, "America Rebuilds," first aired in September 2002, that he gave orders to "pull" Building 7 later in the afternoon on 9-11. Yet the government still claims that this building, like the two main towers, fell because of the fires that were burning within.

As further proof that the WTC towers were taken down by explosives,

FEMA, which was in charge of the cleanup of Ground Zero, refused to allow any of the debris to be properly and systematically examined as it was being removed (this is a felony). Understand that it is STANDARD PROCEDURE (in fact, it's the law) to carefully and meticulously scrutinize the debris left behind after a fire, especially when a fire occurs at a crime scene. This needs to be done, if for no other reason than to improve design and construction of future structures, so that no building would ever suffer the same fate again in a fire. But, again, this was not allowed. Understand that there is absolutely no justification for blocking the investigation of the WTC debris, except that a coverup was taking place. This becomes even more obvious when we consider the fact that then-Mayor Rudolph Giuliani passed a local ordinance forbidding anyone from taking pictures as the debris was being removed from the WTC site. Obviously there was a lot to hide.

The Twin Towers both collapsed in about 10 seconds flat (the speed of gravity), their contents were reduced to powder as they fell, and their massive central columns, composed of 4-inch-thick steel walls, were snapped into relatively small pieces, all the way down to ground level.

Another troubling point to ponder, which lends further support to the notion that the towers were destroyed by demolition charges, is the fact that some of the WTC steel had actually melted and even vaporized, which require temperatures of roughly 2800 and 5100 degrees, respectively. Yet the fires in the buildings, before they collapsed, were said to have only reached a maximum of 800 degrees. Here are a few quotes that support these points:

- "Pieces of steel have also been found that were apparently melted and vaporized...because of a corrosive contaminant that was somehow released in the conflagrations....

"Perhaps the deepest mystery uncovered in the investigation [if you can call it that] involves extremely thin bits of steel collected from the trade towers and from Seven World Trade Center, a forty-seven storey high rise that also collapsed for unknown reasons [well, not unknown any longer]. The steel apparently melted away, but no fire in any of the buildings was believed to be hot enough to melt steel outright." - *New York Times*, February 2, 2002(541).

- "The severe corrosion and subsequent erosion of samples 1 and 2 constitute an unusual event. No clear explanation for the source of the sulfur has been identified." - FEMA's "World Trade Center Building Performance Study," Appendix C, released May 1, 2002(542).

- The November 29, 2001 *New York Times* quoted Dr. Jonathan Barnett, a professor at the Center for Fire Safety Studies at the Worcester Polytechnic

Institute, as saying that some of the "steel members in the debris pile [at Ground Zero]...appear to have been partly evaporated in extraordinarily high temperatures"(543).

- *The Structural Engineer* (September 3, 2002) quoted Dr. Keith Eaton, Chief Executive and Secretary of the Institution of Structural Engineers, as saying that he was shown slides of WTC debris that revealed things "ranging from molten metal which was still red hot weeks after the event, to 4-inch thick steel plates sheared and bent in the disaster."

- The July/August 2002 issue of *The Atlantic Monthly* talked about correspondent William Langewiesche being on the scene during some of the clean-up work at Ground Zero. It stated that he "crawled through 'the pile' with survey parties and descended deep below street level to areas where underground fires still burned and steel flowed in molten streams." In this same article, Langewiesche was quoted as saying that "streams of molten metal...leaked from the hot cores and flowed down broken walls inside the foundation hole."

I also want to stress the point that the fires at Ground Zero continued to rage for over three months after 9-11. As CBS News reported on December 19, 2001: "Firefighters have extinguished almost all but the last remnants of underground fires that have burned at the World Trade Center site for more than three months since the Sept. 11 terrorist attack."

For fires to burn this long, the initial energy that got them started must have been tremendous--far greater than what can be accounted for by the relatively minor fires that burned in the towers before they fell. To give you an idea of just how intense these inextinguishable, long-lived fires actually were, CBS went on to say: "The fires that began with the Sept. 11 attacks had been strong enough that fire trucks had to spray a nearly constant jet of water on them [again, for over 3 months]. At times, the flames slowed the work of clearing the site. 'You couldn't even begin to imagine how much water was pumped in there,' said Tom Manley of the Uniformed Firefighters Association, the largest fire department union. 'It was like you were creating a giant lake'"(544).

Yet another troubling factor we will look at regarding the 9-11 attacks, which further points to a government coverup, is the evidence that Flight 93 was shot down.

First we have the testimony of many local residents in Pennsylvania, who said that they saw a white military jet flying close behind Flight 93, in hot pursuit:

- An unnamed witness of this fighter plane, a woman, was quoted by the

September 13, 2002 edition of the UK's *Mirror* as saying: "It was white with no markings but it was definitely military....It had two rear engines, a big fin on the back like a spoiler....It definitely wasn't one of those executive jets. The FBI came and talked to me and said there was no plane around....But I saw it and it was there before the crash and it was 40 feet above my head. They did not want my story"(547).

- The same *Mirror* article cited above mentioned another eyewitness, Tom Spinelli, who gave this description of the plane that obviously shot down Flight 93: "I saw the white plane. It was flying around all over the place like it was looking for something. I saw it before and after the crash."

- Another "mystery plane" eyewitness that this article quoted from was Lee Purbaugh, who said: "I didn't get a good look but it was white and it circled the area about twice and then it flew off over the horizon."

There were even some air traffic workers who were aware of the presence of this military plane. The September 13, 2001 edition of Nashua, New Hampshire's *Telegraph* newspaper revealed that air traffic controllers in Nashua heard from other controllers that an F-16 fighter was closely following Flight 93.

Some of the local witnesses of this military plane said that they heard a missile being fired at Flight 93:

- According to the November 15, 2001 edition of the *Philadelphia Daily News*, Ernie Stull, the mayor of Shanksville, PA, stated: "I know of two people--I will not mention names--that heard a missile. They both live very close, within a couple of hundred yards....This one fellow's served in Vietnam and he says he's heard them, and he heard one that day." He also said that, based on what he has learned, F-16s were "very, very close."

- The same edition of this paper quoted eyewitness (or in this case, "earwitness") Laura Temyer of Hooversville, PA, as saying: "I didn't see the plane but I heard the plane's engine. Then I heard a loud thump that echoed off the hills and then I heard the plane's engine. I heard two more loud thumps and didn't hear the plane's engine anymore after that."

In regards to the "loud thumps" silencing Flight 93's engines, the August 13, 2002 edition of the *Independent* stated that a one-half ton piece of engine was found over a mile away from the main crash site of Flight 93(548). And according to the November 15, 2001 *Philadelphia Daily News*, this is perfectly consistent with what would be expected from the heat-seeking Sidewinder missiles of an F-16--targeting the engines, which are the hottest parts of a plane.

If Flight 93 was truly shot down, we would expect to find pieces of it far away from the main crash site, since the plane would have continued to fly for some distance after being hit, and pieces of it would have been blown off all along its route, as a result of damage done to it by the impacting missile. And, as fate would have it, this is precisely the case. On September 13, 2001, CNN correspondent Brian Cabell, reporting live, stated: "[I]n the last hour or so, the FBI and the state police here [in Pennsylvania] have confirmed that they have cordoned off a second area about six to eight miles away from the crater here where [the] plane [Flight 93] went down. This is apparently another debris site, which raises a number of questions. Why would debris from the plane--and they identified it specifically as being from this plane--why would debris be located six miles away? Could it have blown that far away? It seems highly unlikely. Almost all the debris found at this site is within 100 yards, 200 yards, so it raises some questions." Questions indeed! This plane crashed because it was shot down, plain and simple.

As still more proof of this fact, the Associated Press reported a 911 emergency phone call made by a man in the bathroom on Flight 93, who said that the plane was "going down" and that he heard an explosion and saw white smoke. Speaking of the recording of this call, the *Washington Post* had this to say on September 12, 2002: "FBI agents quickly took possession of the tape of that 911 call, which constitutes the only public evidence so far of what went on during the doomed plane's last moments. The FBI declined to provide any information about the tape's contents or the identity of the caller" [Endnote 142].

Although the fact of Flight 93 being shot down doesn't, in and of itself, prove government complicity in the events of 9-11, it certainly does further prove that we are being lied to about what really went on that day.

But let us now move on to still another problem with the events of 9-11-- the strange behavior of Bush that morning, acting scandalously unconcerned about what was going on, and exhibiting no response, even after hearing about the second plane hitting the second tower and being told that "the nation is under attack." He continued to sit calmly in a Florida classroom, listening to kids read about a pet goat, without doing ANYTHING.

But still even more strange is the fact that the Secret Service didn't rush in and whisk him off. Why weren't they concerned that Bush might have been a target of the alleged terrorists that morning? As long as Bush remained in that school, not only was his life in danger (since his trip there was announced days in advance), but the lives of all the students and staff as well. Yet the Secret Service never intervened.

Another major troubling factor is the manner in which Bush & Co. not only fought to prevent an investigation of the 9-11 attacks, but then fought the investigation itself, once the 9-11 Commission was finally formed against their wishes, 14 months after 9-11. For example, the Commission was denied free access to government documents pertaining to 9-11, unless the White House could first view them and censor them. The Commission was also denied requests to interview certain government employees unless a representative from the Justice Department could be present (to obviously decide what could and could not be discussed). The Bush team also cut back the already-too-low budget for the investigation, by several million dollars. And then there was the fact, perhaps the most strange one of all, that Bush at first refused to appear before the Commission. Later he finally agreed, but only if a whole list of conditions were first met: Cheney had to be present with him, the proceedings were to be private, there was to be no recording of the meeting in any form, and neither Cheney nor he himself were to testify under oath.

It is obvious that the 9-11 Commission, from the start, was intended to be a whitewash, just like the Warren Commission. How could it have been otherwise, when we consider that Bush personally appointed its chairman, Thomas Kean? (Originally Bush had appointed Henry Kissinger for this position--an obvious coverup artist--but he had to step down because of "conflict of interests" with some of his business partners.) Furthermore, the executive director of this Commission, Philip Zelikow, had formerly worked on the Bush-Cheney transition team, as the new administration first took power, advising his longtime friend, National Security Advisor Condoleezza Rice, on the incoming National Security Council team.

It turns out that Zelikow was not only a close friend of Bush and Rice, but his area of expertise was the creation and dissemination of propaganda. This was brought out by the Internet encyclopedia, Wikipedia, which had this to say about him: "Prof. Zelikow's area of academic expertise is the creation and maintenance of, in his words, 'public myths' or 'public presumptions,' which he defines as 'beliefs (1) thought to be true (although not necessarily known to be true with certainty), and (2) shared in common within the relevant political community.' In his academic work and elsewhere he has taken a special interest in what he has called "'searing" or "molding" events [that] take on "transcendent" importance and, therefore, retain their power even as the experiencing generation passes from the scene'"(545).

Rigging Congressional investigations was apparently quite habit-forming for Mr. Bush. For we find that he also stacked the deck in his favor with a commission that he formed to "investigate" the matter of Iraq's missing weapons of mass destruction (more on this in Appendix 8). Speaking about this commission, Senator Robert Byrd observed: "This commission is 100 percent under the thumb of the White House. Who created the panel's charter? The President. Who chooses the penal members? The President. To whom does the panel report? The President. Whom shall the panel advise and assist? The President. Who is in charge of determining what classified reports the panel may see? The President. Who gets to decide whether the Congress may see the panel's report? The President"(432).

Another problem that emerged with the 9-11 Commission was the revelation that 6 out of the 10 members of the panel had investments in either United or American Airlines, the two airlines involved in the attacks.

Proof that the 9-11 Commission was going to be nothing more than an exercise in damage control came early on in its history, when United Press International, on February 6, 2003, quoted Vice Chairman Lee Hamilton as saying: "The focus of the commission will be on the future [to prevent future attacks]. We're not interested in trying to assess blame, we do not consider that part of the commission's responsibility." He also stated: "...we're not criminal prosecutors...we're not on a witch hunt."

Then, to make matters worse, in early May of 2004, the MSNBC website reported on a *Newsweek* article called "9/11 Commission: The Panel Tones It Down," which was to appear in the upcoming May 10 issue. This article stated: "Fearing that their high-profile inquiry was being dragged into election-year politics, 9/11 commission chair Tom Kean and vice chair Lee Hamilton made powerful private pleas to fellow commissioners to tone down the rhetoric and avoid politically charged questioning, panel sources tell NEWSWEEK." Later in this article, Hamilton was quoted as saying, regarding the private meeting that the panel had with Bush and Cheney on April 29: "I don't think there was a single moment of tension....We weren't there to challenge him [Bush] or ask any contentious questions designed to contradict him"(431).

Well isn't that comforting! They weren't there to challenge Bush or ask him contentious questions? What a farce!

So now we are left with a nagging question: Did the government do 9-11 itself, or did it merely sit back and let it happen? Either way, its treasonous hands are stained with blood. We must pull our heads out of the sand and face the ugly truth that 9-11 happened because the government wanted it to happen, plain and simple.

We talked earlier about the potential of the Patriot Act and similar pieces of post-9-11 legislation being used to label globalization protesters as "terrorists," and thus to strip them of their rights. Well, it so happens that this same false labeling tactic has been applied to those who recognize and expose government culpability in the 9-11 attacks. In early September of 2006, the White House's website posted a brief study called "Strategy for Winning the War on Terror," which stated that "The terrorism we confront today springs from...[s]ubcultures of conspiracy and misinformation. Terrorists recruit more effectively from populations whose information about the world is contaminated by falsehoods and corrupted by conspiracy theories. The distortions keep alive grievances and filter out facts that would challenge popular prejudices and self-serving propaganda"(534). The not-so-subtle message here is that the "conspiracy theory" crowd breeds terrorists. The globalists are obviously setting the stage for silencing those who are aware of, and are exposing, what they are up to.

In the November 17, 2002 edition of the *Toronto Star*, an editorial appeared entitled "Pursue the Truth About Sep. 11." It strongly criticized the government and media regarding 9-11: "Getting the truth about 9/11 has seemed impossible. The evasions, the obfuscations, the contradictions and, let's not put too fine a point on it, the lies have been overwhelming....The questions are endless. But most are not being asked--still--by most of the media most of the time....There are many people, and more by the minute, persuaded that, if the Bushies didn't cause 9/11, they did nothing to stop it."

"We are told our enemy is Osama bin Laden, but, the war crimes of [9-11] were carried out by men who live among us. The enemy is already inside the gates." - Pat Buchanan, *Los Angeles Times*, September 21, 2001.

"You can fool some of the people all of the time, and those are the ones you need to concentrate on." - George W. Bush, BBC News, March 25, 2001.

Regarding our earlier discussion of the globalists viewing 9-11 as an "opportunity," there's one last fascinating quote we need to look at. It's from Gary Hart, Co-Chair of the CFR and former senator of Colorado (D), who, just after 9-11, during a CFR meeting, said: "There is a chance [for] the president of the United States to use this disaster [the 9-11 attacks] to carry out what his father...a phrase his father used...a New World Order"(310).

Hitler was a big fan of the Hegelian Dialectic process. In order to rob the German people of many of their rights guaranteed to them by their constitution, and, consequently to increase his power over them, he made arrangements in 1933 to have the Reichstag set on fire, which he immediately claimed was the work of the Communist Party, one of his main rivals. Soon thereafter he passed the rights-trampling "Enabling Act," which, during a public speech, he claimed was for "the protection of the people and the state." He then went on to explain how this new law called for "restrictions on personal liberty, on the right of free expression of opinion, including freedom of the press; on the rights of assembly and associations; and violations of the privacy of postal, telegraphic, and telephonic communications and warrants for house searches, orders for confiscations as well as restrictions on property..."(136, p. 19).

And what was the result of all of this? Not only did the German people happily give up many of their rights and freedoms, but they pledged their full support to their new dictatorial leader. Notice what Hermann Goering, who was second in command under Hitler, stated at the Nuremberg Trials in this regard: "[P]eople can always be brought to the bidding of the leaders. That is easy. All you have to do is to tell them they are being attacked, and denounce the pacifists for lack of patriotism and [for] exposing the country to danger"(114, p. 59).

Notice also what General Douglas MacArthur stated back in 1957, regarding this same fear-based manipulation of the public during the Cold War: "Our government has kept us in a perpetual state of fear--kept us in a continuous stampede of patriotic fervor--with the cry of grave national emergency. Always there has been some terrible evil at home or some monstrous foreign power that was going to gobble us up if we did not blindly rally behind it [the government]..."(114, p. 59).

The psychology behind this fear-instilling manipulation technique is perhaps best expressed in the words of psychologist William Sargant: "Various types of belief can be implanted in people after brain function has been...disturbed by accidentally or deliberately induced fear, anger, or excitement. Of the results caused by such disturbances the most common one is temporarily impaired judgement and heightened suggestibility. Its various group manifestations are sometimes classed under the heading of 'herd instinct,' and appear most spectacularly in wartime, during severe epidemics, and all similar periods of common danger, which increase anxiety and so individual and mass suggestibility....We would be advised not to underestimate the effect on the collective psyche in terms of fear and a desire for the authorities to 'protect people' from that fear"(137).

Bertrand Russell, in his book *The Impact of Science on Society*, put it this way: "[W]henever an organization [government] has a combatant purpose, its members are reluctant to criticize their officials, and tend to acquiesce in usurpations and arbitrary exercises of power which, but for the war mentality, they would bitterly resent. It is the war mentality that gives officials and governments their opportunity. It is therefore only natural that officials and governments are prone to foster war mentality"(154).

To accentuate just how desperate our situation has become through Bush's post-9-11 policies, the *Washington Post* reported on November 25, 2004, about how many Americans were faced with a battle over "whether theirs will be a free country, with an independent press and courts and leaders who are chosen by genuine democratic vote. Corporate America, who channeled hundreds of millions of dollars into Mr. Bush's campaign, is backing the imposition of an authoritarian system--with a propagandistic regime, controlled media, official persecution of dissent, business executives who take orders from the state, and elections that are neither free nor fair"(450).

* * * * * * *

"[L]iberty...cannot flourish in a country that is permanently on a war footing, or even a near-war footing. Permanent crisis justifies permanent control of everybody and everything by the agencies of the central government. And permanent crisis is what we have to expect in a world in which...dictatorship...becomes almost inevitable." - Aldous Huxley, *Brave New World Revisited*(412).

"No nation could preserve its freedom in the midst of continual warfare." - James Madison(555).

"They that can give up essential liberty to obtain a little temporary safety deserve neither liberty nor safety." - Benjamin Franklin, *Historical Review of Pennsylvania*, 1759.

"You're free. And freedom is beautiful. And, you know, it'll take time to restore chaos and order--order out of chaos. But we will." - George W. Bush, Washington, D.C., April 13, 2003(471).

Appendix 8

The U.N. and the U.S.--war-waging partners

From its inception, the U.N. has been an instrument of war, and it has used U.S. military might, more than that of any other nation, to do its dirty work. Between 1945 and 2002, for example--the first 57 years of its existence--the U.N. was involved in 62 wars around the world. That's more than one war per year, on average. And with each one of these wars, the U.N. has always left behind "peacekeeping" troops (occupation forces) in every country as it went along, to ensure that they all remained "imperial outposts" of the emerging global empire [Endnote 143].

The U.N.'s first big blunder was the Korean War, which, as we saw earlier, was deliberately prolonged, unnecessarily costing tens of thousands of lives. However, to the U.N. and those who have supported it and its agenda, those lives were not lost unnecessarily, as we see from these treasonous words of President Truman, spoken before the U.N. General Assembly on October 24, 1950: "The men who laid down their lives for the United Nations in Korea....They died in order that the United Nations might live"(112, p. 83).

The Vietnam War--the other major U.S. "Cold War" quagmire that was deliberately dragged on, and also unnecessarily cost tens of thousands of American lives--was likewise fought under the fully-approving eye of the U.N. In fact, take a look at what Section 3 of the Gulf of Tonkin Resolution had to say on this matter: "This resolution shall expire when the President shall determine that the peace and security of the area is reasonably assured by international conditions created by action of the United Nations..."

J. Ruben Clark Jr., former undersecretary of state and U.S. ambassador to Mexico, who was also widely recognized as one of our nation's foremost international lawyers, wrote insightfully about the U.N. Charter, saying that it "is a war document not a peace document....[It] makes us a party to every international dispute arising anywhere in the world..." He then went on to say: "Not only does the Charter Organization [the U.N.] not prevent future wars, but it makes it practically certain that we shall have future wars, and as to such wars it takes from us [the U.S.] the power to declare them, to choose the side on which we shall fight, to determine what forces and military equipment we shall use in war, and to control and command our sons [and daughters] who do the fighting"(376, p. 48).

Examples abound of the U.N. waging war through U.S. military forces (or with the aid of U.S. military supplies). But let's single out one particularly notorious example--the Persian Gulf War in Iraq, in 1991--to attain a clear understanding of how these U.N.-embraced conflicts actually work.

The globalists targeted this nation then, not only because they wanted to pressure it into compliance with U.N. dictates, but because they wanted to make an example of it to other potentially resistant countries, that if they followed in Iraq's path of resistance, they too would be decimated through bombings and starved through sanctions.

In order to justify the massive assault on Iraq that was being planned, the globalists found it necessary to set up Saddam Hussein. Thus, just prior to Iraq's invasion of Kuwait, the Bush-Baker State Department (both Bush and Baker were CFR members) told April Glaspie, the U.S. ambassador to Iraq at that time, to inform Hussein that the United States "had no opinion" on the Iraq-Kuwait border dispute. Glaspie was told to say this to Hussein because it was known full well that this would encourage him to go ahead with his Kuwait invasion plans, which he did, of course, on August 2, 1990. Tragically, Glaspie was later unfairly blamed for giving Hussein the OK for this invasion, when all the while she was just an innocent pawn in the game(238, p. 760)[Endnote 144].

Interestingly, back in the 1980s the U.S. supplied a tremendous amount of "financial aid" to Iraq, to help in its war against Iran. It could be argued that this was done in anticipation of Iraq being a future target of a globalist-inspired U.S. military aggression--the old dominos game of "set 'em up and knock 'em down." This is a favorite trick of the globalists, which they also played out--again, through the U.S.--on many other nations and leaders around the world, such as Noriega and the Taliban. In this game, the friends of today make great enemies of tomorrow.

As always, though there be other hidden motives behind the playing of the war-orchestration game, the biggest one of all is the advancement of the globalist/U.N. cause of world government, or the New World Order. Let us now take a second look at a George Bush Sr. quote cited earlier, to see that the 1991 Persian Gulf War was indeed intended as a progressive step toward this goal: "For two centuries [referring back to the days of Weishaupt], we've done the hard work of freedom [the push for world government]. And tonight, we lead the world in facing down a threat to decency and humanity. What is at stake is more than one small country; it is a big idea: a New World Order....

"We have within our reach the promise of a renewed America. We can find meaning and reward by serving some higher purpose than ourselves--a shining purpose, the illumination of a thousand points of light....Join the community of conscience...[and] the world can therefore seize this opportunity to fulfill the long-held promise of a New World Order...."

Later on in this same speech, Bush also declared: "If we do not follow the dictates of our inner moral compass and stand up for human life, then his

[Saddam's] lawlessness will threaten the peace and democracy of the emerging New World Order we now see, this long dreamed-of vision we've all worked toward for so long [who is this "we" here, anyway?]"(130).

Now notice what Stansfield Turner, CFR member and former CIA director, said when asked about Iraq and the Gulf War crisis, on CNN's "Crossfire" in late July of 1991: "We have a much bigger objective. We've got to look at the long run here. This is an example--the situation between the United Nations and Iraq--where the United Nations is deliberately intruding into the sovereignty of a sovereign nation....Now this is a marvelous precedent...[to be used in] all countries of the world..."(254)[Endnote 145].

The Gulf War, an international cooperative effort to force a nation to comply with U.N. resolutions, brilliantly demonstrates what the U.N. was really intended for--unchallengeable global power, as we see revealed in this next quote from an NEA publication, which dates back to 1948: "The idea has become established that the preservation of international peace and order may require that force be used to compel a nation to conduct its affairs within the framework of an established world system. The most modern expression of this doctrine of collective security is in the United Nations Charter....Many persons believe that enduring peace cannot be achieved so long as the nation-state system continues as at present constituted....Enduring peace cannot be attained until the nation-states surrender to a world organization"(255).

The intended function of the U.N. set forth in this last quote has, unfortunately, already become a reality, and, as time progresses, this reality is becoming ever more frightening. Today we are indeed seeing "force" being used to "compel" nations to conduct themselves "within the framework of the established world system." It is now possible for a country to incite the wrath of the U.N. simply by refusing to comply with just about any demand that is placed upon it by the Security Council, as the proceeding *New York Times* quote confirms: "[T]he [U.N.] Security Council widened its definition of what constitutes a threat to peace and security in today's world, saying this now includes 'proliferation of all weapons of mass destruction' as well as 'non-military sources of instability in the economic, social, humanitarian, and ecological fields.' Such language seems to cover just about anything that could go wrong in the present-day world. So a more politically intrusive United Nations may be the real price the world must pay if it wants fewer conflicts and smaller peacekeeping bills in the future"(256).

Consider also the following relevant quote, from the former U.N. Secretary General Kofi Annan: "It is important to define [U.N.] intervention as broadly as possible, to include actions along a wide continuum from the most pacific to the most coercive"(257).

Now we can make sense of what the U.N. Charter means when it states in Article 1, Section 2, Chapter 1, that the U.N.'s purpose is "To develop friendly relations among nations...and to take other appropriate measures to strengthen international peace."

If you have any question as to what is meant by these "other appropriate measures," take a look at the next few quotes:

- "Over the next 20 to 30 years [as of 1995], we are going to end up with world government. It's inevitable....[W]e have to empower the United Nations and...we have to govern and regulate human interaction....There's going to be conflict, coercion and consensus. That's all part of what will be required as we give birth to the first global civilization." - *San Francisco Weekly*(258).

- "We must exercise responsibility not just at home, but around the world....America must stand against the poisoned appeals of extreme nationalism....To meet these challenges we are helping to write international rules of the road of the twenty-first century, protecting those who join the family of nations and isolating [imposing sanctions upon and/or bombing] those who do not." - President Bill Clinton, state of the Union address, January 28, 1998(259, pp. 130, 131).

- "As for the New World Order...[t]he basic rules...[are]: the rule of law for the weak, the rule of force,...state power and intervention for the strong." - Noam Chomsky(45, p. 271).

The United States military has expressed these same sentiments on numerous occasions--that its goal is to dominate the world scene in cooperation with other major military powers around the world (ultimately operating under the direction of the U.N., of course). One noteworthy example of this is found in "Joint Vision 2020," a document produced by the United States Department of Defense (released on May 30, 2000), which states: "'The ultimate goal of our military force is to accomplish the objectives directed by the National Command Authorities. For the joint force of the future, this goal will be achieved through full spectrum dominance--the ability of US forces, operating unilaterally or in combination with multinational and interagency partners, to defeat any adversary and control any situation across the full range of military operations.

"The full range of operations includes maintaining a posture of strategic deterrence. It includes theatre engagement and presence activities. It includes conflict involving employment of strategic forces and weapons of mass destruction, major theatre wars, regional conflicts and smaller-scale contingencies. It also includes those ambiguous situations residing between peace and war, such as peace-keeping and peace enforcement operations, as well as non-combat humanitarian relief operations and support to domestic authorities.

"The label full spectrum dominance implies that US forces are able to conduct prompt, sustained, and synchronised operations with combinations of forces tailored to specific situations, and with access to and freedom to operate in all domains--space, sea, land, air and information. Additionally, given the global nature of our interests and obligations, the United States must maintain its overseas presence forces and the ability to rapidly project power worldwide in order to achieve full spectrum dominance"(551).

In other words, total global domination. Do notice how this document stresses the use of "weapons of mass destruction" in pursuit of this goal. Maybe now you can understand why the globalist sell-outs in Washington are so concerned about disarming non-compliant nations of such weapons--they obviously don't want any competition.

Considering the aforementioned globalist goal of world domination through multinational military engagements, can you guess what the real agenda was behind the 1999 U.S.-led bombing of Kosovo? If not, perhaps the following few quotes will help:

- "Europe's long war [in history] has...[been] a war against the nation-state....The idea is on the march again today....And what is this idea? It is world government....This, after all, is why we are today attacking a sovereign nation, Yugoslavia, which has a legally elected government and which threatens none of its neighbors." - *Guardian*(377).

- "In an article for *Newsweek* magazine, the Prime Minister [Tony Blair] suggests that NATO's action in Kosovo could be a model for future international relations. Mr. Blair says: 'This is a conflict we are fighting...for a new internationalism [New World Order].' Establishing the principle that outside countries can intervene in a sovereign state...would mark a shift in the basic norms of international relations..." - London *Times*(260).

- "I think it's a U.S.-NATO thing. They want to show that they're the New World Order....I guess they're giving notice if you don't follow the dictates of the New World Order, this is what can happen to you." - Douglas Mattern, president of the Association of World Citizens, Marlin Maddoux radio program, "Point of View," June 11, 1999(18, pp. 245, 246).

A careful consideration of the last several quotes should be enough to convince you that the Kosovo bombing was yet another U.N. operation of taking "appropriate measures to strengthen international peace" through "conflict, coercion, and consensus," on the way toward world government. But in case you're still not convinced, consider the fact that the Kosovo campaign, being a NATO effort, places U.N. fingerprints all over it, since the U.N. Charter, under articles 52-54, declares NATO (along with any other such alliance) to be a U.N. "regional arrangement." This only makes sense, seeing that both NATO and the U.N. are globalist creations. And it must also be kept in mind that, just after the Kosovo bombing ceased, U.N. "peacekeeping" troops were sent in to occupy the region as a new outpost of the ever-expanding globalist empire--such a typical pattern!

The operation in Kosovo provides us with a good glimpse at how the globalists use propaganda to aid their military efforts of whipping nations into submission to their authority. In the August 16, 1999 edition of the *New York Times*, an article entitled "NATO Peacekeepers Plan a System of Controls for the News Media in Kosovo" was printed, which stated: "The United States and its allies charged with peacekeeping in Kosovo are establishing a system to control the news media in the province that would write a code of conduct for journalists, monitor their compliance with it and establish enforcement mechanisms to punish those who violate its rules." The article then went on to say that a Media Regulatory Commission was to be established that would "have the right to censor material, to fine stations or to order certain journalists or stations off the air." This is how the U.S. and U.N. spread "freedom" and "democracy" (whatever that means) abroad.

The Kosovo intervention also provides us with a good glimpse at the domestic propaganda that always accompanies globalist-instituted U.S. foreign policy. The declared justification for this intervention was "to stop ethnic cleansing." Actually, considering the dismal record of U.S. human rights abuses, we must hold in high suspicion any claim of the U.S. government to be concerned with this issue. But if the U.S. government was really so concerned about stopping Milosevic's human rights violations (where about 10,000 ethnic Albanians were said to have been murdered), then why didn't it (or the U.N., for that matter) intervene in the 1994 Rwanda genocide incident, where 800,000 Tutsis died at the hand of the Hutus in just 100 days? Both men, women, and children were brutally murdered while the U.S. (and the U.N.) sat idly by. Not only were troops not sent in, but the few that were already there were withdrawn. Obviously the murderous Hutus of Rwanda were being compliant with globalist policies, whereas Milosevic was not. Also, Rwanda is not exactly a politically or economically strategic piece of prime real estate, if you catch my drift.

And why was it, you may ask, that Milosevic wasn't compliant with the policies of the globalists?--For the same reasons that the entire Serbian Parliament wasn't: the outrageous demands made by NATO in the Rambouillet Accord. Here are some startling excerpts from it: "NATO personnel shall enjoy, together with their vehicles, vessels, aircraft, and equipment, free and unrestricted passage and unimpeded access throughout the FRY [Federal Republic of Yugoslavia] including associated airspace and territorial waters. This shall include, but not be limited to,...utilization of any areas or facilities as required for support, training, and operations....

"NATO shall be immune from all legal process, whether civil, administrative, or criminal....NATO personnel, under all circumstances and at all times, shall be immune from...any civil, administrative, criminal, or disciplinary offenses which may be committed by them in the FRY....NATO personnel shall be immune from any form of arrest, investigation, or detention by the authorities in the FRY....

"NATO shall be exempt from duties, taxes, and other charges and inspections and custom regulations including providing inventories or other routine customs documentation, for personnel, vehicles, vessels, aircraft, equipment, supplies, and provisions entering, exiting, or transiting the territory of the FRY in support of the operation....

"The authorities in the FRY shall facilitate, on a priority basis and with all appropriate means, all movement of personnel, vehicles, vessels, aircraft, equipment, or supplies, through or in the airspace, ports, airports, or roads used....Vehicles, vessels, and aircraft used in support of the operation shall not be subject to licensing or registration requirements, nor commercial insurance...and the right to use all of the electromagnetic spectrum for this purpose, free of cost....

"The Parties shall provide, free of cost, such public facilities as NATO shall require to prepare for and execute the operation....NATO and NATO personnel shall be immune from claims of any sort which may arise out of activities in pursuance of the operation"(261).

What nation would have agreed to such outrageous demands? This was certainly no "peace accord." Like the Versailles Treaty, it was a setup designed to bring about a war. While keeping these demands in mind, notice what Bill Clinton said when speaking at Spangdahlem Air Base in Germany, on May 5, 1999: "Our mission in Kosovo has nothing to do with trying to acquire territory or dominate others"(114, p. 204). Sure, Bill.

Coming back to Iraq and the 1991 Gulf War for just a moment, it is important to draw attention to one final point: It has often been asked why Saddam was never removed from power after this war. This, of course, is a very good question, and the power-hungry globalists have a very good answer. After the Gulf War, with the severe reduction of Saddam's war machine--previously the largest in the Arab world--it was initially hoped, as stated before, that Saddam, as well as other radical Arab leaders, would be coerced into submission through fear. But when this didn't happen, it was decided that leaving the Iraqi leader in power (at least for a time) would better serve their purposes. This fact was vividly disclosed in the proceeding blatant admission of Fareed Zakaria, former managing editor of the CFR's journal, *Foreign Affairs*: "Yes, it's tempting to get rid of Saddam. But his bad behavior actually serves America's [i.e. the CFR's] purposes in the region....If Saddam Hussein did not exist, we would have to invent him....The end of Saddam Hussein would be the end of the anti-Saddam coalition. Nothing destroys an alliance like the disappearance of the enemy....Maintaining a long-term American presence in the gulf would be difficult in the absence of a regional threat"(262)[Endnote 146].

After the 9-11 tragedy, of course, Saddam had worn out his usefulness to the globalists. With the "war on terror" in the Middle East, the maintenance of his position as the Iraqi leader was no longer necessary to justify a strong U.S. military presence in the region. Thus, removing Saddam from power became most appealing to the globalists, especially since Iraq had the second largest oil reserves on the planet, and since Iraq would serve as a good launching point for future invasions in the region. So remove him they did, initiating a preemptive strike on Baghdad on March 19, 2003.

Just as the Gulf War against Iraq in 1991 was planned in advance by the globalists, so too was the 2003 attack. In fact, it was planned several years before Bush Jr. even entered office. ABC's Ted Koppel brought this point out on the March 5, 2003 edition of Nightline. Later, on the following Monday, March 10, the ABC News website featured a story on this broadcast, titled "The Plan: Were Neo-Conservatives' 1998 Memos a Blueprint for Iraq War?" In this article, it was stated: "Years before George W. Bush entered the White House, and years before the Sept. 11 attacks set the direction of his presidency, a group of influential neo-conservatives hatched a plan to get Saddam Hussein out of power.

"The group, the Project for the New American Century, or PNAC, was founded in 1997. Many of its members would later end up in the administration of President George W. Bush. Among its supporters were three Republican former officials who were sitting out the Democratic presidency of Bill Clinton: Donald Rumsfeld, Dick Cheney and Paul Wolfowitz [all CFR members].

"In open letters to Clinton and GOP congressional leaders the next year, the group called for 'the removal of Saddam Hussein's regime from power' and a shift toward a more assertive U.S. policy in the Middle East, including the use of force if necessary to unseat Saddam.

"And in a report just before the 2000 election that would bring Bush to power, the group predicted [this report was produced in September of 2000] that the shift would come about slowly, unless there were 'some catastrophic and catalyzing event, like a new Pearl Harbor [Endnote 147].'

"That event came on Sept. 11, 2001. By that time, Cheney was vice president, Rumsfeld was secretary of defense, and Wolfowitz his deputy at the Pentagon.

"The next morning--before it was even clear who was behind the attacks-- Rumsfeld insisted at a Cabinet meeting that Saddam's Iraq should be 'a principal target of the first round of [war against] terrorism,' according to Bob Woodward's book, *Bush At War*.

"What started as a theory in 1997 was now on its way to becoming official U.S. foreign policy.

"Some critics of the Bush administration's foreign policy, especially in Europe, have portrayed PNAC as, in the words of Scotland's *Sunday Herald*, 'a secret blueprint for U.S. global domination.'

"The group was never secret about its aims. In its 1998 open letter to Clinton, the group openly advocated unilateral U.S. action against Iraq....

"...[T]he group's thinking stemmed from the principles of Ronald Reagan: 'A strong America. A morally grounded foreign policy...that defended American security and American [globalist] interests....'

"...In reports, speeches, papers and books, they pushed for an aggressive foreign policy to defend U.S. [globalist] interests around the globe.

"Clinton did order airstrikes against Iraq in 1998, but through the rest of his presidency and the beginning of Bush's, America's 'containment' policy for Saddam lay dormant--until September 2001.

"'Before 9/11, this group...could not win over the president to this extravagant image of what [globalist] foreign policy required,' said Ian Lustick, a Middle East expert at the University of Pennsylvania. 'After 9/11, it was able to benefit from the gigantic eruption of political capital, combined with the supply of military preponderance in the hands of the president. And this small group, therefore, was able to gain direct contact and even control, now, of the White House.'

"Like other critics, Lustick paints PNAC in conspiratorial tones: 'This group, what I call the tom-tom beaters, have set an agenda and have made the president feel that he has to live up to their definitions of manliness, their definitions of success and fear, their definitions of failure...'"(263).

Proof that the Bush crowd had plans to invade Iraq very early on is overwhelming. Here's another compelling piece of evidence: The *Sunday Herald* reported on January 11, 2004, that Paul O'Neill, Bush's former treasury secretary, revealed that "The President took office in January 2001 fully intending to invade Iraq and desperate to find an excuse for pre-emptive war against

Saddam Hussein"(473).

Recall that initially, in order to drum up public support for the 2003 war against Iraq, the idea was proposed that Saddam was somehow involved in the 9-11 terrorist plot. In this regard, the *USA Today* website reported on September 17, 2003: "Most Americans suspect that Saddam Hussein was somehow connected to the Sept. 11, 2001, attacks, polls show. The Bush administration has said since before the war with Iraq that Iraq has ties to al-Qaeda, which carried out the plot....[H]owever, President Bush said [on September 17], 'We have no evidence that Saddam Hussein was involved with...September 11th.'...Critics charge that the president and members of his administration have misled the public about the former Iraqi leader's connection to the Sept. 11 attacks to justify the U.S. invasion of the country"(264).

On a related note, the February 27, 2003 *New York Times* talked about a letter written by John Brady Kiesling, a diplomat at the U.S. embassy in Athens, announcing his resignation to Secretary of State Colin Powell. Kiesling resigned because of his disgust over this false 9-11/Iraq connection being used as a pretext for war. In this letter, he stated: "We spread disproportionate terror and confusion in the public mind, arbitrarily linking the unrelated problems of terrorism and Iraq. The result, and perhaps the motive, is to justify a vast misallocation of shrinking public wealth to the military and to weaken the safeguards that protect American citizens from the heavy hand of government."

The main reason given for this war, as you may recall, was the claim that Saddam indisputably had huge stockpiles of "weapons of mass destruction." But as the weeks went by after this conflict began, and no such weapons were being found, it became painfully obvious that this claim was a complete fabrication. In fact, notice what Deputy Secretary of Defense Paul Wolfowitz said in a *Vanity Fair* interview on May 10, 2003: "The truth is that for reasons that have a lot to do with the U.S. government bureaucracy we settled on the one issue that everyone could agree on which was weapons of mass destruction as the core reason [for the war]..."(265).

Furthermore, on May 1, 2005, the *Sunday Times* of London reported on a secret document known as the Downing Street memo. It was the minutes of a meeting on Iraq between British Prime Minister Tony Blair and President George W. Bush that was held on July 23, 2002. Written by Matthew Rycroft, a Downing Street foreign policy aide, it stated: "Bush wanted to remove Saddam through military action, justified by the conjunction of terrorism and WMD....[T]he intelligence and facts were being fixed around the policy." In other words, fake intelligence was being created that would support the preconceived war agenda.

This story was later expanded upon by the June 12, 2005 edition of *The*

Times: "Ministers were warned in July 2002 that Britain was committed to taking part in an American-led invasion of Iraq and they had no choice but to find a way of making it legal. The warning, in a leaked Cabinet Office briefing paper [Downing Street memo], said Tony Blair had already agreed to back military action to get rid of Saddam Hussein at a summit at the Texas ranch of President George W Bush three months earlier. The briefing paper, for participants at a meeting of Blair's inner circle on July 23, 2002, said that since regime change was illegal it was 'necessary to create the conditions' which would make it legal. This was required because, even if ministers decided Britain should not take part in an invasion, the American military would be using British bases. This would automatically make Britain complicit in any illegal US action"(478).

So what we have here is a phony excuse of "weapons of mass destruction" being used to launch a war that Washington and London were bent on waging. It didn't matter how many people had to die on either side of the conflict--they wanted war, and that's all there was to it.

Of course, even if Saddam did have weapons of mass destruction, it was the most outrageous hypocrisy for the U.S. to take on the responsibility of disarming him, since no other nation in the world possesses more of such weapons than the U.S. itself, which does not hesitate to use them at will. For example, during the 2003 Iraq campaign, weapons such as the MOAB (Massive Ordinance Air Blast) bomb was used, which is said to deliver the same force as a nuclear bomb, minus the radiation.

And there's another, even more outrageous sign of hypocrisy on the part of the U.S. wanting to disarm Saddam: Any mass destruction weapons that he once had were obtained via aid from the U.S. government, back in the 1980s.

In addition to the MOAB bomb, the U.S. military used another weapon of mass destruction in the 2003 Iraq campaign--depleted uranium, or DU, as reported by, among others, CNN, on May 24, 2003. And this was by no means the first time this had happened. In fact, DU was used in 1991, during the first Iraq campaign, which has been linked, at least in part, to what has become known as "Gulf War Syndrome." Thus we see that even our own servicemen mean nothing to the bigwigs at the Pentagon, let alone innocent civilians in foreign countries like Iraq. Notice what Senator Russell Feingold had to say about this: "[The Pentagon's] assertion that no Gulf War veterans could be ill from exposure to DU...contradicts numerous pre- and post-war reports, some from the U.S. Army itself"(266)[Endnote 148].

Then we had the reports of a sharp increase in cancer rates in post-Gulf-War Iraq, particularly among children. Speaking on such shameful statistics, the *San Jose Mercury News* reported back in 1998: "The number of cancer cases among Iraqi civilians...has grown at least threefold since the 1991 Persian Gulf

War, according to Iraqi doctors and medical records....Most alarming, doctors say, is a sharp rise in leukemia cases among children"(374).

There can be little doubt that all of this was directly attributable to the use of DU in the 1991 Gulf War, which is highly carcinogenic.

Cancer-causing DU was also dumped in large quantities in Kosovo, back in 1999. Here's what the BBC said about this: "A British biologist, Roger Coghill, says he expects the depleted uranium weapons used by U.S. aircraft over Kosovo will cause more than 10,000 fatal cancer cases....In mid-June scientists at Kozani in northern Greece were reporting that radiation levels were 25% above normal whenever the wind blew from the direction of Kosovo. And Bulgarian researchers reported finding levels eight times higher than usual within Bulgaria itself, and up to 30 times higher in Yugoslavia"(375).

Now on to another important point about the 2003 campaign against Iraq: The idea, so often portrayed in the media, that the U.N. was against this war, you can bet, was a blatant lie on the part of U.N. officials. This idea had to be gotten across to the public, however, in order for the U.N. to create, maintain, or restore the image of itself as the "good guy" in world affairs. But understand that, at the highest levels of power, the U.N., from the beginning, wanted this war, just like it has wanted so many other wars around the world, since the time it was founded. Notice, for instance, what the Fox News website reported on January 18, 2003, about two months before the Iraq war broke out: "Top U.N. officials warned Iraq on Saturday that the January 27 deadline for the results of weapons inspections is fast approaching, and that time is running out for the country to cooperate and avoid a war. 'Iraq has not cooperated sufficiently with the United Nations weapons inspectors, and we will impress the seriousness of the situation to them,' top U.N. inspector Hans Blix told reporters Saturday in Cyprus. 'The world would like to be assured that Iraq is rid of weapons of mass destruction. Until we, the inspectors, have been convinced of that we cannot so report to the Security Council.'" This same article then went on to report about an Iraqi physicist, Faleh Hassan, who was questioned by U.N. inspectors about some documents in his possession. Hassan told Fox News that these documents "were from his private research projects and students' theses. He accused the inspectors of 'Mafia-like' tactics"(378).

Is it not obvious what was going on here? Were these inspectors really interested in averting a war? Of course not! And neither was the Bush administration.

Don't think for one moment, as was also often portrayed in the media, that Bush was going against the U.N. by invading Iraq. Bush was not "defying" the U.N.--he was doing exactly what the U.N. wanted. Just like his father before him, Bush Jr. had always been a major fan of the U.N., which is why he officially signed the U.S. back on to UNESCO [Endnote 149]. And let's not forget that he said he was enforcing U.N. Resolution 1441 through his Iraq invasion. The apparent discordance over this war between the U.N. and the Bush administration was just that--apparent. William Shakespear was right when he wrote, "All the world's a stage." But in this case, it's the globalists putting on the show. In fact, check out this bold admission made by an unnamed White House Aide to a *New York Times* reporter: "We're an empire now, and when we act, we create our own reality. And while you're studying that reality--judiciously, as you will--we'll act again, creating other new realities, which you can study too, and that's how things will sort out. We're history's actors...and you, all of you, will be left to just study what we do." - *New York Times*, October 17, 2004(554).

Many erroneously believed that the U.N. was against the preemptive nature of the strike that the U.S. launched against Iraq in 2003. However, this belief was based on a complete misunderstanding of the true nature of the U.N., at its top echelons of power. In fact, as the December 1, 2004 *Independent* reported, the U.N. had developed plans to make preemptive strikes an official policy of its Security Council: "The United Nations secretary general is poised to recommend the first major overhaul of the UN in its 60-year history which will back the use of pre-emptive military strikes with the approval of a more proactive Security Council." In other words, the U.N. hierarchy was calling for purging the Security Council of members who did not favor preemptive strikes, and replacing them with people who did favor such actions.

This article then went on to say: "Kofi Annan is due to present a report tomorrow by a team of 16 high-level experts after he formed the panel a year ago in the midst of the Iraq crisis and asked it to come up with solutions for dealing with the challenges to global security in the 21st century....[T]he report recognises the international community needs to be concerned about the 'nightmare scenarios combining terrorists, weapons of mass destruction and irresponsible states and much more besides, which may conceivably justify the use of force, not just reactively, but preventively and before a latent threat becomes imminent'"(407).

Such a policy obviously leaves the door wide open for invading any country of the U.N.'s choosing, under the vague pretext that the target country might pose a future threat. So much for the U.N. being an instrument for peace!

On the very next day (December 2, 2004), the *Washington Times* covered a speech that Bush Jr. gave in Halifax, Nova Scotia, which clearly revealed that this preemptive strike policy was to be the standard procedure to follow for advancing the cause of the New World Order: "President Bush yesterday challenged international leaders to create a new world order, declaring pre-September 11 multilateralism outmoded and asserting that freedom from terrorism will come only through pre-emptive action against enemies of democracy....'Defense alone is not a sufficient strategy,' he said. 'There is only one way to deal with enemies who plot in secret and set out to murder the innocent and the unsuspecting: We must take the fight to them'"(408).

Later, on February 13, 2005, Kofi Annan, speaking at the 41st Munich Conference on Security Policy, stated that the European Union and the United States (in cooperation with the U.N., of course) needed to work more closely together to "combat terrorism" with an attitude of "collective security," and to form "the backbone of a new world order in the 21st century"(455).

The truth is, ever since May 3, 1994, when President Clinton signed Presidential Decision Directive 25 (PDD-25), U.S. soldiers have been wearing U.N. shoulder patches and berets, and have been placed officially under U.N. control. As a matter of fact, as the December 24, 2004 edition of the *New York Sun* reported, a federal court has approved of these treasonous measures: "A federal judge in Washington [Paul Friedman] has upheld the right of the American military to place its personnel under United Nations command and force those soldiers to wear insignia designed by the world body"(433). Thus it should be clear that any actions the U.S. military takes are in total agreement with U.N. directives, regardless the spin we hear in the media. This is as true for the 2003 campaign in Iraq as it is for any other.

Incidentally, don't you find it just a LITTLE strange that the U.N., the supposed champion of human rights, never so much as questioned the official U.S. policy of torturing Iraqi prisoners? Isn't it obvious that the U.S. and the U.N., at the highest levels of power, are two sides of the same coin?

On June 8, 2004, the U.N. Security Council produced a draft resolution regarding the steps that were to be taken after the proposed upcoming U.S. pullout from Iraq on June 30. It basically called for an international force (under U.N. direction, naturally) to remain in Iraq and "maintain peace." Rest assured that this was the plan all along--for the U.S. to do the dirty work of bombing the country so that the U.N. could later move in and take over the reins, being welcomed as a "better alternative" to U.S. occupation forces. It's a virtually foolproof method of conquest that has worked almost flawlessly for the U.N. for decades.

Of course, things didn't quite go so well for the U.N. to move in and set up shop, in the time-frame it had hoped for. Because of an increase in uprisings by Iraqi "insurgents" (freedom fighters), the U.N. decided to pull back and wait until U.S. forces could crush out all resistance and make things safe for its "peacekeeping" forces to enter the country.

So, do you now understand the deadly game of global conquest that is being played out here? Do you not see that all these military operations of the U.S. and the U.N. are complete miserable frauds?

Appendix 9

Hi-tech weather modification

"As one specialist [Gordon J.F. McDonald] noted, 'By the year 2018, technology will make available to the leaders of the major nations a variety of techniques for conducting secret warfare.....Techniques of weather modification could be employed to produce prolonged periods of drought or storm, thereby weakening a nation's capacity and forcing it to accept the demands of the competitor'" - Zbigniew Brzezinski, *Between Two Ages*(48).

Weather modification technology is rarely discussed in the mainstream media. On the sparse occasions that it has been mentioned, such references have almost exclusively pertained to its use by foreign governments. One instance of this nature was in the November 13, 1997 edition of the *Wall Street Journal*, in which staff reporter Chen May Yee wrote an article called "Malaysia to Battle Smog With Cyclones," on page A19, where he stated: "Malaysia's war on smog is about to get a new twist. The government wants to create man-made cyclones to scrub away the haze that has plagued Malaysia since July. 'We will use special technology to create an artificial cyclone to clean the air,' said Datuk Law Hieng Ding, minister for science, technology and the environment.

"The plan calls for the use of new Russian technology to create cyclones...to cause torrential rains, washing the smoke out of the air. The Malaysian cabinet and the finance minister have approved the plan, Datuk Law said. A Malaysian company, BioCure Sdn. Bhd., will sign a memorandum of understanding soon with a government-owned Russian party to produce the cyclone. Datuk Law declined to disclose the size of the cyclone to be generated, or the mechanism.

"'The details I don't have,' he said. He did say, though, that the cyclone generated would be 'quite strong.' Datuk Law also declined to disclose the price of creating the cyclone. But, he said, Malaysia doesn't have to pay if the project doesn't work."

On those extremely rare occasions that we find mainstream media discussion of the employment of weather modification by the U.S. government, it is almost always by a foreign press agency. One such occasion was the November 23, 2000 edition of the London *Times*, which quoted world-renowned scientist Dr. Rosalie Bertell as saying that "US military scientists are working on weather systems as a potential weapon." This rather revealing article then went on to say that "The methods [of weather control] include the enhancing of storms and the diverting of vapor rivers in the Earth's atmosphere to produce targeted droughts or floods."

Efforts to prevent the use of weather-altering technology for military purposes date back to the 1970s. A good example of this is found in a 1994 U.N. publication titled "Basic Facts About the United Nations." On the inside of the front cover, a list was given of some of the major agreements that the U.N. has negotiated with the nations of the world over the years. The second item on the list was a treaty dating back to 1977. It was referenced as "1977--The Convention on the Prohibition of Military or Any Other Hostile Use of Environmental Modification Techniques." This agreement was then described as follows: "ENMOD Convention prohibits the use of techniques that would have widespread, long-lasting or severe effects through deliberate manipulation of natural processes and cause such phenomena as...tidal waves...and changes in climate and in weather patterns."

Here you have an example of a U.N. treaty that had good intentions, which, if adhered to, would be beneficial to mankind (obviously the result of sincere delegates who were blissfully unaware that the top dogs of the U.N. did not share their concerns for the good of mankind, but have generally allowed such treaties to pass since they at least look good on paper, serving as effective public relations propaganda). But, as has almost always been the case with any useful and sensible U.N. treaty, apparently no one is adhering to it.

One of the people who pushed early on for such a treaty, which was reported in the June 24, 1975 edition of the *Providence Journal Bulletin*, was Senator Claiborne Pell (D-RI), who stated that "The U.S. and other world powers should sign a treaty to outlaw the tampering with weather as an instrument of war....We need a treaty now to prevent such actions--before the military leaders of the world start directing storms...[and] manipulating climates...against their enemies.

"The basic idea of environmental warfare is simple--if a nation can learn to trigger natural events it can inflict terrible damage on an enemy through rainfall, flooding, tidal waves...and even climate changes that could devastate an enemy nation's agriculture. It may seem a great leap of imagination to...such science-fiction ideas as...melting the polar ice cap, changing the course of warm ocean currents, or modifying the weather of an adversary's farm belt. But, in military technology, today's science fiction is tomorrow's strategic reality."

Senator Pell's references to "directing storms," "manipulating climates," "flooding," "melting the polar ice cap," and "changing the course of warm ocean currents" are particularly interesting when one considers the strange extremes in weather that have been occurring around the world, beginning especially in the early 1990s--floods, hurricanes, tornadoes, droughts, extremes of hot and cold, el nino, global warming, ozone depletion, etc.

In the August 1998 issue of *Life*, in an article called "Weather: Special Report," on p. 40, we find an illuminating report on just how strange global weather patterns have become: "The rain is biblical, bucketing down as if God meant to drown Manhattan's haughty towers....Everyone's talking about the weather--or cursing it, or trembling before it, or theorizing as to cause and effect--and you needn't be paranoid to conclude that climatic conditions have gone batty in recent months....

"In the U.S. it started early last year when the Truckee River invaded Reno, Nev....A few months later, more than 30 died as rivers in the Ohio Valley burst their banks. The Red River swallowed Grand Forks, N.Dak., displacing 50,000. Not long after that, the rogue Pacific current known as El Nino began wreaking havoc around the world.

"Indonesia's jungles burned while Chile's Atacama Desert got a foot of rain. Snow fell in Guadalajara for the first time since 1881. Canada suffered its worst-ever ice storm. Floods killed thousands in Africa. In Peru endless downpours created a 2,300-square-mile lake on which President Alberto Fujimori Jet-Skied to promote tourism.

"Back in the States, daffodils popped up in midwinter Chicago, and Washington, D.C.'s cherry blossoms were three months early. Winter storms that usually hit Alaska veered toward California, pitching mudslides onto mansions. Throughout the West, this spring was the soggiest on record. The tornado season was the deadliest since '74, with a body count of 124, as the worst twisters skipped the Great Plains' Tornado Alley for the more densely populated Southeast.

"All that was prelude to the wild summer of '98. Thunderstorms with hurricane-force winds trashed Moscow. The rain-swollen Yangtze River killed more than 400 as it cut a swath through central China.

"One weekend, six rafters were killed on California rivers that were running at least 50 percent higher and faster than normal; the next weekend two dozen people were killed by storms that rampaged through the Midwest and East, dumping a foot of rain in parts of Ohio and West Virginia. In Frame, W.Va., a four-month-old baby was seized from his mother's arms by the rising current and swept away. Florida, cleaning up after its twisters, was plagued again, this time by fire caused by aberrant weather patterns. The state suffered its worst rash of wildfires in history, with more than 2,000 outbreaks. A half million acres were incinerated and property losses ran to a quarter billion dollars.

"To sum up: Since the beginning of 1997, more than 16,000 have been killed world-wide by the weather and nearly $50 billion in damage has been done. In the U.S., the figures are 456 dead and $13 billion lost. While there have been cataclysms of greater immensity and intensity in our century, the distribution, variety and frequency of the recent rotten weather has been extraordinary. The new movie, 'The Avengers,' has a villain who specializes in climate manipulation. You peer from the window and wonder: Is he out there?"

Yes, it makes you wonder, doesn't it?

In the first ten days of May 2003, record tornado statistics were set, with a total of 412 tornadoes touching down in several states from Kansas to Georgia, 22 of which were F5s. In all, a total of 44 deaths resulted. This broke the previous record set in 1999, where about 200 tornadoes were reported within a ten-day time period. On March 28, 2007, 65 tornadoes ripped through parts of Oklahoma, Texas, Colorado, and Nebraska, leaving a massive trail of destruction in their wake.

Such record-setting weather extremes appear to have become the norm, and seem to be getting progressively worse. What is going on here? Are the globalists playing with their hi-tech toys? Are they using them for purposes that go far beyond military strategy?

If the technology exists to create "natural" disasters--and clearly it does--then why would anyone suppose that the globalist boys wouldn't use it? Not only does it have tremendous potential as a military weapon, to overpower and control populations, but it also provides a great opportunity to rake in huge profits in damage repairs and rebuilding projects. Wouldn't this last factor, by itself, be reason enough for this technology's utilization domestically, especially knowing the lust that the globalists have for massive wads of cash?

As far as the U.S. goes, most weather manipulations are conducted and coordinated at the HAARP (High-frequency Active Auroral Research Program) facility near the village of Gakona, Alaska. This facility bombards the ionosphere with extremely high and low frequency energy emissions (primarily radio waves). In conjunction with similar facilities around the country (like the magnetic-field-altering GWEN towers located in places like Mechanicsville and Ledyard, Iowa; Chelsea, Wisconsin; Shephard, Minnesota; Curryville and Dudley, Missouri; Whitney, Nebraska, and several other locations in Colorado and Montana) and multiple satellites in orbit, weather manipulation of just about any type can be conducted virtually anywhere, and with any desired intensity.

Interestingly, U.S. Patent No. 4,686,605, held by ARCO Power Technologies, Inc., the ARCO subsidiary that was contracted by the U.S. government to build HAARP, describes an ionospheric heater very similar to the HAARP heater. According to this patent, "Weather modification is possible by...altering upper atmospheric wind patterns or altering solar absorption patterns..." This patent then goes on to mention how "Alaska provides easy access to magnetic field lines that are especially suited to the practice of this invention, since many field lines which extend to desirable altitudes for this invention intersect the earth in Alaska." Given this revelation, is it not obvious why Alaska was chosen as the site for HAARP? [Endnote 150]

While it is clear that the U.S. government is modifying the weather, it does not yet have a total monopoly on this technology, or the use thereof. But it is definitely working toward this goal. For we find that, following President Clinton's re-election in 1996, a report called "Weather as a Force Multiplier: Owning the Weather in 2025" was submitted to the Chief of Staff of the U.S. Air Force, Ronald R. Fogleman, as part of an important directive called "Air Force 2025." The seven military officers who produced this report, presenting it on June 17, 1996, were Col. Tamzy J. House, Lt. Col. James B. Near Jr., Lt. Col. William B. Shields, Maj. Ronald J. Celentano, Maj. David M. Husband, Maj. Ann E. Mercer, and Maj. James E. Pugh. This report stated, in part: "Today, weather-modification is the alteration of weather phenomena over a limited area for a limited period of time. [But within] the next three decades, the concept of weather-modification could expand....Achieving such a highly accurate and reasonably precise weather-modification capability in the next 30 years will require overcoming some challenging but not insurmountable technological and legal hurdles....As more countries pursue, develop, and exploit increasing types and degrees of weather-modification technologies, we must be able to detect their efforts and counter their activities when necessary....[T]he technologies and capabilities associated with such a counter weather role will become increasingly important."

As you can see, the concept of weather control is very real, very serious, and very frightening. Ultimately, the globalists naturally want to exploit it to help hasten the attainment of their goal of global government. Bearing this in mind, look at what the February 24, 2004 *Miami Herald* said: "A new report ordered by the Pentagon warns that a sudden change in climate could become a violent global battle for control of scarce resources...." This report, according to the *Herald*, states that, although a dramatic change in climate is unlikely, it "'would challenge United States national security in ways that should be considered immediately." "The plausible consequences," continued the *Herald*, "include famine in Europe and nuclear showdowns over who controls what's left of the world's water, the futurists concluded.

"The report, commissioned by the Department of Defense's Office of Net Assessment, its internal think tank, reflects the Pentagon's policy of planning for the worst, said author and long-time Pentagon consultant Peter Schwartz...."

Do you suppose the globalists, with their weather-altering toys, are gearing up for something? Apparently so. For this article then went on to say: "While the Bush [Jr.] administration generally has not considered global warming much of an immediate threat, 'I did not write an impossible scenario,' Schwartz said. It could play out, he said, in the next 5 to 15 years.

"Unlike most climate-change studies, which examine global warming over more than a century, the Pentagon study is based on an 'abrupt climate change' that scientists say has happened in the past and could happen again soon."

And what would be the result of such a sudden climate change? The *Herald*, quoting from the Pentagon's report, supplied the answer: "Imagine eastern European countries, struggling to feed their populations with a falling supply of food, water and energy, eyeing Russia, whose population is already in decline, for access to its grains, minerals and energy supply. Or, picture Japan, suffering from flooding along its coastal cities and contamination of its fresh water supply, eyeing Russia's Sakhalin Island oil and gas reserves as an energy source....Envision Pakistan, India and China--all armed with nuclear weapons--skirmishing at their borders over refugees, access to shared rivers and arable land."

Next, the *Herald* added these comments: "Military showdowns could be fast and furious, the report speculates: In 2015, conflict in Europe over food and water supplies leads to strained relations. In 2022, France and Germany battle over the Rhine River's water. The U.S. Defense Department seals off America's borders to staunch floods of refugees from Mexico and the Caribbean.

"In 2025, as energy costs increase in nations struggling to cope with warmer and colder weather, the United States and China square off over access to Saudi Arabian oil.

"America would weather the climate changes best, albeit with declining agricultural fertility, according to the report. Europe would be hit hard with food shortages and streams of people leaving. China would be hurt by colder winters and hotter summers triggering widespread famine"(481).

In other words, the results of this "potential" climate change would be a globalist dream come true. With all the shortages, starvation, and warfare, the globalist boys would emerge as our saviors, offering their tyrannical world government as the solution to the problems that they themselves set up in the first place. I can just see them rubbing their hands together in anticipation of this.

As it turns out, the same technology that is used to modify the weather can also be used to create earthquakes and other geologic disruptions, simply by directing beams of energy near a fault or volcano, which create powerful vibrations that cause the earth's crust to locally crack or shift. This fact was admitted by former Secretary of Defense William Cohen, for example, on April 28, 1997, while speaking at a counterterrorism conference at the University of Georgia, Athens, sponsored by former Senator Sam Nunn. Cohen said: "Others are engaging even in an eco-type of terrorism whereby they can alter the climate, set off earthquakes, volcanoes remotely through the use of electromagnetic waves.

So there are plenty of ingenious minds out there that are at work finding ways in which they can wreak terror upon other nations. It's real, and that's the reason why we have to intensify our efforts, and that's why this is so important"(499).

With all this in mind, do you suppose the Asian Tsunami that resulted from the December 26, 2004 earthquake in the Indian Ocean may have been manufactured? It's awful funny how no warning was given of this disaster, even though it was known 2 hours in advance that it was headed for Sri Lanka. Neither were other locations given warning that were struck hours after Sri Lanka was hit.

And then there was the devastation wrought by Hurricane Katrina, which struck the coasts of Alabama, Mississippi, and Louisiana on August 28-29, 2005. Let us consider some highly suspicious occurrences surrounding this tragic event:

- President George W. Bush had cut back federal funding, beginning in 2003, for improving the levee system in New Orleans, citing the costs of the war in Iraq and the large Homeland Security budget as the justification(508).

- The Associated Press reported on September 2, 2005: "A group of Loudoun County sheriff's deputies heading to Louisiana to help maintain order among hurricane refugees had to turn around at the Virginia border when they couldn't get confirmation from emergency management officials, the Loudoun County sheriff said.

"After attempting for 12 hours to reach officials at the Federal Emergency Management Agency and the Louisiana Emergency Operations Center, the deputies were told to head home. The group of 22 officers and six emergency medical technicians was expected to arrive back in Leesburg by 2 a.m. Friday, according to a statement from the sheriff's office"(502).

- By the next day, September 3--a full five days after the storm struck--desperately-needed help was still not being provided by federal agencies, nor were they allowing non-governmental agencies to provide any help. As Louisiana Senator Mary Landrieu complained: "I understand that the U.S. Forest Service had water-tanker aircraft available to help douse the fires raging on our riverfront, but FEMA has yet to accept the aid. When Amtrak offered trains to evacuate significant numbers of victims--far more efficiently than buses--FEMA again dragged its feet. Offers of medicine, communications equipment and other desperately needed items continue to flow in, only to be ignored by the agency"(500).

- Yahoo News reported on the same day, September 3, that "Several states ready and willing to send National Guard troops to the rescue in New Orleans didn't get the go-ahead until days after the storm struck--a delay nearly certain to be investigated by Congress"(501).

- While on Meet the Press on September 4, Aaron Broussard, the president of Jefferson Parish in New Orleans, told Tim Russert: "We have been abandoned by our own country. Hurricane Katrina will go down in history as one of the worst storms ever to hit an American coast. But the aftermath of Hurricane Katrina will go down as one of the worst abandonments of Americans on American soil ever in U.S. history....Whoever is at the top of this totem pole, that totem pole needs to be chainsawed off and we've got to start with some new leadership. It's not just Katrina that caused all these deaths in New Orleans here. Bureaucracy has committed murder here in the greater New Orleans area and bureaucracy has to stand trial before Congress now....

"...We had Wal-Mart deliver three trucks of water. FEMA turned them back. They said we didn't need them. This was a week ago....[W]e had 1,000 gallons of diesel fuel on a Coast Guard vessel docked in my parish. When we got there with our trucks, FEMA says don't give [them] the fuel. Yesterday...FEMA comes in and cuts all of our emergency communication lines. They cut them without notice. Our sheriff, Harry Lee, goes back in, he reconnects the line. He posts armed guards and said no one is getting near these lines...."

- Not only was FEMA blocking domestic efforts to help the victims of Katrina, but even foreign assistance was being denied. For example, CBS News reported on September 1: "The U.S. Federal Emergency Management Agency has rejected a Russian offer to send rescue teams and other aid in the wake of Hurricane Katrina, a Russian emergency official said Thursday.

"Russia offered to send two transport planes with rescue teams, helicopters and other equipment to help deal with Katrina's aftermath"(503).

In all, about 50 countries offered aid of some sort, and every single one of these offers got turned down by FEMA.

- In addition to the government preventing help and supplies from getting to the suffering people in New Orleans, it also prevented these people from leaving the city to get their own help. Shepard Smith, reporting live for Fox News on September 3, revealed that the thousands of people who were told to take refuge in the Convention Center and the Superdome had been trapped inside for 6 days without food or water, and that nobody was allowed to leave the city across a nearby, easily-accessible bridge. He stated: "They've locked them in there. The government said, 'You go here [in the Convention Center], and you'll get help; or you go in that Superdome, and you'll get help.' And they didn't get help.

They got locked in there....

"And you know what they're doing now?...They have set up a check point at the bottom of this bridge....This is the bridge that takes you from New Orleans over into Gretna--from Orleans Parish into Jefferson Parish. It's the only way out--it's the connection to the rest of the world. And they've set up a check point. And anyone who walks up out of that city now is turned around. You are not allowed to go to Gretna, Louisiana from New Orleans, Louisiana. Over there, there's hope. Over there, there's electricity. Over there, there's food and water. But you cannot go from there to there [as he points]. The government will not allow you to do it. It's a fact."

Please notice how it was FEMA that was thwarting all of this aid to victims of this disaster. And who was it that placed FEMA specifically in charge of coordinating disaster relief for this storm? On August 27, 2005, the White House's website reported that "The President...authorizes the Department of Homeland Security, Federal Emergency Management Agency (FEMA), to coordinate all disaster relief efforts which have the purpose of alleviating the hardship and suffering caused by the [hurricane]"(504). And what was Bush's response to FEMA's performance? On September 2, he told Michael Brown, the agency's director: "Brownie, you're doing a heck of a job"(507).

And then came the typical coverup activities. Reuters revealed on September 6: "The U.S. government agency leading the rescue efforts after Hurricane Katrina said on Tuesday it does not want the news media to take photographs of the dead as they are recovered from the flooded New Orleans area.

"The Federal Emergency Management Agency, heavily criticized for its slow response to the devastation caused by the hurricane, rejected requests from journalists to accompany rescue boats as they went out to search for storm victims.

"An agency spokeswoman said space was needed on the rescue boats and that 'the recovery of the victims is being treated with dignity and the utmost respect'"(509). Well, it's good to know that FEMA had respect for these people after they died. But too bad they didn't have such respect for them when they were still alive, because THEY LET THEM DIE.

Predictably, on September 19, the Los Angeles Times carried an article called "House GOP Scraps Plan for Joint Probe on Hurricane Response"(513). Now why do you suppose they didn't want such an investigation?

Even up to almost a year later, the coverup activities were still underway. The Associated Press reported on July 20, 2006: "Residents of trailer parks set up by the Federal Emergency Management Agency to house hurricane victims in Louisiana aren't allowed to talk to the press without an official escort....

"In one instance, a security guard ordered an Advocate reporter out of a trailer during an interview in Morgan City. Similar FEMA rules were enforced in Davant, in Plaquemines Parish.

"FEMA spokeswoman Rachel Rodi wouldn't say whether the security guards' actions complied with FEMA policy, saying the matter was being reviewed. But she confirmed that FEMA does not allow the news media to speak alone to residents in their trailers.

"'If a resident invites the media to the trailer, they have to be escorted by a FEMA representative who sits in on the interview,' [said Rodi]....'That's just a policy'"(530).

Is it not obvious that this storm was exactly what the globalist-controlled Bush Jr. administration wanted? And isn't it clear that the Bushites went out of their way to see to it that maximum carnage resulted? Why would they do this, you ask? Here are some reasons:

- So that Haliburton, which was awarded the New Orleans cleanup contract, could reap maximum profits from maximum damage, as unchecked and undrained flood waters continued to reek havoc. I should also point out that, in order to further maximize the profiteering of Haliburton, Bush passed an executive order on September 8, which enabled post-Katrina rebuilding contractors to pay workers below the prevailing wage.

- To get people to beg for martial law, conditioning the public to accept such a measure as the standard operating procedure during a time of crisis.

- To purge the area of a significant portion of its unwanted, poverty-stricken black population, and thereby make it easier to grab up land for redevelopment. As Representative Richard Baker of Baton Rouge put it: "We finally cleaned up public housing in New Orleans. We couldn't do it, but God did"(512). And then, on October 5, 2005, CNN reported: "As Hurricane Katrina-ravaged cities begin the laborious process of rebuilding, there is increasing speculation that government officials may turn to the controversial--and often disparaged--use of eminent domain to revitalize the destroyed region.

"It's a prospect that's raising eyebrows among critics who fear that land developers will take advantage of the desperation in the region and push devastated homeowners out of their homes in the name of redevelopment"(514).

To ensure that the damage to New Orleans was maximized in the poor section of the city and minimized in the richer areas, it appears that the breaching of the levee may have actually been caused by explosives. There were several earwitnesses who testified to hearing a massive explosion coming from the area of the levee's breach. Though the reason given for this breaching was the presence of a barge found nearby, one would have to wonder why this barge was even left in the area, knowing that a powerful storm was on its way. Was it left there to provide a cover for the bombing of the levee?

As sinister as these exploitive and criminally-negligent activities were, you are probably asking what this all has to do with weather modification. Well, I would like to strongly suggest that this whole catastrophe was manmade, in order to expedite these exploitative criminal activities. Notice what Bush said, just prior to his tour of the areas devastated by this storm: "I'm not looking forward to this trip. It's as if the entire Gulf Coast were obliterated by the worst kind of weapon you can imagine"(505).

The technology to manipulate and intensify hurricanes and other storm systems has been employed by the U.S. government for a long time, by its own admission. For example, the official website of the Navy's Air Weapons Station, China Lake, contains this astonishing confession: "Weather modification was another area of China Lake preeminence. Between 1949 and 1978 China Lake developed concepts, techniques, and hardware that were successfully used in hurricane abatement, fog control, and drought relief. Military application of this technology was demonstrated in 1966 when Project Popeye was conducted to enhance rainfall to help interdict traffic on the Ho Chi Minh Trail"(529).

Realizing that weather modification technology involves ultra high and low frequency radiation, which can also cause the earth's crust to vibrate, triggering earthquakes and/or volcanic eruptions, it is profoundly important to take careful notice of what the *New Scientist* website said about Hurricane Charley that touched down in Florida in August of 2004: "[T]he storm...caused the Earth to vibrate. The planet's surface in the vicinity of the hurricane started moving up and down at several frequencies ranging from 0.9 to 3 millihertz. Such low-frequency vibrations have been detected following large earthquakes, but this is the first time a storm has been found to be the cause"(506).

Of course, the same phenomenon was detected at the time that Katrina tore through the Gulf. The website of the Center for Earthquake Research and Information in Memphis, Tennessee, gave this report shortly after Katrina had passed: "The microseisms [grew] relentlessly as Katrina approach[ed] slowly for at least 2 days. On August 28 the microseisms [were] so strong that the lines [were] overwriting each other"(510).

Was Hurricane Charley a practice run for Hurricane Katrina? And was the Pacific submarine earthquake that spawned the Asian tsunami a warmup for something bigger yet to come? It should be pointed out that Katrina was followed by Rita and Wilma in the following 6 weeks, which were also Category 5 storms. Rita was roughly 400 miles in diameter and Wilma had 959 millibars of pressure, setting a new record for hurricanes. Does this sound natural to you?

In case you can't come to grips with the fact that the government would use weather modification technology for such destructive purposes, I would ask, Why hasn't the government at least been using this technology, which clearly exists, to diminish or destroy highly destructive storms like Katrina?

The massive flooding in Des Moines, Iowa, in June 2008, is another good example of sinister weather modification. Pictures of this storm system taken from the ground by the *Boston Globe* revealed strange-looking concentric clouds around the top of the funnel, looking like they had aligned themselves around magnetic field lines--just the thing we would expect from hi-tech human intervention, but not from natural processes.

As a result of this calamity, almost all of the nation's ethanol production plants were either destroyed by the disaster or driven out of business because of the damage to the corn crops. Thus the major oil corporations had no competition as they soared their prices, at this same time, to well over $4.00 per gallon.

But coming back to our discussion of the possibility of earthquakes being orchestrated by HAARP and related systems, it's profoundly important to note the frequency and intensity of powerful earthquakes that have been occurring in recent years, as compared to what is on record for the past thousand years or so. Note the following statistics for earthquakes ranking 7.0 and higher over this time-frame:

9th century -1
10th-15th centuries -none
16th century -1
17th century -none
18th century -2
19th century -1
1900-1975 -9
1975-1978 -10
1979-1998 - about 364

And the numbers have continued to rise ever since. Pretty strange, wouldn't you say?

* * * * * * *

"From space, the masters of infinity would have the power to control the earth's

weather, to cause drought and flood, to change the tides and raise the level of the sea, to divert the gulf stream and change temperate climates to frigid. " - Lyndon Baines Johnson, 1958(519).

Appendix 10

Mandatory sterilization and other forms of population control

Mandatory sterilization and other methods of population control have been high priorities on the globalists' agenda for a long time. Even many scientific journals have featured articles on population control. The following quote from a 1970 article in *Science* is a good example of this: "The 'right' to breed implies ownership of children. This concept is no longer tenable....If parenthood is a right, population control is impossible"(150). Biologist Paul Silverman, speaking at the 1970 Earth Day conference, made this similar propagandic statement: "If voluntary restraints on population growth are not forthcoming, we will be faced with a need to consider coercive measures"(151, p. 31).

The globalist-controlled U.S. government has had a long history of practicing eugenics, particularly through unsolicited sterilization of certain "undesirables." As ABC News reported on May 15, 2005: "From the early 1900s to the 1970s, some 65,000 men and women were sterilized in this country, many without their knowledge, as part of a government eugenics program to keep so-called undesirables from reproducing. 'The procedures that were done here were done to poor folks,' said Steven Selden, professor at the University of Maryland. 'They were thought to be poor because they had bad genes or bad inheritance, if you will. And so they would be the focus of the sterilization'"(466).

And you thought only Adolf Hitler did things like this? But don't think that sterilization in this country is a thing of the past. And don't think that this is as sinister as it gets. Unfortunately, sterilization is only the tip of the iceberg.

Have you noticed all the talk about "overpopulation" in the media in recent years? Have you also noticed how the media are all-too-happy to lend an ear to supporters of the abortion rights, gay rights, and euthanasia rights movements? Is this because the media are so concerned about giving these activists a chance to voice their opinions? Not at all! Rest assured that all the globalist-controlled media are doing here is taking advantage of the supporters of these movements, exploiting their ambitions to serve their own twisted interests in population control.

And what interests they are! For not only do they want to halt population growth, but they seek to significantly reduce the present population as well, in order to be able to hoard the world's resources for their own selfish, greedy pursuits. Also, it is easier to control a smaller population--a population of "worker bees" that will serve as a global slave force to keep the gears of their machine turning.

The elderly, the poor, the handicapped, and the sick will, of course, find no welcome mat laid out for them under this emerging system [Endnote 151]. Regarding specifically the treatment of the elderly in the future, notice what demographer Barbara Logue, speaking at the annual conference of the American Economic Association, had to say, which was recorded in the January 12, 1997 edition of the *Minneapolis Star-Tribune*, in an article entitled "The Methuselah Dilemma: Can America Afford Grandma and Grandpa?": "It's time for the U.S. to consider moving from birth control to 'death control.'...Death control clearly has considerable potential as a reallocative mechanism for scarce resources such as health care."

Even the late Jacques Cousteau had gotten into the act. Here's what he had to say about "death control," as quoted in a U.N. publication, nonetheless: "It's terrible to have to say this. World population must be stabilized and to do that we must eliminate 350,000 people per day"(152, pp. 8-13).

In a 1972 population control propaganda book, *Population and Survival*, author Jack Nelson talked about a coming "International Mortality Lottery" which "would solve the world over-population crisis. Each year, five percent of the earth's inhabitants between the ages of 30 and 40 would be exterminated"(153, p. 103).

Another such "visionary," Bertrand Russell, mentioned some additional sinister methods that may be employed in the future, to reduce the world's population: "I do not predict that birth control is the only way in which population can be kept from increasing....War...has hitherto been disappointing in this respect, but perhaps bacteriological war may prove more effective. If a Black Death could be spread throughout the world once in every generation, survivors could procreate freely without making the world too full....The state of affairs might be somewhat unpleasant, but what of that? Really high-minded people are indifferent to happiness, especially other people's. There are three ways of securing a society that shall be stable as regards population. The first is that of birth control, the second that of infanticide or really destructive wars, and the third that of general misery, except for a powerful minority"(154, pp. 103, 104).

Did you notice Russell's reference to "bacteriological war," or a "Black Death," as a means of population control/reduction? Many have proposed that the AIDS virus was purposely developed for this very reason. While we don't have space here to provide detailed documentation of this, it's most instructive to draw attention to the proceeding statement made before Congress by Dr. Donald M. MacArthur, Deputy Director, Research and Engineering, Department of Defense, on June 9, 1969: "Within the next 5 to 10 years, it would probably be possible to make a new infective microorganism which could differ in certain important aspects from any known disease-causing organisms. Most important of these is that it might be refractory [resistant] to the immunological and therapeutic processes upon which we depend to maintain our relative freedom from infectious disease"(155). (Should you have any doubt that the government would ever unleash a deadly virus on the public, see Appendix 12.)

Another statement of this nature was made in the 1972 Bulletin of the United Nation's World Health Organization, Volume 47, page 251: "An attempt should be made to see if viruses can in fact exert selective effects on immune function. The possibility should be looked into that the immune response to the virus itself may be impaired if the inflicting virus damages, more or less selectively, the cell responding to the virus." Does it sound here like the World Health Organization is really interested in people's health?

In further regards to Bertrand Russell's mention of "bacteriological war," the September 6, 2003 edition of London's *Guardian* had this to say: "We now know that a blueprint for the creation of a global Pax Americana was drawn up...entitled Rebuilding America's Defenses, [which] was written in September 2000 by the neoconservative think tank, Project for the New American Century (PNAC) [which we mentioned earlier]....[This blueprint] hints that the US may consider developing <u>biological weapons 'that can target specific genotypes</u> [and] may <u>transform biological warfare from the realm of terror to a politically useful tool'</u>"(398)[Endnote 152].

Incidentally, the women's rights movement has also been manipulated by the globalists to advance their evil agenda of population control (as well as other things). One good proof of this point emerged on March 11, 1969, when the vice president of Planned Parenthood: World Population, Frederick S. Jaffe, wrote a proposal paper called "Activities Relevant to the Study of Population Policy for the U.S.," which dealt with measures that the U.S. government could undertake in the future to help reduce world population. In this paper he stated that the government should work to "restructure family, encourage increased homosexuality, educate for family limitation, fertility control agents in the water supply, <u>encourage women to work</u> [a major "pillar" of the women's rights movement]...and payment to encourage...abortion...and contraception"(8, p. 84). (Further information about globalist manipulation of the women's rights movement is provided in Appendix 11.)

In further regards to the globalists wanting to reduce the world's population, here's something shocking to consider: In June of 1979, construction began of a stone monument on one of the highest hilltops of Elbert County, Georgia, known as the "Georgia Guidestones." It consists of four giant granite slabs arranged in a standing position. The stones contain a "message for the world" in eight different languages. The project was launched by a man who went by the name of R.C. Christian, but his real identity has never been made public. The message is presented in a ten-point format, relating instructions, or guidelines, on how a world government can be made more feasible. Important to our current discussion is point number 1, which reads as follows:

"1. Maintain humanity under 500,000,000 in perpetual balance with nature."

Are we to understand from this that the globalists intend to reduce the population down to this shockingly low level? Apparently so.

Appendix 11

Abolishing the family

With all that we have studied about the globalists and their evil designs, it shouldn't be too startling to come to the realization that they also have plans to abolish the family unit, in order to maximize their control over the rearing of the young. However, this task is obviously not something that can so easily be done in one broad move. Thus the globalists have chosen to take small, gradual strides in this direction, which, unfortunately but not surprisingly, have been proving quite effective.

One of the main avenues that they have worked through to achieve this has been the women's rights movement. Over the years, the globalist-controlled media have pushed the idea on women that if they seek equality with men, and if they desire to achieve their "true potential," they should find a suitable career. (Of course, a great many women have entered the workforce without a choice, out of economic necessity--but even this, of course, has been rigged by the globalists.)

It has been primarily through this means that the traditional American family arrangement has been eroding away. As both parents in most families now work full-time jobs, they have consequently been spending less and less time with their children, thereby opening the door for the government to move in and fill this gap with its multitudinous social programs, such as government funded, regulated, and controlled daycare centers. Close family bonds are thus not so close or bonding as they used to be, which is just how the globalists want it [Endnote 153].

In no way is it being suggested here that activists for women's rights (or feminism) are trying to break up the family. On the contrary, most of the activists in this camp have the utmost pure motives. But what many of them fail to realize is that they and their movement have been hijacked and are being used to support an agenda that is entirely antithetical to the interests of most of them, and to those of society as a whole. A very revealing article in *The Nation* put it like this: "[F]eminism is not just an issue or a group of issues; it is the cutting edge of a revolution in cultural and moral values....The objective of every feminist reform, from legal abortion to the E.R.A. to child-care programs, is to undermine traditional family values..."(176).

Destroying the family naturally involves destroying respect for the institution of marriage, which has obviously already happened in this country, to an alarming degree. And, as the next quote will demonstrate, this has come about according to plan. This quote comes from a 1971 treatise called *The Document:*

Declaration of Feminism, which stated that "Marriage is the institution that has failed us and we must work to destroy it....The nuclear family must be replaced with a new form of family where individuals live and work together to help meet the needs of all people in the society....With the destruction of the nuclear family must come a new way of looking at children. They must be seen as the responsibility of an entire society rather than individual parents"(112, p. 86).

Did you catch that? Children must be seen as the responsibility of an entire society? This should help you to understand what the real agenda was behind Hillary Clinton's book, *It Takes a Village*.

Earlier we talked about the state-sponsored game of child snatching, where out-of-control child welfare agencies have been stealing kids from their parents, often without any legitimate cause, all for fun and profit. But there is another purpose behind this scheme, as you can probably now guess--it greatly aids the globalists' "war on the family."

Abolition of the family is something else that Karl Marx, and particularly his partner, Frederich Engels, had called for. In his 1884 book *The Origin of the Family, Private Property and the State*, Engels wrote: "[T]he first condition for the liberation of the wife is to bring the whole female sex back into public industry, and this in turn demands the abolition of the monogamous family as the economic unit of society....Private housekeeping is transformed into a social industry. The care and education of the children becomes a public affair; society looks after all children alike, whether they are legitimate or not." Right in the *Communist Manifesto* itself we find a specific call for "abolition of the family." Do you see where this all comes from? (Refer also to Appendix 14.)

* * * * * * *

"In the 1960's, the elite media invented second-wave feminism as part of the elite agenda to dismantle civilization and create a New World Order." - Henry Makow, "Gloria Steinem: How The CIA Used Feminism To Destabilize Society," NewsWithViews.com, July 1, 2002(565).

Appendix 12

Use of chemical and biological weapons on the public by the U.S. Army and the CIA

The Army has acknowledged that between 1949 and 1969, 239 populated areas from coast to coast were blanketed with chemical and biological agents(267). The public was treated as guinea pigs as it was sprayed with toxic agents for the purpose of measuring patterns of dissemination in the air, weather effects, dosages, optimum placement, etc. Sometimes the CIA assisted the U.S. Army in these experiments. At other times, the Army acted alone. Here are a few examples(156):

1950, San Francisco Bay area: Clouds of spray from a ship were created that engulfed an area 200 miles long up and down the coast. The spray contained Bacillus globigii and Serratia marcescens to test the feasibility of a military application of these cultures for biological warfare. 11 infections and 1 death resulted from this "experiment"(268).

1953, Minneapolis: 61 releases of zinc cadmium sulfide occurred in 4 sections of the city. No report was released of any casualties, but this substance is known to cause lung damage, kidney inflammation, and fatty degeneration of the liver(269).

1953, D.C. area: Zinc cadmium sulfate was sprayed from a height of 75 feet, combined with lycopodium spores(270).

1969, Cambridge, MD area: Zinc cadmium sulfate, 115 open-air tests(271).

Early 1960s, Washington's National Airport and the Washington Greyhound bus terminal: The Army released Bacillus subtilis. The effects of this bacteria are especially harmful, even deadly, to the elderly and the sick(272).

1955, Tampa Bay area: The CIA conducted an open-air test with whooping cough bacteria. The number of reported whooping cough cases jumped from 339 and one death in 1954 to 1,080 and 12 deaths in 1955(273).

1956-58, Savannah, GA and Avon Park, Florida: The Army released hundreds of thousands of Aedes aegypti mosquitos that are known for carrying yellow fever and dengue fever. Though the Army claimed they were uninfected, one would have to wonder why they were released at all, if this was true. Irregardless, judging from the Army's previous involuntary use of the public as its guinea pigs, there's no reason to believe this denial(274, pp. 101-103).

1956, New York City: CIA-Army team sprayed the Holland and Lincoln tunnels using trick suitcases and a car with dual mufflers. The agent used this time was Bacillus subtilis variant niger. This agent was also released in subway systems during rush hours. One method was to fill light bulbs with the bacteria and then smash them on the sidewalk near subway ventilation grills(275).

The U.S. Army has also used servicemen as human guinea pigs, to develop and perfect chemical and biological warfare agents over the years. For example, the Senate Committee on Veterans' Affairs released a report in 1994, which stated: "Approximately 60,000 military personnel were used as human subjects in the 1940s to test two chemical agents, mustard gas and lewsite [blister gas]. Most of these subjects were not informed of the nature of the experiments and never received medical followup after their participation in the research. Additionally, some of these human subjects were threatened with imprisonment at Fort Leavenworth if they discussed these experiments with anyone, including their wives, parents and family doctors. For decades, the Pentagon denied that the research had taken place, resulting in decades of suffering for many veterans who became ill after the secret testing"(325).

Of course, it's not just the Army and the CIA that have played such games on U.S. citizens. Many other federal institutions have conducted, and continue to conduct, tests on people, unbeknownst to them. Often it happens that various branches of the military have experimented, or at least have proposed to experiment, on the general public with new, supposedly nonlethal weapons systems. One such instance was reported by CNN on September 12, 2006: "Nonlethal weapons such as high-power microwave devices should be used on American citizens in crowd-control situations before being used on the battlefield, the Air Force secretary said Tuesday.

"The object is basically public relations. Domestic use would make it easier to avoid questions from others about possible safety considerations, said Secretary Michael Wynne.

"'If we're not willing to use it here against our fellow citizens, then we should not be willing to use it in a wartime situation,' said Wynne. '(Because) if I hit somebody with a nonlethal weapon and they claim that it injured them in a way that was not intended, I think that I would be vilified in the world press'"(535).

If all this isn't bad enough, President Bill Clinton admitted during a speech he gave on October 3, 1995, that the U.S. government had conducted thousands of radiation experiments on unsuspecting victims across the country during the second half of the 20th century. Here's what he said: "Thousands of government-sponsored experiments did take place at hospitals, universities and military bases around our nation. The goal was to understand the effects of radiation exposure on the human body.

"While most of the tests were ethical by any standards, some were unethical, not only by today's standards, but by the standards of the time in which they were conducted. They failed both the test of our national values and the test of humanity"(550).

There's no level too low that our globalist-controlled government won't sink to with its human experiments. The Organic Consumers Association reported on their website on November 18, 2005: "[T]he EPA's newly proposed rule, misleadingly titled 'Protections for Subjects in Human Research,' puts industry profits ahead of children's welfare. The rule allows for government and industry scientists to treat children as human guinea pigs in chemical experiments in the following situations: 1. Children who 'cannot be reasonably consulted,' such as those that are mentally handicapped or orphaned newborns....With permission from the institution or guardian in charge of the individual, the child may be exposed to chemicals for the sake of research. 2. Parental consent forms are not necessary for testing on children who have been neglected or abused. 3. Chemical studies on any children outside of the U.S. are acceptable"(517).

In addition to the government experimenting on the public with biological and/or chemical weapons, it has also used such weapons on the public for sleazy political purposes. One good example of this was the anthrax mailing attacks that occurred about a month after 9-11. Let's look at some highly-suspicious circumstances surrounding these assaults.

The *Washington Post* revealed on October 23, 2001, that Cipro, the anthrax antibiotic, was distributed to White House staff a full 6 weeks before the stories of tainted mailings began to pop up in the news(589). The Associated Press later revealed, on June 9, 2002, that Judicial Watch sued the Bush administration for the release of documents showing who knew what in advance about the anthrax attacks, and why presidential staff were protected while Congress and others were not(590). Now how do you suppose the White House had advance knowledge of the anthrax attacks?

What a convenient time for these dirty deeds to have occurred, to keep the public in a state of panic and divert attention away from the inconsistencies of the 9-11 fiasco. But perhaps even more important, these mailings, along with fake "Code Orange" terror alerts, distracted the attention of Congress, making the passage of the anti-Constitutional Patriot Act an easier task. One person in Congress, in particular, that received an anthrax mailing was Senate Judiciary

Committee Chairman Patrick Leahy, who had raised several objections to the Patriot Act(591). Isn't it obvious what was going on here?

Another Congress person who received an anthrax mailing was Senate Majority Leader Tom Daschle, who pushed most aggressively, right from the beginning, for an independent Congressional 9-11 investigation. Daschle had also expressed strong opposition to the Patriot Act, just like Leahy. The strand of anthrax sent to Daschle's office, by the way, as *USA Today* pointed out, was extremely lethal, and its source turned out to be connected with an Army research facility, the Institute for Genomic Research, Rockville, MD(592).

Of great significance here is the fact that, from November 12, 2001, to March 25, 2002, 13 world-renowned microbiologists mysteriously died. Some were world leaders in developing weapons-grade biological plagues. Others were experts in preventing mass deaths from occurring as a result of biological weapons. Still others were experts in the theory of bioterrorism(593). Did these scientists know something about the anthrax mailings that they weren't supposed to know? Did they perhaps threaten to spill the beans?

For the longest time, it seemed like nothing would ever come out of the FBI's "investigation" into the anthrax attacks. For instance, the BBC reported on April 4, 2002, that investigators of these deadly mailings had no suspects at all. They said that they had come up "against some closely held military secrets" which were slowing down the investigation. Furthermore, the BBC stated, "Federal investigators tell ABC NEWS that military and intelligence agencies have withheld a full listing of all facilities and all employees dealing with top-secret anthrax programs where important leads could be found." Now why do you suppose that was?

It wasn't until 2008, due to much public pressure, that the FBI claimed it had finally "solved" the case. The man they fingered as being responsible for the attacks was Bruce Ivins, who had worked at the Army's labs in Rockville. However, there were major problems with the FBI's claims about Mr. Ivins. For example, there's no evidence that he ever worked with weapons-grade anthrax. Furthermore, the FBI's case against him allotted only 7 ½ hours in the evening over a period of only three days for him to prepare his first concoction. Yet, according to the chief biological weapons inspector for the U.N. from 1994 to 1998, Richard Spertzel, "In my opinion, there are maybe four or five people in the whole country who might be able to make this stuff, and I'm one of them. And even with a good lab and staff to help run it, it might take me a year to come up with a product as good"(594).

Before Ivins could be brought to trial, something very tragic, yet very predictable, happened to him--he "committed suicide"! And if that isn't suspicious enough, the FBI was later highly selective in its release of documents pertaining to the case(595).

"I believe the FBI knows exactly who was behind these terrorist anthrax attacks upon the United States Congress in the Fall of 2001, and that the culprits were US government-related scientists involved in a criminal US government bio-warfare program....
[The whole thing] appears to be a cover-up orchestrated by the FBI....
Could the real culprits behind the terrorist attacks on 11 September 2001, and the immediately following terrorist anthrax attacks upon Congress ultimately prove to be the same people? Could it truly be coincidental that two of the primary intended victims of the terrorist anthrax attacks--Senators Daschle and Leahy-- were holding up the speedy passage of the pre-planned USA Patriot Act...an act which provided the federal government with unprecedented powers in relation to US citizens and institutions?" - Francis A. Boyle, former U.S. government biological weapons legislator(596).

Appendix 13

The U.N.--something for everyone

     In this appendix we present a list of some of the major power structures of the U.N. As you look it over, take notice of how the U.N. has left no stone unturned, having set up a multitude of organizations to regulate and control every conceivable aspect, not only of every nation as a whole, but of every individual person's life on earth. It is just a matter of time, if the globalists have their way, before we will see the ugly end results of where all of this is leading--a totalitarian, dictatorial world regime:

International Court of Justice (World Court)
International Criminal Court
Economic and Social Council
Security Council
UNDCP - U.N. International Drug Control Program
UNCTAD - U.N. Conference on Trade and Development
UNCHS - U.N. Center for Human Settlements (Habitat)
UNEP - U.N. Environment Program
WFC - World Food Council
WFP - World Food Program
ILO - International Labor Organization
WTO - World Trade Organization
UNESCO - U.N. Educational, Scientific, and Cultural Organization
WHO - World Health Organization
ICAO - International Civil Aviation Organization
UPU - Universal Postal Union
ITU - International Telecommunications Union
WMO - World Meteorological Organization
IMF - International Monetary Fund
IMO - International Maritime Organization
WIPO - World Intellectual Property Organization
IFAD - International Fund/Agricultural Development
UNICEF - U.N. Children's Fund
UNFPA - U.N. Population Fund
UNIFEM - U.N. Development Fund for Women
INSTRAW - International Research and Training Institute for the Advancement of Women
UNDP - U.N. Development Program

UNITAR - U.N. Institute for Training and Research
UNU - U.N. University
IAEA - International Atomic Energy Agency
UNHRC - Office of the U.N. High Commissioner for Refugees
UNIDO - U.N. Industrial Development Organization
World Bank (also known as IBRD - International Bank for Reconstruction and Development)
IDA - International Development Association
IFC - International Finance Corporation
MIGA - Multicultural Investment Guarantee Agency

...and the list goes on and on. Remember, "Absolute power corrupts absolutely."

One branch of the U.N., in particular, that is (or should be) of great concern, especially to U.S. citizens, is the International Criminal Court. Here's what the book *Taking Sides: Clashing Views on Controversial Global Issues* had to say about this globalist institution: "On July 17, 1998, in Rome, a treaty was drafted up which created a permanent International Criminal Court (ICC) under the auspices of the U.N. If 60 countries ratify this treaty...the ICC would act as police, prosecutor, judge, jury, and jailer....The ICC would be the sole judge of its own power, and there would be no process to appeal its decisions, however irrational or unjust those might be....

"[T]he participation of the United States in this treaty regime runs counter to U.S. national interests. Moreover, U.S. participation would be unconstitutional because it would subject individual Americans to trial and punishment in an extra-constitutional court without affording them all of the rights and protections the U.S. Constitution guarantees. Unfortunately, merely refusing to join the Rome treaty will not protect Americans from the ICC's reach. In an astonishing break with the accepted norms of international law, the Rome treaty would extend the ICC's jurisdiction to the nationals of countries that do not sign and ratify the treaty. Because of this unprecedented and unlawful attempt to assert power over the citizens of non-party states, it is not sufficient for the U.S. government merely to reject the treaty....The Rome ICC treaty, in concept and execution, is utterly antithetical to [the Constitution]. It should be opposed by the United States with all the vigor it has mustered, throughout its history, to fight similar threats to the fundamental values of the Republic"(151, pp. 334, 335).

Appendix 14

The U.N. wages war on parents

As stated earlier, the U.N. is not only working to destroy children's loyalties to their parents and their country, but it is also working to circumvent parental authority. One particular measure that the U.N. has undertaken in pursuit of this goal occurred on November 20, 1989, when the General Assembly unanimously voted in favor of "The United Nations Convention on the Rights of the Child," which outlined what has become the U.N.'s official policy on child rights. Article 3 of the Convention states that in all actions concerning children, the "best interest of the child" shall be the primary consideration. While this may sound noble enough, nothing is mentioned about the parents being the ones to decide, or even playing a role in the decision of, what is in the "best interest of the child."

Article 4 tells us that this treaty is not just a "positive affirmation," but that it is to be implemented under the force of law. To further prove this point, take notice of how UNICEF's report, *The State of the World's Children 1997*, stated that "Once a country ratifies [the Convention on the Rights of the Child], it is obliged...[by] law to undertake all appropriate measures to assist parents and other responsible parties in fulfilling their obligations under the Convention....Fulfilling their obligations sometimes requires States to make fundamental changes in national laws, institutions, plans, policies and practices to bring them into line with the principles of the Convention."

UNICEF also stated that the Convention "makes it clear that children shall be protected from all forms of mental or physical violence or maltreatment. Thus, any forms of discipline involving such violence are unacceptable." Article 29 of the "Rights of the Child" establishes that discipline must be administered in a way that will protect the child's "human dignity." This is precisely the reason why spanking children out of discipline is being called "abuse" today, all across the U.S. As mentioned earlier, children in recent years have often been taken from their parents because of corporal punishment, which brings us to Article 9 of the Convention, which dictates that "a child shall not be separated from his or her parents" unless "competent legal authorities subject to judicial review determine...that such separation is necessary for the best interests of the child." Well, there you have it. The ones to decide what is in the "best interest of the child" are "competent legal authorities subject to judicial review," who dictate that spanking is an abusive practice. Apparently they haven't considered that it isn't in the best interest of the child to be subjected to the trauma of being separated from his/her parents, who are put on trial simply because they were employing a method of discipline that has effectively been used for millennia to help curtail juvenile delinquency. How interesting that in this age of saving children from spankings, delinquency and disrespect among kids have never been higher.

Article 7 requires all parents to register their children at birth (this is apparently in "the best interest of the child" as well).

Article 13 bestows a virtually absolute "freedom of expression" on the child, including the right to "seek, receive and impart information and ideas of all kinds, regardless of frontiers, either orally, in writing or in print, in the form of art, or through any other media of the child's choice." Interesting! So does this mean that parents will eventually have their children taken away if they don't allow them to have the "freedom" to view pornography? (Don't forget that the globalist agenda calls for the complete removal of the concept of morality.)

Article 15 creates "the right of the child to freedom of association." This provision declares that this right shall not be infringed except in the interest of public order. So then, apparently it would be acceptable for our children, in the future, to engage in sexually promiscuous activities, without worrying about interference from "bothersome" parents who would be arrested if they dared to suppress their children's "freedom"!

No wonder the Communist Party favored the U.N. from the very beginning--their philosophies are identical. Notice what the April 1945 issue of *Political Affairs*, the Party's official journal, had to say about the U.N.: "Great popular support and enthusiasm for the United Nations policies should be built up, well organized and fully articulate. But it is also necessary to do more than that. The opposition must be rendered so impotent that it will be unable to gather any significant support in the Senate against the United Nations Charter and the treaties which will follow"(33, p. 86).

Though the Convention on the Rights of the Child has not yet been officially ratified by the U.S. government, it is obvious that it need not be. For our government has been enforcing this treaty's tenets on us for years. Also, back in 1999, President Bill Clinton issued Executive Order 13107, which calls for compliance with all United Nations human rights treaties, even those which have not been ratified by the Senate. How nice of Mr. Clinton to trash the Constitution and transform the United States into a vassal to the suzerain U.N., with hardly anyone even knowing that it happened!

Appendix 15

Environmentalism--another tool of the globalists

Protecting the environment is certainly a commendable cause, and it's an issue that should not be ignored. However, this is not a cause that should be pursued under the direction of the United Nations, or any other globalist institution. Yet this is exactly what has been happening. Few realize that the environmental movement has been manipulated, from the very beginning, to advance the world government agenda. So many sincere environmentalists would be shocked to discover what lies behind this whole thing.

By telling us that the "environmental crisis" is a "global threat" (a threat which the globalists themselves have created, of course, by deliberately polluting and poisoning the environment), the idea is being drilled into our heads that we need a global government to handle it. For the globalists, there's never a shortage of such "global crises" requiring "global solutions," as the quotes that follow will demonstrate:

- "World Federalists believe that the environmental crisis facing planet earth is a global problem and therefore calls for a 'global' solution--a worldwide United Nations Environmental Agency with the power to make its decisions stick." - World Association of World Federalists, 1972(333).

- "Global warming, ozone depletion, deforestation and overpopulation are the four horsemen of a looming 21st century apocalypse....[T]he environment is becoming the No. 1 international security concern." - Michael Oppenheimer, CFR member(334).

- "We've got to ride the global warming issue. Even if the theory is wrong, we will be doing the right thing in terms of economic and environmental policy." - Timothy Wirth, former member of the CFR and the U.S. Senate, as well as a former Under Secretary of State(335, p. 97).

- "No matter if the science of global warming is all phony...climate change [provides] the greatest opportunity to bring about justice and equality in the world." - Christine Stewart, former Canadian Minister of the Environment(573).

- "In searching for a new enemy to unite us, we came up with the idea that pollution, the threat of global warming, water shortages, famine and the like would fit the bill." - The Council of the Club of Rome, 1991(336, p. 115).

- On March 13, 2007, Yahoo News reported: "Gordon Brown, likely to be the next prime minister, will deliver a speech calling for a 'new world order' to combat global warming....

"According to excerpts released by the finance ministry, Chancellor of the Exchequer Brown will also say the United Nations should make the fight against global warming a core 'pillar' of its international mission"(566).

Even people like Rush Limbaugh have recognized the sinister agenda at the highest levels of the environmental movement. During the August 20, 1997 edition of his national radio program, he made reference to an upcoming *National Review* cover story (September 1) by Ronald Bailey, entitled "Who Is Maurice Strong?," and then went on to say: "The article spells out in great detail just exactly what all these global environmental conferences are really all about--the spread of communism, the spread of socialism, global control over as much of the function of the world as they can."

One of the many scams that the globalists have been pulling off, in the name of "protecting the environment," has been to drive people (particularly farmers) off their land through oppressive, severely-restricting, and often impossible-to-comply-with "land management" regulations on the local, state, and federal levels. These regulations are the socialism/communism that Limbaugh was talking about in the above quote. And most of these regulations have originated with the U.N. To prove this point, take a look at the next quote from "Habitat 1," the Conference Report of the 1976 U.N. Conference on Human Settlements: "Land cannot be treated as an ordinary asset, controlled by individuals and subject to the pressures and inefficiencies of the market...." And then, under "Recommendation D.1, Land Resource Management," we read: "(a) Public ownership or effective control of land in the public interest is the single most important means of...achieving a more equitable distribution of the benefits of development whilst assuring that environmental impacts are considered....(b) Land is a scarce resource whose management should be subject to public surveillance or control in the interest of the nation....(d)...Governments must maintain full jurisdiction and exercise complete sovereignty over such land with a view to freely planning development of human settlements"(324).

Another quote from a U.N. document, similar to the ones we just looked at, came out of the U.N.'s 1992 Earth Summit in Rio de Janeiro, under "Agenda 21": "All countries should...develop national land-management plans to guide development"(331). Make no mistake about it--this is land theft under the guise of "the common good."

To show just how intrusive and all-encompassing the globalists intended their Agenda 21 to be, look at what the book *Agenda 21: The Earth Summit Strategy to Save the Planet* had to say: "Effective execution of Agenda 21 will require a profound reorientation of all human society, unlike anything the world has ever experienced--a major shift in the priorities of both governments and individuals and an unprecedented redeployment of human and financial resources. This shift will demand that a concern for the environmental consequences of every human action be integrated into individual and collective decision-making at every level"(332, pp. 69, 70).

The U.N. has been playing another game under the pretext of "environmentalism"--laying claim to most, if not all, of our national parks and historic landmarks, having designated them as "U.N. World Heritage Sites" under the 1972 World Heritage Treaty. The U.N. also lays claim to vast amounts of U.S. wilderness, which it designates as "Biosphere Reserves." These once-public-owned national treasures have been seized by a foreign power, further destroying our national sovereignty. And all of this was done with the full blessing of our sell-out "public servants" in Washington.

Appendix 16

The welcome mat for the illegal alien invasion

Under the Bush Jr. administration, more so than any previous presidency, we saw a massive influx of illegal aliens into this country, because of the U.S./Mexican border being left wide open for so long. This was especially scandalous for Bush Jr., who claimed to be so passionately concerned about protecting the American people from foreign terrorists getting into the country. Here's what the September 20, 2004 edition of *Time* had to say about our unsecured border under Bush Jr.'s watch: "The next time you pass through an airport and have to produce a photo ID to establish who you are and then must remove your shoes, take off your belt, empty your pockets, prove your laptop is not an explosive device and send your briefcase or purse through a machine to determine whether it holds weapons, think about this: In a single day, more than 4,000 illegal aliens will walk across the busiest unlawful gateway into the U.S., the 375-mile border between Arizona and Mexico. No searches for weapons. No shoe removal. No photo-ID checks....

"Who are these new arrivals? While the vast majority are Mexicans, a small but sharply growing number come from other countries, including those with large populations hostile to the U.S....

"[L]ocal law enforcers, ranchers and others who confront the issue daily tell TIME they have encountered not only a wide variety of Latin Americans (from Guatemala, El Salvador, Brazil, Nicaragua and Venezuela) but also intruders from Afghanistan, Bulgaria, Russia and China as well as Egypt, Iran and Iraq. Law-enforcement authorities believe the mass movement of illegals, wherever they are from, offers the perfect cover for terrorists seeking to enter the U.S....

"[T]he U.S. arrests enough of the border crossers to create the illusion that it is enforcing the immigration laws while allowing the great majority to get through...."

One of the main reasons for this open border policy--cheap labor for globalist corporations--was boldly exposed in this same *Time* article: "Many big companies, which have...[a clear] stake in cheap labor, aggressively fend off the enforcement of laws that would shut down their supply of illegal workers....

"[C]orporate managers go so far as to place orders with smugglers for a specific number of able bodies to be delivered. For corporate America, employing illegal aliens at wages so low few citizens could afford to take the jobs is great for profits and stockholders. That's why the payrolls for so many businesses--meat packers, poultry processors, landscape firms, construction companies, office-cleaning firms and corner convenience stores, amongst others--are jammed with illegals. And companies are rarely, if ever, punished for it."

Another major reason for this open border policy, which *Time* was not bold enough to mention, is the fact that the globalists are intent on destroying American sovereignty and bringing this country down to Third-World-status.

As time went by and people became aware of Bush Jr.'s open border policy, and began to complain about it, Bush finally decided to do something about it--he ordered Border Patrol to stand down! As the May 13, 2005 *Washington Times* put it: "U.S. Border Patrol agents have been ordered not to arrest illegal aliens along the section of the Arizona border where protesters patrolled last month because an increase in apprehensions there would prove the effectiveness of Minuteman volunteers, The Washington Times has learned.

"More than a dozen agents, all of whom asked not to be identified for fear of retribution, said orders relayed by Border Patrol supervisors at the Naco, Ariz., station made it clear that arrests were 'not to go up' along the 23-mile section of border that the volunteers monitored to protest illegal immigration.

"'It was clear to everyone here what was being said and why,' said one veteran agent. 'The apprehensions were not to increase after the Minuteman volunteers left. It was as simple as that.'

"Another agent said the Naco supervisors 'were clear in their intention' to keep new arrests to an 'absolute minimum' to offset the effect of the Minuteman vigil, adding that patrols along the border have been severely limited....

"...Rep. Tom Tancredo, Colorado Republican, yesterday said 'credible sources' within the Border Patrol also had told him of the decision by Naco supervisors to keep new arrests to a minimum, saying he was angry but not surprised.

"'It's like telling a cop to stand by and watch burglars loot a store but don't arrest any of them,' he said. "This is another example of decisions being made at the highest levels of the Border Patrol that are hurting morale and helping to rot the agency from within.

"'I worry about our efforts in Congress to increase the number of agents,' he said. 'Based on these kinds of orders, we could spend the equivalent of the national debt and never have secure borders.'

"Mr. Tancredo, chairman of the Congressional Immigration Reform Caucus, blamed the Bush administration for setting an immigration enforcement tone that suggests to those enforcing the law that he is not serious about secure borders.

"'We need to get the president to come to grips with the seriousness of the problem,' he said. 'I know he doesn't like to utter the words, "I was wrong," but if we have another incident like September 11 by people who came through our borders without permission, I hope he doesn't have to say "I'm sorry"""(465).

Do you understand the seriousness of this treasonous fraud? These Border Patrol agents were being told to stand down so that the efforts of the Minuteman volunteers, who wanted to see to it that our border with Mexico was secured, would appear ineffective. This is outrageous!

It wasn't until a year later, by mid-2006, that something was finally done about this problem--construction on the border fence had begun. But this was one of those typical "too little, too late" measures that was only designed to superficially appease a public that had finally become aware of the enormity of this problem, and had demanded that something be done about it. But through the Panamerican Union deal that Bush signed in mid-2005, which will merge the United States with Canada and Mexico by 2010, this fence will be torn down anyway, regardless how minimally effective it might be until then.

Appendix 17

The 2008 fleecing of America

On September 22, 2008, the stock market fell 777 points. The panic that ensued led to a cry from Wall Street banks and businesses for the government to bail them out. Thus a bill was introduced a week later that asked for $700 billion. What was so amazing is that this figure was chosen arbitrarily. The *Los Angeles Times* of September 29 had this to say about this outlandish sum: "'It's not based on any particular data point,' a Treasury spokeswoman told Forbes.com Tuesday. 'We just wanted to choose a really large number'"(576).

Can you believe this? Wall Street plays a risky gambling game with derivatives, and then they make up an exorbitant sum of money that they want the public to reimburse them with?

But it gets even crazier than this. In the text of the bailout bill, this outrageous statement was made: "Decisions by the Secretary pursuant to the authority of this Act are non-reviewable and committed to agency discretion, and may not be reviewed by any court of law or any administrative agency"(577).

In spite of the fact that this monumentally fraudulent bill refused to allow any oversight of its proposal, it was passed on October 3. And, get this, an additional $150 billion was tacked on to it. But how, you may ask, could such a scam have been pulled off? Why would Congress sell us out like this? Well, for one thing, many Congressmen had investments in the companies that were recipients of this money. But there was another (and more shocking) factor that inspired the passage of this bill. Representative Brad Sherman stated before the House on October 2 that "a few members [of the House] were even told that there would be martial law in America if we voted no."

To further show what a scandal this bailout bill was, which massively increased inflation and our national debt, notice what Congresswoman Marcy Kaptur said about it, just prior to its passage: "Let's play Wall Street bailout. Rule 1: Rush the decision. Time the game in the week before Congress is set to adjourn, and just six weeks before an historic election, so your opponents will be preoccupied, pressured, distracted, and in a hurry. Rule 2: Disarm the public through fear. Warn that the entire global financial system will collapse and the world will fall into another Great Depression. Control the media enough to ensure that the public will not know that this bailout will indebt them for generations, taking from them trillions of dollars that they earned and deserved to keep. Rule 3: Control the playing field and set the rules. Hide from the public and most of Congress just who is arranging this deal. Communicate with the public through leaks to media insiders; limit any open Congressional hearings;

communicate with Congress via private teleconferencing calls; heighten political anxiety by contacting each political party separately; treat members of Congress condescendingly, telling them that the matter is so complex that they must rely on those few insiders who really do know what's going on. Rule 4: Divert attention and keep people confused. Manage the news cycle so Congress and the public have no time to examine who destroyed the...banking system....Rule 5: Always keep in mind the goal is to privatize gains to a few and socialize losses to the many.

"For 30 years, in one financial scandal after another, Wall Street game masters have kept billions of dollars of their gain and shifted their losses to American taxpayers. Once this bailout is in place, the greed game will begin again."

To top things off, huge bonuses were handed out to executives of many of the companies that were recipients of big portions of this bailout money. The *Guardian* reported on October 17, 2008: "Financial workers at Wall Street's top banks are to receive pay deals worth more than $70bn, a substantial proportion of which is expected to be paid in discretionary bonuses, for their work so far this year--despite plunging the global financial system into its worst crisis since the 1929 stock market crash, the Guardian has learned.

"Staff at six banks including Goldman Sachs and Citigroup are in line to pick up the payouts despite being the beneficiaries of a $700bn bail-out from the US government that has already prompted criticism"(581). And where did the cash come from for these bonuses? From the bailout money, obviously! This is why the bailout bill forbade oversight by any court or administrative body--it simply isn't a bailout, but is instead a monstrous act of unparalleled thievery!

But, as always, globalist fiascos like this aren't just about making tons of fat wads of cash--they're also about advancing the cause of the New World Order. Speaking of the global financial crisis that arose from the almost-crash that spawned the phony bailout of 2008, Yahoo News reported on November 10 of that year: "Mr. [Gordon] Brown [British prime minister] will use a high-profile speech in the City of London to say that Britain, the US and Europe should join together to provide leadership in the creation of a 'stronger and more just international order.'

"He wants this weekend's emergency summit of world leaders in Washington to reach consensus on a new framework for the international financial system, featuring a reformed IMF which will act as a global early-warning system for financial problems, he will say.

"The Prime Minister promised to work with US President-elect Barack Obama to build a new global society in which the markets are subjected to morality and ordinary people's interests are put first.

"In his annual foreign policy speech to the Lord Mayor of London's Guildhall banquet, Mr. [Gordon] Brown [British prime minister] will say that the transatlantic relationship between Britain and Europe and the USA can be the driving force behind the creation of a new international order.

"'The alliance between Britain and the US--and more broadly between Europe and the US--can and must provide leadership, not in order to make the rules ourselves, but to lead the global effort to build a stronger and more just international order,' Mr Brown will say.

"'The transatlantic relationship has been the engine of effective multilateralism for the past 50 years.

"'As America stands at its own dawn of hope, so let that hope be fulfilled through a pact with the wider world to lead and shape the 21st century as the century of a truly global society.

"'And I believe the whole of Europe can work closely with America to meet the great challenges which will test our resolution and illuminate our convictions'"(578).

Henry Kissinger, in an article he wrote for the *International Herald Tribune* (January 12, 2009 edition) called "The Chance for a New World Order," also talked, as the title of the article clearly implies, about using the financial crisis that led to the bailout as an opportunity to bring the world closer to world government. In fact, reading between the lines of what he wrote indicates that this whole fiasco was orchestrated primarily for that very purpose. Here are some revealing excerpts from this article: "...An international order will emerge if a system of compatible priorities comes into being....

"...The alternative to a new international order is chaos....

"The financial collapse...made evident the absence of global institutions to cushion the shock and to reverse the trend. Inevitably, when the affected publics turned to their national political institutions, these were driven principally by domestic politics, not considerations of world order....

"International order will not come about either in the political or economic field until there emerge general rules toward which countries can orient themselves....

"The ultimate challenge is to shape the common concern of most countries and all major ones regarding the economic crisis...into a common strategy reinforced by the realization that...[there is] no national or regional solution [only a global one]....

"An international order can be permanent only if its participants have a share not only in building but also in securing it. In this manner, America and its potential partners have a unique opportunity to transform a moment of crisis into a vision of hope [the Hegelian Dialectic]"(582).

Astonishingly, the amount of the bailout was later raised to over $8 trillion! Of course, with all the interest added in, the final cost to American taxpayers will wind up being far greater than even this figure. What a swindle job!

Supplement I

The final piece of the puzzle

This study would be inadequate without a discussion of this last piece of the globalist puzzle, which is essential for completing the picture that this puzzle forms. But because it is such a controversial and sensitive puzzle piece, it seemed appropriate to save it for the end, after all the other pieces have been set in place.

Before proceeding, it is a necessity of the highest order to first emphasize the point that the information which follows is not by any means intended to slander a particular ethnic or religious group, although many will undoubtedly claim that to be the case. If I protest the corruption of Hitler's regime (and I certainly do!), this does not make me anti-German. If I protest Mao's or Stalin's murderous rampages, this does not make me anti-Chinese or anti-Russian. With this in mind, let me also say that if I protest a very dangerous and power-hungry movement known as Zionism, I am NOT anti-Semitic.

Many people have erroneously equated the word "Zionism" with "Judaism." They think, because of the prevailing propaganda, that one who protests this political movement is against Jews. Let me stress very strongly that this is a blatant and bold-faced lie. There are many Jews who are not Zionists, and thus do not support the Zionist cause. There are also many Zionists who aren't Jewish. And, there are also many who profess to be Zionists who are entirely ignorant of the real, hidden agenda of this movement. So the indictment set forth herein against Zionism only pertains to those at the top rungs of the ladder of this political system, and not to the many innocent dupes who have no idea what they are supporting. So let me make it clear: This is NOT an indictment against the Jewish people, regardless what some might say to the contrary.

Traditional Jews--that is, Jews who follow the Torah (and the Torah alone)--are one segment of Judaism, in particular, who reject Zionism as being in any way a legitimate representation of Jewry. Let's see what the "Jews Against Zionism" website, for example, has to say on this matter: "Torah Jewry protests at every opportunity against the Zionist rule over the Holy Land, and the Zionist rebellion against the neighboring nations. Torah Jewry has condemned the Zionist oppression of the Palestinians, the land's veteran inhabitants who have been driven from their homes and properties. The Zionists' barbaric and violent deeds are absolutely antithetical to the essence of the Jewish People. Torah Jewry has never ever recognized the Zionist state. Since [the time of] the Zionists succeeding in establishing their state, Torah Jewry has continuously announced to the world that the Zionists do not represent the Jewish People, and that the name

'Israel' that they use is a forgery....

"We implore and beseech our Jewish brethren to realize that the Zionists are not the saviors of the Jewish People and guarantors of their safety, but rather the instigators and original cause of Jewish suffering in the Holy Land and worldwide. The idea that Zionism and the State of 'Israel' is the protector of Jews is probably the greatest hoax ever perpetrated on the Jewish People. Indeed, where else since 1945 [the time of the first mass migration of East European Jews to Israel] have Jews been in such physical danger as in the Zionist state?! Torah-true Jews wish to live in peace and harmony with their neighbors in every country among the community of nations, including in historic Palestine. They deplore acts and policies of violence carried out by those who, misusing the name of Israel..., have substituted the ideal of chauvinist nationalism for the eternal values of the Torah"(277).

It is regrettable that space does not here allow for a full treatment of the subject of Zionism--a very complex and multifaceted topic. Nevertheless, an endeavor will be made to give as comprehensive an overview as possible of this final piece of the globalist puzzle, which we shall now commence.

The mentality of the elite Zionists is that of utter superiority to the swelling masses of humanity, over whom the Zionists plan to exercise complete domination. But it needs to be emphasized that the elitist nature of Zionism does not of necessity restrict itself to those who are of Jewish descent. Zionists highly esteem and accept as fellow-Zionists all who embrace and cooperatively work toward their goal of world domination. To prove this point, let us take note, for example, of the very close ties that exist between Zionism and Freemasonry (recall that Freemasonry is a strong proponent of global government). One Jewish (or, in this case, Zionist) paper wrote: "The connections [between Freemasonry and Judaism--Zionism] are more intimate than one would imagine. Judaism should maintain a lively and profound sympathy for Freemasonry in general, and no...indifference to it....[T]he spirit of Freemasonry is that of Judaism in its most fundamental beliefs, its ideas are Judaic, its language is Judaic"(278).

Freemasonry itself acknowledges its close ties with the *Kabbalah*, an ancient, mystical, and apostate Jewish text that Zionists uphold as the embodiment of their teachings and philosophy. As Albert Pike wrote: "Masonry is a search after Light. That search leads us directly back, as you see, to the Kabbalah. In that ancient and little understood...philosophy, the initiate will find the source of many doctrines....[A]ll the Masonic associations owe to it their Secrets and their Symbols"(5, pp. 741, 744). Let us affirm, therefore, that Zionism is more of a political and mystical philosophy, which transcends ethnicity and religion (just like Freemasonry).

Though Zionists often refer to themselves as Jews, and non-Zionists as "non-Jews," "Gentiles," or "Goyim," the truth is, once again, that a true Zionist is anyone or any group that embraces and supports the Zionist cause. All other people comprise the "inferior" masses who are considered "enemies" by the Zionists, simply because they are seen as potential threats to their aspirations of global power. Note what the *Kabbalah* says about such enemies: "Rabbi Jehuda said to him [Rabbi Chezkia], 'He is to be praised who is able to free himself from the enemies of Israel, and the just are much to be praised who get free from them and fight against them.' Rabbi Chezkia asked, 'How must we fight against them?' Rabbi Jehuda said, 'By wise counsel thou shalt war against them (Proverbs 24:6). By what kind of war?...[B]y deceit and trickery wherever possible. They must be fought against without ceasing, until proper order be restored. Thus it is with satisfaction that I say we should free ourselves from them and rule over them'"(279).

Although the term "Zionism" was coined in the late 19th century, its philosophy and stated goal of world empire date back, through the *Kabbalah*, for example, to long before that time. Though many people believe--even many professed Zionists--that the Zionist objective is, and always has been, a simple dedication to the establishment and continuance of a "Jewish state," the truth is that the REAL Zionist goal, I repeat, is total world domination, as prominent Zionists and Zionist literature readily admit. Let us examine a few such admissions:

- "The Feast of Tabernacles is the period when Israel triumphs over the other peoples of the world. That is why during this feast we seize the loulab and carry it as a trophy to show that we have conquered all the other people..." - *Zohar* (a text that the *Kabbalah* is based upon), Toldoth Noah, 63b.

- "The great ideal of Judaism is that the whole world shall be imbued with Jewish teachings, and that in a Universal Brotherhood of Nations--a greater Judaism, in fact--all the separate races and religions shall disappear." - *Jewish World*(394).

- "The Jews [Zionists] energetically reject the idea of fusion with the other nationalities and cling firmly to their historical hope of world empire." - Max Mandelstam, speaking at the World Zionist Congress, July 1898.

- "Jerusalem...aspires to become the spiritual center of the world." - David Ben-Gurion, former Israeli prime minister, *Jewish Chronicle*(391).

- "In Jerusalem, the United Nations (a truly United Nations) will build a Shrine of the Prophets to serve the federated union of all continents; this will be the seat of the Supreme Court of Mankind, to settle all controversies among the federated continents..." - David Ben-Gurion, *Look* magazine(392).

- Dr. Nahum Goldman, former President of the World Jewish Congress, speaking in Montreal back in 1963, was quoted as saying: "The Jews might have had Uganda, Madagascar and other places for the establishment of a Jewish Fatherland, but they want absolutely nothing except Palestine...because Palestine is the crossroads of Europe, Asia and Africa, because Palestine constitutes the veritable center of world political power, the strategic center for world control." - *L'Unite Nationale*, No. 4, 1963.

- "The Jewish people [again, the Zionists] cannot ever be destroyed, but rather they and their God of History will emerge in days to come triumphant over the evils and the foolishness of all other nations. Zion will and must emerge as the mount to which all other peoples turn." - Rabbi Meir Kahane, *Jewish Press*(393).

It is in this context of the Zionist lust for power that we can finally begin to unravel the mystery behind the Israeli/Palestinian conflict in the Middle East. The reason there has not been peace, and will not be peace, is because the Israeli government simply does not want it. This was admitted by *Ha'aretz*, a major Israeli newspaper, on April 10, 2007: "The moment of truth has arrived, and it has to be said: Israel does not want peace. The arsenal of excuses has run out, and the chorus of Israeli rejection already rings hollow. Until recently, it was still possible to accept the Israeli refrain that 'there is no partner' for peace and that 'the time isn't right' to deal with our enemies. Today, the new reality before our eyes leaves no room for doubt and the tired refrain that 'Israel supports peace' has been left shattered"(567).

And why does the Zionist-controlled Israeli government not want peace? It is the Zionists' stated goal to completely destroy Arab culture and society, en route to their global empire. Take, for instance, the following revealing statement made by former Israeli Prime Minister Menachem Begin: "You shall have no pity on them until we shall have destroyed their so-called Arab culture, on the ruins of which we shall build our own civilization"(280).

This sort of thinking is at the very heart of Zionist philosophy. One of the most influential Zionist figures of the 20th century, who was largely responsible for such Zionist hatred of Arabs, and whose influence still continues to drive Zionist thinking today, was Ze'ev Jabotinsky, the spiritual father, if you will, of such figures as Menachem Begin, Ariel Sharon, and Brooklyn Rabbi Meir Kahane. With this thought in mind, let us draw our attention to an article called "Death Wish in the Holy Land"that appeared in the December 12, 2001 edition of

Village Voice, which mentioned how, in 1923, Jabotinsky wrote that the "sole way" for Jews to deal with Arabs in Palestine was through "total avoidance of all attempts to arrive at a settlement," which he euphemistically termed the "iron wall" approach. This same edition of *Village Voice* also pointed out, not so surprisingly, that a picture of Jabotinsky graced Prime Minister Sharon's desk.

To further demonstrate the pervasive hatred that Zionists have for Arabs in particular, as well as their desire to completely destroy the Arab people, note the following: The April 12, 2001 edition of *Ha'aretz* reported on how the influential Israeli Rabbi Ovadia Yosef delivered a sermon just prior to the 2001 Passover holiday. During this sermon, he was quoted as saying: "May the Holy Name [meaning God] visit retribution on the Arab heads, and cause their seed to be lost, and annihilate them....It is forbidden to have pity on them. We must give them missiles with relish, annihilate them. Evil ones, damnable ones."

Statements such as this are commonly voiced by prominent Zionists. Let us look at yet another one: "We declare openly that the Arabs have no right to settle on even one centimeter of Eretz Israel....Force is all they do or ever will understand. We shall use the ultimate force until the Palestinians come crawling to us on all fours." -Rafael Eitan, chief of staff of the Israel Defense Forces(381).

It's most ironic how the Zionist Israelis constantly cry about being victims of "hate speech," when in reality they are the worst purveyors of such speech themselves. They are also notorious for shooting down criticism of themselves by labeling it "anti-Semitism," when in reality they're hatred of Arabs is itself anti-Semitism, since the Arabs are, in fact, Semites.

While the Palestinians, and the Arabs in general, are often blamed for the troubles in the Middle East, the media in the United States remain ominously silent about the many atrocities committed by the Zionist Israeli government against innocent Palestinian citizens, including women and children, on literally a daily basis. Though it is true that some Arabs have committed terrorist attacks against Israelis, these actions are retaliatory measures for the barbaric acts of aggression against the Palestinians, which are far more devastating than anything the Arabs are capable of doing to the Israelis. This very point was brought out by the *Jerusalem Post* on May 23, 2001: "Israel's actions are much worse [than those of the Palestinians], both because they are state sanctioned and because the force used is much greater and therefore more destructive."

Please don't forget that the Israeli government receives billions of dollars in aid from the U.S. government each year, and has an enormous arsenal of conventional and non-conventional weaponry. In light of this, one must more carefully contemplate just who the real victim is in the Arab-Israeli conflict.

But coming back to our mention of Arab terrorist attacks, it is of great significance to note the following *Washington Star* quote, which will help shed some light on who the real culprit is that is behind much of the terrorism in the Middle East, and indeed in the rest of the world: "Some years ago, the prominent journalist Russel Warren Howe asked [Menachem] Begin whether he considered himself 'the father' of terrorism in the Middle East. Begin answered expansively, 'No, in the entire world'"(281). Another former Israeli prime minister made this similar statement regarding terrorism and Israeli complicity therein: "We must use terror, assassination, intimidation, land confiscation, and the cutting of all social services to rid the Galilee of its Arab population." - David Ben-Gurion, while speaking to the General Staff in May 1948(344).

If you do some research, you will discover that much of the terrorism in the Middle East is actually perpetrated by the Mossad (Israel's equivalent of the CIA), but later falsely attributed to radical Arabs. This is done to gain sympathy for the Zionist-controlled state of Israel, and to justify more tyranny against Arabs, especially the Palestinians. The Mossad, in fact, is perhaps the only entity in the world that is as evil, if not more so, than the CIA. According to Victor Ostrovsky, a defected Mossad agent, the motto of the Mossad is "We shall wage war by means of deception" [Endnote 154]. This point, and so much more, was revealed in his fascinating book *By Way of Deception* (ISBN: 0971759502).

In addition to the Mossad staging fake terrorist attacks, the Israeli government has also supported radical Arab groups like Hamas over the years. This point came to light by United Press International on June 18, 2002: "In the wake of a suicide bomb attack Tuesday on a crowded Jerusalem city bus that killed 19 people and wounded at least 70 more, the Islamic Resistance Movement, Hamas, took credit for the blast.

"Israeli officials called it the deadliest attack in Jerusalem in six years.

"Israeli Prime Minister Ariel Sharon immediately vowed to fight 'Palestinian terror' and summoned his cabinet to decide on a military response to the organization that Sharon had once described as 'the deadliest terrorist group that we have ever had to face.'

"Active in Gaza and the West Bank, Hamas wants to liberate all of Palestine and establish a radical Islamic state in place of Israel. It has gained notoriety with its assassinations, car bombs and other acts of terrorism.

"But Sharon left something out.

"Israel and Hamas may currently be locked in deadly combat, but, according to several current and former U.S. intelligence officials, beginning in the late 1970s, Tel Aviv gave direct and indirect financial aid to Hamas over a period of years.

"Israel 'aided Hamas directly--the Israelis wanted to use it as a counterbalance to the PLO (Palestinian Liberation Organization),' said Tony Cordesman, Middle East analyst for the Center for Strategic Studies.

"Israel's support for Hamas 'was a direct attempt to divide and dilute support for a strong, secular PLO by using a competing religious alternative,' said a former senior CIA official..."(493). Of course, I would argue that another reason for the Israeli government supporting Hamas has been for the purpose of justifying more oppression of the Palestinians, and to gain sympathy from the international community (with the lie that Israel is the victim).

State-sponsored terrorism and murder on the part of Israel's government against the Palestinians has gone on since the creation of the state of Israel in 1948, and amounts to nothing short of ethnic cleansing. Sadly, many people around the world, even government leaders, are afraid to speak out against such atrocities, for fear of being labeled either anti-Semitic or supporters of terrorism. Notice what Leah Harris of the Washington-based Jews for Peace in Palestine and Israel had to say on this matter: "All people who denounce the Israeli occupation are accused of supporting terrorism. According to this twisted logic, if you oppose Israeli state terrorism, then you of course support other forms of terrorism"(282).

Let us now return to our discussion of the Zionist goal of world domination.

If the Zionists have truly been playing a major role in the formation of global government over the years, then we would expect them to have had their hand in major world events, just like any other globalist entity that we have examined in this study. And indeed, as we look at the history of Zionism, this is exactly what we find. Earlier we talked about the dangers of socialism, and how it is being used to help set up world government. Interestingly, many Jewish encyclopedias have boasted over the years that socialism is the creation of Jews (i.e. Zionists). For example: "[Socialism] originated in the combination of Jewish Messianic feeling with German philosophy." - *Universal Jewish Encyclopedia* (1946), under "socialism." Here's another example: "Jews have been prominently identified with the modern Socialist movement from its very inception." - *Jewish Encyclopedia* (1901-5), under "socialism."

Authoritative Jewish (Zionist) sources have even boasted of orchestrating the communist Bolshevik Revolution in Russia, in 1917: "During the [Russian] Revolution Jews played a prominent part in the party organs. The politburo elected on Oct. 23, 1917 had four Jews among its seven members. The Military Revolutionary Committee, appointed to prepare the coup, was headed by Trotsky [a Zionist Jew, whose real name was Lev Davidovich Bronstein][Endnote 155] and had two Jews among its five members. In the early years of the Soviet regime, Jews were in many leading positions in the government and party machinery." - *Encyclopedia Judaica* (1972), pp. 797, 798.

Further confirmation of the major role played by Jews (Zionists) in the

Bolshevik Revolution can be found by examining many varied and reliable non-Jewish (non-Zionist) sources as well. Let us now examine a few of them:

- "There is now definite evidence that Bolshevism is an international movement controlled by Jews; communications are passing between the leaders in America, France, Russia and England, with a view toward concerted action." - Scotland Yard Report to the American Secretary of State, July 23, 1919.

- "It is probably unwise to say this loudly in the United States [unwise?], but the Bolshevik movement is and has been since its beginning guided and controlled by Russian Jews..." - Captain Montgomery Scyler(283).

- "Fifty percent of the Soviet government in each town consists of Jews of the worst type, many of whom are anarchists." - U.S. State Department Report(284).

- Earlier in this study we cited a quote made by Winston Churchill in the *Illustrated Sunday Herald*, February 8, 1920, regarding his knowledge of a pervasive, ongoing conspiracy for world government. In this same edition of this same paper, Churchill was further quoted as saying: "There is no need to exaggerate the part played in the creation of Bolshevism and in the bringing about of the Russian Revolution by these international...Jews [Zionists]. It is certainly a very great one; it probably outweighs all others. With the notable exception of Lenin, the majority of the leading figures were Jews [Zionists]."

At this point, a pressing question is forced upon us: How did the globalist Zionists pull off the orchestration of this revolution in Russia? To answer this question, recall how we quoted earlier from the *Kabbalah*, which gave instruction on the importance of using "deceit and trickery." In other words, propaganda. Along this line, notice what Carroll Quigley wrote in *Tragedy and Hope*: "[T]he Bolsheviks had no illusions about their position in Russia at the end of 1917. They knew that they formed an infinitesimal group in that vast country and that they had been able to seize power because they were a decisive and ruthless minority among a great mass of persons who had been neutralized through propaganda"(28, p. 386). The main piece of propaganda that neutralized the Russian people was the repeated lie told in the Zionist-controlled press that this new movement of communism was for the downtrodden masses. In reality, it kicked the downtrodden even further into the ground. Quigley went on to say: "From 1917 to 1921, Russia passed through a period of...incredible political and economic chaos....[T]here was extreme economic and social collapse." This, of course, was all by design, as always.

The fact that Zionists organized the Bolshevik Revolution is shocking enough. But when one realizes that it is their intention to repeat this pattern all over the world, engulfing the whole planet in a communistic/socialistic (or better yet, fascistic) global dictatorship, it becomes clear that we are dealing here with a most alarming situation. Before writing this off as paranoid speculation, consider the proceeding comments from a New York Senate report: "[T]he immediate suppression of Bolshevism is the greatest issue now before the world...and unless...Bolshevism is nipped in the bud immediately, it is bound to spread in one form or another over Europe and the whole world, as it is organized and worked by Jews who have no nationality, and whose one object is to destroy for their own ends the existing order of things"(285). Even more shocking is the following Zionist admission: "The Bolshevist revolution in Russia was the work of Jewish brains, of Jewish dissatisfaction, of Jewish planning, whose goal is to create a new order in the world [New World Order]. What was performed in so excellent a way in Russia, thanks to Jewish brains, and because of Jewish dissatisfaction, and by Jewish planning, shall also, through the same Jewish mental and physical forces, become a reality all over the world." - *American Hebrew*(384).

The Bolshevik Revolution resulted in mass carnage, slaughter, misery, and rabid corruption in Russia, and yet the Zionists boast that they were the brains behind it all, and that they intend to repeat it worldwide. Can you not see how incredibly evil and dangerous the Zionist movement is, and how it is, in fact, playing a major role in the push for the New World Order?

But what about the communist/socialist movement in the United States? Have the Zionists been behind this as well? Let's allow the Zionists to answer this question for themselves:

- "The list of Jews who played a prominent role in the leadership and factional infighting of the American Communist Party from its inception is a long one....Many American Jewish authors and intellectuals...were active in editing Communist publications and spreading party propaganda in the 1920s, 1930s and even later." - *Encyclopedia Judaica* (1972), under "communism."

- "[S]o pervasive was Jewish influence in Roosevelt's experiment to socialize America that the pejorative epithet 'Jew Deal' became popular among anti-Semitic elements." - Ibid., under "Franklin D. Roosevelt."

- "Jews have been active in the United States in all radical movements, Socialist and Communist, Old Left and New." - Ibid., under "New Left."

Not only have the Zionists been behind the communist/socialist movement in the United States, but they, like all other globalist string-pullers, have been exerting a powerful influence in our government, media, and our society in general, as the next group of quotes will demonstrate:

- "If after having elected their man or group, obedience is not rendered to the Jewish control, then you speedily hear of 'scandals' and 'investigations' and 'impeachments' for the removal of the disobedient. Usually a man with a 'past' proves the most obedient instrument, but even a good man can often be tangled up in campaign practices that compromise him. It has been commonly known that Jewish manipulation of American election campaigns have been so skillfully handled, that no matter which candidate was elected, there was ready made a sufficient amount of evidence to discredit him in case his Jewish masters needed to discredit him." - Henry Ford, *The International Jew: The World's Foremost Problem.*

- "The greatest danger to this country lies in the Jewish ownership and influence in our motion pictures, our press, our radio, and our government." - Congressman Charles Lindbergh(286).

- "I am aware how almost impossible it is in this country to carry out a foreign policy [especially in the Middle East] not approved by the Jews....[T]errific control the Jews have over the news media and...congressmen....I am very much concerned over the fact that the Jewish influence here is completely dominating the scene and making it almost impossible to get Congress to do anything they don't approve of. The Israeli embassy is practically dictating to the Congress through influential Jewish people in the country." - Secretary of State John Foster Dulles(287).

- From a 1972 Oval Office tape-recorded meeting between President Nixon and Reverend Billy Graham, released in February 2002, we find the following interesting exchange:

Graham: "The Jewish stranglehold on the media has got to be broken or this country's going down the drain."

Nixon: "You believe that?"

Graham: "Yes, sir."

Nixon: "Oh boy. So do I. I can't ever say that but I do believe it."

- "Israel controls the United States Senate. We should be more concerned about the United States' interests." - William Fulbright, U.S. Senator(288).

- "The United States Congress is Israeli occupied territory." - Patrick Buchanan(289).

- "The Jewish Problem pops up in the strangest places. In the winter of 1991, at the height of the first gulf war, I [Ian Buruma of the *New York Times*] asked a right-wing Japanese politician who still wields considerable power in the ruling Liberal Democratic Party to explain the Japanese role in the Middle Eastern conflict. After clearing his throat with some perfunctory remarks about oil supplies and United States-Japan relations, he suddenly stopped midsentence, gave me a shrewd look and said: 'Look, we Japanese aren't stupid. We saw Henry Kissinger on TV. We know how America operates. We're perfectly well aware that this war is not about Kuwait. It's about Jewish interests. It's all about Israel.'...Earlier this year, Representative James Moran, a Democrat, said that 'if it were not for the strong support of the Jewish community for this war with Iraq, we would not be doing this.'...Rarely can such a tiny country as Israel...have been assumed to exercise so much influence in world affairs. The special relationship between Israel and the United States, and the supposed dominance of 'Jewish interests' in Washington, is by now encrusted with so many layers of mythology and bad faith that it has become very difficult to discuss Israel's role in American politics critically and dispassionately. Yet not to talk about it invites only more conspiracy theories [there's nothing theoretical about it!]." - *New York Times*(290).

- "I've never seen a President--I don't care who he is--stand up to them [Zionist Jews]. It just boggles the mind. They always get what they want. The Israelis know what is going on all the time. If the American people understood what a grip those people have got on our government, they would rise up in arms. Our citizens certainly don't have any idea what goes on." - Admiral Thomas Moorer(291).

- "Is there any criminal act that Israel can do without being protected from criticism from the United States? If there is I haven't seen it. And I haven't seen it from the Bush administration or from the Clinton administration or from any administration before them. But when you consider the influence of Israel's lobby and its political action committees and the more than $41 million they've given to Congress and the White House, is it any wonder Israel is shielded from any shame? For more than 54 years the Israelis have committed acts that no other nation would dare get away with. But even here in America, where it is not yet illegal to publicly ask the wrong questions, any public figure that does so is subjected to smears, intimidation, and the attempted destruction of his career and reputation by Jewish organizations and by the very cooperative news media." - U.S. Brigadier General James J. David(382).

- On October 3, 2001, I.A.P. (Islamic Association for Palestine) News reported that, according to Israel Radio, Kol Yisrael, Ariel Sharon said: "Don't worry about American pressure, we the Jewish people control America, and the Americans know it."

- One of the most effective means through which the Zionist movement has operated to control the U.S. government has been through AIPAC (American Israel Public Affairs Committee), which is one of the most powerful lobbyist groups in Washington. Speaking of this organization, the November 5, 1992 edition of the *Chicago Tribune* reported: "The president of the powerful pro-Israel lobby has resigned after being secretly taped boasting about his influence with President-elect Bill Clinton and President Bush's chief of staff, James A. Baker III. David Steiner, president of the American Israel Public Affairs Committee, was recorded as saying he was 'negotiating' with Clinton over his choice for secretary of state and had already 'cut a deal' with Baker to get additional aid for Israel."

The 2003 war waged on Iraq serves as a good example of just how true the above quotes are, that the "Jews" (Zionists) control America. Though the lust for oil played a major role in motivating this war, there was another force pushing the U.S. into this conflict, which the following quotes illustrate:

- "The war in Iraq was conceived by 25 neoconservative intellectuals, most of them Jewish [Zionist], who are pushing President Bush to change the course of history." - *Ha'aretz*(385).

- Less than a week before the war began (March 14, 2003), the *Wall Street Journal* reported: "The U.S. is soon likely to go to war in Iraq in no small part because of the arguments of thinkers who have graced the pages of *Commentary* magazine [official publication of the American Jewish Committee] over the years."

- As early as August 17, 2002, the *Guardian* had reported that "Israel signaled its decision yesterday to put public pressure on President George Bush to go ahead with a military attack on Iraq."

- Former Israeli prime minister Benjamin Netanyahu told a congressional committee on September 12, 2002: "I speak for the overwhelming majority of Israelis in supporting a preemptive strike against Saddam's regime"(386).

- The *Washington Post* reported on December 26, 2002: "In private conversation with [Senator Chuck] Hagel and many other members of Congress, [Prime Minister Ariel Sharon] leaves no doubt that the greatest U.S. assistance to Israel would be to overthrow Saddam Hussein's Iraq regime."

- Finally, the Inter Press Service (IPS) revealed on March 29, 2004, that "Iraq under Saddam Hussein did not pose a threat to the United States but it did to Israel, which is one reason why Washington invaded the Arab country, according to a speech made by a member of a top-level White House intelligence group. IPS uncovered the remarks by Philip Zelikow, who is now the executive director of the body set up to investigate the terrorist attacks on the United States in September 2001--the 9-11 commission--in which he suggests a prime motive for the invasion just over one year ago was to eliminate a threat to Israel, a staunch U.S. ally in the Middle East....Zelikow made his statements about 'the unstated threat' during his tenure on a highly knowledgeable and well-connected body known as the President's Foreign Intelligence Advisory Board (PFIAB), which reports directly to the president [in other words, this man is a very informed person in foreign intelligence matters]"(383).

To help this farce war look like a virtuous cause, Bush Jr. called it "Operation Iraqi Freedom" and talked about bringing "democracy" to Iraq. This same mantra of bringing "freedom and democracy," remember, was chanted all during the Cold War as the U.S. invaded country after country, and, as it went along, installed ruthless dictators who were friendly to U.S./globalist policies. Bearing all this in mind, one can easily get that feeling of déja-vu when considering the fact that Representative Tom Lantos assured an Israeli parliament member in September 2002 that, after the U.S. removed Saddam from power, "we'll install a pro-Western dictator, who will be good for us and for you." - *Ha'aretz*(387). Are you starting to understand what is going on here? Are all the strange goings-on in our foreign and domestic policies beginning to come into focus?

Within weeks of the outbreak of the 2003 campaign against Iraq, Bush had already started looking at other countries like Syria, Iran, and Libya as his next possible targets for "regime changes." Were the Zionists also behind this push for yet more wars against Arab nations? Notice these remarks made by a prominent American Jewish (Zionist) newspaper: "Openly pleased with the Bush administration's recent warnings to Syria not to aid Iraq, Israel and its supporters here have begun ratcheting up their accusations against its radical neighbor in apparent hopes of widening the rift between Damascus and Washington." - *Forward*(388). On February 19, 2003, *Ha'aretz* reported: "Prime Minister Ariel Sharon said yesterday that Iran, Libya and Syria should be stripped of weapons of mass destruction after Iraq. 'These are irresponsible states, which must be disarmed of weapons of mass destruction, and a successful American move in Iraq as a model will make that easier to achieve,' Sharon said to a visiting delegation of American congressmen."

Can't you see that the Zionists are using the United States to carry out an agenda that they have had on the drawing board for a very long time--the total destruction of the Arab world and its culture? Let us take a second look at a Menachem Begin quote cited earlier, which stated this objective very clearly: "You shall have no pity on them until we shall have <u>destroyed their so-called Arab culture</u>, on the ruins of which we shall build our own civilization." These words sound so very much like those of Norman Podhoretz, editor emeritus of *Commentary* (a Zionist publication), who urged the United States to have "the will to fight World War IV [WW III being the Cold War]--the war against militant Islam [and thus the Arab world, in general]--to a successful conclusion, and...then have the stomach to impose <u>a new political culture</u> on the defeated parties"(389). Similarly, on April 5, 2003, *Ha'aretz* reported that William Kristol, the *Weekly Standard* editor who helped to persuade the Bush administration to attack Iraq, stated of the Iraq war that "at a deeper level it is a greater war, for the shaping of a new Middle East. It is a war that is intended <u>to change the political culture</u> of the entire region."

Zionist influence in the U.S. government began very early on. Rabbi Stephen Wise, a rabid Zionist who was a personal friend of President Woodrow Wilson, in his book *Challenging Years*, wrote: "[I]n [Woodrow] Wilson we had and would always have understanding sympathy for the Zionist program and purpose....Throughout, it must be added, we received warm and heartening help from Colonel House, close friend of the president and his unofficial secretary of state. House not only made our cause the object of his very special concern but served as liaison officer between the Wilson administration and the Zionist movement"(486, p. 82).

Incidentally, Rabbi Wise was also a close personal friend of F.D.R., and was instrumental in the launching of his political career. Here's what he had to say about F.D.R. in *Challenging Years*: "In 1928...I had full opportunity to support Franklin D. Roosevelt for governor [of New York] and did so wholeheartedly....I felt, because of his able leadership of the state..., that he should be re-elected in 1930. By then he had also begun to loom large as the Democratic candidate for the presidency in 1932"(486, p. 136).

Of course, the Zionists have exerted a powerful influence upon the British government as well, beginning at about the same time that it began influencing the U.S. government. One of the most obvious signs of this was the famous Balfour Declaration. This was a letter written on November 2, 1917 by the British foreign secretary, Arthur James Balfour, to the most powerful man in England at the time, Lionel Rothschild, who was another rabid Zionist. The letter read, in part, as follows: "I have much pleasure in conveying to you, on behalf of his Majesty's government, the following declaration of sympathy with Jewish Zionist aspirations which have been submitted to, and approved by, the Cabinet.

"'His Majesty's government view with favor the establishment in Palestine of a national home for the Jewish people and will use their best endeavors to facilitate the achievement of this object...'

"I would be grateful if you would bring this declaration to the knowledge of the Zionist Federation"(486, p. 88).

Here we have a promise being made by a British government official to the world's chief international banker--a Zionist--that the Palestinians' land would be stolen from them and given to the Zionists. This, of course, did happen, in 1948, when the United Nations awarded 55% of Palestine to the newly-formed Zionist state of Israel. Can you not see the string-pulling that was going on here, and who was behind it? By the way, in Rabbi Wise's book *Challenging Years*, he said that Wilson once promised him: "Have no fear, Palestine will be yours"(486, p. 83).

The Zionist-controlled state of Israel, in spite of its supposed official position as a "close ally" of the United States, has proven itself to be a sworn enemy of this country. On numerous occasions it has launched attacks (sometimes not so successfully) against U.S. targets for various political reasons, and has always gotten away with such acts of betrayal, because of the powerful hold it has over Washington.

One good example of this type of activity was the famous Lavon Affair. In 1954, Israel's secret service set up a spy ring in Egypt for the purpose of blowing up U.S. and British targets. These terrorist attacks were to be blamed on the regime of Egyptian President Gamal Abdul Nasser, in the hope of alienating the U.S. and Britain from Egypt and Nasser. The spies were caught, however, resulting in a scandal that eventually led to the resignation of Israeli Prime Minister Ben-Gurion. A resulting wave of persecution forced the emigration of tens of thousands of Jews from Egypt. But, of course, absolutely no action was ever taken against Israel by U.S. or British officials for this fiasco.

Another good example of a traitorous attack by Israelis against an American target (which was also not successful, but did result in many U.S. casualties--34) was the assault on the U.S. Naval intelligence ship, the U.S.S. Liberty, 13 miles off the coast of the Sinai Peninsula. On June 8, 1967, Israeli air and naval forces attacked this ship without warning and without cause. For at least a half hour this boat was relentlessly fired upon from the air and torpedoed from the sea. All the while a U.S. flag was waving high on this ship, right out in the open and in broad daylight. There can be no question that it was known by the Israelis that this was not an enemy vessel.

Following this attack, President Johnson made no official statements concerning this event (what a surprise!). However, Secretary of State Dean Rusk sent a diplomatic note to the Israeli ambassador to the United States, on June 10, which read in part: "...At the time of the attack, the U.S.S Liberty was flying the American flag and its identification was clearly indicated in large white letters and numerals on its hull. It was broad daylight and the weather conditions were excellent. Experience demonstrates that both the flag and the identification number of the vessel were readily visible from the air. At 1450 hours local time on June 8, 1967, two Israeli aircraft circled the U.S.S. Liberty three times, with the evident purpose of identifying the vessel. Accordingly there is every reason to believe that the U.S.S Liberty was identified, or at least her nationality determined, by Israeli aircraft approximately one hour before the attack. In these circumstances, the later military attack by Israeli aircraft on the U.S.S. Liberty is quite literally incomprehensible. As a minimum, the attack must be condemned as an act of military recklessness reflecting wanton disregard for human life.

"The subsequent attack by Israeli torpedo boats, substantially after the vessel was or should have been identified by Israeli military forces, manifests the same reckless disregard for human life. The silhouette and conduct of the U.S.S Liberty readily distinguished it from any vessel that could have been considered as hostile. The U.S.S. Liberty was peacefully engaged, posed no threat whatsoever to the torpedo boats, and obviously carried no armament affording it a combat capability. It could and should have been scrutinized visually at close range before torpedoes were fired...."

The Israelis tried to justify this outrage by claiming that it was an accident. But this claim just doesn't cut it. When Secretary Rusk later published his memoirs in 1990, he agreed that this excuse was preposterous: "...I was never satisfied with the Israeli explanation. Their sustained attack to disable and sink Liberty precluded an assault by accident or some trigger-happy local commander. Through diplomatic channels we refused to accept their explanations. I didn't believe them then, and I don't believe them to this day. The attack was outrageous"(489, p. 388). But, as always, nothing was done by the U.S. government about this act of war.

So why was the U.S.S. Liberty attacked? The most likely reason was that this intelligence ship's intercepts flatly contradicted Israel's claim, made on June 5, that it was attacked by Egypt, and that Israel's massive air assault on three Arab nations was done in retaliation. However, in reality, Israel began the war by a devastating, unprovoked surprise attack that caught the Arabs totally off guard, completely destroying their air forces.

Israel was also preparing to attack Syria to seize its strategic Golan Heights. But Washington warned Israel not to invade Syria, because this country did not respond to Israel's attack on Egypt. Of course, Israel decided to go ahead with its plans anyway. However, according to James Bamford's *Body of Secrets*, Israel's Syrian offensive was abruptly postponed when the U.S.S. Liberty appeared off Sinai. It was only after this ship was knocked out of commission that Israel finally went ahead with its planned Syrian invasion.

A possible further reason for the Israeli assault on the Liberty was the hope that, had it been successfully sunk, Egypt or Syria could have been falsely blamed, and thus the U.S. would be suckered into fighting a war that Israel wouldn't have to fight itself.

Another fiasco of the Israeli government, which proves that it is by no means an ally of the United States, is the fact that this nation has been caught, on many occasions over the years, spying on our government. For instance, beginning on December 12, 2001, Fox News ran a four-part series by Carl Cameron on a major and highly suspicious Israeli spy ring that had been going on since long before 9-11. In Part I of this series, Cameron reported: "Since September 11, more than 60 Israelis have been arrested or detained, either under the new patriot anti-terrorism law, or for immigration violations. A handful of active Israeli military were among those detained, according to investigators, who say some of the detainees also failed polygraph questions when asked about alleged surveillance activities against and in the United States.

"There is no indication that the Israelis were involved in the 9-11 attacks, but investigators suspect that the Israelis may have gathered intelligence about the attacks in advance, and not shared it. A highly placed investigator said there are 'tie-ins.' But when asked for details, he flatly refused to describe them, saying, 'evidence linking these Israelis to 9-11 is classified. I cannot tell you about evidence that has been gathered. It's classified information' [Endnote 156].

"Fox News has learned that one group of Israelis, spotted in North Carolina recently, is suspected of keeping an apartment in California to spy on a group of Arabs who the United States is also investigating for links to terrorism. Numerous classified documents obtained by Fox News indicate that even prior to

September 11, as many as 140 other Israelis had been detained or arrested in a secretive and sprawling investigation into suspected espionage by Israelis in the United States.

"Investigators from numerous government agencies are part of a working group that's been compiling evidence since the mid '90s. These documents detail hundreds of incidents in cities and towns across the country that investigators say, 'may well be an organized intelligence gathering activity.'

"The first part of the investigation focuses on Israelis who say they are art students from the University of Jerusalem and Bazala Academy. They repeatedly made contact with U.S. government personnel, the report says, by saying they wanted to sell cheap art or handiwork.

"Documents say they, 'targeted and penetrated military bases.' The DEA, FBI and dozens of government facilities, and even secret offices and unlisted private homes of law enforcement and intelligence personnel. The majority of those questioned, 'stated they served in military intelligence, electronic surveillance intercept and or explosive ordinance units.'...

"Why would Israelis spy in and on the U.S.? A general accounting office investigation referred to Israel as country A and said, 'According to a U.S. intelligence agency, the government of country A conducts the most aggressive espionage operations against the U.S. of any U.S. ally.'

"A defense intelligence report said Israel has a voracious appetite for information and said, 'the Israelis are motivated by strong survival instincts which dictate every possible facet of their political and economical policies. It aggressively collects military and industrial technology and the U.S. is a high priority target.'"

Naturally, nothing came out of this "investigation," except that each of these spies, one by one, was sent back to Israel, at American tax-payer expense. Absolutely no legal action was ever taken against any of them. The reason for this is obvious, as this same Fox series pointed out: "Investigators within the DEA, INS and FBI have all told Fox News that to pursue or even suggest Israeli spying...is considered career suicide." So there you have it--a classic example of the tail wagging the dog!

As the above Fox News report mentioned, Israel doesn't just spy on the U.S. for political reasons, but for economic reasons as well. Along this line, the December 16, 2004 *Washington Times* reported: "Israeli defense officials in the United States have been accused by the FBI of industrial espionage, the second spying complaint leveled against Israel in four months, Israel's Army Radio has reported"(490).

As we have seen, one of the stated goals of the Zionist-controlled Israeli government is to completely annihilate Arab culture in general, and the

Palestinian state in particular. And since the Israeli government has a powerful hold on the U.S. government, it should not be surprising that the U.S. has never lifted a finger to prevent Israel from abusing and killing Palestinians. On the contrary, the U.S. government has facilitated such endeavors. Here's what former Congressman Paul Findley had to say about this problem, in the November 13, 2006 edition of *Friday* magazine: "The massive aid we keep sending has long helped Israel to inflict lethal degradation on mostly-Muslim Palestinians. We are silent when Israel makes Gaza a vast, miserable and bloody concentration camp where 1.4 million human beings are denied electricity, clean water, housing, food, and medical care. We look the other way when Israel arrests officials of Palestine's freely-elected government.

"Our Congress approves when Israel herds the rest of the Palestinians like cattle behind high walls and fences. Every U.S. president beginning with Lyndon B. Johnson could have stopped Israel's major crimes, simply by suspending all U.S. aid until Israel behaved. Every Congress could have done the same. But none did. The only U.S. President to stand resolutely against Israel's criminal behavior was Dwight D. Eisenhower. Israel's influence has led America into one awful mess after another"(557).

Echoing similar sentiments, Jimmy Carter wrote an article for the December 10, 2006 *Los Angeles Times*, in which he declared: "The many controversial issues concerning Palestine and the path to peace for Israel are intensely debated among Israelis and throughout other nations--but not in the United States. For the last 30 years, I have witnessed and experienced...severe restraints on any free and balanced discussion of the facts. This reluctance to criticize any policies of the Israeli government is because of the extraordinary lobbying efforts of the American-Israel Political Action Committee and the absence of any significant contrary voices.

"It would be almost politically suicidal for members of Congress to espouse a balanced position between Israel and Palestine, to suggest that Israel comply with international law or to speak in defense of justice or human rights for Palestinians"(559).

In light of our earlier examination of the role that the papacy has been playing in the globalist movement, you may be asking yourself: How could both the Vatican and Zionism be cooperatively working toward the same goal of world domination, when they seem to be at such obvious odds with each other, especially in religious matters? This is a good question. But the truth is that both of them are purely political entities that are only after power, and thus they do indeed have very much in common.

As it turns out, Zionism has nothing to do with true Jewish religion (based on the Torah), although many who support the Zionist cause, such as the Christian

Zionists, do have what they believe to be true religious motives for doing so [Endnote 157]. And the same holds true for Catholicism, whose membership, for the most part, has a sincere but blind religious rationale for supporting the Vatican, being entirely oblivious to its corrupt, power-hungry, purely politically-motivated ambitions.

Because of the mutual interest in power between Zionism and the papacy, both have made official concessions in order that they may work together effectively toward the same end. As one example of such concessions, the Vatican signed an agreement, or concordat, with the Zionist state of Israel on December 30, 1993, called "Fundamental Agreement Between the Holy See and the State of Israel." In it, both agreed, for instance, under Article 2, to remain "committed to appropriate cooperation in combating all forms of antisemitism [anti-Zionism]..., and in promoting mutual understanding among nations [pushing for a New World Order]." Under Article 3 we read: "The Holy See and the State of Israel recognize that both are free in the exercise of their respective rights and powers, and commit themselves to respect this principle in their mutual relations and in their cooperation..."(390).

Remember that Zionists, like all other globalists, warmly embrace all who uphold and support their goal of global dominance. Likewise, the Vatican also has a long history of holding in high esteem all who aid its interests (the monarchs who assisted the medieval Crusades are a good example of this). Therefore, there should no longer be any problem comprehending how these seemingly incompatible systems can actually be very close companions.

The same is true, of course, in regards to the relationship between the U.N. and the Zionist-controlled state of Israel--they are both close partners en route to global control, even though, on the surface, they appear to be incompatible. For instance, so often we have heard, over the years, of the U.N.'s condemnations of Israel, and rightly so, for its abuse of the Palestinians and for unjustifiable aggressions against various Arab countries. But understand that such condemning sentiments do not originate at the top echelons of power at the U.N. The only reason why the top dogs at the United Nations allow such sentiments to be expressed in its name is so that the public, on a global scale, will put more trust in the U.N. and lend it more support, looking to it as the only hope for world peace. Understand, too, that even though the U.N. condemns Israeli (Zionist) acts of aggression, rightly calling them violations of human rights, it never once has done anything to intervene--either by sending in "peacekeeping" troops or imposing sanctions, as it has done in so many other countries. Nor has it even suggested doing either of these things. So is the U.N., at the top levels of power, really against Israeli abuses? Of course not!

Far from taking steps to prevent the Israeli government from committing

314

its atrocities, efforts have been made over the years by U.N. officials, through pressuring voting members, to actually temper down their condemnations of Israel's government. For instance, on December 16, 1991, the United Nations passed General Assembly Resolution 46/86 with a vote of 87 to 25, which overturned Resolution 3379, passed by a vote of 89 to 67 on November 10, 1975, that had declared Zionism as a form of racism. This vote-change alone should tell you who's calling the shots at the U.N., since not only had the racist nature of Zionism not improved between 1975 and 1991, but had actually gotten much worse.

In closing, let it be stressed once again that protesting Zionism has absolutely nothing to do with anti-Semitism. What DOES constitute anti-Semitism, however, is Zionism itself, not only because of the rabid hatred it has for the Arabs, but because of its hatred for real Jews who follow the Torah alone. Zionists have actually incited anti-Semitic sentiments against such Jews worldwide. Why? The Jews Against Zionism website provides us a good answer: "It has been the age-old intention of Zionism to intentionally stir up anti-Semitism anywhere possible, and even more commonly, to take advantage of any Jewish suffering anywhere in order to enhance its cause. Indeed, hatred of Jews and Jewish suffering is the oxygen of the Zionist movement, and from the very beginning [it] has been [its aim] to deliberately incite hatred of the Jew and then, in feigned horror, use it to justify the existence of the Zionist state--this is, of course, Machiavellianism raised to the highest degree. Thus, the Zionists thrive on hatred and suffering of Jews, and seek to benefit thereby through keeping Jews in perpetual fear, causing them to ignore the true nature of Zionism, and instead to consider the Zionist state as their salvation....[T]he founder of [modern] Zionism and apostate, Theodor Herzl, sought to intensify hatred of the Jew in order to enhance the cause of political Zionism. Here are some of his 'pearls': 'It is essential that the sufferings of Jews...become worse....[T]his will assist in realization of our plans....I have an excellent idea...I shall induce anti-Semites to liquidate Jewish wealth....The anti-Semites will assist us thereby in that they will strengthen the persecution and oppression of Jews. The anti-Semites shall be our best friends.' (From his Diary, Part I, p. 16)"(277).

"There's nothing more deep than recognizing Israel's right to exist. That's the most deep thought of all....I can't think of anything more deep than that right." - George W. Bush, March 13, 2002(570).

Supplement II

Excerpts from the Protocols of the Illuminati
(the "blueprints" of the New World Order)

- In our day the power which has replaced that of the rulers...is the power of gold.
- Whether a State exhausts itself in its own convulsions, whether its internal discord brings it under the power of external foes--in any case it can be accounted irretrievably lost if it is in our power. The despotism of Capital, which is entirely in our hands, reaches out to a straw that the State must take hold of: if not--it goes to the bottom.
- The political has nothing in common with the moral. The ruler who is governed by the moral is not a skilled politician, and is therefore unstable on his throne. He who wishes to rule must have recourse both to cunning...and to make-believe. Great national qualities, like frankness and honesty, are vices in politics, for they bring down rulers from their thrones more effectively and more certainly than the most powerful enemy. Such qualities must be the attributes of the kingdoms of the [common people] but we must in no ways be guided by them....
- For us there are no checks to limit the range of our activity. Our Super-Government subsists in extra-legal conditions which are described in the accepted terminology by the energetic and forcible word--Dictatorship....[A]t the proper time we, the lawgivers, shall execute judgment and sentence, we shall slay and we shall spare, we, as head of all our troops, are mounted on the steed of the leader. We rule by force of will, because in our hands are the fragments of a once powerful party, now vanquished by us. And the weapons in our hands are limitless ambitions, burning greediness, merciless vengeance, hatreds and malice.
- The intensification of armaments, the increase of police forces--are all essential for the completion of the aforementioned plans. What we have to get at is that there should be in all the States of the world, besides ourselves, only the masses of the proletariat, a few millionaires devoted to our interests, police and soldiers.
- We must be in a position to respond to every act of opposition by war with the neighbours of that country which dares to oppose us; but if these neighbours should also venture to stand collectively together against us, then we must offer resistance by a universal war.
- In a word, to sum up our system of keeping the governments of the [common people]...in check, we shall show our strength to one of them by terrorist attempts and to all, if we allow the possibility of a general rising against us, we shall respond [with] the guns of America or China or Japan.
- ...From the premier dictators [that we control]...the peoples suffer patiently and bear such abuses as for the least of them they would have beheaded twenty kings.

What is the explanation...? It is explained by the fact that these dictators whisper to the peoples through their agents that through these abuses they [have]...the highest purpose--to secure the welfare of the peoples...their solidarity and equality of rights. Naturally they do not tell the peoples that this unification must be accomplished only under our sovereign rule....

- [T]hey [the common people] will close their eyes: for we shall keep promising them to give back all the liberties we have taken away as soon as we have quelled the enemies of peace and tamed all parties.

- It is from us that the all-engulfing terror proceeds....[W]e will not give them [the common people] peace until they openly acknowledge our international Super-Government and with submissiveness.

- When we at last definitely come into our kingdom by the aid of coups d'etat prepared everywhere for one and the same day, after the worthlessness of all existing forms of government has been definitely acknowledged (and not a little time will pass before that comes about, perhaps even a whole century) we shall make it our task to see that against us such things as plots shall no longer exist. With this purpose we shall slay without mercy all who take arms in hand to oppose our coming into our kingdom. Every kind of new institution of anything like a secret society will also be punished with death.

- All people are chained down to heavy toil by poverty more firmly than ever they were chained by slavery and serfdom; from these, one way and another, they might free themselves, these could be settled with, but from want they will never get away.

- We appear on the scene as alleged saviors of the worker from this oppression when we propose to him to enter the ranks of our fighting forces--Socialists, Anarchists, Communists--to whom we always give support in accordance with an alleged brotherly rule (of the solidarity of all humanity) of our social masonry. The aristocracy, which enjoyed by law the labour of the workers, was interested in seeing that the workers were well fed, healthy and strong. We are interested in just the opposite--in the diminution, the killing out of the [common people]. Our power is in the chronic shortness of food and physical weakness of the worker because by all that this implies he is made the slave of our will, and he will not find in his own authorities either strength or energy to set against our will. Hunger creates the right of capital to rule the worker more surely than it was given to the aristocracy by the legal authority of kings.

- By want and the envy and hatred which it engenders we shall move the mobs with their hands; we shall wipe out all those who hinder us on our way.

- Our countersign is--Force and Make-Believe. Only force conquers in political affairs, especially if it be concealed in the talents essential to statesmen. Violence must be the principle, and cunning and make-believe the rule for governments which do not want to lay down their crowns at the feet of agents of some new power. This evil is the one and only means to attain the end, the good. Therefore we must not stop at bribery, deceit and treachery when they should serve towards the attainment of our end.

- In the hands of the State of today there is a great force that creates the movement of thought in the people, and that is the Press. The part played by the Press is to keep pointing out requirements supposed to be indispensable, to give voice to the complaints of the people, to express and create discontent. It is in the Press that the triumph of freedom of speech finds its incarnation. But the [common people] States have not known how to make use of this force; and it has fallen into our hands. Through the Press we have gained the power to influence while remaining ourselves in the shade; thanks to the Press we have got the gold in our hands, notwithstanding that we have had to gather it out of oceans of blood and tears. But it has paid us...

- The [common people] have lost the habit of thinking unless prompted by the suggestions of our specialists.

- In order to put public opinion into our hands we must bring it into a state of bewilderment by giving expression from all sides to so many contradictory opinions and for such length of time as will suffice to make the [common people] lose their heads in the labyrinth and come to see that the best thing is to have no opinion of any kind in matters political which it is not given to the public to understand, because they are understood only by him who guides the public. This is the first secret.

- The second secret requisite for the success of our government is comprised in the following: To multiply to such an extent national failings, habits, passions, conditions of civil life, that it will be impossible for anyone to know where he is in the resulting chaos, so that the people in consequence will fail to understand one another. This measure will also serve us in another way, namely, to sow discord in all parties, to dislocate all collective forces which are still unwilling to submit to us, and to discourage any kind of personal initiative which might in any degree hinder our affair. There is nothing more dangerous than personal initiative; if it has genius behind it, such initiative can do more than can be done by millions of people among whom we have sown discord. We must so direct the education of the [common people] communities that whenever they come upon a matter requiring initiative they may drop their hands in despairing impotence. The strain which results from freedom of action saps the forces when it meets with the freedom of another. From this collision arise grave mortal shocks, disenchantments, failures. By all these means we shall so wear down the [common people] that they will be compelled to offer us international power of a nature that by its position will enable us without any violence gradually to absorb the State forces of the world and to form a Super-Government. In place of the rulers of today we shall set up a bogey which will be called the Super-Government Administration. Its hands will reach out in all directions...and its organizations will be of such colossal dimensions that it cannot fail to subdue all the nations of the world.

- We must compel the governments of the [common people] to take action in the direction favoured by our widely-conceived plan, already approaching the desired consummation, by what we shall represent as public opinion, secretly prompted by us through the means of that so-called "Great Power"--the Press, which, with a few exceptions that may be disregarded, is already entirely in our hands.

- Not a single announcement will reach the public without our control. Even now this is already attained by us inasmuch as all news items are received by a few agencies, in whole offices they are focused from all parts of the world. These agencies will then be already entirely ours and will give publicity only to what we dictate to them.

- All our newspapers will be of all possible complexions--aristocratic, republican, revolutionary, even anarchical--for so long, of course, as the constitution exists....Like the Indian idol Vishnu they will have a hundred hands, and every one of them will have a finger on any one of the public opinions as required. When a pulse quickens, these hands will lead opinion in the direction of our aims, for an excited patient loses all power of judgment and easily yields to suggestion. Those fools who will think they are repeating the opinion of a newspaper of their own camp instead will be repeating our opinion or any opinion that seems desirable for us. In the vain belief that they are following the organ of their party, they will in fact follow the flag which we hang out for them.

- Methods of organization like these, imperceptible to the public eye but absolutely sure, are the best calculated to succeed in bringing the attention and the confidence of the public to the side of our government. Thanks to such methods we shall be in a position, as from time to time may be required, to excite or to tranquilize the public mind on political questions, to persuade or to confuse, printing now truth, now lies, facts or their contradictions, according as they may be well or ill, received, always very cautiously feeling our ground before stepping upon it....We shall have a sure triumph over our opponents since they will not have at their disposition organs of the press in which they can give full and final expression to their views, owing to the aforesaid methods of dealing with the press. We shall not even need to refute them except very superficially.

- [O]ur orators will expound great problems which have turned humanity upside down in order to bring it at the end under our beneficent rule.

- Who will ever suspect then that all these peoples were stage-managed by us according to political plan which no one has so much as guessed at in the course of many centuries?

- We have fooled, bemused and corrupted the youth of the [common people] by rearing them in principles and theories which are known to us to be false although it is by us that they have been inculcated.

- In a word, knowing by the experience of many centuries that people live and are guided by ideas, that these ideas are imbibed by people only by the aid of education provided with equal success for all ages of growth, but of course by varying methods, we shall swallow up and confiscate to our own use the last scintilla of independence of thought, which we have for long past been directing towards subjects and ideas useful for us. The system of bridling thought is already at work in the so-called system of teaching by object lessons, the purpose of which is to turn the [common people] into unthinking submissive brutes waiting for things to be presented before their eyes in order to form an idea of them.

- [I]t is essential to teach in national schools one simple, true piece of knowledge, the basis of all knowledge--the knowledge of the structure of human life, of social existence, which requires division of labour, and, consequently, the division of men into classes and conditions....In the present state of knowledge, and the direction we have given to its development to the people, blindly believing things in print--cherishes--thanks to promptings intended to mislead and to its own ignorance--a blind hatred towards all conditions which it considers above itself, for it has no understanding of the meaning of class and condition.

- This hatred will be still further magnified by the effects of an economic crisis, which will stop dealings on the exchanges and bring industry to a standstill. We shall create by all the secret subterranean methods open to us and with the aid of gold, which is all in our hands, a universal economic crisis whereby we shall throw upon the streets whole mobs of workers simultaneously in all the countries of Europe. These mobs will rush delightedly to shed the blood of those whom, in the simplicity of their ignorance, they have envied from their cradles, and whose property they will then be able to loot.

- "Ours" they will not touch, because the moment of attack will be known to us and we shall take measures to protect our own.

- Remember the French Revolution...the secrets of its preparations are well known to us for it was wholly the work of our hands.

- We shall create an intensified centralization of government in order to grip in our hands all the forces of the community. We shall regulate mechanically all the actions of the political life of our subjects by new laws. These laws will withdraw one by one all the indulgences and liberties which have been permitted by the [common people], and our kingdom will be distinguished by a despotism of such magnificent proportions as to be at any moment and in every place in a position to wipe out any [common people] who oppose us by deed or word.

- Who and what is in a position to overthrow an invisible force? And this is precisely what our force is....[T]he plan of action of our force, even its very abiding-place remains for the whole people an unknown mystery.

- [T]here is not one State which would anywhere receive [financial] support [from us] if it were to raise its arm, for every one of them must bear in mind that any agreement against us would be unprofitable to itself. We are too strong--there is no evading our power. The nations cannot come to even an inconsiderable private agreement without our secretly having a hand in it.

- Capital...must be free to establish a monopoly of industry and trade: this is already being put in execution by an unseen hand in all quarters of the world. This freedom will give political force to those engaged in industry, and that will help to oppress the people. Nowadays it is more important to disarm the peoples than to lead them into war; more important to use for our advantage the passions which have burst into flames than to quench their fire; more important to catch up and interpret the ideas of others to suit ourselves than to eradicate them. The principal object of our directorate consists in this: to debilitate the public mind by criticism; to lead it away from serious reflections calculated to arouse resistance; to distract the forces of the mind toward a sham fight of empty eloquence.

- In order to give the [common people] no time to think and take note, their minds must be diverted towards industry and trade. Thus, all the nations will be swallowed up in the pursuit of gain and in the race for it will not take note of their common foe.

- In order that the masses themselves may not guess what [is going on]...we further distract them with amusements, games, pastimes, passions....Soon we shall begin through the press to propose competitions in art, in sport, in all kinds: these interests will finally distract their minds from questions in which we should find ourselves compelled to oppose them. Growing more and more disaccustomed to reflect and form any opinions of their own, people will begin to talk in the same tone as we, because we alone shall be offering them new directions for thought...of course through such persons as will not be suspected of solidarity with us.

- In all ages the peoples of the world, equally with individuals, have accepted words for deeds, for they are content with a show and rarely pause to note, in the public arena, whether promises are followed by performance. Therefore we shall establish show institutions which will give eloquent proof of their benefit to progress.

- It is easy to understand that in these conditions the key of the shrine will lie in our hands, and no one outside ourselves will any longer direct the force of legislation.

- We have got our hands into the administration of the law, into the conduct of elections, into the press, into liberty of the person, but principally into education and training as being the corner-stones of a free existence.
- We must arm ourselves with all the weapons which our opponents might employ against us. We must search out in the very finest shades of expression and the knotty points of the lexicon of law justification for those cases where we shall have to pronounce judgments that might appear abnormally audacious and unjust, for it is important that these resolutions should be set forth in expressions that shall seem to be the most exalted moral principles cast into legal form. Our directorate must surround itself with all these forces of civilization among which it will have to work. It will surround itself with publicists, practical jurists, administrators, diplomats and, finally, with persons prepared by a special super-educational training in our special schools. These persons will have cognizance of all the secrets of the social structure, they will know all the languages that can be made up by political alphabets and words; they will be made acquainted with the whole underside of human nature, with all its sensitive chords on which they will have to play.
- Above the existing laws without substantially altering them, and by merely twisting them into contradictions of interpretations, we have erected something grandiose in the way of results. These results found expression first in the fact that the interpretations masked the laws: afterwards they entirely hid them from the eyes of the governments owing to the impossibility of making anything out of the tangled web of legislation.
- [U]ntil there will no longer be any risk in entrusting responsible posts in our States to others...we shall put them in the hands of persons whose past and reputation are such that between them and the people lie an abyss, persons who, in case of disobedience to our institutions, must face criminal charges or disappear--this in order to make them defend our interests to their last gasp.
- [W]e shall arrange elections in favour of such presidents as have in their past some dark, undiscovered stain...then they will be trustworthy agents for the accomplishment of our plans out of fear of revelations and from the natural desire of everyone who has attained power, namely, the retention of the privileges, advantages and honour connected with the office of president. The chamber of deputies will provide cover for, will protect, will elect presidents, but we shall take from it the right to propose new, or make changes in existing laws, for this right will be given by us to the responsible president, a puppet in our hands....[W]e shall invest the president with the right of declaring a state of war....The president will, at our discretion, interpret the sense of...the existing laws...he will further annul them when we indicate to him the necessity to do so....[B]esides this, he will have the right to propose temporary laws, and even

new departures in the government constitutional working, the pretext both for the one and the other being the requirements for the supreme welfare of the state. By such measures we shall obtain the power of destroying little by little, step by step,...every kind of constitution, and then the time is come to turn every government into our despotism....

- [T]he blind force of the people remains our support and we, and we only, shall provide them with a leader and, of course, direct them along the road that leads to our goal.

- [We shall] transfer into our hands all the money of the world, and thereby throw all the [common people] into the ranks of the proletariat. Then the [common people] will bow down before us, if for no other reason but to get the right to exist....We shall raise the rate of wages which, however, will not bring any advantage to the workers, for at the same time, we shall produce a rise in prices of the first necessaries of life.

- ...It is essential...for us at whatever cost to deprive [the people] of their land....At the same time we must intensively patronize trade and industry....[W]hat we want is that industry should drain off from the land both labour and capital and by means of speculation transfer into our hands all the money of the world....

- In order that the true meaning of things may not strike the [common people] before the proper time, we shall mask it under an alleged ardent desire to serve the working classes and the great principles of political economy about which our economic theories are carrying on an energetic propaganda.

- What...indeed is, in substance, a loan, especially a foreign loan? A loan is an issue of government bills of exchange containing a percentage obligation commensurate to the sum of the loan capital. If the loan bears a charge of 5 percent, then in twenty years the State vainly pays away in interest a sum equal to the loan borrowed, in forty years it is paying a double sum, in sixty--treble, and all the while the debt remains an unpaid debt.

- From this calculation it is obvious that with any form of taxation per head the State is bailing out the last coppers of the poor taxpayers in order to settle accounts with wealthy foreigners, from whom it has borrowed money instead of collecting those coppers for its own needs without the additional interest.

- So long as loans were internal the [common people] only shuffled money from the pockets of the poor to those of the rich, but when we bought up the necessary person in order to transfer loans into the external sphere all the wealth of States flowed into our cash-boxes and all the [common people] began to pay us the tribute of subjects....

- Our power in the present tottering condition of all forms of power will be more invincible than any other, because it will remain invisible until the moment when it has gained such strength that no cunning can any longer undermine it.

- Our international rights will then wipe out national rights...and will rule the nations precisely as the civil law of States rules the relations of their subjects among themselves.

- When the hour strikes for our Sovereign Lord of all the World to be crowned [referring to the globalist-appointed leader of the coming New World Order], it is these same hands which will sweep away everything that might be a hindrance thereto.

- What we want...from...the peoples of the world...[is that] they should recognize once and for all that we are so strong,...so super abundantly filled with power, that in no case shall we take any account of them, and so far from paying any attention to their opinions or wishes, we are ready and able to crush with irresistible power all expression or manifestation thereof at every moment and in every place, that we have seized at once everything we wanted and shall in no case divide our power with them...(276).

* * * * * * *

"The only statement I care to make about the Protocols is that they fit in with what is going on...and they have fitted the world situation up to this time. They fit it now." - Henry Ford, *New York World*, February 17, 1921.

Endnotes

1. The plan to establish a New World Order is nothing new. For example, just look at the wording on the back of a one dollar bill, under the pyramid. There you will find the Latin words *Novus Ordo Seclorum*, which mean "New World Order." How fitting that this logo should "just happen" to wind up on the dollar--the very means through which the globalists (those pushing for this tyrannical world government) are working to bring this nation, and thereby the rest of the world, under their control (more on this shortly).

2. Weishaupt once wrote: "The great strength of our Order [the Bavarian Illuminati] lies in its concealment; let it never appear in any place in its own name, but always covered by another name and another occupation"(1, p. 112).

3. It is important to understand that the bulk of the members of secret societies, such as the Masons, are kept in complete ignorance of the world-domination agenda of their leaders, who alone are "in the know." Prominent secret society officials themselves have admitted this on occasion. For example, note the following statement made by a famous and influential 33rd-degree Mason, Manly P. Hall: "Freemasonry is a fraternity within a fraternity--an outer organization concealing an inner brotherhood of the elect....It is necessary to establish the existence of these two separate yet independent orders, the one visible and the other invisible. The visible society is a splendid camaraderie of...men enjoined to devote themselves to ethical, educational, fraternal, patriotic, and humanitarian concerns. The invisible society is a secret and most August fraternity whose members are dedicated to the service of a mysterious arcanum acandrum [a secret]. In each generation, only a few are accepted into the inner sanctuary of the Work"(3, p. 433).

   Another famous 33rd-degree Mason, Albert Pike (perhaps the *most* famous), who lived in the 19th century, made the following, even more revealing similar statement: "Masonry conceals its secrets from all except the Adepts and Sages, or the elect, and uses false explanations and misinterpretations of its symbols to mislead those who deserve only to be misled; to conceal the Truth, which it calls Light, from them, and to draw them away from it"(5, pp. 104, 105).

4. Of all the clandestine organizations working toward world government, perhaps none are as pervasive and influential as the Trilateral Commission, the Council on Foreign Relations, and the Bilderbergers. Over the years, the very biggest names in government, business, academia, and the media have belonged to one or more of these organizations. All three of them, by the way, are "private clubs" that meet regularly, and privately, to decide the direction they want to take the world en route to their total domination of it (more will be said on their private meetings later).

5. This term,"Establishment," is one that is often used to refer to the elitist clique that controls our government from behind the curtain--and rightly so, given its definition as found in the *American Heritage Dictionary*: "An exclusive group of powerful people who rule a government or society by means of private agreements or decisions." This type of political arrangement is also known as an oligarchy. And as we shall see, this is the very type of arrangement that has been running the U.S. government (along with many other governments around the world) for quite some time now.

6. Indeed, the world government conspirators do view constitutions as irrelevant, particularly the Constitution of the United States. In their New World Order propaganda book, *Creating A New*

Civilization, authors Alvin and Heidi Toffler wrote: "The Constitution of the United States needs to be reconsidered and altered...to create a whole new structure of government....The [constitutional] system that served us so well must, in its turn, die and be replaced"(10, pp. 90, 91). (Note: This book was strongly endorsed by Newt Gingrich, former Speaker of the U.S. House of Representatives. In fact, he wrote the Foreword to it. Incidentally, Gingrich is a 33rd-degree Mason and a member of the CFR.)

As another example of globalist anti-constitutional sentiments, notice what historian James MacGregor Burns wrote: "Let us face reality. The framers of the Constitution have simply been too shrewd for us. They have outwitted us. They designed separated institutions that cannot be unified by mechanical linkages, frail bridges, tinkering. If we are to 'turn the founders upside down'--to put together what they put asunder--we must directly confront the constitutional structure they erected"(11). Perhaps you won't be so surprised to discover that this anti-constitutionalist is a member of the CFR as well.

7. It is significant to note that every CIA director has been a member of the CFR.

8. Until the turn of the twentieth century, the U.S. had maintained a policy of political isolationism, confining its foreign relations to the realm of trade only. This was a policy that began with George Washington, who, during his farewell address on September 17, 1796, stated: "The great rule of conduct for us in regard to foreign nations is in extending our commercial relations, to have with them as little political connection as possible."

To see how far we've fallen from this ideal, notice what George Bush Sr. stated during an address he gave before Duke University graduates on May 17, 1998: "The United States must stay involved in the world and we must lead. Today there is a strange coalition at work in Washington and across the country consisting of people on the political right and the political left coming together to keep us from staying involved. Big labor and liberal Democrats are joining some Republicans on the right in calling for America to come home, [saying] we have done our part and that it's time for others to do the heavy lifting on international leadership. And we must not listen to that siren's call of protection and isolation"(448).

9. And how was it, exactly, that the United Nations "came to life"? This next quote has the answer: "The planning of [the] UN can be traced to the 'secret steering committee' established by Secretary [of State Cordell] Hull in January 1943. All of the members of this secret committee, with the exception of Hull, a Tennessee politician, were members of the Council on Foreign Relations [and most of them, such as Alger Hiss and Dexter White, later turned out to be communist spies]. They saw Hull regularly to plan, select, and guide the labors of the [State] Department's Advisory Committee. It [the CFR] was, in effect, the coordinating agency for all the State Department's postwar planning"(21).

And how is it that the CFR was able (and still is able) to direct the State Department (and just about every other branch of the U.S. government) with the manipulative power of a puppeteer? Perhaps no one has answered this question better than Rear Admiral Chester Ward, who himself was a CFR member for 16 years: "Once the ruling members of the CFR have decided that the U.S. Government should adopt a particular policy, the very substantial research facilities of CFR are put to work to develop arguments, intellectual and emotional, to support the new policy, and to confound and discredit, intellectually and politically, any opposition"(22, p. 151).

10. The Marx-Weishaupt connection becomes very apparent when one reads things like John

Robison's *Proofs of a Conspiracy*, published 21 years before Marx was even born, which reveals that Weishaupt was the source of inspiration for all of the "10 Planks" of Marx's *Manifesto*. Marx was also a member of a secret society known as the League of the Just, which was an offshoot of Weishaupt's Bavarian Illuminati.

11. As one globalist, Percy Ellwood Corbett, wrote: "World government is the ultimate aim, but there is more chance of attaining it by gradual development"(24).

12. The Federal Reserve is not the first central bank that this country has had. Nevertheless, even though there were a couple others that preceded it (well, they were early stages of what was hoped would become a central bank, anyway), the Federal Reserve has been by far the longest lasting, the most powerful, and thus the most destructive. Previous attempts at central banks failed because the American people were more awake, and their leaders were, for the most part, honest and patriotic. (More will be said on these early efforts to establishing a U.S. central bank later on.)

13. Regarding Quigley's comment about the central banks of the world collaborating to create a world government, note this relevant quote: "[T]here is...emerging...a world government composed of...the central banks of the leading industrial nations." - Alexander Cockburn, journalist(27).

14. In a chapter of this book called "Selwyn Seeks a Candidate," Selwyn (i.e. House) is depicted as asking Rockland (i.e. Wilson) to "dine with me in my rooms at the Mandell House." Is it not obvious, then, who this "Senator Selwyn" character really was?

15. More will be said on the income tax shortly. But for now, let us take note of what T. Coleman Andrews, former commissioner of the IRS, said back in 1956: "I don't like the income tax...it's written into the Communist Manifesto....Maybe we ought to see that every person who gets a tax return receives a copy of the Communist Manifesto with it so that he can see what's happening to him"(311). (Note: The income tax, at first, only targeted businesses. It wasn't until WWII, with the so-called "Victory Tax," that it began targeting individual citizens.)

16. War profiteering, on the part of U.S. corporations trading with enemy nations, was again done, on an even grander scale, during WW II, also under provisions in the Trading With the Enemy Act. In fact, this same thing was done during ALL wars and "military engagements" that the U.S. has been involved in since 1917. A great book to read for thorough documentation of these crimes during WW II is *Trading With the Enemy: The Nazi-American Money Plot 1933-1949*, by Charles Higham (ISBN: 0-7607-0009-5).

    Such revelations shouldn't shock us when we realize that big, big money is, and always has been, the real power behind every political entity. As James Stewart Martin, a former lawyer with the U.S. Justice Department, wrote in his 1950 book *All Honorable Men*: "The relative powerlessness of governments in the growing economic power is of course not new....[N]ational governments have stood on the sidelines while bigger operators arranged the world's affairs"(484).

17. One of the biggest profiteers of WW I was famous Wall Street tycoon Bernard Baruch. Curtis B. Dall, in his book *FDR: My Exploited Father-in-Law*, said of his war profits: "Before WW I, it was said that 'Barney' Baruch was worth a million dollars or more. After World War I was over,

it was alleged that he was worth about two hundred million dollars, a suitable figure for a titan"(82).

18. Wilson wasn't a total sellout--he did have some sense of loyalty to his country, and did not go along with all of what the international banking crowd wanted. For example, in 1916, while giving a speech, he said: "A great industrial nation is controlled by its system of credit. The growth of the nation, therefore, and all our activities are in the hands of a few men. We have come to be one of the worst ruled, one of the most completely controlled governments in the civilized world--no longer a government of free opinion, no longer a government of conviction and the vote of the majority, but a government by the opinion and duress of a small group of dominant men"(29).

　　　Not long before his death, looking back at his signing of the Federal Reserve Act, Wilson said: "I have unwittingly ruined my country"(30, p. 3).

19. In the July 1928 issue of *Foreign Affairs*, Franklin D. Roosevelt wrote an article which stated: "The United States has taken two negative steps. It has declined to have anything to do with either the League of Nations or the World Court [another globalist front]....The time has come when we must accept not only certain facts but many new principles of a higher law, a newer and better standard in international relations....[W]ith the cooperation of others we shall have more order in this hemisphere." (In other words, give up our national sovereignty and become slaves to an external system of world-government.)

　　　Speaking of the U.S. giving up its national sovereignty, notice this next quote from the Rothschild publication, *The Economist*, in its cover story of June 28, 1991, entitled "The World Order Changeth": "...America needs to remember that a willingness to involve others is not enough to make a collective world order work. There must also be readiness to submit to it. If America really wants such an order, it will have to be ready to take its complaints to the GATT [more on GATT later], finance the multilateral aid agencies, submit itself to the International Court, bow to some system to monitor arms exports, and make a habit of consulting the U.N." Of course, world government will involve ALL nations giving up their sovereignty, as the next quote will demonstrate: "In the next century, nations as we know it [sic] will be obsolete; all states will recognize a single, global authority. National sovereignty wasn't such a great idea after all." - Strobe Talbot, who served as Deputy Secretary of State under Clinton(31).

　　　The United Nations, naturally, is all for destroying national sovereignty. In July of 1994, the U.N. released a study financed by the Ford Foundation, called *Renewing the United Nations System*. The authors, Erskine Childers and Sir Brian Urquhart, both former U.N. officials, talked over and over in this study about the need to "chip away" at the edges of traditional sovereignty. They emphasized that the "limitation of sovereignty" must be taken in "small steps" to achieve a "trans-sovereign society," i.e. world government. As you can see, this study made no attempt to hide the U.N.'s power-seeking agenda.

20. James P. Warburg, a CFR member, a member of Roosevelt's "brain trust," and the son of Paul M. Warburg (one of the original organizers of the Federal Reserve System), revealed just how determined he and his globalist friends have been, down through the decades, to establish a world government, when he told the Senate Foreign Relations Committee on February 17, 1950: "We shall have world government whether or not we like it. The only question is, whether world government will be achieved by conquest or consent"(14, p. 61).

21. Yes, you are reading correctly--WW I, WW II, the 1929 stock market crash, and a whole host

of other catastrophes from history were planned and directed by the world government conspirators, simply to fatten their wallets and increase their power. (For more information on how the globalists have rigged wars to advance world government, see Appendix 1.)

22. Note the proceeding additional legal requirement regarding the creation of money: Art. 1, Sect. 10, Clause 1 of the Constitution declares that "No state shall...make anything but gold and silver coin a tender in payment of debts." Also, Title 12, Sec. 152 of the U.S. Code states: "Lawful money of the United States shall be construed to mean gold and silver coin."

Not only are we no longer using gold and silver coin for currency, but our paper money is no longer backed by any precious metal. This destabilization of our monetary system came about through the crafty and sinister planning of the globalists. It began with F.D.R., who took us off the gold standard in 1933. This meant that unlimited amounts of phony paper money could be printed, regardless of how much gold reserves the nation had. Given this arrangement, it was only a matter of time before the dollar would no longer be exchangeable for gold. And sure enough, on August 15, 1971, President Nixon internationally suspended the convertibility of the dollar for gold, completing what F.D.R. had begun nearly forty years earlier.

To show how our dollar has lost its value as a result of no longer being backed by gold, it's enlightening to notice how the wording in the redemption "guarantee" on the dollar bill has changed over the years. The 1928 Federal Reserve Certificate, for instance, contained this promise: "Redeemable in gold on demand at the U.S. Treasury..." Later, in 1934, a year after Roosevelt had taken us off the gold standard, the new Federal Reserve Note read: "This note is legal tender for all debts, public and private, and is redeemable in lawful money at the Treasury or at any Federal Reserve Bank." Naturally, the reference to these new notes being "redeemable in gold" was removed, because there was no longer any guarantee that they would be backed by the precious metal. But then, in 1963, the situation degenerated even further (as intended). Beginning in that year, the Notes now stated, "This note is legal tender for all debts, public and private," with no promise of redeemability of any kind (in obvious anticipation of what Nixon declared 8 years later--that the dollar was indeed no longer redeemable).

23. Yes, our banker friends have made a shambles of our economy, destroying our right to life, liberty, and the pursuit of happiness. (For more information on how the globalists create poverty for economic and political control, see Appendix 2.)

24. The Federal Reserve, the most important and powerful financial institution in the country, has NEVER been audited, nor has it ever been willing to consent to an audit. As Congressman Wright Patman put it: "[T]he Federal Reserve System has never been subjected to a complete, independent audit, and it is the only important agency that refuses to consent to an audit by...the General Accounting Office....GAO audits of the Federal Reserve will...fill the glaring gap that now exists in our information about the Fed's activities and programs. As things now stand, the only information that we get on the programs of the Fed is what the Fed itself wants us to have!"(410)

25. Indeed, monopoly is the name of the game. As John D. Rockefeller once said: "competition is a sin." And in perfect harmony with this philosophy, the globalists have been working to consolidate all major banks and businesses into one massive, all-powerful conglomerate. This will eliminate all competition and will eventually allow them to charge ANY price they choose for any product or service desired. Have you been noticing recent mergers of big banks and big corporations, or buy-outs of small banks and businesses by larger ones? Have you also noticed

how many small businesses have been closing or laying off, being unable to keep up with the "big boys"? And then you have many big corporations downsizing, not out of necessity, but in order to drive up profits and stock values by replacing full-time employees with "temps" or "contract workers" who are paid much lower wages and receive little or no benefits. You also have big corporations sending jobs overseas by the millions, or "outsourcing," where labor is much cheaper and regulations are minimal or non-existent. Under Bush Jr.'s administration, companies were actually awarded with tax breaks for sending jobs overseas. Do you see what is going on here?

The wealth of this country is being concentrated in the hands of a few, while being sucked out of the hands of the working class. Just look, for instance, at the ever-widening gap between corporate profits and the wages of workers. If the wages of workers had kept pace with corporate profits over the years between 1970 and 2000, then the average wage by the year 2000 should have been $24.56 per hour, instead of $13.74, and the minimum wage should have been $13.80 per hour, instead of $5.15. This is Robin Hood in reverse--robbing from the poor and giving to the rich. And what's even more disgusting is the manner in which many major corporations receive massive government subsidies, and other forms of "corporate welfare" giveaways, taking the public's tax money (and keep in mind that most major corporations pay little if any taxes themselves) and returning nothing to the public except more downsizing layoffs or stealing of jobs through outsourcing. The following Noam Chomsky quote is very instructive in this regard: "For the executives of a transnational corporation, professionals linked to the power structure, and other privileged sectors, it is important for the world to be properly disciplined, for advanced industry to be granted its huge public subsidies, and for the wealthy to be guaranteed security. It does not matter much if public education and health deteriorate, the useless population rots in slums and prisons, and the basis for a livable society erodes for the public at large"(45, p. 19).

26. Though Kennedy appeared to approve of this "redistribution" of U.S. gold (he was, after all, at least for a time, a member of the CFR), he was not in favor of the monetary system of the Federal Reserve (more on this later).

27. Another major fleecing of the American people took place under the presidency of George W. Bush. To find out more about this, see Appendix 17.

28. Speaking of the Emergency Banking Relief Act, Curtis B. Dall, F.D.R.'s son-in-law, wrote: "Gold was taken away from Americans....FDR did not initiate that particular legislation. That was ordered 'from above.'

"The C.F.R. Advisors 'advised,' all right, aided by their top-level friends on the Federal Reserve Bank Board"(82, p. 90).

29. As it turned out, though Reagan didn't belong to either the CFR or the TC, this didn't really matter very much, since his cabinet was dominated mostly by CFR members, with a few belonging to the TC as well. For example: Vice President George Bush Sr. (CFR/TC), Treasury Secretary Donald Regan (CFR), Secretary of State Alexander Haig (CFR) and then George Schultz (CFR), Deputy Secretary of State John Whitehead (CFR), Secretary of Defense Casper Weinberger (TC), Deputy Secretary of Defense Frank Carlucci (CFR), Ambassador to China Winston Lord (CFR), Commerce Secretary Malcolm Baldrige (CFR), Labor Secretary William Brock (CFR), Federal Reserve Board Chairman Alan Greenspan (CFR), to name but a few.

The globalist elites allowed Reagan, a non-club-member, to become president, not only because they knew that most of his cabinet would be dominated by those who *were* club members, but also because they wanted to reduce public suspicions about their actions which arose under the Carter administration, where Carter himself was a member of the TC, along with nearly every one of his cabinet members. So obvious was the influence of the TC during the Carter years, in fact, that it became impossible for the mainstream media to avoid discussing it, as the public was aware of it and was highly concerned. Note, for instance, the following *U.S. News and World Report* quote: "The 'Trilateralists' have taken charge of foreign policy making in the Carter administration, and already the immense power they wield is sparking some controversy. Active or former members of the Trilateral Commission now head every key agency involved in mapping U.S. strategy for dealing with the rest of the world....[S]ome see this concentration of power as a conspiracy at work"(61).

On March 17, 1980, while campaigning for the presidency, Reagan was asked if he planned to allow Trilateral Commission members in his cabinet. In response to this question, notice what he said: "No, I ...think [the Trilateral Commission's] interests are devoted to international banking, multinational corporations, and so forth. I don't think that any administration of the U.S. Government should have the top nineteen positions filled by people from any one group or organization representing one viewpoint [referring to Carter's Trilateralist-dominated administration]. No, I would go in a different direction"(62).

The promise that Reagan made here was misleading, to say the least. While it is true that he did have relatively few TC members in his cabinet, this lack was more than made up for by the large number of CFR members that he appointed. Thus there was no movement away from the globalist agenda during his administration. But even if it truly wasn't his intention to support the globalist agenda during his presidency, it's quite obvious that he found out pretty quick that being president is more a public relations position than anything else. Whether Reagan was a willing servant of "the plan" or not, the truth is that this non-club-member served the globalists more effectively than other previous presidents who WERE a part of the club. For example, during Reagan's presidency this nation fell into greater debt than it had done under all previous presidencies combined. (That record was later beaten by George Bush Jr.)

30. See, for example, Vincent Bugliosi's and Molly Ivins's *The Betrayal of America: How the Supreme Court Undermined the Constitution and Chose Our President*, ISBN: 156025355X and Douglas Kellner's *Grand Theft 2000: Media Spectacle and a Stolen Election*, ISBN: 0742521036.

As further proof of the Supreme Court's role in the stolen election of 2000, the October 18, 2004 Fort Wayne *Journal Gazette* carried an article called "Clerks Spill Bush v. Gore Details," which was based on an article in the October 2004 *Vanity Fair* that quoted an anonymous Supreme Court clerk who decided to break his pledge of confidentiality by saying: "We feel that something illegitimate was done with the Court's power [in regards to the role it played in Bush winning the election], and such an extraordinary situation justifies breaking an obligation we'd otherwise honor. Our secrecy was helping to shield some of those actions"(399).

Of course, the 2004 election was also stolen. *PC World* reported on November 2, 2004: "Reports of problems with electronic voting technology cropped up across the country Tuesday....Malfunctioning machines, ill-trained poll workers, and an inadequate supply of voting terminals were among the problems reported to state election officials and to a host of groups monitoring the election"(400). Reuters stated on November 3, 2004: "Voters across the United States have reported problems with electronic touch-screen systems in what critics say could be a sign that the machines used by one-third of the population are prone to error. Voters calling in to an election-day hotline reported more than 1,100 problems with the ATM-like machines, from improperly tallied choices to frozen screens that left their votes in limbo"(401).

Even though exit polling on the evening of election day, November 2, 2004, showed a major lead for John Kerry, Bush still managed to win. It would appear, then, that the reason for this can be traced to the above-mentioned problems with the electronic voting machines. In this regard, it is crucial to take notice of the fact that the *New York Times*, on December 2, 2003, quoted Walden O'Dell, chief executive of Diebold Inc., the company that made these touch-screen voting machines, as saying: "I am committed to helping Ohio deliver its electoral votes to the president next year"(402).

After the 2004 election, the General Accounting Office investigated allegations of election fraud through the Diebold machines and concluded that "some of [the] concerns about electronic voting machines have...caused problems with recent elections, resulting in the loss and miscount of votes"(522).

This is not to imply that Kerry was any better a candidate than Bush, of course. But just like in the rigged 2000 election, Bush was more the man that the globalists wanted in office. Why? Because, under Kerry, they would have had to temper things down a bit, in order to maintain the illusion of bipartisanship in this country. Whereas, under Bush, whom many Americans naively believed to be a "Christian conservative republican," they could move important pieces of their agenda forward much quicker, such as amnesty for illegal aliens, massive movement of jobs overseas, more constitution-trampling legislation, more deficit spending, etc.

31. Add to NAFTA the GATT/WTO (General Agreement on Tariffs and Trade/World Trade Organization) economic globalization noose (along with other similar organizations), and you can see the disaster we are headed for. (See Appendix 3 for more information on the WTO/NAFTA fiasco.)

32. Interestingly, Henry Ford Sr., the inventor of the automobile assembly line, once made a statement very similar to this last Jackson statement cited above: "It is well enough that the people of the nation do not understand our banking and monetary system, for if they did I believe there would be a revolution before tomorrow morning"(67). Speaking of international bankers, Ford also once remarked: "The one aim of these financiers is world control by the creation of inextinguishable debts"(67).

In the earliest days of his presidency, F.D.R., our great socialist president himself, acknowledged his awareness that the money power had been running the show in this country since the days of Andrew Jackson. In a letter that he addressed to Colonel Edward M. House (the globalist-appointed top advisor to Woodrow Wilson) on November 23, 1933, F.D.R. wrote: "The real truth of the matter is, as you and I know, that a financial element in the large centers has owned the government ever since the days of Andrew Jackson....The country is going through a repetition of Jackson's fight with the Bank of the U.S.--only on a far bigger and broader basis [referring to the Great Depression]"(68).

33. Some have postulated that the global power- and money-grabbing nature of major corporations, which seek to abolish tariffs, stems from an innate problem with capitalism. But this is not true. The problem lies with monopolistic capitalism driven by unbridled greed, without constitutional/congressional restraints. Article 1, Section 8, Clause 3 of the U.S. Constitution states that Congress shall "regulate commerce with foreign nations." But today, Congress basically sits back while NAFTA, the WTO, etc., perform this function for them, which is always done in the interest of big business, and with no regard for the interests of the American people (or any other people, for that matter, except the ones in big business).

34. Isn't this where we are at today? Isn't the government "wasting the labor of the people under the pretense of caring for them"? And aren't the people unhappy because of this abuse? No wonder there are so many who are turning to a life of crime in this country today! The logic of the modern criminal mind, because of our sabotaged economy, runs like this: "Why should I struggle to make a living within the confines of the established system, barely scraping by, when I can turn to a much more profitable life of crime? And why should I obey the law when the government doesn't even do that?"

35. I should mention, too, that all the countries with central banks have also implemented an income tax. But then again, you've probably already assumed that to be the case, knowing the globalists' modus operandi.

As each country around Europe began establishing central banks and income taxes during the 19th century, it should go without saying that wars started breaking out between these countries, to strengthen the hold the bankers had on them, while at the same time making massive wads of cash. In his book *None Dare Call It Conspiracy*, Gary Allen quoted from Stuart Crane, an economics professor (formerly with the University of Michigan, Ann Arbor, and Bob Jones University, Greenville, SC), who said: "If you will look back at every war in Europe during the Nineteenth Century, you will see that they always ended with the establishment of a 'balance of power.' With every re-shuffling there was a balance of power in a new grouping around the House of Rothschild in England, France, or Austria. They grouped nations so that if any king got out of line a war would break out and the war would be decided by which way the financing went. Researching the debt positions of the warring nations will usually indicate who was to be punished"(33, p. 39).

36. The following list of False Beliefs was adapted from *Do You Love America? How About the IRS?* by Gordon Phillips of the Save-A-Patriot Fellowship, Westminster, MD. This will serve as the source for all quotations in this section that are not referenced.

37. Does the term "politically correct" ring a bell? Can you guess where this philosophy comes from? Today in this country, people are being conditioned to conform to specially-designed majoritarian thought patterns. Those who refuse to comply are deemed as trouble-making extremists. Thus the individual's right to freedom of speech is being trampled underfoot, without anyone even realizing what is going on. In fact, just about all individual rights and freedoms in this country are under attack today. The government has been invading our private lives to the point where nobody can do anything, go anywhere, conduct any type of business, etc., without government interference and outright oppression. Nearly every aspect of our lives is government-controlled on the federal, state, and local levels. And yet, all the while, we are continually bombarded with propagandic reminders that we live in a "free country." (For more information on how our rights and liberties are being stolen away from us, right under our noses, see Appendix 5.)

38. But, of course, it is also not the job of the courts to ignore or trample your rights either, which is just what they are doing!

39. Note: On July 30, 2002, Traficant was sentenced to 8 years in prison for "bribery," in a sham trial that was based totally on hearsay evidence. Traficant had opened his mouth about government corruption too many times over the years, and had to learn the hard way that, in this globalist-controlled outlaw government of ours, crime DOES pay, and honesty will get you locked up.

40. The income tax helps, amongst other things, to conceal this "inflation by design." (More on this later.)

41. In another Supreme Court case, Brushaber vs. Union Pacific (1915), it was ruled that "The 16th Amendment, as correctly interpreted, is limited to indirect taxes and for that reason is constitutional." Did you catch that? The 16th Amendment only allows for indirect taxes (for example, taxation on purchases) and has nothing to do with taxation of the wages of a resident citizen (a direct tax), which is unconstitutional!

42. Article IV of the Constitution (Bill of Rights) presents another problem for the 16th Amendment being used to justify the income tax. Notice what former IRS commissioner T. Coleman Andrews, who was quoted from earlier, had to say on this matter: "It [the 16th Amendment] has robbed you and me [in the way it has been construed and enforced] of the guarantee of privacy and the respect for our property that was given to us in Article IV of the Bill of Rights. This invasion is absolute and complete as far as the amount of tax that can be assessed is concerned. Please remember that under the 16th Amendment [again, in the way it has been construed and enforced], Congress can take 100% of our income anytime it wants to....[T]his is downright confiscation and cannot be defended on any other grounds....[T]he income tax is fulfilling the Marxist prophecy that the surest way to destroy a capitalist society is by steeply graduated taxes on income and heavy levies on the estates of people when they die"(71).

      Can any law or amendment that contradicts the Constitution (or that is construed and enforced in such a way that it contradicts the Constitution) be considered legally binding? To find the answer to this question, note the following: "All laws which are repugnant to the Constitution are null and void." - Marbury vs. Madison, 5 US (2 Cranch) 137, 174, 176, (1803). "Where rights secured by the Constitution are involved, there can be no rule making or legislation which would abrogate them." - Miranda vs. Arizona, 384 US 436, p. 491. "An unconstitutional act is not law; it confers no rights; it imposes no duties; affords no protection; it creates no office; it is, in legal contemplation, as inoperative as though it had never been passed." - Norton vs. Shelby County, 118 US 425, p. 442. "No one is bound to obey an unconstitutional law and no courts are bound to enforce it." - 16 Am Jur 2d, Sec. 177, late 2d, Sec. 256.

43. Several U.S. presidents, such as Nixon and Clinton, have capitalized on this fear of the IRS to intimidate and silence political opposition. The January 25, 1997 edition of *Technopolitics*, the TV news magazine of the Public Broadcasting Service, reported that the IRS was "aggressively auditing conservative public policy groups who oppose Clinton administration policies." In such cases as this, it doesn't matter that there is no evidence of "tax evasion." When the IRS wants to target someone, it simply makes up false evidence, just to entrap the "trouble-maker."

44. On June 23, 2005, Banister was acquitted. He was found not guilty of all charges launched against him. In other words, the IRS couldn't prove its case (of course it couldn't!).

45. It should be kept in mind that the above-mentioned so-called "foreign aid" never benefits the people of the countries that this money is sent to, nor is it intended to. Such money is sent overseas to bribe corrupt foreign leaders into compliance with globalist aims, which, as you may have guessed, are never in the interest of the people that these corrupt leaders are supposed to represent.

It should also be kept in mind that such "foreign aid" given by our globalist-controlled government amounts to taxation without representation, since the foreign leaders who receive the funds are not held accountable to American taxpayers, as to how the money is spent.

46. The true definition of "income" is money earned beyond your wages (for example, profits on investments), while the word "wages" refers exclusively to financial reimbursements for services rendered. Neither of them, of course, are constitutionally taxable for U.S. citizens (who live and work in the U.S.), since taxation of either of them amounts to a direct tax.

47. This document then goes on to refer the reader to another form (Publication 15, Circular E, *Employer's Tax Guide*) for additional information. However, as you may have guessed, this information does not apply to any American citizen who is earning income (wages) in the U.S., unless, of course, that citizen has volunteered to have his wages taxed.

48. Europeans, almost all of which now fully embrace socialism, are often baffled by Americans who are opposed to this form of government. They frequently defend socialism on the basis of the wonderful fruits it has borne in their respective countries. However, this is all part of the setup. The globalists, who are pulling the strings behind the scenes, have not yanked the rug out from underneath them yet, because they want socialism to look more appealing to Americans, so that they will become more accepting of it. Only when this happens, along with the U.S. government itself becoming more socialistic, will the true totalitarian nature of this form of government be openly manifested--when it is too late to do anything about it.

49. Tens of thousands of well-informed U.S. citizens have already quit Social Security--100% legally--by submitting an Affidavit of Revocation and Rescission to the Secretary of the Treasury, revoking their voluntary application for a Social Security number. (Note: This information is only being provided for educational purposes. The present author does not encourage or discourage anyone who wishes to take such action. This is an issue that all must decide for themselves.)

50. Another obvious reason for Bush Jr. pushing this Social Security privatization scam, of course, was so that his backers in the corporate world could have the values of their companies' stocks substantially driven up.

51. Note, for instance, what Walter Cronkite wrote in his 1997 book, *A Reporter's Life*: "If we are to avoid catastrophe, a system of world order--preferably a system of world government--is mandatory. The proud nations someday will...yield up their precious sovereignty"(89).

52. Some high-profile media officials have admitted that withholding truth is not only something they engage in, but that it is an absolute necessity. One such person was Reese Schoenfeld, a co-founder of CNN. On February 14, 2005, while being interviewed on Fox's "Your World" with Neil Cavuto, he said: "The government has the right and sometimes the duty to lie. The press must never lie, but has no duty to tell the truth....This whole idea [that] 'the public has a right to know'--the public does not have a right to know. The editor has a right to publish, that's what the First Amendment is about. The editor...doesn't have to tell everything he knows, and God forbid that he ever should."

53. The truth is, there are actually a good number of journalists in the mainstream media who are completely oblivious to the whole globalist plot (although such individuals are usually low on the totem pole). Those in this category can remain in the newscasting business their entire lives, in fact, and retain complete ignorance of how things really work. This is because they never actually do their own investigative journalism. This work is done for them by others. All they do is read off of a paper that is handed to them, and they just assume that what they are reporting is "unbiased news."

54. You would think that the FCC (Federal Communications Commission) would intervene to prevent such high concentration of ownership of our media, right? Wrong! On the contrary, this federal bureaucracy has fought to protect this monopoly, and has taken measures to ensure that the public not find out about the threat that it poses. This point was brought to light by MSNBC on September 14, 2006, when it reported: "The Federal Communications Commission ordered its staff to destroy all copies of a draft study that suggested greater concentration of media ownership would hurt local TV news coverage....

"Adam Candeub, now a law professor at Michigan State University, said senior managers at the agency ordered that 'every last piece' of the report be destroyed. 'The whole project was just stopped--end of discussion,' he said"(537).

55. To illustrate what Chomsky is talking about, it helps to note the board member interlocks that exist between big media and big business. Here are a few examples:
1. The *New York Times* interlocks with the Carlyle Group, Eli Lilly, Ford, Johnson and Johnson, Hallmark, Staples, Pepsi, and Lehman Brothers.
2. The *Washington Post* interlocks with Lockheed Martin, Coca-Cola, Dun & Bradstreet, Gillette, G.E. Investments, J.P. Morgan, and Moody's.
3. The *Chicago Tribune* and the *Los Angeles Times* interlock with 3M, Allstate, Caterpillar, Conoco Phillips, Kraft, McDonalds, Pepsi, Quaker Oats, Shering Plough, and Wells Fargo.
4. News Corp (Fox) interlocks with British Airways and Rothschild Investments.
5. GE (NBC) interlocks with Anheuser-Busch, Avon, Bechtel, Chevron/Texaco, Coca-Cola, Dell, GM, Home Depot, Kellogg, J.P. Morgan, Microsoft, Motorola, and Procter & Gamble.
6. Disney (ABC) interlocks with Boeing, Northwest Airlines, Clorox, Estee Lauder, FedEx, Gillette, Halliburton, Kmart, Staples, Yahoo, and McKesson.
7. Viacom (CBS) interlocks with American Express, Consolidated Edison, Oracle, and Lafarge North America.
8. AOL-Time Warner (CNN) interlocks with Citigroup, Estee Lauder, Colgate-Palmolive, and Hilton.
...and the list keeps going.

My point here is simply to draw attention to these happy little friendships that have emerged, and the threats they pose to "we the people." For example, the above list contains the names of several major Pentagon contractors. This should help you to understand why the media offer little or no criticism of Washington's eagerness to involve us in foreign conflicts. In fact, to the contrary, the media are the ones who cry the loudest in support of such military efforts, and demonize protesters as "unpatriotic." Are you starting to see how this whole thing works?

56. Inevitably, down through the years it has happened, on occasion, that certain statements made at Bilderberger conferences (such as the Rockefeller one cited above and a Kissinger one that we'll look at later) have been leaked out to the public, usually because of an attendee with a conscience who was able to sneak a pocket recorder onto the premises. But, as a whole, the tight

seal on these conferences has made such leaks virtually impossible.

57. You might be interested to know that the whole focus of education in this country today on "interculturalism" has absolutely NOTHING to do with "world brotherhood." The whole scheme was conjured up by the globalist "scholars" to prepare students "psychologically, socially, and in good time politically" to embrace the concept of global government, where we will all be united in one common cause--service to the globalist oligarchy. Pushing interculturalism also helps to dilute patriotism, nationalism, and constitutionalism, and thus leads people away from the notion of national sovereignty. While the concept of interculturalism certainly sounds like a worthy cause, and surely WOULD be a worthy cause under ordinary circumstances, the truth is that it can never work as long as the motives behind it are corrupt, and as long as it is being imposed upon people, instead of being encouraged.

There's another agenda behind "interculturalism"--cheap labor for globalist corporations. Bush Jr., who pushed aggressively for legalizing all illegal aliens, admitted this very thing, saying: "[I]f someone is willing to do jobs others in America aren't willing to do, we ought to welcome that person to the country and we ought to make that a legal part of our economy"(345). This traitorous president's first director of Homeland Security, Tom Ridge, further stated in this regard: "[A]s a country we have to come to grips with the presence of 8 to 12 million illegals, [and] afford them some kind of legal status some way..."(346). Is this what he considered "Homeland Security"? What a joke! (Further information on the open-door policy for illegal aliens is provided in Appendix 16.)

The push for interculturalism is a major piece of UNESCO's agenda, and has been since its inception. To better understand the philosophy of UNESCO, consider a quote from Julian Huxley, brother of the famous Aldous Huxley (both of which were major advocates of the globalist cause). Julian was the founding director-general of UNESCO, and in the 1946 UNESCO publication *UNESCO, Its Purpose and Its Philosophy*, he stated: "The general philosophy of UNESCO should be a scientific world humanism, global in extent....It can stress...the transfer of full sovereignty from separate nations to a world political organization....Political unification in some sort of world government will be required...to help the emergence of a single world culture."

Incidentally, Julian Huxley was also president of the Eugenics Society. Eugenics is the so-called science of creating better people through genetic manipulation. Over the years it has embraced ethnic cleansing and various sinister methods of what is often referred to as "population control," which we shall touch upon later. But for now, let's notice what else Julian Huxley wrote in the above-cited document, in regards to eugenics: "Even though it is quite true that any radical eugenic policy will be for many years...politically impossible, it will be important for UNESCO to see that the eugenic problem is examined with the greatest care, and that the public mind is informed of the issues at stake so that much that is now unthinkable may at least become thinkable." Do you suppose that the interest in cloning humans is a part of what Huxley was talking about here?

58. Despite the NEA's propaganda about being dedicated to academics, the truth is that its only interest lies in mind controlling our youth. (For more information on how the NEA is sabotaging our educational system, see Appendix 6.)

59. Hitler also recognized the importance of education for shaping the minds of the youth to think in harmony with his twisted, power-hungry agenda. During a public speech he gave in 1937, he had this to say about the education of youth: "This New Reich will give its youth to no one, but will itself take youth and give to youth its own education and its own upbringing"(103, p. 249).

During a speech he delivered two years later, in 1939, he further stated: "When an opponent declares: 'I will not come over to your side,' I calmly say, 'Your child belongs to us already. What are you? You will pass on. Your descendants, however, now stand in the new camp. In a short time they will know nothing else but this new community'"(103, p. 249).

60. At the same time that the U.N. has been working to rob children of their national and parental loyalties, it has also been working to circumvent parental authority, which is elaborated upon in Appendix 14.

61. The *New York Times* was here referring to L.B.J.'s 1965 Elementary and Secondary Education Act, when globalist control of our education system kicked into high gear, with Washington becoming the ultimate education authority. It was at this time that a de-emphasis on academics had begun, and the psycho-social development of students became more the focus.

    Over time, the government has used "public education" for all sorts of sinister purposes, none of which have anything to do with educating children. Here's a good example of this: As part of the No Child Left Behind Act, high schools across the country are now required to turn over names, addresses, and phone numbers of all students to their local draft boards. Thus it should be clear what "no child left behind" actually means--the government doesn't want any child left out from serving the war machine.

62. Such pieces of legislation are always passed off as "education reform," in order to make them look attractive to Congress and the general public. But notice what Noam Chomsky had to say about this: "'Reform' is one of those words you should watch out for. Changes are called reforms if the powerful are in favor of them....'Reforms' is an Orwellian term. You use it for the changes that you're supposed to support. What are called educational reforms should be evaluated on their own terms, but not on the assumption that because they're called reforms they're necessarily positive. Many are quite destructive"(106, p. 215).

    The truth is, every "reform" proposed and implemented by Washington over the years has been designed to systematically "dumb down" education further and further, persistently lowering standards nationally. The globalists wouldn't have it any other way.

63. As we have already seen, the federal government sticks its nose in MANY areas over which it has no authority. Thus its involvement in education should not seem so unexpected.

    Article 1, Section 8 of the Constitution is very specific as to what the limited powers of Congress actually are. Therein, Congress is only given authority to levy certain taxes; regulate commerce with foreign governments and among the States; create and define bankruptcy laws; coin money; protect the currency of the U.S.; establish a Post Office; create a national system of roads; legislate patent laws; determine the rules by which citizenship is granted; define the laws of the admiralty and prosecute felonies on the high seas; raise, support, and maintain an army and a navy to protect the confederation; and, whenever necessary, to declare war on nations that pose a threat to the people of the U.S. Beyond these boundaries, Congress has no legal authority to legislate ANYTHING, including, of course, education.

64. While those who fail the test are free to take it again, the globalists are also free to fail them again.

65. The time factor should also be mentioned here. After failing the test, a person usually has to

wait three months to retake it. And then, after passing the test, it can take several more months to receive the license or certification. In the meantime, the would-be teacher's student loan bills start coming in, which cannot be paid because a job cannot be had without the license/certification. What a scam!

66. In regards to the hidden agenda behind Rhodes' "secret society," notice what Carroll Quigley wrote in another one of his books: "The [Rhodes] scholarships were merely a facade to conceal the secret society, or, more accurately, they were to be one of the instruments by which members of the secret society could carry out Rhodes' purpose"(111).

67. Bill Clinton, as you may recall, was, amongst other things, a Rhodes Scholar. And, as such, he served the globalist agenda of his "private club" quite well, being a major supporter of the NAFTA and GATT/WTO fiascos, as well as the U.N. In this regard, look what Robert Rotberg, himself a Rhodes Scholar and author of the book *The Founder: Cecil Rhodes and the Pursuit of Power*, wrote in an article called "A Rhodes Scholar Reaches the Top," which appeared in the December 7, 1992 edition of *The Christian Science Monitor*: "Rhodes was a man of unparalleled vision....Mr. Clinton's accession to the American presidency fulfills Rhodes' deepest aspiration....Rhodes believed...[in] an idea that could lead 'to the cessation of all wars' [quoting from Rhodes' letter to W.T. Stead that we cited above]....In the ninety years of [Rhodes] scholarships, only Clinton has taken Rhodes' dream to the top."

It was Clinton's intention, very early on in life, to penetrate the hidden forces running the world, so that he could reach "the top." This point was brought out by an article in a 1993 edition of *The Wanderer*: "Clinton told reporters in an interview that Quigley's work [*Tragedy and Hope*, which we quoted from earlier] centered on the existence of a permanent shadow government of powerful bankers and businessmen and government officials that controls the agenda of our political life from behind the scenes. Clinton spoke in that interview of coming to the conclusion, while still a young man, that it was necessary for him to gain access to the inner circle of this group in order to become part of the decision-making process that shapes our world"(322).

68. All leaders of the major world religions have a fond respect for the pope. Most of them have already expressed a desire to see all world religions unite, with the pope as their head. This has also been a desire expressed by various U.N. leaders over the years. For example, at the 1990 Global Survival Conference, Robert Mueller, Assistant Secretary General of the U.N., made a speech in which he declared: "We need a world of cosmic spirituality. I hope that religious leaders will get together and define...the cosmic laws which are common to all their faiths....They should tell the politicians what the cosmic laws are, what God, or the gods, or the cosmos are expecting from humans....We must also hope that the Pope will come before the year 2000 to the United Nations [this did in fact happen, in October 1995] and will speak for all the religions on this planet and give the world the religious view of how the third millennium should be a spiritual one"(116). Mueller also once said: "We must move as quickly as possible to a one-world government; a one-world religion; under a one-world leader"(17, p. 81). Finally, in his book *The New Genesis*, Mueller wrote that all religions should "accelerate their ecumenism and create common religious institutions which would bring the resources and inspirators of the religions to bear upon the solution of world problems [and to] display the UN flag in all their houses of worship"(117).

The U.N., along with its proponents, since the turn of the 21st century, have been aggressively pursuing this goal of uniting the major religions of the world. As proof of this, the NewsMax website reported on July 14, 2003: "At the next meeting of the General Assembly of the United Nations in September, President Gloria Macapagal Arroyo of the Philippines is to present a formal proposal for the establishment of an Inter-religious Council at the world body. It would be an institutional part of the United Nations, with status like that of the U.N.'s Economic and Social Council or the Trusteeship Council.

"At her meeting with President Bush at the White House in May, Arroyo suggested the United States might want to co-sponsor the proposal. Bush, a practicing Christian with a keen sense of the power of religion, expressed deep interest....

"[Speaker of the Philippines House of Representatives Jose] de Venecia then wrote to [National Security Advisor Condoleezza] Rice...[saying], 'And while the really grievous need is for a global Christian-Muslim dialog, the effort must also encompass Buddhists, Hindus, Confucians and Jews, heads of churches, temples, synagogues and mosques, political leaders as well as representatives of global civil society.'...

"The proposal for an Inter-religious Council to become a formal part of the U.N. structure is ambitious and new, and de Venecia has put his formidable energies behind the task of winning political support through his connections with 'Christian Democrat' parties around the world, and particularly in Europe. This may be an idea whose time has come"(437).

69. Some might object, at this point, to the notion of a conspiracy for world government involving the Catholic Church and Masonry, since Catholicism traditionally has, at least on the surface, renounced the Masonic Order as being "of the devil," and since Masonry has pretty much given the same assessment of the Catholic Church, at least in a public setting. However, at the highest levels of power, outside the public's field of view, the Vatican has, on many occasions, enjoyed mutually advantageous arrangements with Freemasonry (such as investment deals involving the P2 Lodge and the Vatican Bank, back in the late '60s and early '70s)(447), not to mention the fact that many Vatican officials over the years have been high-ranking Masons. The official, publicly-declared position of the Vatican as being opposed to Masonry must remain in place, however, in order to conceal its collusion with this obviously unsavory secret society. And Masonry plays the same "public relations" game through its professed aversion to Catholicism. Neither side wants its average members to know about the clandestine operation they have in place to form a single world religion. (More will be said on Masonry and its role in the emerging world religion in a later section.)

70. Of course, there are other problems with Protestant churches today, besides forming an alliance with Rome. Traditionally, churches have been the place where, if nowhere else, people could go to hear the "unadulterated" truth from the pulpit, and discuss, without fear of government censure, current events and their impact on the lives of citizens. But this is sadly no longer the case. One particular reason for this is the IRS's 501(c)3 non-profit, tax exempt corporation status that churches have been pressured into receiving (which they are not required to have in order to be tax exempt, by the way, since the Constitution already guarantees tax exemption to churches). Through the 501(c)3 designation, the government has basically slapped a gag order on the pulpits of America, threatening to shut down, or remove tax exemption status from, any church that speaks out against government policies, since doing so is in violation of their IRS "contractual agreement."

By incorporating, churches today have, in effect, given up their constitutional protections and have literally become extensions of the globalist-controlled U.S. government. As the Supreme Court has asserted: "[T]he corporation is a creature of the state. It is presumed to be incorporated for the benefit of the public. It receives certain special privileges and franchises, and holds them subject to the laws of the state and the limitations of its charter. Its powers are limited by law. It can make no contract not authorized by its charter. Its rights to act as a corporation are only preserved to it so long as it obeys the laws of its creation." - Hale vs. Henkel, 201 US 43 at 74 (1906). In other words, these "steepled corporations" are now pawns in the hand of the government, being controlled as to what they can and can't say and do. No wonder the sermons in the big churches today are so "politically correct." So much for "separation of church and state," as Thomas Jefferson had understood the establishment and free exercise clauses. Freedom of religion is yet another one of our rights that has been stolen away from us, and most don't even realize it.

Should you be harboring any doubts that the 501(c)3 status has given the government control over churches, here's a specific instance where the IRS exercised such power: On September 16, 2006, Yahoo News carried an article called "IRS Investigating Liberal Calif. Church," which stated: "The Internal Revenue Service has ordered a prominent liberal church to turn over documents and e-mails it produced during the 2004 election year that contain references to political candidates.

"The IRS is investigating whether All Saints Episcopal Church in Pasadena violated the federal tax code when its former rector, Rev. George F. Regas, delivered an anti-war sermon on the eve of the last presidential election.

"Tax-exempt organizations are barred from intervening in political campaigns and elections, and the church could lose its tax-exempt status"(536).

So why is it that almost all churches today have registered as non-profit, tax-exempt corporations? Primarily because receipt of this status has offered to them the "benefit" of their contributing parishioners being able to claim their contributions as tax write-offs (which helps to serve, of course, as an encouragement for more generous donations to be given). As IRS Publication 557 states: "By [a corporation] establishing its exemption, potential contributors are assured by the [Internal Revenue] Service that contributions will be deductible." (For more information on incorporated churches and the negative consequences thereof, see Peter Kershaw's *Sanctuary of Silence*. Boulder, CO: Heal Our Land, 1997.)

Pressuring churches to incorporate is only one of many measures that have been taken to control them, turning each of them into an arm of big government. Other measures of control include programs like Bush Jr.'s "Faith Based Initiative," where churches are provided with government funding for assistance with "humanitarian services." It's easy to see how such funding can (and surely will) be denied to churches that refuse to abide by whatever demands the government places upon them.

In the year 2003 alone, according to the *Guardian*, "The [U.S.] government gave more than $1 billion...to organizations it considers 'faith-based,' with some going to programs where prayer and spiritual guidance are central..."(446). Also, through Executive Order 13397, created on March 7, 2006, all churches and other institutions that receive Faith Based Initiative funds were made a part of the Homeland Security apparatus. Now why do you suppose that was done?

Still another example of government control over "private" churches is the manner in which church-run colleges have lost much of their independence. Today the pressure is on for such institutions to conform to government policies if they want any kind of grant money. And, on the college and grade school levels alike, receiving accreditation is a problem which turns so-called "private church schools" into mirror images of their government-controlled public education counterparts, since, in most states, all accredited educational establishments are required to embrace the same basic curriculum, teaching methods, and textbooks.

71. Speaking of the fall of the Iron Curtain, it is important to point out that John Paul II had actually played a major role in the Soviet Union's collapse. Understand that the Soviet Union had

once served as a major barrier to the papacy's ascent to power. But thanks largely to John Paul II, this is no longer the case.

If you are interested in reading up on how John Paul II helped to bring down the Iron Curtain, check out the cover story of the February 24, 1992 issue of *Time*, entitled "Holy Alliance: How Reagan and the Pope Conspired to Assist Poland's Solidarity Movement and Hasten the Demise of Communism."

It was under Reagan, by the way, that the U.S. first appointed an ambassador to the Vatican, William Wilson, who was confirmed by the Senate for this position on March 7, 1984--an action that has set a most dangerous and unconstitutional precedent.

72. Another pope who pushed openly for a New World Order, calling it by name, was Paul VI, who wrote in his *Populorum Progressio*, on March 26, 1967: "Who can fail to see the need and importance of...coming to the establishment of a world authority capable of taking effective action on the juridical and political planes?...Delegates to international organizations, public officials, gentlemen of the press, teachers and educators--all of you must realize that you have your part to play in the construction of a new world order"(112, p. 108).

73. Along this line, notice what one concerned and alert Catholic author, Penny Lernoux, wrote in her 1989 book *The People of God*: "John Paul's Vatican longs for the past; the pope wishes to restore an authoritarian church model based on that of the <u>Middle Ages</u>..."(128, p. 11).

74. Far from being a model of wholesome morals and deep religious convictions, notice what the June 14, 2004 edition of *Capitol Hill Blue* had to say about Bush: "A new book by a prominent Washington psychoanalyst says President George W. Bush is a 'paranoid megalomaniac' as well as a sadist and 'untreated alcoholic.' The doctor's analysis appears to confirm earlier reports the President may be emotionally unstable.

"Dr. Justin Frank, writing in *Bush on the Couch: Inside the Mind of the President*, also says the President has a 'lifelong streak of sadism, ranging from childhood pranks (using firecrackers to explode frogs) to insulting journalists, gloating over state executions...[and] pumping his fist gleefully before the bombing of Baghdad'"(445).

Incidentally, speaking of Bush Jr. gloating over state executions, you might be interested to know that, while governor of Texas, he set the record for having more executions under his watch (a total of 152) than any other governor in U.S. history.

75. Author and educator George Grant has had a profound influence upon the thinking of the Religious Right in America over the years. In his 1987 book *The Changing of the Guard: Biblical Principles for Political Action*, he further confirmed the real underlying motive of the Religious Right's political activism. He wrote: "Christians have an obligation, a mandate, a commission, a holy responsibility to reclaim the land for Jesus Christ--to have dominion in civil structures, just as in every other aspect of life and godliness.

"But it is dominion we are after. Not just a voice.

"It is dominion we are after. Not just influence.

"It is dominion we are after. Not just equal time.

"It is dominion we are after.

"World conquest. That's what Christ has commissioned us to accomplish. We must win the world with the power of the Gospel. And we must never settle for anything less....Thus, Christian politics has as its primary intent the conquest of the land--of men, families, institutions, bureaucracies, courts, and governments for the Kingdom of Christ"(441, pp. 50, 51).

76. For a history of how the globalists have used the U.S. government to rig fake crises in the past, see Appendix 7.

77. As we saw earlier, one of the main reasons for the Federal Reserve's creation was so that an economic collapse could be easily engineered whenever the globalists wanted one, like in 1929. Understand that such collapses only affect the masses whose wealth is based on worthless paper money. But the globalists are not affected, of course, since their wealth is based on tangible assets like gold and real estate.

78. It was this very type of numbering system, and the total control that it would bring about, that Carroll Quigley was referring to (although minus the hi-tech dimension) when he wrote in *Tragedy and Hope*: "[H]is [the individual's] freedom and choice will be controlled within very narrow alternatives by the fact that he will be numbered from birth and followed [literally, via satellite!], as a number, through his educational training, his required military or other public service, his tax contributions, his health and medical requirements, and his final retirement and death benefits."

79. Many people fail to recognize the serious threat posed by these chips. A major reasons for this is the sugar-coated manner in which they are presented to the public. One way they are sold is by encouraging parents to have their children injected with chips so that they could quickly be found if ever lost or abducted. While this sales pitch certainly makes this technology sound appealing, what happens if these same children grow up to be, let's say, anti-war activists, and the government issues a warrant for their arrest? Where could they hide?

Another common sales pitch that is used to attract people to receive chip implants is the promise of identity theft prevention, so that no one can access a person's bank and/or credit card accounts except the person whose name is on the account(s). Understandably, this also sounds like an attractive reason to make use of this technology. But such a system could (and surely will!) also be used to deny a person access to his/her own account(s), if the government blacklists this person as an "enemy of the state" (i.e. an advocate of freedom and human rights).

Plans to exert this type of complete control through credit denial have been in the works for a long time. In his 1980 book *Charge It!--Inside the Credit Card Conspiracy*, Terry Galanoy wrote these seemingly prophetic words about the coming cashless society: "The gruesome fact is that if for some reason you had no [card or chip]..., you would have no credit....[S]ince checking accounts will have been discontinued and cash made obsolete..., you won't be able to buy anything, probably not even food....[Y]ou could literally starve to death....

"[Y]ou will become a code or a number....If the officials [controlling the system]...decide to drop you, the inter-tied computers will...erase that number. Although you may be alive..., you will have been effectively 'liquidated.'...

"George Orwell's notorious character 'Big Brother' from the book *1984* will actually turn out to be Big Banker; all-seeing, all-knowing, all-controlling, capable of destroying any resistance.

"The bankers are already putting that...system into place"(453).

80. One measure, in particular, that has been implemented to help condition us toward eventually accepting mandatory microchip implants was Bush Jr.'s national ID card legislation (Real ID Act). The tactic here was to get the public accustomed to having their private information being made available, through a national (and eventually global) database, to local, state, and federal prying

eyes, without a search warrant and without a person being guilty of any wrong-doing to justify such prying.

By the way, the Real ID Act did not originate with the Bush Jr. administration. The globalists tried to push this exact same thing, under a different name (the aborted Health Security Act of 1994), during the Clinton administration.

I should also point out that Europeans already have the equivalent of a "national ID card." All nations belonging to the EU require their citizens to have a standardized EU driver's license.

81. Some have brought the authenticity of this document into question, even claiming it to be some sort of political satire. However, John Kenneth Galbraith, Harvard professor and CFR member, wrote in the November 26, 1967 *Washington Post*, under the alias of Herschel McLandress: "As I would put my personal repute behind the authenticity of this document, so would I testify to the validity of its conclusions. My reservations relate only to the wisdom of releasing it to an obviously unconditioned public." He was later quoted in the February 12, 1968 London *Times* as saying: "I was in general a member of the [Iron Mountain report] conspiracy but I was not the author."

82. For more information on how the globalists utilize the environmental movement to advance their twisted agenda, see Appendix 15.

83. Such a thing could very well have happened in the wake of the 9-11 terrorist attacks, but the globalists obviously didn't want to take such a bold step just yet. Nevertheless, notice the proceeding quote along this line, from the *Washington Times*: "Simply by proclaiming a national emergency on Friday [September 14, 2001], President Bush activated some 500 dormant legal provisions [executive orders], including those allowing him to impose censorship and martial law [a police state!]"(166).

84. Speaking of carting off dissenters, the August 8, 2005 *Washington Post* reported on a Pentagon plan to deploy U.S. troops to police American cities in case of a major terrorist attack. The article, "War Plans Drafted To Counter Terror Attacks in U.S.," stated: "He [Timothy Keating, the head of NorthCom] cited a potential situation in which Guard units might begin rounding up people..."(492).

85. These executive orders were not the first of their kind--only the most detailed. The idea of executive orders being used to void the Constitution (or at least portions thereof) in time of an emergency dates back to F.D.R. In fact, since his passage of the Emergency Banking Relief Act of March 9, 1933 (mentioned earlier), this country has been under an officially-declared state of emergency that has never been lifted. Thus a whole slew of "emergency" executive orders have been passed over the years, some of which have not yet been put into effect, because they are awaiting the outbreak of a yet future national emergency crisis situation that will be significant enough in scope to justify their implementation.

This state of emergency that we have been under since 1933 was elaborated upon thusly by a 1973 Senate report: "Since March 9, 1933, the United States has been in a state of declared emergency. In fact, there are now in effect four presidentially proclaimed states of emergency....These proclamations give force to 470 provisions of Federal law [that] delegate to the President extraordinary powers, ordinarily exercised by Congress, which affect the lives of American citizens in a host of all-encompassing manners. This vast range of powers, taken together, confer enough authority to rule the country without reference to normal constitutional processes.

"Under the powers delegated by the statutes, the President may: seize property; organize and control the means of production; seize commodities; assign military forces abroad; institute martial law; seize and control all transportation and communications; regulate the operation of private enterprise; restrict travel; and [in a] plethora of particular ways, control the lives of American citizens"(442).

Roosevelt alone, during just his first term in office, issued 1,489 executive orders that created a massive anti-constitutional bureaucracy. Most of these orders still remain in place today--some have even been greatly expanded. And, of course, many more such orders have been created by every president since Roosevelt.

I should point out that the National Emergencies Act, passed September 14, 1976, is believed by most people to have ended the national emergency crisis created by F.D.R. However, this Act was nothing but a whole lot of window dressing, since there has been no decrease in the creation of executive orders since its passage, and none of the emergency powers that were seized before its passage have been relinquished.

86. Some might argue that suspending the Constitution is a non-issue, since the Constitution itself actually provides for its own suspension in time of emergency. However, this provision presupposes that the people are armed to prevent the government from abusing any extra-constitutional powers it attains during such an emergency. And it also presupposes that such an emergency would arise from a threat that was not foreseen and could not be avoided, with the government responding in the interest of the people. Another thing that this provision presupposes is that any new powers gained by the government during an emergency would be TEMPORARY, until the crisis has passed. But what we are instead looking at, of course, is the government planning an emergency in order to void the Constitution on a permanent basis, seeking first to disarm the people and leave them defenseless against oppression (more will be said on the issue of the government disarming the people shortly).

87. There are also plans to utilize private contractors to handle the chaos when martial law is implemented. On February 8, 2008, reporter Matthew Rothschild, writing for *The Progressive*, revealed these shocking insights: "Today, more than 23,000 representatives of private industry are working quietly with the FBI and the Department of Homeland Security. The members of this rapidly growing group, called InfraGard, receive secret warnings of terrorist threats before the public does--and, at least on one occasion, before elected officials. In return, they provide information to the government, which alarms the ACLU. But there may be more to it than that. One business executive, who showed me his InfraGard card, told me they have permission to 'shoot to kill' in the event of martial law. InfraGard is 'a child of the FBI,' says Michael Hershman, the chairman of the advisory board of the InfraGard National Members Alliance and CEO of the Fairfax Group, an international consulting firm"(571).

88. To the U.N. globalists, "tranquility" and "safety" simply mean the absence of all opposition to their sinister plot. For years now, the U.N. has been putting tremendous pressure on resistant or potentially resistant nations, often through the use of economic sanctions and/or outright military force, to compel them to "play ball" and become a cooperative part of the "global family" by submitting to U.N. authority. (For more information on this coercive U.N. war-waging and sanction-imposing game [working in conjunction primarily with U.S. forces], see Appendix 8.)

89. On June 13, 2005, Representative Ron Paul reported: "This week Congress will vote on a bill to expand the power of the United Nations beyond the dreams of even the most ardent left-wing, one-world globalists. But this time the UN power grabbers aren't European liberals; they are American neo-conservatives, who plan to use the UN to implement their own brand of world government.

"The 'United Nations Reform Act of 2005' masquerades as a bill that will cut US dues to the United Nations by 50% if that organization does not complete a list of 39 reforms. On the surface any measure that threatens to cut funding to the United Nations seems very attractive, but do not be fooled: in this case reform 'success' will be worse than failure. The problem is in the supposed reforms themselves--specifically in the policy changes this bill mandates.

"The proposed legislation opens the door for the United Nations to routinely become involved in matters that have never been part of its charter. Specifically, the legislation redefines terrorism very broadly for the UN's official purposes--and charges it to take action on behalf of both governments and international organizations.

"What does this mean? The official adoption of this definition by the United Nations would have the effect of making resistance to any government or any international organization an international crime. It would make any attempt to overthrow a government an international causus belli for UN military action. Until this point a sovereign government retained the legal right to defend against or defeat any rebellion within its own territory. Now any such activity would constitute justification for United Nations action inside that country. This could be whenever any splinter group decides to resist any regime--regardless of the nature of that regime"(479).

What this means is that, as the U.S. government becomes more and more oppressive, any attempt to overthrow it by freedom-loving Americans would be met with an invasion by U.N. troops.

90. Interestingly, State Department Paper 72-77, titled "Blueprint for World Peace," actually provides for policing of the U.S. by foreign troops. (If the Founding Fathers could only be alive today to see what has happened to this nation!)

91. Yes, U.N. foreign troops will be used to fire upon American citizens (and citizens of any other country, for that matter) who resist the coming global system. But most people will welcome these troops, hailing them as heroes who have come to save them from the planned crisis that we are headed for. On this note, look at the following astonishing statement made by Henry Kissinger during a speech he gave at the 1992 Bilderberger conference in Evian-Les-Bains, France, on May 21, 1992: "Today America would be outraged if U.N. troops entered Los Angeles to restore order [referring to the 1992 Los Angeles riots that resulted from the Rodney King verdict]. Tomorrow they will be grateful. This [will be] especially true if they were told that there was an outside threat from beyond, whether real or promulgated, that threatened our very existence. It is then that all peoples of the world will plead to deliver them from this evil. The one thing every man fears is the unknown. When presented with this scenario, individual rights will be willingly relinquished for the guarantee of their well-being granted to them by the World Government"(174).

92. Speaking of banning assault weapons, look at this next quote, going back to 1996: "Ultimately, a civilized society must disarm its citizenry....Passing a law like the assault weapons ban is a symbolic--purely symbolic--move in that direction. Its only real justification is not to reduce crime but to desensitize the public to the regulation of weapons in preparation for their ultimate confiscation." - Charles Krauthammer (nationally syndicated columnist), "Civilized

Society Must Disarm Its Citizenry," *Detroit News*, April 9, 1996.

93. This haunting quote sounds so much like something that Marx wrote: "There is but one way of simplifying, shortening, and concentrating the death agony of the old society as well as the bloody labor of the new world's birth--Revolutionary Terror"(63, pp. 46, 47).

94. This is the reason, by the way, that we are seeing militia and patriot groups being demonized by the media. The globalists need to build up public prejudice, fear, and ultimately hatred toward these "public enemies," in order that their coming planned demise will be viewed as a "necessary evil" to rid society of such "menaces." Hitler employed this same tactic, and it worked most effectively.

Snuffing out the lives of those who resist, or even protest, the coming world government has been the plan all along. Notice what H.G. Wells said about this: "Countless people...will hate the new world order...and will die protesting against it. When we attempt to evaluate its promise, we have to bear in mind the distress of a generation or so of malcontents..."(148).

95. Regarding mandatory sterilization, and population control in general, see Appendix 10.

96. For more on abolishing the family, see Appendix 11.

97. The CFR-controlled CIA has played a leading role in researching such drugs for controlling human behavior, beginning in the late 1940s, just after its inception. In this regard, it is significant to take note of a particularly disturbing statement made by a commission formed by President Gerald Ford, just five months after assuming office. Chaired by Nelson Rockefeller, this commission was largely a sham designed to minimize warranted public suspicions about CIA abuses. Nevertheless, it did make the following admission: "Beginning in the late 1940s, the CIA began to study the properties of certain behavior-influencing drugs and how such drugs might be put to use in intelligence activities....The drug program was part of a much larger CIA program to study possible reasons for controlling human behavior. Other studies explored the effects of radiation, electric shock, psychology, psychiatry, sociology, and harassment substances [whatever that means!]"(177, p. 172).

98. Should you have any doubt that "brainwashing enhanced by pharmacological methods" could happen in the U.S., pay close attention to what follows: In the June 19, 2004 edition of the *British Medical Journal*, we find this astonishing account: "A sweeping mental health initiative will be unveiled by President George W Bush in July....[T]he New Freedom Commission on Mental Health [was established] in April 2002 to conduct a 'comprehensive study of the United States mental health service delivery system.' The commission issued its recommendations in July 2003. Bush instructed more than 25 federal agencies to develop an implementation plan based on those recommendations. The president's commission found that 'despite their prevalence, mental disorders often go undiagnosed' and recommended comprehensive mental health screening for 'consumers of all ages,' including preschool children. According to the commission, 'Each year, young children are expelled from preschools and childcare facilities for severely disruptive behaviours and emotional disorders.' Schools, wrote the commission, are in a 'key position' to screen the 52 million students and 6 million adults who work at the schools. The commission also recommended 'Linkage [of screening] with treatment and supports' including 'state-of-the-art treatments' using 'specific medications for specific conditions'"(404).

So, as we can see, Bush Jr.'s "New Freedom Initiative" not only involved mind control through mandated medications (every tyrant's dream), but it came attached with an added bonus: a tremendous amount of loot to boot for his campaign contributors in the pharmaceutical industry. As the August 8, 2004 edition of *Intervention* magazine put it: "Never mind that it couldn't have less to do with freedom; if you're a thinking American, this initiative should scare the hell out of you.

"The New Freedom Initiative proposes to screen every American, including you, for mental illness....It's interesting to note that many on the staff appointed to the [New Freedom] Commission [on Mental Health] have served on the advisory boards of some of the nation's largest drug companies....

"...It is no coincidence that the treatments recommended for specific conditions are the newest state-of-the-art treatments that will bring in the most revenues for the drug companies. One of these emerging treatments is a capsule implanted within the body that delivers doses of medication without the patient having to swallow pills or take injections. If a government wanted to exert control of its citizens, think of the implications of using this device....

"...Masquerading in the lamb's fleece of providing mental health treatment to needy folk is the greedy wolf called Big Pharma....

"The destruction of America is evident in many ways. Do not be fooled; the Bushites intend to control all they can, and if that can include your brain, they will do it. If Big Pharma benefits, all the better. The New Freedom Initiative is an early step toward both..."(405).

I should mention, too, that the globalists have set up kids to be put on behavioral meds through, among other things, the food additives that they place in junk food. As the BBC reported on October 25, 2002: "Additives in popular snacks can cause hyperactivity and tantrums in young children, a study suggests. Research carried out by the independent watchdog the Food Commission found that so-called 'E-numbers' [artificial food colorings such as tartrazine (E102), sunset yellow (E110), carmoisine (E122), and ponceau 4R (E124), as well as the preservative Sodium Benzoate (E211)] may adversely affect one in four toddlers"(485). This one-in-four ratio, no surprise, corresponds with the ratio of kids who are on behavioral drugs today. Rest assured that this is all being done deliberately.

99. George Orwell, under the cloak of "novels" (*Animal Farm* and *1984*), was able to openly reveal exactly where he knew the globalists were planning to take us. In his classic 1948 work, *1984*, he depicted the character O'Brien talking to another character, Winston, telling him: "[T]he Party [the globalist party, or "Big Brother"] seeks power entirely for its own sake....We are interested solely in power....We are priests of power....We shall crush you down to the point from which there is no coming back....There will be no love, except the love of Big Brother....If you want a picture of the future, imagine a boot stamping on a human face--forever."

Another author who exposed the globalist agenda through this same novel-writing medium was Taylor Caldwell, who we quoted from earlier. In her book *Ceremony of the Innocent*, she wrote: "[T]here will be no peace in the tormented world, only a programmed and systematic series of wars and calamities--until the plotters have gained their objective: an exhausted world willing to submit to a planned Marxist economy and total and meek enslavement--in the name of peace"(178, p. 289). Doesn't this sound familiar? Interestingly, one of the mottos of Orwell's Big Brother was "War is peace" (the other two were "ignorance is strength" and "freedom is slavery").

100. Weather modification, on a technologically advanced scale that far surpasses mere "cloud seeding," is actually no longer confined to the future. In fact, it began before Brzezinski's book

was even published, but did not become fully refined until the early 1990s. (For more information on this subject, see Appendix 9.)

101. Alice Bailey, as well as being a Co-Mason, was also a key pioneer of the modern New Age movement. This is to be expected, since the two are intimately connected. In her 1950 book *Glamour: A World Problem*, for example, Bailey talked about how the world was in the midst of "the inauguration of the New Age," which would be based upon "the Masonic ritual." Interestingly enough, the magazine *New Age* was the official publication of the Supreme Council, 33rd Degree Scottish Rite of Freemasonry until 1990 (it's now called the *Scottish Rite Journal*).

So, since the New Age movement is obviously connected with Freemasonry, which is itself connected with the push for a New World Order, would it not then follow that the New Age movement is connected with the push for a New World Order? Indeed, this is precisely the case. Often it happens that major supporters of the New World Order agenda are also involved to some degree in the New Age movement, and vice versa, whether or not they, as individuals, have direct connections with Freemasonry. For instance, notice this next quote from the May 18, 1990 issue of *Time*: "Fans of Harmonic Convergences and the like have been noting Mikhail Gorbachev's frequent use of phrases associated with the New Age movement, that mystical universal philosophy that preaches--as the Soviet president does--of the need for 'a New World Order.' As Gorbachev said in California, 'All mankind is entering a New Age, and world trends are beginning to obey new laws and logic.' More strikingly, he [Gorbachev] held a private meeting in Canada earlier in the week with one of the leading gurus of the New Age movement, Sri Chinmoy, who read him a 'spiritual song' and gave him a volume of admiring letters"(181).

Not so surprisingly, five months later, on October 1, 1990, President George Bush Sr. addressed the United Nations General Assembly, asking the nations of the world "to press forward to cap a historic movement toward a New World Order." He later ended his speech by saying: "And so let it be said of the final decade of the twentieth century, this was a time when humankind came into its own...to bring about a revolution of the spirit and the mind and began a journey into a new day, a New Age, and a new partnership of nations. The U.N. is now fulfilling its promise as the world's parliament of peace"(8, p. 150). Do recall, by the way, that both Bush presidents (Sr. and Jr.) were/are members of the Order of Skull and Bones--an "offshoot" of Freemasonry, and that Bush Sr. is a 33rd-degree Mason.

A moment ago we talked about *New Age* magazine, and how it's the official publication of the Supreme Council, 33rd Degree Scottish Rite of Freemasonry. Keeping this in mind, let's take a look at what contributing author C. William Smith wrote in the September 1950 issue of this magazine: "This [world government] plan [is] dedicated to the new order of things...to make all things new--a new nation, a new race, a new civilization...to bring in and unfold the new order of the world [New World Order]."

Earlier we discussed the papacy becoming the head of the emerging world religion. Yet it must be stressed that this world religion will contain aspects of all major religions and philosophies from around the world--a "tossed salad," if you will, with the Vatican only serving as its epicenter of control. But the New Age "religion" of Freemasonry will, of course, also be exerting a powerful influence on this global religious conglomerate. In her twisted 1948 book, *The Reappearance of the Christ*, Alice Bailey underscored this point: "Is it not possible... [that] Masonic teaching...may provide all that is necessary for the formulation of a universal religion?...[Masonry] is the descendant of, or is founded upon, a divinely imparted religion....[This religion]...was the first United World Religion. Then came the era of separation of many religions and sectarianism. Today we are working again towards a World Universal Religion."

Believe it or not, there actually is precious little difference between the papacy and

Freemasonry. For instance, both put a heavy emphasis on symbols and monuments that are of obvious pagan origins. One good example is the obelisk, or phallic symbol. It's common knowledge that the Washington Monument in Washington D.C. was constructed by Masons, and right in the center of St. Peter's Square in the Vatican is found another giant phallic symbol. And it rests right in the center of another favorite Masonic symbol--a solar wheel.

On occasion, some Catholic sources have admitted the pagan origins of papal beliefs, practices, and symbols. Cardinal J. H. Newman, in *An Essay on the Development of Christian Doctrine*, London, 1890, p. 373, made a confession of this very nature: "The use of temples, especially those dedicated to concrete saints, and adorned on occasion with tree branches; incense, lamps and candles; votive offerings upon the healing of a sickness; holy water...holy days and periods...processions, and the blessing of fields; priestly vestments, tonsures, the wedding ring, facing the East,...statues...are all part of pagan origins, sanctified by their adoption into the church."

102. In the case of the U.S., through agencies like OSHA, FCC, FDA, EPA, USDA, etc., private enterprise is indeed being regulated--utilities companies, manufacturing firms, human services facilities, you name it--all are being regulated in the interests of the globalist lust for power and profit. With all the socialistic controls and restrictions placed on businesses today (which began back in the days of F.D.R.), only the largest corporations can afford to meet the demands of legislation (or buy off the regulation officials) that dictate standards of safety, quality control, environmental protections, etc., which serves to smoke out smaller companies and secure the globalist-owned monopolies. At the same time, deregulation has been occurring in some sectors of the business world, such as communications, since the globalist monopolization in such areas has been complete. But as time goes on, we may yet see communications being regulated again, should any significant competition arise outside the globalist sphere.

103. To see just how pervasive the U.N.'s jurisdiction is becoming, in order that it may "make and enforce law on the individual," see Appendix 13.

104. One of the most ridiculous examples of Cold War propaganda used by the government to legitimize the "Soviet threat" was when it encouraged public schools across the country, in the heart of the Cold War, to conduct Soviet nuclear attack drills. These drills involved telling school children to practice ducking under their desks ("duck and cover") to protect themselves from a possible nuclear missile strike. Now what, pray tell, do you suppose ducking under a desk would accomplish during a nuclear strike? These exercises were an absolute sham, simply designed to heighten fears and keep people compliant and dependent on the government to "save" them from the "bogeyman," and thereby to gain public support for military and CIA interventionism abroad.

105. Somoza was not alone in his thinking. There were some, in the U.S. government itself, who recognized, during the Cold War, that the real threat to the United States, instead of Russia or any other country, was actually right here in our midst. One such person was Senator Joseph McCarthy. He clearly saw--and wasn't afraid to voice what he saw--that our government was loaded with what he called "communist infiltrators." What he had really discovered, however, were the globalist infiltrators (mostly CFR members) who were using the U.S. to set up their Marxist world government.

Of course, McCarthyism, as a movement, got extremely carried away and wound up targeting innocent people. But this was surely the work of the globalists themselves, using the "Red Scare" to purge government of those not compliant with their globalist aims. Nevertheless, notice what McCarthy had said: "How can we account for our present situation unless we believe that men high in government are concerting to deliver us to disaster? This must be the product of a great conspiracy, a conspiracy on a scale so immense as to dwarf any previous such venture in the history of man. A conspiracy of infamy so black that, when it is finally exposed, its principals shall be forever deserving of the maledictions of all honest men"(195, p. 17). McCarthy also once stated, referring to our globalist/Marxist-dominated foreign and domestic policies: "What can be made of this unbroken series of decisions and acts contributing to the strategy of defeat? They cannot be attributed to incompetence....The laws of probability would dictate that part of...[the] decisions would serve this country's interest"(196, p. 4). And let's not forget what George Kennan said: "I sometimes wonder what use there is in trying to protect the West against fancied external threats when the signs of disintegration within are so striking"(191).

106. Victor Marchetti, a former officer in the CIA's Clandestine Services branch, wrote an eye-opening article about the CIA in the Institute for Historical Review's *Journal of Historical Review*. In this article, Marchetti stated: "The CIA, functioning as a secret instrument of the U.S. government and the presidency, has long misused and abused history and continues to do so. I first became concerned about this historical distortion in 1957, when I was a young officer in the Clandestine Services of the CIA.

"One night, after work, I was walking down Constitution Avenue with a fellow officer, who previously had been a reporter for United Press.

"'How are they ever going to know,' he asked....'How are the American people ever going to know what the truth is...about what we are doing and have done over the years?...We operate in secrecy, we deal in deception and disinformation, and then we burn our files. How will the historians ever be able to learn the complete truth about what we've done in these various operations, these operations that have had such a major impact on so many important events in history?'"(462)

107. Long after the Cold War, not only did torture continue to be used by U.S. forces, but it had actually become official policy, endorsed at the highest levels of government, which declared this outrageous practice to be "legal." As the June 9, 2004 *Boston Globe* reported: "What have we learned so far about officially sponsored torture by the US government? First, it is unambiguously clear that the torture of prisoners in Afghanistan, at Guantanamo [in Cuba], and at Abu Ghraib [in Iraqi] was official policy. Lawyers for the Pentagon and the White House, reporting directly to Defense Secretary Donald Rumsfeld and President [George W.] Bush, wrote contorted legal briefs trying to define a category of person immune to both due process of law and the Third Geneva Convention. As recently disclosed Pentagon memos divulge, one explicit purpose was to justify torture as a technique of interrogation.

"Second, the grotesque abuses at Abu Ghraib were therefore not the work of a few renegade freaks. Official policy was that coercion should be used to pry information out of prisoners. The torture techniques were at first wielded by military and CIA interrogation specialists and limited to 'high value' captives.

"But as torture moved down the chain of command, it further degenerated from a twisted and illegal means of interrogation into a sadistic sport for ordinary soldiers to apply to ordinary prisoners. This deterioration is predictable. It has happened under every totalitarian regime, from Stalin to Hitler to Torquemada. When torture is official policy, ordinary soldiers and police let their frustrations and imaginations run wild. This is why civilized nations ban torture categorically.

"Third, as details of the freestyle tortures at Abu Ghraib reached Rumsfeld and other top officials, they treated it mainly as a potential public relations problem, not as a sign that the entire policy was flawed and illegal. Indeed, even as the then-secret report by General Taguba on Abu Ghraib was being discussed internally, the government's lawyers continued to contend that the Third Geneva Convention on prisoners of war did not apply to alleged terrorists and that even US citizens, if accused of certain crimes, could be treated outside the law.

"For nearly three years, the Bush administration has resorted to the most preposterous fictions to define either locales or categories of people to whom the law does not apply. If you connect the dots, the torture at Abu Ghraib is part of a larger slide toward tyranny as the Bush administration tries to exempt itself from the rule of law.

"White House lawyers have contended in court briefs that the US base at Guantanamo, which the United States governs in perpetuity under a treaty, is actually under Cuban sovereignty. They contend that the president's powers as commander in chief override both international and domestic laws and even constitutional due process protections for US citizens as well as aliens accused of 'terrorism.'

"These legal claims are complete fabrications. The Third Geneva Convention is airtight. Its language allows for no special cases where torture is permitted and no gradations of acceptable forms of torture. Prisoners are not required to give their captors information beyond name, rank, and serial number, period. Captors are not allowed to resort to coercion, either physical or psychological. There is no category of alleged crime beyond the rule of law.

"Moreover, the legal protections of the US Constitution do not speak of citizens; they speak of 'persons.' And even if there were some special justification for torturing alleged terrorists--and there is none--most prisoners in Iraq are not 'illegal combatants' but POWs from a defeated army, exactly those whom the Geneva Convention was intended to protect. Indeed, the United States demands that any American captive abroad be treated with scrupulous respect. (This is the whole point of a universal agreement to ban torture--it covers everyone.)

"US officials darkly mention war crimes prosecutions whenever there are hints that American captives have been abused. Yet the US government, in every official forum, tries to negotiate special exemptions so that US personnel abroad are exempt from any such prosecutions. By definition, we are the good guys; so by definition, Americans cannot be guilty of war crimes.

"After Abu Ghraib, even America's allies are no longer willing to grant Washington special exemptions....

"It is appalling that a few grunts are taking the fall for torture that was official government policy. Donald Rumsfeld should not just be impeached. He should be tried as a war criminal. As for Bush, he can be dispatched by the electorate while we are still a democracy"(419).

108. During the Cold War, Russia was, of course, globalist-controlled as well. However, it was obviously not the nation of choice for the globalists to work through for their world empire-building enterprise. It simply did not have the readily-available resources for the globalists to exploit toward that end. Thus Russia's job was simply to play the "bad guy" in the Cold War.

109. For more information on how the world government conspirators have worked backstage to create wars and other calamities, see G. Edward Griffin's *The Creature from Jekyll Island* (ISBN: 0-912986-18-2), Des Griffin's *Descent Into Slavery* (ISBN: 0-941380-01-7), A. Ralph Epperson's *The Unseen Hand* (ISBN: 0-9614135-0-6), and Carroll Quigley's *Tragedy and Hope* (ISBN: 094500110X). For a mind-blowing exposure of the Cold War fiasco, specifically, see William Blum's *Killing Hope* (ISBN: 1-56751-052-3).

110. One-third of these victims--a full 500,000--were said to have been children. When asked if this price was worth the imposition of sanctions on Iraq, CFR member Madeleine Albright, then serving as U.S. ambassador to the U.N., responded by saying: "I think this is a very hard choice, but the price? We think the price is worth it"(349).

111. The threat of "competition" from a potential "new rival" mentioned in the above quote is not limited to the military and economic realms, of course, but extends to the political and social realms as well. Controlling all of these realms has been a goal of our military and intelligence for decades. And why? Because this is the goal of the globalists who control our military and intelligence agencies. Observe what Elmo Roper, CFR member and treasurer of the Atlantic Union Committee (another globalist front group), stated in this regard in a pamphlet he wrote in 1960, titled "The Goal Is Government of All the World": "For it becomes clear that the first step toward World Government cannot be completed until we have advanced on the four fronts: the economic, the military, the political and the social"(207).

112. Globalization not only ignores national boundaries and barriers, but it seeks to completely erase them, in order to destroy the sovereignty of nations around the world and make them more susceptible to world government. During a National Address in early 1988, President Ronald Reagan talked favorably about this emerging global economy, and confirmed that it truly was eroding away national boundaries: "I want to talk to you about...the developing economy of the future, an economy of great challenges and even greater opportunities [for who?], if only we have the courage to embrace them...and open our arms to economic freedom on a world scale [freedom, that is, for a select few, but servitude for the masses].

"I speak of the economy of the future but it is forming now in the mind and imaginations of the entrepreneurs around the globe. It is...linked by a global network of investment and communications, it is transforming our lives so fast that the so-called conventional wisdom can barely keep up. But the dramatic changes we have already witnessed are only the foreshadowing of things to come [indeed!]....

"We are moving to a new era of seemingly limitless horizons....This new world economy is a one world economy...a global electronic network, on line 24-hours a day....In this new world economy, national boundaries are increasingly becoming obsolete"(63, p. 92).

113. GATT became the WTO in 1995.

114. In addition to NAFTA and the EU, you can add CAFTA (Central American Free Trade Agreement), NATO, SEATO (South East Asia Treaty Organization), OAS (Organization of American States), AU (African Union), and a host of others to this list of regional organizations, all of which are designed to first unite countries together regionally, on an economic, political, and/or military basis. From there, the plan has been, and continues to be, to integrate these regional unions under a global government.

Joseph Stalin, in his book *Marxism and the National Question*, laid this plan out a long time ago, when he talked about the need to "Divide the world into regional groups as a transitional stage to world government. Populations will more readily abandon their national loyalties to a vague regional loyalty than they will for a world authority. Later the regions can be brought all the way into a single world dictatorship."

President Nixon said the same thing back in 1967: "The developing coherence of Asian regional thinking is reflected in a disposition to consider problems and loyalties in regional terms, and to evolve regional approaches to development needs and to the evolution of a new world order"(379).

Furthermore, Zbigniew Brzezinski, at the Gorbachev State of the World Forum in 1995, stated: "We cannot leap into world government in one quick step....[T]he precondition for eventual globalization--genuine globalization--is progressive regionalization, because thereby we move toward larger, more stable, more cooperative union"(380).

115. As part of the merger deal between Canada, the U.S., and Mexico, it was proposed that a new currency b e created for this new union--the "amero" (the equivalent of the EU's euro). This, of course, will mean the complete end of the U.S. economy.

116. The IMF and the World Bank were, in fact, created at the same time, by the same people, and at the same place that GATT was created at--the 1944 Bretton Woods, New Hampshire, "economic planning" conference.

117. Our globalist-controlled government is no newcomer to inciting violence and/or riots. The same thing happened back in the 1960s, for instance, with the civil rights riots in Newark, Cleveland, Cincinnati, Detroit, and Los Angeles. In each of these cities, local police stated that racial tensions didn't exist until they were aroused by "outside sources" (agent provocateurs), such as Stokely Carmichael and H. Rap Brown, who encouraged blacks during public speeches to "fight police and burn the city."

The *St. Louis Globe Democrat*, from August 9th to the 16th, 1967, ran a series of articles on the Detroit riots, written by Louis Lomax. He revealed that these riots occurred because "an organized group, largely from outside the Detroit area, had been operating in the city for more than a month....This group had an assignment: burn and destroy." Lomax then went on to describe the methods employed by these professional agitators: "Methodically breaking store windows, the revolutionaries urged the milling Negro people to loot and to steal."

Later, when Dr. James Boyce, a black professor at Wayne University, asked a policeman why the police didn't stop the riots, he was told, "We followed orders"(486, pp. 262, 263). Does this sound familiar?

The reasons for instigating these riots were threefold: They were intended to justify police brutality toward blacks (thereby instilling fear in them, to silence their dissenting voices); to draw attention away from the Vietnam fiasco; to arouse and magnify racial tensions in order to keep the American people divided.

118. The G7/G8 annual meetings, which amount to thinly-veiled measures to further advance the cause of globalization, have also resulted in police brutality against protesters. For example, the massive police attacks at the 2001 session in Genoa caused the death of one of the protesters, Carlo Giuliani.

119. Then-FBI-director, J Edgar Hoover, who hated Kennedy with a passion, did essentially the same thing as the CIA--sold the official bunk story that Oswald was the sole assassin, in order to give the false impression that the murder was solved. On November 24, 1963, just hours after Oswald was murdered, Hoover said, according to the 1975 Report of the Select Committee on Assassinations, that he wanted "something issued so we can convince the public that Oswald is the real assassin."

120. Incidentally, the "magic bullet" theory was concocted by 33rd-degree Mason Arlen Specter.

Speaking of phony bullet evidence surrounding Kennedy's assassination, ABC News reported on May 17, 2007: "Bullet analysis used to justify the lone assassin theory behind President John F. Kennedy's assassination is based on flawed evidence, according to a team of researchers including a former top FBI scientist.

"Writing in the Annals of Applied Statistics, the researchers urged a reexamination of bullet fragments from the 1963 shooting in Dallas to confirm the number of bullets that struck Kennedy"(569).

Do you really think it took them nearly 44 years to figure this out? Be assured that they knew this from day one, and were covering it up. They only come out with stuff like this years after the fact, when nearly all the perpetrators are dead, and when the public, as a whole, doesn't care anymore.

121. One of the many ways that our right to property has been attacked under the guise of "the common good" was revealed by CNN on June 23, 2005: "The Supreme Court on Thursday ruled that local governments may seize people's homes and businesses--even against their will--for private economic development....

"[C]ities [now] have wide power [called "eminent domain"] to bulldoze residences for projects such as shopping malls and hotel complexes to generate tax revenue.

"Local officials, not federal judges, know best in deciding whether a development project will benefit the community, justices said"(482).

Can't you see what's going on here? This is perfectly in line with the U.N.'s "Habitat I" document, which states that "Public ownership of land is justified in favor of the common good." What this document failed to mention, however, is that "common good" is to be defined by corrupt local officials who will unblushingly hand your property over to the corporation that has the greatest potential to generate huge tax revenues (or that hands over the biggest bribery check).

I should also mention another tactic that the new American communist property stealers employ: After seizing a person's home, they often call upon corrupt inspectors to falsely condemn the building, severely dropping its market value so that the rightful owner will receive the least amount of monetary compensation for his loss. And you didn't think this could happen in America? Well, think again!

122. For instance, the *Washington Post* reported on December 14, 2006: "Widely used antidepressants double the risk of suicidal behavior in young adults, from around three cases per thousand to seven cases per thousand, according to a huge federal analysis of hundreds of clinical trials. It marks the first time regulators have acknowledged that the drugs can trigger suicidal behavior among patients older than 18"(560).

123. As the U.K.'s *Daily Telegraph* reported on August 7, 1995: "Nearly three million tons of fruit and vegetables, including almost a million tons of apples, were destroyed in 1993, at a cost of £439 million, under the European Union's Common Agricultural Policy. More than 720,000 tons of peaches, over half a million tons of oranges and 165,000 tons of nectarines were also taken off the market by farmers paid by Brussels to destroy their own produce. British taxpayers alone paid £57 million towards the cost of destroying fruit and vegetables of almost every type grown in Europe. All were fit for human consumption. Here you have a scheme whereby European taxpayers are funding a scheme which keeps the price of fruit and vegetables artificially high by destroying perfectly good produce. The fruit is destroyed by being buried in the ground and allowed to rot."

124. In the spring of 2008, a world-wide "food shortage" crisis began that resulted in food costs soaring to unprecedented heights. This crisis, too, was a scam, of course--orchestrated to generate huge profits for the big agribusinesses. This was all documented in a London *Independent* article called "Multinationals Make Billions in Profit Out of Growing Global Food Crisis," in the May 4, 2008 edition.

125. The "brain" behind this program was none other than John Poindexter, Reagan's National Security Advisor, who was convicted in 1990 of conspiracy, lying to Congress, defrauding the government, and destroying evidence in the Iran-Contra scandal. So, aren't you glad that our globalist-controlled government was so careful in selecting the right kind of person to dream up such an important program like TIA?

It is important to point out that the TIA program was defunded by Congress in September 2003. However, the Bush Jr. administration, anticipating that this might happen, had created several "backup" programs that serve the same function. The most notorious of these programs is Homeland Security's Computer Assisted Passenger Profiling System (or CAPPS II), which is a national database used to assess the "threat level" of each potential airliner passenger. Whether a person is assigned a red, yellow, or green color code determines if he/she is either allowed to fly, detained for questioning, or prevented from flying altogether. Hitler never had it so good!

126. Speaking of government-orchestrated child abductions, this discussion would not be complete without mentioning a most shocking account given in the book *The Franklin Cover-Up* by former Nebraska Republican Senator John DeCamp (ISBN: 0963215809). It meticulously documents how during the '80s and early '90s, local and state Nebraska officials, with cooperation from federal officials, were involved in trafficking children (mostly orphaned boys). These children were taken to private parties around the country (including the 1984 and 1988 Republican National Conventions) that were attended by very prominent and powerful individuals in the world of politics and big business. At these parties, the children were sexually abused--some were even used in snuff films that were shown at some of these parties. Because these outrageous crimes involved very high profile individuals like Nebraska billionaire Warren Buffet and George Bush Sr., as well as elements within the CIA, DeCamp ran into all sorts of barriers in his investigation, particularly at the hand of the FBI. One of his key investigators was even killed during a mysterious small plane crash. Though he was able to bring some of the lower level conspirators to justice, he was only allowed to go just so far.

As an interesting side note, the Discovery Channel planned to air a documentary on this story called "Conspiracy of Silence." It was scheduled to be shown on May 3, 1994. *TV Guide* even had a large ad announcing the upcoming show. But at the last minute, it got canceled. However, it can easily be found and downloaded off the Internet from a plethora of different websites. Although it doesn't mention the snuff films or the involvement of George Bush Sr., nevertheless it is a well-done documentary, and is well worth watching.

Here's another interesting side note: Former CIA Director William Colby (perhaps the only person with a conscience who ever held this position), who was most helpful in assisting DeCamp with research for his book, disappeared on April 27, 1996. About a week later, his body was found in the Wicomico River near his Maryland home. His death was said to have been the result of a "boating accident," but I highly doubt it! When he left to go on his "boat ride," he failed to turn off his computer and several lights throughout his home. He also left half of his dinner uneaten on the table. At the time of his death, the second edition of DeCamp's book was soon to come out, which contained even more damning evidence about corruption within the CIA. And Colby was the main source of this new information.

127. For a more thorough and shocking exposure of how our rights and freedoms are being stolen away from us, see James Bovard's *Lost Rights* (ISBN: 0-312-12333-7), and his other work, *Freedom in Chains* (ISBN: 0-312-22967-4). For more information on the CIA and its drug dealing activities over the years, as well as a host of other crimes committed by it and other government agencies, see, for example, Rodney Stich's *Defrauding America: Encyclopedia of Secret Operations by the CIA, DEA, and Other Covert Agencies* (ISBN: 0932438091), Michael Levine's and co-author Laura Kavanau-Levine's *The Big White Lie: The CIA and the Cocaine/Crack Epidemic* (ASIN: 156025064X), Gary Webb's *Dark Alliance: The CIA, the Contras, and the Crack Cocaine Explosion* (ISBN: 1888363932), and Celerino Castillo's *Powderburns: Cocaine, Contras and the Drug War* (ISBN: 0889625786).

128. In addition to teaching children "not to respect their tradition-bound elders," the globalists, through the NEA and similar institutions that focus on "education" in this country, are working hard to directly usurp the authority of parents over their own children. This is being done in a variety of ways, and always under false pretenses. One of the most common methods used today is hidden behind the mask of "special education services." Here's how it works: There is a big push today, in public schools across the country, to designate as many children as possible as having "special needs," and to assign them an IEP (Individualized Education Program). There are two main reasons for this: a) It means more federal funding. b) It enables schools, when giving standardized tests at the end of the school year, to grant special concessions to these students with "special needs" (such as allowing them to use a calculator, giving them extended time periods for taking the tests, and even dropping them hints so they get the answers right). Schools are eager to grant such concessions because they fear losing federal funding altogether if a certain percentage of their student body fails these tests.

So it's obvious that schools are being tremendously pressured to maximize the number of students that are put into special education programs. But why are they thusly being pressured?

The real problem with all of this arises from the "contractual agreement" that parents must sign, in order for their child to receive special education services. Before agreeing with and signing this contract, parents are first asked to review the "Parents' Rights Brochure," which states under the heading "Providing Your Written Consent": "Once you have consented to an initial placement in a special education program, if you refuse to provide consent to any subsequent actions related to special education, the school district cannot use your refusal to consent as a basis to deny you or your child any other service, benefit or activity to which you or your child may be entitled."

As you can see, this contract, which comes from Washington bureaucrats, is designed to circumvent parental authority. Once it is signed, "any other service, benefit or activity" that the school district wishes to implement (such as putting your child on "behavioral medication") can be potentially imposed upon your child, whether you like it or not. Do you see how serious this is?

This same brochure further states: "...after your child is first placed in a special education program, if a school district believes your refusal to consent [to future recommendations] would deny your child a free appropriate public education (FAPE), the school district must take steps to ensure that FAPE is provided. Such steps may include mediation and/or initiation of a due process hearing...to resolve the dispute."

The way to avoid this trap is to NEVER sign the contract, and thereby not sign your child over to the "special education" cageless zoo.

129. This sounds so much like a quote we cited earlier from Aldous Huxley, in *Brave New World*

Revisited: "And it seems to me perfectly in the cards that there will be within the next generation or so a pharmacological method of making people love their servitude, and producing...a kind of painless concentration camp for entire societies, so that people will in fact have their liberties taken away from them but will rather enjoy it, because they will be distracted from any desire to rebel by propaganda, brainwashing, or brainwashing enhanced by pharmacological methods"(412). Recall, also, our discussion earlier of Bush Jr.'s New Freedom Initiative, which calls for the mandatory psychological testing and drugging of students nationwide.

While we're back on the subject of psychological testing and drugging, let's remember that we're not just dealing with mind control as the hidden agenda here--we're also dealing with mega-profits for the pharmaceutical companies. As the *Washington Post* reported on April 20, 2006: "Every psychiatric expert involved in writing the standard diagnostic criteria for disorders such as depression and schizophrenia has had financial ties to drug companies that sell medications for those illnesses, a new analysis has found"(521).

130. This "discontent with the current values," designed to "produce a passion for change," is what Values Clarification and Outcome-Based Education are all about--poking around inside of kids' heads and subtly removing or diluting what has been instilled therein by their parents. Do you remember our discussion earlier of Mikhail Gorbachev's "new way of thinking"? Is this all starting to fit together now? Are you seeing the big picture?

The agenda behind Outcome-Based Education and Values Clarification was set a long time ago. This can be seen by reading quotes like the following, from the 1938 NEA-published book, *The Purposes of Education in American Democracy*: "Measurement of outcomes must be directly related to the objectives....Education has, on the whole, been altogether too much concerned with facts, and too little concerned with values....There should be a much greater concern with the development of attitudes, interests, ideals and habits....Our schools should give prizes not to the one who wins more credit for himself, but to the one who operates more effectively with others....The educated citizen is a cooperating member of the world community....Are students becoming more skillful in doing some type of useful work? [Remember Clinton's "School to Work" program?]...Are they acquiring skills?...Are they learning to be fair and tolerant in situations where conflicts arise?...Education is not gained in a few years in school; it is a lifetime enterprise..."

131. Another stunning similarity between F.D.R. and Wilson is the fact that both of them got reelected on the basis of promises to keep the U.S. out of war--promises that obviously neither of them intended to keep.

During a campaign speech in Boston on October 30, 1940, Roosevelt assured his listeners, "I have said this before, but I shall say it again, and again, and again: your boys are not going to be sent into any foreign wars." Yet, all the while, he had been quietly assuring Churchill that he was committed to getting the U.S. involved in WW II (see Churchill quote above).

Likewise, Wilson's 1916 campaign slogan, "He Kept Us Out of War," was a great vote-catcher. Yet, on February 22, 1916, Colonel House sent a memo to Sir Edward Grey, the British foreign secretary, promising him that Wilson would attempt to negotiate a peace settlement between Germany and the Allied Powers, and that if Germany refused to participate in the conference, the U.S. would enter the war on England's side(483, p. 935).

132. The deficits created under Bush Jr. were absolutely staggering. In the year 2006 alone, the Bush administration reported a deficit of $248.2 billion. Yet, as bad as that figure was, the Treasury Department stated that the reality was far worse--around $4.6 trillion!(562)

133. It needs to be mentioned here that, just after the 9-11 attacks, on September 28, the United Nations Security Council passed Resolution 1373--a new set of rules for member states to follow in order to combat terrorism. It called for stringent state controls on financial transactions, arms sales and possession, and extended government powers of surveillance. Sound familiar?

134. Ashcroft continued to play this Congress-dodging game all throughout his tenure, acting as he pleased and refusing to give account of his actions. As another good example of this, on June 25, 2004, the *Salt Lake Tribune* ran an article on the Senate Judiciary Committee's oversight hearing with John Ashcroft, held on June 8. The article quoted Senator Patrick Leahy as saying to Ashcroft, during the proceedings: "Mr. Attorney General, I must speak frankly about an issue that has emerged as a basic problem during your tenure. There are two words that succinctly sum up the Justice Department's accountability and its cooperation with congressional oversight on your watch. Those two words are 'sparse,' and 'grudging.' Even those of us who have served through several presidents cannot recall a worse performance record when it comes to responsiveness.

"Just days ago we learned of Justice Department involvement in devising legal arguments to minimize our obligations under such U.S. laws and international agreements as the convention on torture. Yet a letter I wrote to you last November, well before most of these abuses came to light [referring to the scandal of U.S. soldiers abusing and torturing Iraqi prisoners], went unanswered for months, and when we are lucky enough to get responses, the premium is on unresponsiveness. Few of the answers we get are worth much more than the paper they are printed on. We often learn more about what's really happening in the Justice Department in the press than we do from you"(395).

135. The Bush Jr. administration played this "public distraction" deception game over and over again. One way, in particular, was its issuance of false Code Orange terrorist alerts. For example, when the news broke in May 2002 about the Bush administration (including Bush himself) having specific prior knowledge of the 9-11 attacks, suddenly there was a convenient outbreak of terrorist alerts, which served as a great distraction to divert the public's attention from such damaging revelations. These May 2002 alerts were, of course, an absolute scam. As the *Washington Times* noted: "The Bush administration issued a spate of terror alerts in recent days to mute criticism that its national security team sat on intelligence warnings in the weeks before the September 11 attacks. The warnings, including yesterday's uncorroborated FBI report that terrorists might target the Statue of Liberty, quieted some of the lawmakers who said President Bush failed to act on clues of the September 11 attacks, although Senate Majority Leader Tom Daschle yesterday reiterated his demand for an independent investigation. The latest alerts were issued 'as a result of the controversy that took place last week,' said Bush spokesman Ari Fleischer, referring to reports that the president received a CIA briefing in August [the August 6 Presidential Daily Briefing] about terror threats, including plans by Osama bin Laden's al Qaeda network to hijack U.S. commercial airliners"(363).

Naturally, all the other terrorist alerts were fake as well, launched for various political reasons. In January 2003 it was reported by *WorldNetDaily*: "[S]ources within the bureau [FBI] and the Central Intelligence Agency said the [Bush] administration is pressuring intelligence agencies to develop 'something, anything' to support an array of non-specific terrorism alerts issued by the White House and the Department of Homeland Security....FBI and CIA sources said a recent White House memo listing the war on terrorism as a definitive political advantage and fund-raising tool is just one of many documents discussing how to best utilize the terrorist threat"(364). In case you're wondering why the Democrats weren't jumping all over these particular false terror alerts, to expose them as the frauds that they were, perhaps the answer was best provided by Democratic strategist Russ Barksdale, who was quoted by *Capitol Hill Blue* as saying: "Of course the White House is going to exploit the terrorism threat to the fullest political advantage, they would be fools not to. We'd do the same thing"(365).

But what was the real motive behind the January 2003 terrorist alerts? As you may recall, the claim was initially made that Saddam Hussein was involved in 9-11, and that he was a supporter of al Qaeda. So the fear of a terrorist attack was being revived at this time, just two months before the outbreak of the Iraq war, to drum up public support for this military campaign.

Perhaps you would not be surprised to discover that on October 12, 2001, the day that the rights-trampling Patriot Act was passed by the House, a *Washington Post* front page headline read, "Terrorist Attacks Imminent, FBI Warns." The *New York Times* reported the next day, October 13: "[B]oth the House and the Senate adopted complex, far-reaching antiterrorism legislation with little debate in an atmosphere of edgy alarm, as federal law enforcement officials warned that another attack could be imminent." And then a *Washington Post* editorial noted on the 16th that, although many Democrats opposed the Patriot Act, they "voted for it anyway, lest there be a further terrorist attack and they be accused of not having provided the government sufficient means to defend against it."

In May of 2004, the Bush boys were at it again, issuing more vague warnings about terrorist attacks over the upcoming summer. And once again it was such good timing, with the election drawing near, and with Bush's approval ratings dropping low because of rising body counts of U.S. troops in Iraq. Here's what Reuters said about this, on May 26: "A vague new U.S. warning that al Qaeda may be planning a massive attack smacks of political back-covering and campaigning, not just a call for heightened vigilance, analysts and former government officials say.

"Stung by accusations that the Bush administration ignored key intelligence in the run-up to the Sept. 11, 2001, attacks, officials may now be issuing warnings to prove to Americans they are on the ball this time, say terrorism analysts on both sides of the political fence....

"...One former national security official in the Bush administration told Reuters: 'This is more butt-covering than anything else.'...Critics say the new threat warnings may also just be a ploy to shore up the president's job approval ratings or divert attention from the increasingly unpopular Iraq campaign....

"Some critical voices say the government may also be hoping the warnings could score political points on national security that could boost President Bush's flagging popularity ahead of the November elections....

"One prominent terrorism expert, who would only speak on condition of anonymity, said Bush may also be trying to staunch increasing criticism of the Iraq campaign by underlining the link in the public's mind between Iraq and security at home.

"'The president is running as a war president, so the timing is interesting,' he said, pointing to a speech by Bush on Monday that made frequent references to terrorist threats.

"'I wonder if there's not a connection to the president's speech when he mentioned terrorism 18 times in the context of Iraq. Isn't this a very convenient way of linking back to the United States that Iraq is part of the broader war on terrorism?' he said"(587).

Another possible reason for the May 2004 terror alerts was the reports surfacing about U.S. servicemen abusing and torturing Iraqi prisoners of war, which were also driving down Bush's approval ratings. Yes, there's nothing like a nice distraction when a scandal breaks.

On August 3, 2004, yet another fake terror alert was issued. The following day, London's *Independent* had this to say on the matter: "The Bush administration was forced into the embarrassing admission yesterday that 'new' intelligence about al-Qa'ida's plans to attack US financial institutions--information that led to an official alert and a slew of fresh security measures--was up to four years old and predated the 11 September attacks.

"Intelligence officials were forced into retreat just a day after they had said fresh and 'alarmingly' specific information indicated terrorists were planning attacks on institutions in Washington, New York and New Jersey and had been carrying out surveillance of the targets. One investigator had even said that al-Qa'ida operatives had recently carried out a 'test-run' for an attack against a bank....

"The *Washington Post* , one of many newspapers to carry the claims, yesterday quoted one senior law enforcement official briefed on the intelligence who said: 'There is nothing right now that we're hearing that is new. Why did we go to this level? I still don't know that'"(420).

Well, this law enforcement official may not have known why this terror threat level was reached, but the August 8, 2004 *Chicago Sun-Times* sure did, which stated: "Terror alerts are...ready to be employed anytime President Bush wants to move the Kerry-Edwards campaign off the front page for a few days. The 'cry wolf' factor is high. Tom Ridge's claim that his Homeland Security Department 'doesn't do politics' rings hollow, given his political background and the boss he is beholden to. Bush can shout, 'We're a nation in danger' in the Rose Garden anytime he wishes, but the public may yet conclude that the danger is the president's judgment"(421).

136. Did you catch how Brzezinski referred to a PERCEIVED threat here? Bearing this thought in mind, take careful notice of the proceeding quote from a book published back in 1972: "[P]ower is viewed as a means of achieving change....During the period of a perceived crisis, the pace of change can be speeded up tremendously. It matters more that a crisis is perceived than whether a crisis actually exists"(347).

137. In addition to the oil motive for the Afghanistan invasion, we must also mention another important, hidden agenda behind this campaign--the revival of the highly-profitable opium farming business. The November 25, 2001 *Observer* reported that Afghan farmers were being encouraged by warlords allied with the U.S. to plant "as much opium as possible." Now isn't that interesting!

138. It might appear confusing to see Cronkite, a staunch globalist, speak like this against his fellow globalists in the Bush administration. But this "doublespeak" is actually quite typical of the world government conspirators, which is designed to confuse the public. Another good example of this was Zbigniew Brzezinski's 2004 book *The Choice: Global Domination or Global Leadership*, in which he gave the impression that he was totally opposed to the policies of the Bush administration. Yet this same administration had actually been carrying out everything that he called for in his 1997 book *The Grand Chessboard*, as we saw earlier.

139. It is also worth noting that just a few days after 9-11, 11 members of the bin Laden family were allowed to fly out of the U.S., via Boston's Logan Airport, at a time when all other Arabs were being closely scrutinized as potential terrorists, and at a time when no one else in the country was allowed to fly. There were also reports of Saudi officials (Bush business partners) being secretly flown out of the country as well(372). Commenting on this fiasco, Tom Kinton, director of aviation at Logan Airport, said: "We were in the midst of the worst terrorist act in history and here we were seeing an evacuation of the bin Ladens!"(373).

140. The only pictures ever released from any of the airports that the hijacked planes left from on 9-11 were from Dulles, from whence Flight 77 departed. But there are some problems with these

pictures. First of all, they weren't released until late July 2004 (the evening before the 9-11 Commission report came out). Why weren't these pictures released earlier?

Also, none of these pictures had the date, time, or camera identification number on them, which indicates that they were either tampered with, or were outright fakes.

141. Another problem with the named 19 hijackers is the total lack of experience and capabilities of the pilots among them, contrasted with the complicated fashion in which some of the hijacked planes were flown on 9-11. For instance, Flight 77, just prior to hitting the Pentagon, followed a very complicated flight path. CBS News had this to say about it, on September 26, 2001: "The hijacker-pilots...[executed] a difficult high-speed descending turn. Radar shows Flight 77 did a downward spiral, turning almost a complete circle and dropping the last 7,000 feet in two-and-a-half minutes. The steep turn was so smooth, the sources say, it's clear there was no fight for control going on. And the complex maneuver suggests the hijackers had better flying skills than many investigators first believed. The jetliner disappeared from radar at 9:37 and less than a minute later it clipped the tops of street lights and plowed into the Pentagon at 460 mph." Now notice what Rick Garza, a flying instructor at Sorbi's Flying Club in San Diego, had to say about Khalid al-Mihdhar and Nawaq (or Nawaf) al-Hamzi (the supposed hijacker-pilots of Flight 77), whom he had taught: "It was like Dumb and Dumber. I mean, they were clueless. It was clear to me they weren't going to make it as pilots"(435).

There was a third hijacker supposedly aboard Flight 77 who was also "pilot-trained," Hani Hanjour. But according to the 9-11 Commission Report, he was a "terrible pilot" as well, and as late as July 2001, just 2 months before the attacks, his flying instructor had refused to fly with him again.

142. The same fate that befell Flight 93 is probably what also befell Flight 77--it was probably shot down as well. For we find that its official flight path ended in a remote area over West Virginia (or perhaps eastern Kentucky), with a dotted line continuing on toward Washington. This means that this plane literally disappeared off radar, and was not able to be tracked for the rest of its flight to the nation's Capitol. Thus, as implied earlier, it was probably a remote controlled "missile with wings" that struck the Pentagon.

It appears that Flight 77 was taken down in a remote area where its tragic fate, and the subsequent clean-up of its wreckage, could not be witnessed by anyone. In any case, there are several credible reports which reveal that this plane did indeed go down: *Newsday* said on September 23, 2001, that there were rumors floating around which hinted that Flight 77 may have "exploded in midair." *USA Today* further stated on August 13, 2002, that FAA head Jane Garvey had notified the White House the morning of 9-11 that Flight 77 had crashed. Also, Dale Watson, FBI counterterrorism chief, mentioned during a teleconference with Richard Clarke the morning of 9-11 that "a large jet crashed in Kentucky, near the Ohio line"(588).

143. The U.S., of course, has been doing the same thing, building bases in every country that it conquers on behalf of the globalist cause. In fact, the U.S. now maintains over 700 military installations in 132 countries around the world.

144. Funny it was how Saddam was condemned by Bush Sr. for invading Kuwait, when, not only was he set up to do so, but a year earlier Bush had invaded Panama, a nation that posed no threat to the U.S. whatsoever. During this invasion, civilian areas were the ONLY targets hit. And, for some very strange reason, it just so happened that the U.N. never said or did anything about this travesty.

145. One of the many outrages that occurred during the 1991 Iraq conflict was the bombing raid that Bush Sr. ordered AFTER Iraq had surrendered. As the unarmed Iraqi troops were exiting Kuwait in civilian vehicles, heading toward Basra, a massive aerial bombardment needlessly and sinisterly slaughtered tens of thousands in this twenty-mile-long caravan(461). Funny that the U.N.--that great bastion of human rights advocacy--never complained about this atrocity either.

146. This, of course, is the same reason why the U.S. and its allies didn't march forward into Russia at the close of WW II, after crushing the Nazi regime. The globalists needed an "enemy" to justify NATO (and, of course, to justify "Cold War" policies and military campaigns).

147. The title of this report was "Rebuilding America's Defenses: Strategies, Forces and Resources for a New Century," available at http://www.newamericancentury.org. Or go directly to the document at http://www.newamericancentury.org/RebuildingAmericasDefenses.pdf.

148. Since DU has had such devastating effects on veterans of the first Iraq war, costing the government huge sums for veterans' healthcare, and since DU was again used in the second Iraq war, it should come as no surprise to discover that Bush Jr. severely cut back on veterans' healthcare benefits.

149. Reagan had dropped the U.S. out of UNESCO, at least on paper, in 1984, because, as he rightly put it, "It has exhibited a hostility toward the basic institutions of a free society, especially a free market and a free press."

150. I should mention that the earliest theoretical and experimental groundwork for weather modification technology was laid by the genius inventor Nikola Tesla (1856-1943). Of course, his dream was to see this technology utilized for the benefit of mankind, and not for destructive purposes. In the September 9, 1915 *Manufacturer's Record*, he wrote an article called "The Wonder World To Be Created By Electricity," in which he stated: "[T]he time is very near when we shall have the precipitation of the moisture of the atmosphere under complete control, and then it will be possible to draw unlimited quantities of water from the oceans, develop any desired amount of energy, and completely transform the globe by irrigation and intensive farming. A greater achievement of man through the medium of electricity can hardly be imagined." If he only knew what was to become of his discoveries!

Interestingly, Congressman Dennis Kucinich introduced legislation in 2001 that was designed to prevent the use of space-based and HAARP-type systems from being used as weapons, not only in the realm of weather modification, but in other areas that are even more sinister. Known as H.R. 2977, the Space Preservation Act of 2001, it forbids the use of "land-based, sea-based, or space-based systems using radiation, electromagnetic, psychotronic, sonic, laser, or other energies directed at individual persons or targeted populations for the purpose of information war, mood management, or mind control of such persons or populations." It also forbids the use of "high altitude ultra low frequency weapons systems." It even prohibits the use of "chemtrails"--harmful chemical agents that are released into the atmosphere via military planes, every day all over the country, and indeed all around the world, which has been going on for a long time now. The reasons for releasing these toxins are too numerous to elaborate on here. But suffice it to say that none of these reasons have anything to do with general public interest.

Other bills like this have been introduced since 2001, but it's obvious that the federal thugs who utilize such technologies have no intention of complying with them, whether or not they get passed.

151. There has been much talk (and action) in recent years regarding the termination of the lives of unborn (and born) mentally and physically handicapped babies, and even adults (recall how Terri Schiavo, for example, a crippled and brain-damaged car-crash victim, was allowed to slowly die from dehydration in a Florida nursing home in late March 2005). But it's not just from the secular world that we see a push in this direction--it's from the religious world as well. On November 12, 2006, the UK's *Daily Mail* carried an article called "Outrage as Church backs calls for severely disabled babies to be killed at birth," which stated: "The Church of England has broken with tradition[al] dogma by calling for doctors to be allowed to let sick newborn babies die.

"Christians have long argued that life should [be] preserved at all costs--but a bishop representing the national church has now sparked controversy by arguing that there are occasions when it is compassionate to leave a severely disabled child to die.

"And the Bishop of Southwark, Tom Butler, who is the vice chair of the Church of England's Mission and Public Affairs Council, has also argued that the high financial cost of keeping desperately ill babies alive should be a factor in life or death decisions"(558).

152. Apparently great strides have been made toward this goal. According to the March/April 2004 issue of *Mother Jones*, "It has been called a modern-day Manhattan Project--a spending spree so vast and rapid that it might change the face of biological science. In the wake of 9/11, the U.S. government is funding a massive new biodefense research effort, redirecting up to $10 billion toward projects related to biological weapons such as anthrax. The Pentagon's budget for chemical and biological defense has doubled; high-security nuclear-weapons labs have begun conducting genetic research on dangerous pathogens; universities are receiving government funding to build high-tech labs equipped to handle deadly infectious organisms; and Fort Detrick, Maryland, once the home of America's secret bioweapons program, is about to break ground on two new high-tech biodefense centers"(451).

This massive research and development project was the natural outgrowth of a directive that went back about 30 years. On December 10, 1974, the National Security Council produced National Security Study Memorandum 200, "Implications of Worldwide Population Growth for US Security and Overseas Interests," which stated that there was a "special US political and strategic interest" in population reduction or limitation in many developing sector nations due to potential competition with the U.S. over control of natural resources.

153. The globalists have rigged the economy to force many women into the workforce that would otherwise not be there, not only to assist in the breakdown of the family, but to provide themselves with a whole new "human resource" to exploit.

The same holds true with the push in recent years to get as many mentally handicapped people into the workforce as possible. Rest assured that this has NOTING to do with concern for these disabled individuals, even though they might benefit from it.

154. This motto comes right from the pages of the *Kabbalah*, which states, as we saw earlier: "By what kind of war?...[B]y deceit and trickery wherever possible."

Of further interest here is a statement made about the Mossad in a report produced by the U.S. Army's School of Advanced Military Studies (SAMS) in September 2001. It referred to the Mossad as "Ruthless and cunning. Has capability to target US forces and make it look like a Palestinian/Arab act"(475).

155. We should not find it so unusual to discover that Trotsky, by his own admission, was heavily influenced by Freemasonry. In his book *My Life: The Rise and Fall of a Dictato*r, he wrote: "The work [study] on freemasonry [that I did]...influenced the whole course of my intellectual development"(472). This is only natural, since Freemasonry and Zionism go hand-in-hand.

156. In regards to information about these post-9-11 Israeli spy arrests being classified, and to the possibility of there being "tie-ins" between them and 9-11, the September 12, 2001 issue of *The Record*, a Bergen County, New Jersey paper, carried this further suspicious account about some of these very Israeli spies: "About eight hours after terrorists struck Manhattan's tallest skyscrapers, police in Bergen County detained five men who they said were found carrying maps linking them to the blasts.

"The five men, who were in a van stopped on Route 3 in East Rutherford around 4:30 p.m., were being questioned by police but had not been charged with any crime late Tuesday. The Bergen County Police bomb squad X-rayed packages found inside the van but did not find any explosives, authorities said.

"However, sources close to the investigation said they found other evidence linking the men to the bombing plot.

"'There are maps of the city in the car with certain places highlighted,' the source said. 'It looked like they're hooked in with this. It looked like they knew what was going to happen when they were at Liberty State Park.'

"Sources also said that bomb-sniffing dogs reacted as if they had detected explosives, although officers were unable to find anything. The FBI seized the van for further testing, authorities said....

"Sources close to the investigation said the men said they were Israeli tourists, but police had not been able to confirm their identities. Authorities would not release their names...."

How did the local police even know about this van and its suspicious occupants? According to the article: "'We got an alert to be on the lookout for a white Chevrolet van with New Jersey registration and writing on the side,' said Bergen County Police Chief John Schmidig. 'Three individuals were seen celebrating in Liberty State Park after the impact. They said three people were jumping up and down'"(491).

Interestingly, on the day of the attacks, former Israeli Prime Minister Benjamin Netanyahu was asked what the attack would mean for US-Israeli relations. His quick reply was: "It's very good....Well, it's not good, but it will generate immediate sympathy [for Israel]." Stories like these force one to speculate: Was 9-11 another Lavon Affair, or another U.S.S. Liberty?

157. One of the biggest advocates of "Christian Zionism" has been Pat Robertson--and quite aggressively so. As the Townhall.com website reported on December 17, 2003, "American conservative Christian leader Dr. Pat Robertson warned Israel on Wednesday against agreeing to political initiatives with the Palestinians and especially allowing the establishment of a Palestinian state. Surrendering their ancient Biblical claim to the land, he said, would be tantamount to committing suicide. Robertson's advice clashed with the goals of President Bush, who is backing the road map peace plan that envisions the establishment of a Palestinian state by the end of 2005. Robertson, who is founder of the Christian Broadcasting Network in Virginia Beach, Va., and host of the internationally syndicated 700 Club, is part of the large conservative Christian movement, which ardently supported Bush during the last presidential election. But since then, Bush became the first U.S. president to ever formally call for the establishment of a Palestinian state in the Gaza

Strip and West Bank, which millions of Christians as well as Jews believe God promised to the Jewish people as an eternal inheritance in the land of Judea and Samaria. Robertson warned Israel against agreeing to the establishment of a Palestinian state"(436).

So adamant was Robertson about his support for the Zionist state of Israel, that he threatened the Bush administration with repercussions if it backed away from supporting it. As *Ha'aretz* reported on October 4, 2004: "Influential American evangelist Pat Robertson said Monday that Evangelical Christians feel so deeply about Jerusalem [Israel], that if President George W. Bush were to 'touch' Jerusalem [back away from fully supporting Israel], Evangelicals would abandon their traditional Republican leanings and form a third party. 'The President has backed away from [the road map] but if he were to touch Jerusalem, he'd lose all evangelical support,' Robertson said. 'Evangelicals would form a third party.'"

By the way, don't think for a moment that Bush's claim to support a Palestinian state in any way implied that he was going against Israel. This was nothing but a political ploy. Notice, for example, what Bush said about Israel in early May of 2006: "America's commitment to Israel's security is strong, enduring and unshakeable." He also said that the United States and Israel were "natural allies and these ties will never be broken" and that these ties were "unshakeable"(523). (See also the quote at the very end of Supplement I.)

References

1. John Robison, *Proofs of a Conspiracy*. Belmont, MA: Western Islands, 1967. (This book was originally published in 1797.)

2. Nesta Webster, *World Revolution*. London: Constable and Company, 1921.

3. Manly P. Hall, *Lectures on Ancient Philosophy*. Los Angeles: The Philosophical Research Society. As quoted by Texe Marrs in *Circle of Intrigue*, pp. 166, 167.

4. http://www.lucistrust.org/goodwill/ngws.shtml#plan

5. Albert Pike, *Morals and Dogma of the Ancient and Accepted Scottish Rite of Freemasonry*.

6. U.S. George Washington Bicentennial Commission, *The Writings of George Washington*, Vol. 20. Washington, D.C.: U.S. Government Printing Office, 1941.

7. Alexander Addison, *Rise and Progress of Revolution: A Charge to the Grand Juries of the County Courts of the Fifth Circuit of the State of Pennsylvania at December Sessions, 1800*, 1800. As quoted by Dennis Laurence *Cuddy* in *Now is the Dawning of the New Age New World Order*, p. 26.

8. Dennis Laurence *Cuddy*, *Now is the Dawning of the New Age New World Order*. Oklahoma City, OK: Hearthstone Publishing, 2000.

9. *Hansard's Parliamentary Debates*. As quoted by A. Ralph Epperson in *The Unseen Hand: An Introduction to the Conspiratorial View of History*. Tucson, AZ: Publius Press, 1988, pp. 76, 77.

10. Alvin and Heidi Toffler, *Creating A New Civilization*. Atlanta, GA: Turner Publishing, Inc., 1995.

11. James MacGregor Burns, *The Power To Lead: The Crisis of the American Presidency*. New York: Simon and Schuster, 1984.

12. *Congressional Record*, December 15, 1987, Vol. 133, 100th Congress, 1st Session, p. S 18146.

13. *Congressional Record*, February 23, 1954, Vol. 100, Part 2, p. S 2121.

14. James Perloff, *The Shadows of Power: The Council on Foreign Relations and the American Decline*. Belmont, MA: Western Islands, 1988.

15. *New York Times*, March 27, 1922.

16. Woodrow Wilson, *The New Freedom*. New York: Doubleday Page, 1913. As quoted by

Dwight L. Kinman in *The World's Last Dictator*, p. 28.

17. Dwight L. Kinman, *The World's Last Dictator*. Springdale, PA: Whitaker House, 1995.

18. Dennis Laurence Cuddy, *The Globalists: The Power Elite Exposed*. Oklahoma City, OK: Hearthstone Publishing, 2001.

19. Philip Agee, *Inside the Company: CIA Diary*. New York: Stonehill Publishing Company, 1975.

20. Suzanne Keller, *Beyond the Ruling Class: Strategic Elites in Modern Society*. New York: Random House, 1963.

21. Laurence H. Shoup and William Minter, *Imperial Brain Trust: The CFR and United States Foreign Policy*. New York: Monthly Review Press, 1977.

22. Phyllis Schlafly and Chester Ward, *Kissinger on the Couch*. New Rochelle, NY: Arlington House, 1975.

23. *New York* magazine, October 7, 1996.

24. Percy Ellwood Corbett, *Post-War Worlds*. New York: International Secretariat, Institute of Pacific Relations, 1942.

25. Charles A. Lindbergh Sr., *Lindbergh on the Federal Reserve*. Costa Mesa, CA: Noontide Press, 1923.

26. *Congressional Record*, February 1, 1971.

27. *Seattle Times*, May 4, 1995.

28. Carroll Quigley, *Tragedy and Hope: A History of the World in Our Time*. London: The Macmillan Company, 1966.

29. *National Economy and the Banking System*, Senate Documents, Col. 3, No. 23, 75th Congress, 1st Session, 1939.

30. Catherine B. Dalton, *Constitutional Money and the Banking Procedure*. Oreana, Ill: Illinois Committee to Restore the Constitution, 1985.

31. *Time*, July 20, 1992.

32. William Bryan, *The United States' Unresolved Monetary and Political Problems*. As quoted by Gary Allen in *None Dare Call it Conspiracy*, pp. 54, 55.

33. Gary Allen, *None Dare Call it Conspiracy*. Rossmoor, CA: Concord Press, 1972.

34. Milton Friedman, *Capitalism and Freedom*. University of Chicago Press, 1963.

35. James W. Wardner, *The Planned Destruction of America*. DeBary, FL: Longwood Communications, 1994.

36. *Liberty in the Balance: America, the Fed, and the IRS*. Washington, D.C.: Common Law, Mosaic Media, 1993.

37. Frank Vanderlip, "From Farm Boy to Financier," *Saturday Evening Post*, February 9, 1935. (See also Frank Vanderlip's *From Farm Boy to Financier*. New York: D. Appleton-Century Company, 1935, pp. 210-219 and Eustace Mullins' *The Secrets of the Federal Reserve*. Staunton, VA: Bankers Research Institute, 1993, Library of Congress Catalog Card No. 83-072665.)

38. Frederick Lewis Allen, *Life*, April 25, 1949.

39. *Congressional Record*, December 22, 1913, Vol. 51, part 2, 63rd Congress, 2nd Session, pp. 1446-7.

40. Alfred Aldrich, *The Independent*, July 1914.

41. *Congressional Record*, May 23, 1933.

42. Sheldon Emry, *Billions for the Bankers, Debts for the People*, published by J. A. Thauberger, Regina, Saskatchewan, Canada S4P2Z6, updated 4th ed.

43. Martin Larson, *Tax Revolt*. Greenwich, CT: Devin-Adair, 1985.

44. The Federal Reserve Accountability Act, 1993.

45. Noam Chomsky, *World Orders Old and New*. New York: Columbia University Press, 1996.

46. Barry Goldwater, *With No Apologies*. New York: Morrow, 1979.

47. "From a China Traveler," *New York Times*, August 10, 1973, p. 31.

48. Zbigniew Brzezinski, *Between Two Ages*. New York: The Viking Press, original 1970 edition.

49. Zbigniew Brzezinski, *Between Two Ages: America's Role in the Technetronic Era*. New York: Penguin Books, 1976 edition.

50. Gary Allen, *The Rockefeller File*. Seal Beach, CA: '76 Press, 1976.

51. Congressman Wright Patman, *Money Facts*. House Banking and Currency Committee, 1964, p. 9. As quoted by Eustace Mullins in *The Secrets of the Federal Reserve*, p. 165.

52. G. Edward Griffin, *The Creature from Jekyll Island: A Second Look at the Federal Reserve*. Westlake Village, CA: American Media, 1998.

53. David C. Korten, *When Corporations Rule the World*. San Francisco, CA: Berrett-Koehler Publishers, 2001.

54. *Congressional Record*, March 4, 1846.

55. Christopher Weber, *"...Good as Gold"? How We Lost Our Gold Reserves and Destroyed the Dollar*. Berryville, VA: The George Edward Durrell Foundation, 1988.

56. *Congressional Record*, March 9, 1933.

57. *New York Times*, October 1, 1963, p. 16.

58. Gerry Spence, *Give Me Liberty!* New York: St. Martin's Press, 1998.

59. *Secrets, Lies and Democracy*, part of the *Chomsky Trilogy* series interviewed by David Barsamian. Tucson, AZ: Odonian Press, 1994.

60. Kevin Phillips, *Wealth and Democracy: A Political History of the American Rich*. New York: Broadway Books, 2002.

61. *U.S. News and World Report*, February 21, 1977.

62. "Ronald Reagan," *American Opinion* (now *The New American*), September 1980, p. 99. As quoted in James W. Wardner's *The Planned Destruction of America*, p. 56.

63. Robert Sessler, *To Be God of One World*. Merlin, OR: Let There Be Light Publications, 1992.

64. *Beyond JFK: The Question of Conspiracy*, Danny Schechter and Barbara Kopple, directors. Embassy International Pictures, 1992.

65. Archibald E. Roberts, *Bulletin: Committee to Restore the Constitution*, February 1989, p. 6.

66. *Sierra Times*, April 21, 2002, http://www.sierratimes.com/02/04/22/venable.htm

67. Gordon Phillips, *The Truth Behind the Income Tax*. Westminster, MD: Save-A-Patriot Fellowship.

68. Elliott Roosevelt, ed., *F.D.R.: His Personal Letters 1928-1945*, Vol. I. New York: Duell,

Sloan & Pearce, 1950, pp. 371-373.

69. *The Intimate Papers of Colonel House*, Charles Seymour, ed., 1926, Vol. I, p. 114.

70. Olive Cushing Dwinell, *The Story of Our Money*, 2nd ed. Boston: Forum Publishing Co., 1946.

71. *The Utah Independent*, March 29, 1973. As quoted by Cliff Ford in *Blood, Money, and Greed: The Money Trust Conspiracy*. Beverly Hills, CA: Western Front, Ltd., 1998, pp. 58, 59.

72. William Roth and William Nixon, *The Power to Destroy*. New York: Atlantic Monthly Press, 1999, p. 32.

73. "Address on the Proposed Constitutional Amendment to Grant Income Tax Powers to the Federal Government," March 3, 1910. As quoted by Thomas A. Lane in *The Breakdown of the Old Politics*, pp. 288, 289.

74. Thomas A. Lane, *The Breakdown of the Old Politics*. New Rochelle, NY: Arlington House Publishers, 1974.

75. *Congressional Record*, Volume 54, February 9, 1917, pp. 2947-2948.

76. *The Spotlight*. Washington, D.C.: Liberty Lobby, June 24, 1996, p. 1.

77. *1990 Annual Report: Council on Foreign Relations*. New York: Council on Foreign Relations, 1990, p. 182.

78. *Asia Times*, May 10, 2005, http://www.atimes.com/atimes/Front_Page/GE10Aa02.html

79. G.B. Chisholm, "The Reestablishment of Peacetime Society," *Psychiatry*, IX, February 1946, pp. 7, 9.

80. Rene Wormser, *Foundations: Their Power and Influence*. New York: The Devin-Adair Company, 1958, pp. 142, 143.

81. Treasury Department Decision 2313, issued on March 21, 1916.

82. Curtis B. Dall, *FDR: My Exploited Father-in-Law*. Washington, D.C.: Action Associates, 1970.

83. Mikhail Gorbachev, *Perestroika: New Thinking for Our Country and the World*. New York: Harper and Row, 1988.

84. Rose L. Martin, *Fabian Freeway*. Chicago: Heritage Foundation, 1966.

85. *Handbook for Special Agents*, Section 342.12. As quoted by Irwin Schiff in *The Federal Mafia*. Las Vegas, NV: Freedom Books, 1990, p. 32.

86. *Bulletin of the Committee to Restore the Constitution*, No. 347, January 1991, p. 1. As quoted by Texe Marrs in *Dark Majesty*, pp. 227, 228.

87. Texe Marrs, *Dark Majesty*. Austin, TX: Living Truth Publishers, 1992.

88. Amy and David Goodman, *The Exception to the Rulers: Exposing Oily Politicians, War Profiteers, and the Media that Love Them*. Hyperion, 2004.

89. Walter Cronkite, *A Reporter's Life*, Knopf, 1997.

90. *Into the Buzzsaw: Leading Journalists Expose the Myth of a Free Press*, Kristina Borjesson, ed. Amherst, NY: Prometheus Books, 2002.

91. Noam Chomsky, *Necessary Illusions: Thought Control in Democratic Societies.* Boston, Mass.: South End Press, 1989.

92. Edward Bernays, *Propaganda*. London: Kennikat Press, 1928.

93. Ben H. Bagdikian, *The Media Monopoly*. Boston, MA: Beacon Press, 2000.

94. Benjamin Ginsberg, *The Captive Public*. Basic Books, 1986.

95. *The Panama Deception: Exposing the Cover-up*, Los Angeles, CA: Rhino Home Video, 1993.

96. As quoted by Harry Stein in *TV Guide*, June 13-19, 1992.

97. Michael Sturdza, *Betrayal by Rulers*. Belmont, MA: Western Islands, 1976.

98. *Los Angeles Times*, "Lenin's Aims Like U.N.'s, Thant Says," April 7, 1970.

99. *Higher Education for American Democracy: A Report of the President's* [Truman's] *Commission on Higher Education*, Vol. 1, "Establishing The Goals," 1947, pp. 8, 15-20.

100. "Feeling, Valuing, and the Art of Growing," *NEA Yearbook*, 1977, p. 240.

101. "The Teacher and World Government," NEA Journal, January 1946.

102. William Carr, "On the Waging of Peace," NEA Journal, October 1947, p. 496.

103. William L. Shirer, *The Rise and Fall of the Third Reich*. New York: Simon and Schuster, 1960.

104. UNESCO, *In the Classroom With Children Under Thirteen Years of Age*, vol. 5, p. 9. As quoted by Robert Sessler in *To Be God of One World*, p. 115.

105. *Congressional Record*, March 20, 1953.

106. *Propaganda and the Public Mind*, a collection of Chomsky interviews by David Barsamian. Cambridge, MA: South End Press, 2001.

107. Dennis Laurence Cuddy, *The Road to Socialism and the New World Order*. Highland City, Florida: Florida Pro Family Forum, 1995.

108. Sam Lambert, NEA Journal, December 1967.

109. George Fischer, former NEA president, speaking before an NEA assembly on July 3, 1970. As quoted by Dennis Laurence Cuddy in *NEA: The Grab for Power*. Oklahoma City, OK: Hearthstone Publishing, 2000, p. 28.

110. Larry Bates, *The New Economic Disorder*. Orlando, Florida: Creation House Books, 1994.

111. Carroll Quigley, *The Anglo-American Establishment*. New York: Books in Focus, 1981 (originally written in 1949).

112. Dennis Laurence Cuddy, *Secret Records Revealed: The Men, the Money and the Methods Behind the New World Order*. Oklahoma City, OK: Hearthstone Publishing, Ltd., 1999.

113. Thomas and Kathleen Schaeper, *Cowboys Into Gentlemen: Rhodes Scholars, Oxford, and the Creation of an American Elite*. Oxford: Berghahn Books, 1998.

114. David McGowan, *Derailing Democracy: The America the Media Don't Want You to See*. Monroe, ME: Common Courage Press, 2000.

115. *Congressional Record*, April 28, 1972.

116. *World Goodwill Newsletter*, 1989, No. 4, pp. 1, 3.

117. Robert Mueller, *The New Genesis: Shaping a Global Spirituality*. New York: Image Books, 1984.

118. John J. Wright, *National Patriotism In Papal Teaching*. Westminster, MD: The Newman Press, 1942.

119. *America* (Catholic periodical), January 4, 1941, Vol. 64, p. 343.

120. Malachi Martin, *The Keys of This Blood: The Struggle for World Dominion Between Pope*

John Paul II, Mikhail Gorbachev and the Capitalist West. New York: Simon and Schuster, 1990.

121. *Time*, March 16, 1942, pp. 44-48.

122. Norman Hill and Doniver Lund, *If The Churches Want World Peace.* New York: The Macmillan Company, 1958.

123. Peter DeRosa, *Vicars of Christ: The Dark Side of the Papacy.* New York: Crown Publishers, Inc., 1988.

124. F. Cavalli, S. J., *La Civilta Catholica* (a Jesuit organ published at Rome), April 1948.

125. *The Fatima Crusader.* Constable, NY: Servants of Jesus and Mary. Issue 38, Fall 1991, pp. 55, 57.

126. *The Catholic World*, August, 1871, p. 589.

127. http://edition.cnn.com/2004/WORLD/europe/01/01/pope.ny.ap/

128. Penny Lernoux, *The People of God: The Struggle for World Catholicism.* New York: Penguin Books, 1989.

129. "Time is Running Out for Bush, Too," *Guardian Weekly*, an insert of the *Washington Post*, January 6, 1991, p. 14.

130. President George Bush Sr., State of the Union address, January 29, 1991.

131. Edwin A. Sherman, *The Engineer Corps of Hell*, 1883, starting on p. 118. See also *Congressional Record*, House Bill #1523, contested election case of Eugene C. Bonniwell against T. S. Butler, February 15, 1913, pp. 3215-16.

132. Malcolm C. Duncan, *Masonic Ritual and Monitor.* New York: David McKay, 1986.

133. J. Blanchard, *Scottish Rite Masonry Illustrated: The Complete Ritual of the Ancient and Accepted Scottish Rite.* Chicago: Charles T. Powner, 1979.

134. H.L. Haywood, *The Great Teachings of Masonry.* Richmond, VA: Macoy, 1971.

135. *Holy Bible: Masonic Edition*, Cyclopedic Index, 1951.

136. Gore Vidal, *Perpetual War for Perpetual Peace.* New York: Thunder's Mouth Press/Nation Books, 2002.

137. Dr. William Sargant, *The Battle for the Mind: A Physiology of Conversion and Brainwashing.* New York: Harper and Row Publishers, 1957.

138. *Atlantic Magazine,* October 1987. As quoted by James W. Wardner in *The Planned Destruction of America,* p. 70.

139. Dr. Harold Ruggs, *The Great Technology,* 1933.

140. Donald S. McAlvany, *Toward A New World Order.* Phoenix, AZ: Western Pacific Publishing Co., 1992.

141. Attorney General Janet Reno, December 10, 1993 (Associated Press).

142. Sarah Brady, Chairman, Handgun Control, Inc., *The National Educator,* January 1994, p. 3.

143. Charles J. Hanley, "World Gun Control Is U.N. Body's Aim," *Washington Times,* May 24, 1994, p. A1.

144. From combined dispatches, "U.S. OKs Study of U.N. Gun Control," Ibid.

145. Noah Webster, *Examination into the Leading Principles of the Federal Constitution,* 1787.

146. James Madison, *Federalist Paper* #48.

147. Sharif M. Aboullah, *The Power of One: Authentic Leadership in Turbulent Times.* Philadelphia, PA: New Society Publishers, 1995.

148. H.G. Wells, *The New World Order,* 1939 (ISBN: 0837173183).

149. Johanna Michaelsen, *Like Lambs to the Slaughter.* Eugene, OR: Harvest House Publishers, 1989.

150. Garrett Hardin, "Parenting: Right or Privilege?" *Science,* July 31, 1970, p. 427.

151. Julian Simon, *Taking Sides: Clashing Views on Controversial Global Issues.* James Harf and Mark Lombardi, eds. Guilford, CT: McGraw-Hill/Dushkin, 2001.

152. Bahgat Elmadi and Adel Rifaat, "Interview with Jacques-Yves Cousteau," *The UNESCO Courier* (notice that this is a U.N. publication), November 1991.

153. Jack Nelson, *Population and Survival.* Englewood Cliffs, NJ: Prentice Hall, 1972.

154. Bertrand Russell, *The Impact of Science on Society.* New York: Simon and Schuster, 1953.

155. From hearings before a House Subcommittee of the Committee on Appropriations, "Department of Defense Appropriations for 1970." As quoted by William Blum in *Rogue State,* p. 119.

156. William Blum, *Rogue State: A Guide to the World's Only Superpower*. Monroe, ME: Common Courage Press, 2000.

157. *The Men Who Killed Kennedy*, a television series produced by Nigel Turner, appearing on the History Channel for the first time in November 1995.

158. Reuters, February 28, 2002.

159. Amnesty International, "United States of America--Rights for All," October 1998. As quoted by David McGowan in *Derailing Democracy*, p. 134.

160. *CounterPunch*, "America's Private Gulag," January 1997. As quoted in Ibid., p. 136.

161. Michael Moore, *Downsize This*. Perennial; Harper, 1997.

162. House Permanent Select Committee on Intelligence, IC 21: *The Intelligence Community in the 21st Century*. Washington, D.C.: Government Printing Office, April 9, 1996.

163. *New York Times*, November 14, 2002.

164. James Bovard, *Terrorism and Tyranny: Trampling Freedom, Justice, and Peace to Rid the World of Evil*. New York: Palgrave Macmillan, 2003.

165. http://www.newsmax.com/archives/articles/2003/11/20/185048.shtml

166. *Washington Times*, September 18, 2001.

167. http://www.cnn.com/2002/LAW/08/columns/fl.ramasastry.detainees/

168. *The Nation*, May 31, 1999.

169. House of Representatives, *Investigation into the Activities of Federal Law Enforcement Agencies Toward the Branch Davidians*, Report 104-749, August 2, 1996. Washington, D.C.: U.S. Government Printing Office, 1996.

170. *McAlvany Intelligence Advisor*, Durango, CO, May-June, 1994.

171. Cliff Kincaid, *Global Taxes for World Government*. Lafayette, LA: Huntington House Publishers, 1997.

172. "Next Hot Spot for UN Troops--the United States," *San Francisco Chronicle*, October 7, 1993.

173. *The Spotlight*, November 21, 1994.

174. *Free American.* Bingham, NM, May 2000, p. 16.

175. Linda Thompson, *America Under Siege.* Indianapolis, IN: American Justice Federation, 1994.

176. Ellen Willis, *The Nation*, November 14, 1981. As quoted by Dennis Laurence Cuddy in *Secret Records Revealed*, p. 129.

177. David McGowan, *Understanding the F-Word: American Fascism and the Politics of Illusion.* San Jose, CA: Writers Club Press, 2001.

178. Taylor Caldwell, *Ceremony of the Innocent.* Greenwich, CT: Fawcett Books, 1976.

179. *The Independent*, April 3, 1902. From an article called "The Next Step: A Benevolent Feudalism," by W.J. Ghent (who at one time had been the editor of *The American Fabian*, a paper that pushed for socialism in America as a major leap toward world government).

180. *Look* magazine, January 16, 1962.

181. David Ellis, "Gorby, The New Age Guru?" *Time*, May 18, 1990.

182. Alice Bailey, *Externalization of the Hierarchy.* New York: Lucis Publishing Company (a division of Lucis Trust, a United Nations NGO), 1957.

183. *Bulletin.* Fort Collins, CO: The Committee to Restore the Constitution, 1978, p. 1. As quoted by A. Ralph Epperson in *The Unseen Hand*, p. 257.

184. Charles A. Beard, *Saturday Evening Post*, October 4, 1947.

185. R.E. McMaster Jr., *The Power of Total Perspective.* A.N. International Inc., 1994.

186. Charles A. Willoughby and John Chamberlain, *MacArthur: 1941-1951.* New York: McGraw-Hill, 1954.

187. Douglas MacArthur, *Reminiscences.* New York: McGraw-Hill, 1964.

188. General Mark W. Clark, *From the Danube to the Yalu.* New York: Harper and Bros., 1954.

189. Walter LaFeber, *America, Russia, and the Cold War, 1945-1996.* New York: McGraw-Hill, 1997.

190. *American Public Opinion and Postwar Security Commitments*, p. 10. As quoted by James Perloff in *The Shadows of Power*, p. 90.

191. "A Conversation with George Kennan," interviewed by George Urban, *Encounter*, September 1976.

192. John Stormer, *None Dare Call it Treason*. Florissant, MO: Liberty Bell Press, 1998.

193. Charles L. Mee Jr., *The Marshall Plan*. New York: Simon and Schuster, 1984.

194. Colonel James A. Donovan, *Militarism, U.S.A.* New York: Charles Scribner's Sons, 1970.

195. William F. Buckley Jr. and L. Brent Bozell, *McCarthy and His Enemies*. Chicago: Henry Regnery Company, 1954.

196. David Brion Davis, *The Fear of Conspiracy*. Ithaca and London: Cornell Paperbacks, 1971.

197. Anastasio Somoza, *Nicaragua Betrayed*. Belmont, MA: Western Islands, 1980.

198. *What Uncle Sam Really Wants*, part of the *Chomsky Trilogy* series interviewed by David Barsamian. Tucson, AZ: Odonian Press, 1994.

199. *New York Times*, October 17, 1984, pp. 1, 12.

200. *New York Times*, October 19, 1984, p. 8; *Covert Action Information Bulletin*, Washington, D.C., No. 22, Fall 1984, p. 28.

201. "Dulles Outlines World Peace Plan," *New York Times*, October 28, 1939.

202. Susan George, *How the Other Half Dies: The Real Reasons for World Hunger*. Totowa, NJ: Rowman & Allanheld, 1977.

203. Michael Parenti, *Against Empire: A Brilliant Expose of the Brutal Realities of U.S. Global Domination*. San Francisco: City Lights Books, 1995.

204. Zbigniew Brzezinski, *The Grand Chessboard: American Primacy and its Geostrategic Imperatives*. New York: Basic Books, 1997.

205. Thomas L. Friedman, "A Manifesto for the Fast World," *New York Times Magazine*, March 28, 1999.

206. "Pentagon's Planning Guidance for the Fiscal Years 1994-1999," *New York Times*, March 8, 1992, p. 14.

207. *The New American*, November 29, 1993.

208. Bob Woodward and Carl Bernstein, *The Final Days: The Classic Behind-the-Scenes Account of Richard Nixon's Dramatic Last Days in the White House*. Touchstone Books, 1994.

209. Arianna Huffington, *Pigs at the Trough: How Corporate Greed and Political Corruption are Undermining America.* New York: Crown Publishers, 2003.

210. R.C. Longworth, *Chicago Tribune*, March 27, 1994, in a review of a book entitled *Global Dreams: Imperial Corporations and the New World Order*, by Richard Barnet and John Cavanagh.

211. Richard J. Barnet and Ronald E. Muller, *Global Reach: The Power of the Multinational Corporation.* New York: Simon and Schuster, 1974.

212. Sir James Goldsmith, a member of the European Parliament, from his testimony to the Senate Commerce Committee, November 15, 1994. As quoted by Dennis Laurence Cuddy in *The Road to Socialism and the New World Order*, p. 48.

213. Charles Derber, *Corporation Nation: How Corporations are Taking Over Our Lives and What We Can Do About It.* New York: St. Martin's Griffin, 1998.

214. *USA Today*, December 3, 1999.

215. Mark Hertsgaard, *On Bended Knee: The Press and the Reagan Presidency.* Farrar Straus & Giroux, 1988.

216. William Blum, *Killing Hope: U.S. Military and CIA Interventions Since World War II.* Monroe, ME: Common Courage Press, 1995.

217. *Los Angeles Times*, July 18, 1993.

218. Greg Palast, *The Best Democracy Money Can Buy: An Investigative Reporter Exposes the Truth About Globalization, Corporate Cons, and High Finance Fraudsters.* London: Pluto Press, 2002.

219. "International Debt, the Banks and U.S. Foreign Policy," Staff Report of the Subcommittee on Foreign Economic Policy of the Senate Committee on Foreign Relations, Washington, D.C., August 1977, p. 66.

220. "COINTELPRO: The FBI's Covert Action Programs against American Citizens," Final Report of the Senate Committee to Study Governmental Operations with Respect to Intelligence Activities, Book III, April 23, 1976.

221. John Ashcroft, "Remarks of Attorney General John Ashcroft," Justice Department Office of Public Affairs, May 30, 2002. As quoted by James Bovard in *Terrorism and Tyranny*, 148.

222. Warren Bennis and Philip Slater, *The Temporary Society: Under the Impact of Accelerating Change.* San Francisco, CA: Jossey-Bass Publishers, 1998.

223. Benjamin Bloom, *All Our Children Learning*. New York: McGraw-Hill Book Company, 1981.

224. Harold Drummon (former president of ASCD--Association for Supervision and Curriculum Development), "Leadership for Human Change," *Educational Leadership*, December 1964, p. 147.

225. James Guines, former Associate School Superintendent for Washington, D.C., *Washington Post*, August 1, 1977, p. 1.

226. David Krathwohl, Benjamin Bloom, and Bertram Massia, *Taxonomy of Educational Objectives, The Classification of Educational Goals, Handbook II: Affective Domain*. McKay Publishers, 1956.

227. Jon Christian Ryter, *Whatever Happened to America?* Tampa, FL: Hallberg Publishing, 2001.

228. *Global Mandate: Pedagogy for Peace*, Philip Vander Velde and Hyung-Chan Kim, eds. Bellingham, WA: Bellwether Press, 1985.

229. John Goodlad, in the Foreword to *Schooling for a Global Age*. James Becker, ed. New York: McGraw-Hill, 1979.

230. President George Bush Sr., while announcing America 2000 at the White House on April 18, 1991. *America 2000: An Education Strategy*. Washington, D.C.: U.S. Department of Education, 1991, pp. 50, 51, 55.

231. Samuel Blumenfeld, *N.E.A.: Trojan Horse in American Education*. Boise, ID: Paradigm Co., 1984.

232. Thomas Sowell, "Indoctrinating the Children," *Forbes*, February 1, 1993, p. 65.

233. James Bamford, *Body of Secrets: Anatomy of the Ultra-Secret National Security Agency*. New York: Doubleday, 2001.

234. Winston Churchill, *The World Crisis*. New York: Scribner's Sons, 1949.

235. British War Cabinet Minutes, August 19, 1941, CAB65 84 (41), British Public Record Office.

236. John Toland, *Infamy: Pearl Harbor and its Aftermath*. New York: Doubleday, 1982.

237. Robert A. Theobald, *The Final Secret of Pearl Harbor*. Old Greenwich, CT: Devin-Adair, 1954.

238. Walter LaFeber, *The American Age: U.S. Foreign Policy at Home and Abroad*. New York:

W.W. Norton and Company, 1994.

239. U.S. Senate Committee on Foreign Relations, 90th Congress, 2nd Session, 1968.

240. Assistant Attorney General Michael Chertoff, Associated Press, June 1, 2002.

241. Senator Richard Shelby, *San Francisco Chronicle*, June 3, 2002.

242. Senator Arlen Specter, *Daily News* (New York), June 6, 2002.

243. *The New American*, Vol. 18, No. 1, January 14, 2002, p. 24.

244. Secretary of Defense William Cohen, speaking before the Senate Armed Services Committee in February 1999. As quoted by Dennis Laurence Cuddy in *The Globalists*, p. 251.

245. Associated Press, September 16, 2001.

246. *Insight*, August 26, 2002.

247. *New York Times*, September 29, 2001.

248. *The Oregonian*, October 2, 2001.

249. *Congressional Record*, October 12, 2001.

250. John Gerard Ruggie, *Winning the Peace: America and World Order in the New Era.* New York: Columbia University Press, 1996.

251. *New York Times*, February 3, 1992, p. 8.

252. Joseph Trento, Introduction to *Forbidden Truth: U.S.-Taliban Secret Oil Diplomacy and the Failed Hunt for Bin Laden* by Jean-Charles Brisard and Guillanne Dasquie. New York: Thunder's Mouth Press/Nation Books, 2002.

253. *New York Times*, March 5, 2001.

254. Gurudas, *Treason: The New World Order.* San Rafael, CA: Cassandra Press, 1994.

255. *Education for International Understanding in American Schools: Suggestions and Recommendations*, NEA publication, 1948.

256. Paul Lewis, "As the U.N.'s Armies Grow, the Talk is of Preventing War," *New York Times*, March 1, 1992.

257. U.N. Secretary General Kofi Annan, during his annual report to the U.N. General Assembly

on September 20, 1999.

258. James Garrison, president of the Gorbachev Foundation/USA, "One World, Under Gorby" (Gorbachev), *San Francisco Weekly*, May 31-June 6, 1995.

259. Joan Veon, *The United Nations Global Straitjacket*. Oklahoma City, OK: Hearthstone Publishing, 2000.

260. James Landale, "Blair Sees New World Order in Kosovo Conflict," London *Times*, April 12, 1999.

261. Interim Agreement for Peace and Self-Government in Kosovo, Appendix B: Status of Multi National Military Implementation Force, Articles 6-10, 15-17, February 23, 1999. As quoted by David McGowan in *Derailing Democracy*, pp. 217, 218.

262. "Thank Goodness for a Villain," *Newsweek*, September 16, 1996, p. 43.

263. http://www.abcnews.go.com/sections/nightline/DailyNews/pnac_030310.html See also http://www.emjournal.pwp.blueyonder.co.uk/aaadec045.html

264. http://www.usatoday.com/news/washington/2003-09-17-bush-saddam_x.htm

265. http://www.defenselink.mil/transcripts/2003/tr20030509-depsecdef0223.html

266. Senator Russell Feingold (D-WI), September, 1998. As quoted by David McGowan in *Derailing Democracy*, p. 190.

267. Leonard Cole, *Clouds of Secrecy: The Army's Germ Warfare Tests Over Populated Areas*. Maryland, 1990, chapter 1.

268. *San Francisco Examiner*, December 22, 23, 1976; September 17, 79; October 19, 1980.

269. *Baltimore Sun*, August 15, 1980.

270. *Washington Post*, June 9, 1980.

271. *San Francisco Chronicle*, October 14, 1980.

272. *Washington Post*, December 5, 1984.

273. *San Francisco Chronicle*, December 17, 1979; December 29, 1980.

274. *U.S. Army Chemical Corps, Summary of Major Events and Problems of Fiscal Year 1959*

275. *San Francisco Chronicle*, December 4, 1979.

276. *Protocols of the Illuminati* (more commonly known as *Protocols of the Learned Elders of Zion*). This document first surfaced publicly in 1905, and was later translated into English by Victor Marsden, circa 1910, in London, England. The *Protocols* excerpts cited herein come from a 1975 publication of this document by the Christian Nationalist Crusade, Los Angeles, CA.

277. http://www.jewsagainstzionism.com

278. *La Verite Israelite*, vol. 5, p. 74.

279. *Kabbalah*, I, 160a, Pranaitis Translation, pp. 74, 75.

280. Menachem Begin, at a Tel Aviv Conference, October 28, 1956. As quoted in the *South African Observer*, June 1977.

281. *The Washington Star*, June 15, 1981, in a column by Georgie Anne Geyer.

282. *CounterPunch*, December 28, 2002.

283. Captain Montgomery Scyler, "American Expeditionary Forces, Siberia," *Military Intelligence Report of Captain Montgomery Scyler*, National Archives, March 1, 1919. Declassified September 21, 1958, pp. 2, 3.

284. U.S. State Department Report, Foreign Relations, 1918, Russia, Vol. 11, p. 240.

285. "Revolutionary Radicalism, its History, Purpose, and Tactics, with an Exposition and Discussion of the Steps Being Taken and Required to Curb it," report of the Joint Legislative Committee investigating Seditious Activities, filed April 24, 1920 in the Senate of the State of New York.

286. Congressman Charles Lindbergh, during a speech he gave in Des Moines, Iowa, on September 11, 1941.

287. Secretary of State John Foster Dulles. As quoted by Donald Neff in *Fallen Pillars: U.S. Policy Towards Palestine and Israel Since 1945*. Institute for Palestine Studies, 2002, p.99.

288. William Fulbright, U.S. Senator and Chairman of the U.S. Foreign Relations committee, while speaking before a national audience on ABC's Face the Nation, October 7, 1973.

289. Patrick Buchanan. As quoted in the *St. Louis Post Dispatch*, October 20, 1990.

290. Ian Buruma, *New York Times*, August 31, 2003.

291. Admiral Thomas Moorer, Chairman of the U.S. Joint Chiefs of Staff under Ronald Reagan. As quoted in the *Jerusalem Post*, September 27, 2000.

292. *America and the World Revolution and Other Lectures.* New York: Oxford University Press, 1962. As quoted by David McGowan in *Derailing Democracy.*

293. Merle Miller, *Plain Speaking: An Oral Biography of Harry S. Truman.* New York: Berkeley Publishing, 1974.

294. *New York Times*, December 7, 2001.

295. http://larouchein2004.net/pages/other/2001/0101116ashcrofttest.htm

296. *San Francisco Chronicle*, September 8, 2002.

297. *Washington Post*, August 21, 2002.

298. ABC News, March 12, 2003.

299. Molly Ivans and Lou Dubose, *Bushwhacked: Life in George W. Bush's America.* New York: Random House, 2003.

300. NBC's Meet the Press, August 31, 2003.

301. NBC's Meet the Press, February 8, 2004.

302. Kelly Patricia O'Meara, "Rumsfeld Inherits Financial Mess," *Insight*, August 2001.

303. "The Final Frontier: The U.S. Military's Drive to Dominate Space," *Colorado Springs Independent*, December 13, 2001.

304. Hans Schmidt, Maverick Marine: *General Smedley D. Butler and the Contradictions of American Military History.* Lexington: University Press of Kentucky, 1987.

305. Alistair Cooke, "Letter from America: The Pursuit of Self-Determination," http://news.bbc.co.uk/hi/english/world/letter_from_america/newsid_288000/2882_50.stm

306. Chalmers Johnson, *The Sorrows of Empire: Militarism, Secrecy, and the End of the Republic.* New York: Metropolitan Books, Henry Holt and Company, 2004.

307. CNN, December 18, 2000.

308. Bob Woodward, *Bush At War.* New York: Simon and Schuster, 2002.

309. J. Edgar Hoover, *The Elks* magazine, August 1956.

310. As aired on C-Span, September 14, 2001.

311. *U.S. News and World Report*, May 25, 1956.

312. BBC News, March 22, 2004, http://news.bbc.co.uk/2/hi/americas/3559153.stm

313. James Bovard, *Lost Rights: The Destruction of American Liberty*. New York: St. Martin's Griffin, 1995.

314. Howard Zinn, *A People's History of the United States*. New York: HarperCollins, 2003.

315. *Defense News*, April 8, 1991.

316. *U.S. Army Training Manual* No. 2000-25, 1928.

317. *IRS In Action*. Sherwood Communications Associates, 1983 (ISBN: 0-914877-00-3).

318. John Steinbacher, *Bitter Harvest*. Educator Publications, 1970 (ISBN: 091355801X).

319. A. Ralph Epperson, *The New World Order*. Tucson, AZ: Publius Press, 1990.

320. John Hargrave, *Montagu Norman*. New York: Greystone Press, 1942.

321. Bill Moyers, Bill Moyers Journal (PBS), "The World of David Rockefeller," February 7, 1980.

322. James K. Fitzpatrick, *The Wanderer* (Catholic paper), November 18, 1993.

323. *Congressional Record*, February 21, 1958, p. 2560.

324. U.N. Conference on Human Settlements, Habitat I, Vancouver, British Columbia, Canada, May 31-June 11, 1976. See http://www.undp.org/un/habitat/back/vp-intr.html

325. Senate Committee on Veterans' Affairs, "Is Military Research Hazardous to Veterans' Health? Lessons Spanning Half a Century," December 8, 1994, p. 5.

326. Martin Luther King Jr., from a speech entitled "A Time to Break the Silence," which he delivered at the Riverside Church in New York City, April 4, 1967.

327. Dr. George Sylvester Counts, *Dare the School Build a New Social Order?* Southern Illinois University Press, 1982, pp. 28, 29. (Note: This book was originally published in 1932.)

328. *A Catholic Home Encyclopedia*. Chicago: The Catholic Press, Inc., 1954.

329. http://www.state.gov/r/pa/ei/bgn/3819.htm

330. Kenneth Cauthen, *Christian Biopolitics: A Credo & Strategy for the Future*. New York: Abingdon Press, 1971.

331. William F. Jasper, *The United Nations Exposed*. Appleton, WI: John Birch Society, 2001.

332. Daniel Sitarz, ed., *Agenda 21: The Earth Summit Strategy to Save the Planet*. Boulder, CO: EarthPress, 1993.

333. *The Humanist*, January-February 1972.

334. *New York Times*, March 27, 1990.

335. Robert James Bidinotto, "What is the Truth About Global Warming?," *Reader's Digest*, February 1990.

336. Alexander King and Bertrand Schneider, *The First Global Revolution*, A Report by the Council of the Club of Rome. New York: Pantheon Books, 1991.

337. Donnela H. and Dennis L. Meadows, et al, The Limits to Growth: A Report for the Club of Rome's Project on the Predicament of Mankind. New York: Universe Books, 1972.

338. Herman Kahn and Anthony J. Wiener, "World Federal Government," essay in *Uniting the Peoples and Nations: Readings in World Federalism*, compiled by Barbara Walker. Washington, D.C.: World Federalist Association, 1993.

339. *Wall Street Journal*, January 10, 1995.

340. Eugene *Register Guard* newspaper, December 5, 2002.

341. Noreena Hertz, *The Silent Takeover: Global Capitalism and the Death of Democracy*. New York: The Free Press, 2002.

342. Lester W. Grau, "Hydrocarbons and a New Strategic Region: The Caspian Sea and Central Asia," *Military Review*, May-June, 2001.

343. *Lenin Collected works*, Vol. 41.

344. Michael Ben-Zohar, *Ben-Gurion, A Biography*. New York: Delacorte, 1978.

345. *Washington Times*, September 7, 2001.

346. *WorldNetDaily*, December 10,2003, http://www.wnd.com/news/article.asp?ARTICLE_ID=36064

347. Lyle Schaller, *The Change Agent*, Abigon Press, 1972.

348. Catherine Bertini, speaking at the Beijing Woman's Conference, September 1995, http://www.sierratimes.com/cgi-bin/ikonboard/topic.cgi?forum=14&topic=98

349. Madeleine Albright, interview on CBS's 60 Minutes, May 6, 1996.

350. W.J. Ghent, *Our Benevolent Feudalism*, 1902.

351. *New York Times*, January 20, 1906.

352. CNBC-TV, October 8, 1996.

353. *New York Times*, October 12, 2001.

354. *New Yorker*, April 2002.

355. http://www.cfr.org/publication.php?id=4379

356. London *Times*, July 17, 2002.

357. http://www.cbsnews.com/stories/2002/05/17/attack/main509434.shtml

358. http://www.whitehouse.gov/news/releases/2001/11/20011101-12.html

359. http://www.cbsnews.com/stories/2001/07/26/national/main303601.shtml

360. http://www.pbs.org/newshour/updates/intelligence_09-18-02.html

361. http://www.whitehouse.gov/news/releases/2001/09/20010920-8.html

362. *Miami Herald*, April 30, 2002. See also *Los Angeles Times*, April 22, 2002.

363. *Washington Times*, May 22, 2002.

364. *WorldNetDaily*, January 6, 2003.

365. *Capitol Hill Blue*, January 2, 2003.

366. *Los Angeles Times*, September 16, 2001.

367. ABC News, September 17, 2001.

368. Associated Press, August 19, 2002.

369. *Washington Post*, October 1, 2002.

370. http://www.whitehouse.gov/news/releases/2002/03/text/20020313-8.html

371. http://www.defenselink.mil/news/Apr2002/t04082002_t407genm.html

372. *New York Times*, September 30, 2001; *Tampa Tribune*, October 5, 2001; London *Times*, November 25, 2002; *Minneapolis Star Tribune*, August 16, 2002.

373. *Vanity Fair*, October 2003.
374. *San Jose Mercury News*, March 19, 1998.

375. BBC News, July 30, 1999.

376. Steve Bonta, *Inside the United Nations: A Critical Look at the UN*. Appleton, WI: JBS, 2003.

377. *Guardian*, March 28, 1999.

378. http://www.foxnews.com/story/0%2C2933%2C75945%2C00.html

379. Richard Nixon, *Foreign Affairs*, October 1967.

380. http://www.sierratimes.com/02/04/11/farrell.htm

381. Rafael Eitan, chief of staff of the Israel Defense Forces, *New York Times*, April 14, 1983.

382. U.S. Brigadier General James J. David, *Hizbollah*, March 1, 2003.

383. http://www.ipsnews.net/interna.asp?idnews=23083

384. *American Hebrew*, September 8, 1920.

385. *Ha'aretz*, April 5, 2003.

386. http://www.counterpunch.org/hughes1018.html

387. *Ha'aretz*, September 30, 2002.

388. *Forward*, April 4, 2003.

389. http://www.counterpunch.org/faruqui1126.html

390. http://www.mfa.gov.il/MFA/MFAArchive/1990_1999/1993/12/Fundamental%20 Agreement%20-%20Israel-Holy%20See

391. David Ben-Gurion, former Israeli prime minister, *Jewish Chronicle* (London), December 16, 1949.

392. David Ben-Gurion, *Look* magazine, January 16, 1962.

393. Rabbi Meir Kahane, *Jewish Press* (Brooklyn, New York), November 9, 1973.

394. *Jewish World* (London), February 9, 1883.

395. http://www.sltrib.com/2004/Jun/06252004/commenta/commenta.asp

396. Kevin Danaher, *10 Reasons to Abolish the IMF and World Bank*. New York: Seven Stories Press, 2004.

397. Katharine Graham, from a 1988 speech she delivered to CIA recruits at CIA headquarters, http://www.counterpunch.org/graham.html

398. http://politics.guardian.co.uk/iraq/comment/0,12956,1036687,00.html

399. http://www.fortwayne.com/mld/journalgazette/news/nation/9949251.htm

400. http://www.pcworld.com/news/article/0,aid,118431,00.asp

401. http://www.reuters.co.uk/newsPackageArticle.jhtml?type=topNews&storyID=614477&section=news

402. http://www.nytimes.com/2003/12/02/opinion/02KRUG.html

403. L. Fletcher Prouty, *The Secret Team: The CIA and its Allies in Control of the United States and the World*. Ballantine Books, 1974 (ISBN: 0345237765).

404. http://bmj.bmjjournals.com/cgi/content/full/328/7454/1458

405. http://www.interventionmag.com/cms/modules.php?op=modload&name=News&file=article&sid=830

406. http://usinfo.state.gov/xarchives/display.html?p=washfile-english&y=2004&m=November&x=20041118153831EneerG0.9969141&t=livefeeds/wf-latest.html

407. http://news.independent.co.uk/world/politics/story.jsp?story=588521

408. http://www.washingtontimes.com/national/20041202-122549-7793r.htm

409. http://www.washingtonpost.com/wp-dyn/articles/A53452-2004Dec9.html

410. *Congressional Record*, May, 5, 1975.

411. See http://www.seniorjournal.com/NEWS/Opinion/4-12-15BushSelling.htm

412. Aldous Huxley, *Brave New World Revisited.* New York: Bantam Books, 1959.

413. John D. Marks, *The Search for the Manchurian Candidate: The CIA and Mind Control.* New York: W.W. Norton & Co., 1991.

414. Manly P. Hall, *The Secret Destiny of America.* Los Angeles: Philosophical Research Society, 2000 ed.

415. Mark Crispin Miller, *Cruel and Unusual: Bush/Cheney's New World Order.* New York: W.W. Norton & Co., 2004.

416. Gary Kah, *En Route to Global Occupation.* Lafayette, LA: Huntington House Publishers, 1992.

417. Thomas R. Dye and L. Harmon Zeigler, *The Irony of Democracy: An Uncommon Introduction to American Politics.* Harcourt, 1999, 11th ed. (ISBN: 0155058002).

418. Edward Mandell House, *Philip Dru: Administrator.* IndyPublish.com, 2003 ed.

419. http://www.boston.com/news/globe/editorial_opinion/oped/articles/2004/06/09/the_torturers_amo ng_us/

420. http://news.independent.co.uk/world/americas/story.jsp?story=547719

421. http://www.suntimes.com/output/orourke/cst-edt-rour08.html

422. See Ted Rall's *Gas War: The Truth Behind the American Occupation of Afghanistan* (ISBN: 0595261752).

423. See James Bovard's *"feeling your pain": The Explosion and Abuse of Government Power in the Clinton-Gore Years.* New York: St. Martin's Press, 2000, pp. 125, 126.

424. BBC News Online, September 18, 2001; *Guardian*, September 22, 2001.

425. See Dan Briody's *The Iron Triangle: Inside the Secret World of the Carlyle Group* (ISBN: 0471281085).

426. http://www.guardian.co.uk/september11/story/0,11209,601550,00.html

427. http://www.guardian.co.uk/september11/oneyearon/story/0,12361,784541,00.html

428. See, for example, http://www.cnn.com/SPECIALS/2001/trade.center/victims/main.html

429. *Portugal News*, August 3 and 8, 2002.

430.   Newsday.com,   September   23,   2001,
http://www.newsday.com/ny-uspent232380681sep23.story

431. http://msnbc.msn.com/id/4881058/

432. Robert Byrd, *The Congressional Record*, March 3, 2004, p. S 2072.

433. http://www.nysun.com/article/6763

434. CNN, October 29, 2004, http://transcripts.cnn.com/TRANSCRIPTS/0410/29/lkl.01.html

435. *Washington Post*, September 24, 2001.

436. http://www.townhall.com/news/politics/200312/FOR20031217d.shtml

437. http://www.newsmax.com/archives/articles/2003/7/14/161446.shtml

438. Adolf Hitler, *Mein Kampf*. Ralph Mannheim, ed., New York: Mariner Books, 1999, p. 65.

439. *USA Today*, January 2, 2004,
http://www.usatoday.com/news/politicselections/nation/2004-01-02-god-bush_x.htm

440. http://www.au.org/site/News2?page=NewsArticle&id=6949&abbr=cs_

441. George Grant, *The Changing of the Guard: Biblical Principles for Political Action*. Dominion Press, 1987 (ISBN: 0930462270).

442. *Report of the Special Committee on the Termination of the National Emergency*, United States Senate, November 19, 1973, Report 93-549.

443. Representative James Traficant, *Congressional Record*, March 17, 1993, Vol. 33, p. H-1303.

444. *St. Petersburg Times*, February 16, 2001,
http://www.times.spb.ru/archive/times/645/opinion/o_2201.htm

445. http://www.capitolhillblue.com/artman/publish/article_4687.shtml

446. *Guardian*, January 2, 2005,
http://www.guardian.co.uk/worldlatest/story/0,1280,-4706525,00.html

447. See Luigi DiFonzo's *St. Peter's Banker*, 1983 (ISBN: 0531098893).

448. *USA Today*, May 29, 1998.

449. *The Collected Works of Abraham Lincoln*, Roy P. Basler, ed., Volume I. Rutgers University Press, 1990, p. 109.

450. http://www.washingtonpost.com/wp-dyn/articles/A11910-2004Nov25.html?sub=AR

451. http://www.motherjones.com/news/outfront/2004/03/02_400.html

452. http://www.worldnetdaily.com/news/article.asp?ARTICLE_ID=32572

453. Terry Galanoy, *Charge It: Inside the Credit Card Conspiracy*. New York: G.P. Putnam's Sons, 1980.

454. Manly P. Hall, *The Secret Teachings of All Ages*. Jeremy P. Tarcher, 2003 ed. (ISBN: 1585422509).

455. Associated Press, February 14, 2005,
http://www.canada.com/national/nationalpost/news/story.html?id=82ea71ef-62f8-4813-941e-dd3f51cdfff4

456. http://www.cbsnews.com/stories/2002/01/29/eveningnews/main325985.shtml

457. *Washington Post*, December 24, 2002,
http://www.washingtonpost.com/ac2/wp-dyn/A31589-2002Dec23

458. David Ovason, *The Secret Architecture of Our Nation's Capital: The Masons and the Building of Washington, D.C.* New York: HarperCollins, 1999.

459.
http://www.canoe.ca/NewsStand/Columnists/Toronto/Eric_Margolis/2005/02/06/922316.html

460. John Perkins, *Confessions of an Economic Hit Man*. San Francisco: Berrett-Koehler Publishers, Inc., 2004.

461. *Washington Post*, February 27, 1991.

462. Victor Marchetti, "Propaganda and Disinformation: How the CIA Manufactures History," *Journal of Historical Review*, Vol. 9, No. 3, pp. 305-320,

http://www.ihr.org/jhr/v09/v09p305_Marchetti.html

463. Tom Fenton, *Bad News: The Decline Of Reporting, The Business Of News, And The Danger To Us All.* New York: HarperCollins, 2005.

464. http://www.narconews.com/goff1.html

465. http://www.washtimes.com/national/20050513-122032-5055r.htm

466. http://abcnews.go.com/WNT/Health/story?id=708780

467. http://www.defenselink.mil/pubs/space20010111.html

468. Department of Defense News Briefing on Pentagon Attack, September 11, 2001, http://www.defenselink.mil/cgi-bin/dlprint.cgi

469. http://www.worldnetdaily.com/news/article.asp?ARTICLE_ID=44354

470. *Washington Post*, May 25, 2005, http://www.washingtonpost.com/wp-dyn/content/blog/2005/05/25/BL2005052501250.html

471. http://slate.msn.com/id/76886

472. Leon Trotsky, *My Life: The Rise and Fall of a Dictator.* London: Thornton Butterworth Ltd, 1930.

473. http://www.sundayherald.com/39221

474. http://www.boston.com/news/nation/articles/2005/06/06/papers_reveal_jfk_efforts_on_vietnam/

475. "US Troops Would Enforce Peace Under Army Study," *Washington Times*, September 10, 2001.

476. http://www.worldnetdaily.com/news/article.asp?ARTICLE_ID=17023

477. http://transcripts.cnn.com/TRANSCRIPTS/0506/09/ldt.01.html

478. http://www.timesonline.co.uk/article/0,,2087-1650822,00.html

479. http://www.house.gov/paul/tst/tst2005/tst061305.htm

480. http://www.salon.com/news/feature/2005/06/16/thimerosal/index_np.html

481. http://www.miami.com/mld/miamiherald/news/nation/8025845.htm

482. http://www.cnn.com/2005/LAW/06/23/scotus.property.ap/index.html

483. William L. Langer, *An Encyclopedia of World History*. Houghton Mifflin, 1956.

484. James Stewart Martin, *All Honorable Men*. Boston: Litle, Brown, 1950.

485. http://news.bbc.co.uk/2/hi/health/2356163.stm

486. Des Griffin, *Descent Into Slavery*. Clackamas, OR: Emissary Publications, 1996.

487. Fred Hirsh, Cryus Vance, et al, *Alternatives to Monetary Disorder*. Council on Foreign Relations 1980s Project. McGraw-Hill, 1977.

488. William Engdahl, *A Century of War: Anglo-American Oil Politics and the New World Order*. London: Pluto Press, 2004.

489. Dean Rusk, *As I Saw It*. W.W. Norton & Co., Inc., 1990.

490. http://washingtontimes.com/world/20041215-101444-5836r.htm

491. http://www.fpp.co.uk/online/01/12/WTC_Mysteries3.html

492. http://www.washingtonpost.com/wp-dyn/content/article/2005/08/07/AR2005080700843.html?referrer=emailarticle

493. http://www.upi.com/view.cfm?StoryID=18062002-051845-8272r

494. *Washington Post*, November 21, 2001.

495. CNN, February 27, 2003.

496. See, for example, BBC, September 23, 2001, http://news.bbc.co.uk/1/hi/world/middle_east/1559151.stm

497. http://www.sierratimes.com/03/07/02/article_tro.htm

498. Peter Irons, *War Powers: How the Imperial Presidency Hijacked the Constitution*. New York: Metropolitan Books, 2005, p. 117.

499. http://www.defenselink.mil/transcripts/1997/t042897_t0428coh.html

500. http://www.newschannel6.tv/news/default.asp?mode=shownews&id=8695%20

501. http://news.yahoo.com/s/ap/20050903/ap_on_re_us/katrina_national_guard

502. http://www.fredericksburg.com/News/Web/2005/092005/0902deputies

503. http://www.cbsnews.com/stories/2005/09/02/katrina/main812561.shtml

504. http://www.whitehouse.gov/news/releases/2005/08/20050827-1.html

505. Yahoo News, September 2, 2005,
http://news.yahoo.com/s/afp/20050902/wl_afp/usweatherbush_050902171225

506. *New Scientist*, July 1, 2005, http://www.newscientist.com/article.ns?id=mg18625065.900

507. MSNBC, September 6, 2005, http://www.msnbc.msn.com/id/9232927/

508. Yahoo News, September 2, 2005,
http://news.yahoo.com/s/afp/20050902/ts_alt_afp/usweatherwarnings_050902165417

509.
http://today.reuters.com/news/newsArticleSearch.aspx?storyID=21550+07-Sep-2005+RTRS&src
h=fema+photographs

510. http://www.ceri.memphis.edu/katrina/

511. http://news.yahoo.com/s/afp/20050902/ts_alt_afp/usweather_050902082649

512.
http://rawstory.com/news/2005/Congressman_Hurricane_finally_cleaned_out__public_housing_in
_N_0909.html

513.
http://www.latimes.com/news/nationworld/nation/la-091905probe_lat,0,3302428.story?coll=la-ho
me-headlines

514. http://money.cnn.com/2005/10/05/news/economy/eminent_domain_katrina/index.htm

515. As quoted by David Model in *Lying for Empire: How To Commit War Crimes With A Straight Face.* Monroe, ME: Common Courage Press, 2005.

516. Edward Herman, *Beyond Hypocrisy: Decoding the News in an Age of Propaganda.* Cambridge, MA: South End Press, 1992.

517. http://www.organicconsumers.org/epa6.cfm

518.

http://www.dailymail.co.uk/pages/live/articles/news/news.html?in_article_id=369910&in_page_id=1770

519. http://www.thespacereview.com/article/405/2

520. Yahoo News, December 26, 2005, http://au.news.yahoo.com/051225/2/p/xcry.html

521. http://www.washingtonpost.com/wp-dyn/content/article/2006/04/19/AR2006041902560_pf.html

522. http://www.gao.gov/new.items/d05956.pdf

523. http://www.news.com.au/story/0,10117,19033387-23109,00.html

524. http://today.reuters.com/news/newsarticle.aspx?type=worldNews&storyid=2006-05-10T220153Z_01_N05283609_RTRUKOC_0_US-VENEZUELA-ENERGY-GASOLINE.xml&src=rss&rpc=22

525. http://transcripts.cnn.com/TRANSCRIPTS/0506/09/ldt.01.html

526. http://www.brusselsjournal.com/node/1121

527. http://www.washingtonpost.com/wp-dyn/content/article/2005/09/17/AR2005091700657.html

528. WorldNetDaily,   July   13,   2006, http://www.worldnetdaily.com/news/article.asp?ARTICLE_ID=51038

529. http://www.nawcwpns.navy.mil/clmf/weapdig.html

530. http://www.firstamendmentcenter.org/news.aspx?id=17178

531. http://archives.cnn.com/2002/US/06/03/florida.child.welfare/

532. David Allen Rivera, *Final Warning: A History of the New World Order*. Oakland, CA: InteliBooks Publishers, 2004.

533. http://www.cnn.com/2006/LAW/08/21/padilla.charge/

534. http://www.whitehouse.gov/nsc/nsct/2006/sectionV.html

535. http://www.cnn.com/2006/US/09/12/usaf.weapons.ap/index.html

536. http://news.yahoo.com/s/ap/20060916/ap_on_re_us/anti_war_sermon

537. http://msnbc.msn.com/id/14836500/

538. http://www.fbi.gov/wanted/terrorists/terbinladen.htm

539.
The Ithaca Journal, June 29, 2006,

http://www.theithacajournal.com/apps/pbcs.dll/article?AID=/20060629/OPINION02/606290310/1
014

540.
http://www.nytimes.com/2002/07/11/opinion/11TAHE.html?ex=1100840400&en=9373d61912f4
1156&ei=5070&oref=login&ex=1089432000&en=373a282aeff2716a&ei=5070&todaysheadlines

541.
http://www.nytimes.com/2002/02/02/nyregion/02SITE.html?ex=1157860800&en=4523d11f7994
20ab&ei=5070

542. http://www.fema.gov/pdf/library/fema403_apc.pdf

543.
http://www.nytimes.com/2001/11/29/nyregion/29TOWE.html?ex=1149220800&en=380feb84a2f
40fa8&ei=5070

544. http://www.cbsnews.com/stories/2001/12/19/archive/main321907.shtml

545. http://en.wikipedia.org/wiki/Philip_D._Zelikow

546. http://www.mcsweeneys.net/2001/09/19perkal.html

547. See also http://www.worldnetdaily.com/news/article.asp?ARTICLE_ID=30682

548. http://news.independent.co.uk/world/americas/story.jsp?story=323958

549. Jim Marrs, *The Terror Conspiracy: Deception, 9/11, and the Loss of Liberty*. New York:
The Disinformation Company, 2006.

550. "Remarks by the President on Accepting Human Radiation Final Report," The White House,
Office of the Press Secretary, October 3, 1995,
http://www.clintonfoundation.org/legacy/100395-remarks-by-president-on-accepting-human-radia
tion-final-report.htm

551. http://www.dtic.mil/jointvision/jv2020.doc

552. http://www.cnn.com/2006/US/10/10/Dobbs.Oct11/

553.
http://www.nytimes.com/2006/09/28/opinion/28thu1.html?ex=1317096000&en=3eb3ba3410944ff
9&ei=5090&partner=rssuserland&emc=rss

554. http://www.cs.umass.edu/~immerman/play/opinion05/WithoutADoubt.html

555. Thom Hartmann, *Screwed: The Undeclared War Against the Middle Class.* San Francisco,
CA: Berrett-Koehler Publishers, Inc., 2006.

556. http://www.armytimes.com/news/2008/09/army_homeland_090708w/

557.
http://www.aljazeerah.info/Opinion%20editorials/2006%20Opinion%20Editorials/November/13%
20o/America's%20Pro-Israel%20Foreign%20Policy%20Is%20Wrong%20on%20All%20Counts%
20By%20Paul%20Findley.htm

558.
http://www.dailymail.co.uk/pages/live/articles/news/news.html?in_article_id=416003&in_page_id
=1770

559. http://www.latimes.com/news/opinion/commentary/la-oe-carter8dec08,0,7999232.story

560. http://www.washingtonpost.com/wp-dyn/content/article/2006/12/13/AR2006121300452.html

561. http://transcripts.cnn.com/TRANSCRIPTS/0701/08/ldt.01.html

562. http://www.worldnetdaily.com/news/article.asp?ARTICLE_ID=53413

563.
http://www.nytimes.com/2007/02/19/opinion/19mon3.html?_r=1&n=Top%2fOpinion%2fEditoria
ls%20and%20Op%2dEd%2fEditorials&oref=slogin

564. http://leahy.senate.gov/press/200609/091906a.html

565. http://www.newswithviews.com/NWO/newworld22.htm

566. http://news.yahoo.com/s/afp/20070312/wl_uk_afp/britainpolitics_070312082025

567. http://www.haaretz.com/hasen/spages/846420.html

568.
http://www.wxyz.com/entertainment/weirdnews/story.aspx?content_id=69c22563-45ff-46f7-9bcc-
99aa5804cffd

569. http://abcnews.go.com/Technology/wireStory?id=3185540

570. http://www.whitehouse.gov/news/releases/2002/03/20020313-8.html

571. http://www.alternet.org/rights/76388/

572. http://www.sfgate.com/cgi-bin/article.cgi?f=/c/a/2008/02/04/ED5OUPQJ7.DTL

573. Christine Stewart, speaking before the editors and reporters of the *Calgary Herald*, and quoted in the December 14, 1998 edition of this paper.

574. http://www.aflcio.org/aboutus/thisistheaflcio/publications/magazine/0404_manufacturing.cfm

575. Dwight Eisenhower, *The White House Years: Mandate for Change, 1953-1956*. New York: Doubleday and Co., 1963.

576. http://latimesblogs.latimes.com/washington/2008/09/bailout-plan.html

577. http://www.huffingtonpost.com/2008/09/22/dirty-secret-of-the-bailo_n_128294.html

578. http://uk.news.yahoo.com/4/20081110/tuk-brown-calls-for-new-world-order-dba1618.html

579. *Newhouse News*, January 25, 2002.

580. *Aviation Week and Space Technology*, June 3, 2002.

581. http://www.guardian.co.uk/business/2008/oct/17/executivesalaries-banking

582. http://www.iht.com/articles/2009/01/12/opinion/edkissinger.php?page=1

583. William Longgood, *The Poisons in Your Food*. Pyramid Books, 1971.

584. http://www.naturalnews.com/024246.html

585. http://www.berkeley.edu/news/media/releases/2007/02/16_AAAS.shtml

586. http://www.washingtonpost.com/wp-dyn/content/story/2008/02/28/ST2008022803016.html

587. http://news.yahoo.com/news?tmpl=story&u=/nm/20040526/pl_nm/security_threat_politics_dc_1

588. Richard Clarke, *Against All Enemies*. Free Press (ISBN: 0743260244), p. 13.

589. http://www.washingtonpost.com/wp-srv/aponline/20011023/aponline201158_000.htm

590. http://www.judicialwatch.org/1967.shtml

591. *Washington Post*, October 4, 2001.

592. *USA Today*, May 10, 2002.

593. *New York Times*, August 11, 2002.

594.
http://www.opednews.com/articles/FBI-Frame-up-of-Bruce-E-I-by-Michael-Green-080812-624.html

595. http://www.salon.com/opinion/greenwald/2008/08/06/fbi_documents/index.html

596. Francis A. Boyle, *Biowarfare and Terrorism*. Atlanda, GA: Clarity Press, 2005.

Printed in Great Britain
by Amazon.co.uk, Ltd.,
Marston Gate.